An Introduction to the International Criminal Court

Arguably the most significant international organization to be created since the United Nations, the International Criminal Court ushers in a new era in the protection of human rights. The direct descendant of the Nuremberg and Tokyo trials, as well as those of the more recent international criminal tribunals for the former Yugoslavia and Rwanda, the International Criminal Court will prosecute genocide, crimes against humanity and war crimes when national justice systems are either unwilling or unable to do so themselves. This volume reviews the history of international criminal prosecution, the drafting of the Rome Statute of the International Criminal Court and the principles of its operation, including the scope of its jurisdiction and the procedural regime. The Court's fundamental documents – the Rome Statute itself, the Rules of Procedure and Evidence, and the Elements of Crimes – form an annex to the book.

WILLIAM A. SCHABAS is Professor of Human Rights Law at the National University of Ireland, Galway and Director of the Irish Centre for Human Rights. His numerous publications include *Genocide in International Law* (2000), *The Abolition of the Death Penalty in International Law* (third edition to be published in 2001), *International Human Rights Law and the Canadian Charter* (1996), *The Death Penalty as Cruel Treatment and Torture* (1996), *Précis du droit international des droits de la personne* (1997) and *Les instruments internationaux, canadiens et québécois des droits et libertés* (1998). He is also editor-in-chief of *Criminal Law Forum*.

International Centre

AN INTRODUCTION TO THE INTERNATIONAL CRIMINAL COURT

WILLIAM A. SCHABAS

CAMBRIDGE
UNIVERSITY PRESS

PUBLISHED BY THE PRESS SYNDICATE OF THE UNIVERSITY OF CAMBRIDGE
The Pitt Building, Trumpington Street, Cambridge, United Kingdom

CAMBRIDGE UNIVERSITY PRESS
The Edinburgh Building, Cambridge CB2 2RU, UK
40 West 20th Street, New York, NY 10011-4211, USA
10 Stamford Road, Oakleigh, VIC 3166, Australia
Ruiz de Alarcón 13, 28014 Madrid, Spain
Dock House, The Waterfront, Cape Town 8001, South Africa

http://www.cambridge.org

First published 2001

Printed in the United Kingdom at the University Press, Cambridge

Typeface Adobe Minion 10.5/14 pt   *System* QuarkXpress™   [SE]

A catalogue record for this book is available from the British Library

Library of Congress Cataloguing in Publication data

Schabas, William, 1950–
An introduction to the International Criminal Court / by William A. Schabas.
p.   cm.
Includes bibliographical references and index.
ISBN 0 521 80457 4 (hardback) ISBN 0 521 01149 3 (paperback)
1. International Criminal Court. 2. International criminal courts.
3. International offenses. I. Title.
KZ6310.S33 2001
341.7′7–dc21 01-069751

ISBN 0 521 80457 4 hardback
ISBN 0 521 01149 3 paperback

CONTENTS

PREFACE

On 17 July 1998, at the headquarters of the Food and Agriculture Organization of the United Nations in Rome, 120 States voted to adopt the Rome Statute of the International Criminal Court. This complex and detailed international treaty provides for the creation of an international criminal court with power to try and punish the most serious violations of human rights in cases when national justice systems fail at the task. It was a benchmark in the progressive development of international human rights, something whose beginning dates back fifty years, to the adoption on 10 December 1948 of the Universal Declaration of Human Rights by the third session of the United Nations General Assembly.[1] The previous day, on 9 December, the Assembly had adopted a resolution mandating the International Law Commission to begin work on the draft statute of an international criminal court.[2]

Establishing the international criminal court took considerably longer than many had hoped. In the early years of the Cold War, in 1954, the General Assembly essentially suspended work on the project.[3] It did not resume until 1989.[4] The end of the Cold War gave the idea of a court the breathing space it needed. The turmoil created in the former Yugoslavia provided the laboratory for international justice that propelled the agenda forward.[5] The final version of the Rome Statute is not without serious flaws, and yet it 'could well be the most important institutional innovation since the founding of the United Nations'.[6] The institution itself will come into being when sixty States have ratified the Statute.

---

[1] GA Res. 217A(III), U.N. Doc. A/810.

[2] 'Study by the International Law Commission of the Question of an International Criminal Jurisdiction', GA Res. 216B(III).   [3] GA Res. 897(IX) (1954).   [4] GA Res. 44/89.

[5] *Statute of the International Criminal Tribunal for the Former Yugoslavia*, UN Doc. S/RES/827, Annex.

[6] Robert C. Johansen, 'A Turning Point in International Relations? Establishing a Permanent International Criminal Court', 13 (1997) *Report* No. 1, p. 1 (published by the Joan B. Kroc Institute for International Peace Studies, Notre Dame, IN).

Because participation in the Court imposes upon States important obligations with respect to cooperation and support of its activities, ratification
is not something to be undertaken lightly, and most will insist on adopting
relatively sophisticated implementing legislation before confirming their
acceptance. But the process of ratification began in earnest, and it is likely
that the Court will actually come into being sometime in the year 2001 or
early 2002.

The new International Criminal Court (ICC) will sit in The Hague,
capital of the Netherlands, alongside its long-established cousin, the
International Court of Justice (ICJ). The ICJ is the court where States liti-
gate matters relating to their disputes as States. The role of individuals
before the ICJ is marginal, at best. As will be seen, not only does the ICC
provide for prosecution and punishment of individuals, it also recognizes
a legitimate participation for the individual as victim. In a more general
sense, the ICC is concerned, essentially, with matters that might generally
be described as serious human rights violations. The ICJ, on the other
hand, spends much of its judicial time on delimiting international bound-
aries and fishing zones, and similar matters. Yet, because it is exposed to
the same trends and developments that sparked creation of the ICC, the
ICJ finds itself increasingly involved in human rights matters.[7]

The literature on the ICC is already abundant, and several sophisticated
collections of essays addressed essentially to specialists have already been
published.[8] The goal of this work is both more modest and more ambitious: to provide a succinct and coherent introduction to the legal issues
involved in the creation and operation of the ICC, and one that is accessible to non-specialists. References within the text signpost the way to rather
more detailed sources where readers may find detailed analysis. As with all

---

[7] Recent cases have involved genocide in the former Yugoslavia, the use of nuclear weapons, self-
determination in East Timor, the immunity of international human rights investigators, and
the imposition of the death penalty in the United States.

[8] Roy Lee, ed., *The International Criminal Court, The Making of the Rome Statute, Issues,
Negotiations, Results*, The Hague: Kluwer Law International, 1999; Otto Triffterer, ed.,
*Commentary on the Rome Statute of the International Criminal Court, Observers' Notes, Article
by Article*, Baden-Baden: Nomos, 1999; Herman von Hebel, Johan G. Lammers and Jolien
Schukking, eds, *Reflections on the International Criminal Court: Essays in Honour of Adriaan
Bos*, The Hague: T.M.C. Asser, 1999; Flavia Lattanzi and William A. Schabas, eds, *Essays on the
Rome Statute of the ICC*, Rome: Editrice il Sirente, 2000; Dinah Shelton, ed., *International
Crimes, Peace, and Human Rights: The Role of the International Criminal Court*, Ardsley, NY:
Transnational Publishers, 2000; Antonio Cassese, ed., *Commentary on the Rome Statute*,
Oxford: Clarendon Press (forthcoming).

international treaties and similar documents, students of the subject are also encouraged to consult the original records of the 1998 Diplomatic Conference and the meetings that preceded it. But the volume of these materials is awesome, and it is a challenging task to distil meaningful analysis and conclusions from them.

It would be impossible here to thank my many friends involved in the drafting of the Statute, whose insights and observations have all contributed in various ways to this volume, and I trust they will understand if I do not acknowledge them individually here, although I cannot fail to mention Roger Clark and Otto Triffterer. Dan Préfontaine of the International Centre for Criminal Law Reform in Vancouver arranged for me to attend the Rome Conference as the representative of his organization. The Social Sciences and Humanities Research Council of Canada facilitated my attendance at the Rome Conference by awarding me the Bora Laskin Research Fellowship in Human Rights. Sergio D'Elia offered me a room in his beautiful apartment in Rome overlooking the Lateran Palace for the duration of the Conference. Marco Perduca was always obliging in ensuring that I had a badge to attend the sessions of the Preparatory Committee, prior to Rome, and the Preparatory Commission, afterwards. Cherif Bassiouni invited me to the centre he directs in Siracusa on several occasions, for stimulating and enriching exchanges on these questions. I learned much from colleagues who participated in the August 2000 summer course held at the Irish Centre for Human Rights: Fabricio Guariglia, John Holmes, Philippe Kirsch, Leila Sadat, Michael Scharf and Sharon Williams.

I wish to thank my new institution, the Irish Centre for Human Rights of the National University of Ireland, Galway, where I have been based since January 2000, and my former one, the University of Quebec at Montreal, for the time to work on this project. My research assistants at the Centre, particularly Nancie Prud'homme and Barbara Ann Rieffer, helped me revise the text in its final stages. Finola O'Sullivan of Cambridge University Press has been enthusiastic and helpful about the work since I first proposed it. Finally, as always, thanks are due to my wife Penelope, who encourages and supports me in this work.

WILLIAM A. SCHABAS
Oughterard, County Galway

ABBREVIATIONS

CHR   Commission on Human Rights
GA   General Assembly
ICC   International Criminal Court
ICJ   International Court of Justice
ICTR   International Criminal Tribunal for Rwanda
ICTY   International Criminal Tribunal for the Former Yugoslavia
ILC   International Law Commission
LRTWC   *Law Reports of the Trials of the War Criminals*
SC   Security Council
TWC   *Trials of the War Criminals*

1

Creation of the Court

War criminals have been prosecuted at least since the time of the ancient Greeks, and probably well before that. The idea that there is some common denominator of behaviour, even in the most extreme circumstances of brutal armed conflict, confirms beliefs drawn from philosophy and religion about some of the fundamental values of the human spirit. The early laws and customs of war can be found in the writings of classical authors and historians. Those who breached them were subject to trial and punishment. Modern codifications of this law, such as the detailed text prepared by Columbia University professor Francis Lieber that was applied by Abraham Lincoln to the Union army during the American Civil War, proscribed inhumane conduct and set out sanctions, including the death penalty, for pillage, raping civilians, abuse of prisoners and similar atrocities.[1] Prosecution for war crimes, however, was only effected by national courts, and these were and remain ineffective when those responsible for the crimes are still in power and their victims remain subjugated. Historically, the prosecution of war crimes was generally restrained to the vanquished or to isolated cases of rogue combatants in the victor's army. National justice systems have often proven themselves to be incapable of being balanced and impartial in such cases.

The first genuinely international trial for the perpetration of atrocities was probably that of Peter von Hagenbach, who was tried in 1474 for atrocities committed during the occupation of Breisach. When the town was retaken, von Hagenbach was charged with war crimes, convicted and beheaded.[2] But what was surely no more than a curious experiment in medieval international justice was soon overtaken by the sanctity of State sovereignty resulting from the Peace of Westphalia of 1648. With the

---

[1] Instructions for the Government of Armies of the United States in the Field, General Orders No. 100, 24 April 1863.
[2] M. Cherif Bassiouni, 'From Versailles to Rwanda in 75 Years: The Need to Establish a Permanent International Court', (1997) 10 *Harvard Human Rights Journal* 11.

development of the law of armed conflict in the mid-nineteenth century, concepts of international prosecution for humanitarian abuses slowly began to emerge. One of the founders of the Red Cross movement, which grew up in Geneva in the 1860s, urged a draft statute for an international criminal court. Its task would be to prosecute breaches of the Geneva Convention of 1864 and other humanitarian norms. But Gustav Monnier's innovative proposal was much too radical for its time.[3]

The Hague Conventions of 1899 and 1907 represent the first significant codification of the laws of war in an international treaty. They include an important series of provisions dealing with the protection of civilian populations. Article 46 of the Regulations that are annexed to the Hague Convention IV of 1907 enshrines the respect of '[f]amily honour and rights, the lives of persons, and private property, as well as religious convictions and practice'.[4] Other provisions of the Regulations protect cultural objects and private property of civilians. The preamble to the Conventions recognizes that they are incomplete, but promises that until a more complete code of the laws of war is issued, 'the inhabitants and the belligerents remain under the protection and the rule of the principles of the law of nations, as they result from the usages established among civilized peoples, from the laws of humanity, and the dictates of the public conscience'. This provision is known as the Martens clause, after the Russian diplomat who drafted it.[5]

The Hague Conventions, as international treaties, were meant to impose obligations and duties upon States, and were not intended to create criminal liability for individuals. They declared certain acts to be illegal, but not criminal, as can be seen from the absence of anything suggesting a sanction for their violation. Yet within only a few years, the Hague Conventions were being presented as a source of the law of war crimes. In 1913, a commission of inquiry sent by the Carnegie Foundation to investigate atrocities committed during the Balkan Wars used the provisions of the Hague Convention IV as a basis for its description of war

---

[3] Christopher Keith Hall, 'The First Proposal for a Permanent International Criminal Court', (1998) 322 *International Review of the Red Cross* 57.

[4] Convention Concerning the Laws and Customs of War on Land (Hague IV), 3 *Martens Nouveau Recueil* (3d) 461. For the 1899 treaty, see Convention (II) with Respect to the Laws and Customs of War on Land, 32 Stat. 1803, 1 Bevans 247, 91 British Foreign and State Treaties 988.

[5] Theodor Meron, 'The Martens Clause, Principles of Humanity, and Dictates of Public Conscience', (2000) 94 *American Journal of International Law* 78.

crimes.[6] Immediately following World War I, the Commission on Responsibilities of the Authors of War and on Enforcement of Penalties, established to examine allegations of war crimes committed by the Central Powers, did the same.[7] But actual prosecution for violations of the Hague Conventions would have to wait until Nuremberg. Offences against the laws and customs of war, known as 'Hague Law' because of their roots in the 1899 and 1907 Conventions, are codified in the 1993 Statute of the International Criminal Tribunal for the Former Yugoslavia[8] and in Article 8(2)(b), (e) and (f) of the Statute of the International Criminal Court.

As World War I wound to a close, public pressure mounted, particularly in England, for criminal prosecution of those generally considered to be responsible for the war. There was much pressure to go beyond violations of the laws and customs of war and to prosecute, in addition, the waging of war itself in violation of international treaties. At the Paris Peace Conference, the Allies debated the wisdom of such trials as well as their legal basis. The United States was generally hostile to the idea, arguing that this would be *ex post facto* justice. Responsibility for breach of international conventions, and above all for crimes against the 'laws of humanity' – a reference to civilian atrocities within a State's own borders – was a question of morality, not law, said the American delegation. But this was a minority position. The resulting compromise dropped the concept of 'laws of humanity' but promised prosecution of Kaiser Wilhelm II 'for a supreme offence against international morality and the sanctity of treaties'. The Versailles Treaty formally arraigned the defeated German emperor and pledged the creation of a 'special tribunal' for his trial.[9] Wilhelm of Hohenzollern had fled to neutral Holland which refused his extradition, the Dutch government considering that the charges consisted of retroactive criminal law. He lived out his life there and died, ironically, in 1941 when his country of refuge was falling under German occupation in the early years of World War II.

The Versailles Treaty also recognized the right of the Allies to set up

---

[6] *Report of the International Commission to Inquire into the Causes and Conduct of the Balkan Wars*, Washington: Carnegie Endowment for International Peace, 1914.

[7] *Violations of the Laws and Customs of War, Reports of Majority and Dissenting Reports of American and Japanese Members of the Commission of Responsibilities, Conference of Paris, 1919*, Oxford: Clarendon Press, 1919.

[8] Statute of the International Criminal Tribunal for the Former Yugoslavia, UN Doc. S/RES/827, Annex.

[9] Treaty of Peace between the Allied and Associated Powers and Germany ('Treaty of Versailles'), (1919) TS 4, Art. 227.

military tribunals to try German soldiers accused of war crimes.[10] Germany never accepted the provisions, and subsequently a compromise was reached whereby the Allies would prepare lists of German suspects, but the trials would be held before the German courts. An initial list of nearly 900 was quickly whittled down to about forty, and in the end only a dozen were actually tried. Several were acquitted; those found guilty were sentenced to modest terms of imprisonment, often nothing more than time already served in custody prior to conviction. The trials looked rather more like disciplinary proceedings of the German army than any international reckoning. Known as the 'Leipzig Trials', the perceived failure of this early attempt at international justice haunted efforts in the inter-war years to develop a permanent international tribunal and were grist to the mill of those who opposed war crimes trials for the Nazi leaders. But two of the judgments of the Leipzig court involving the sinking of the hospital ships *Dover Castle* and *Llandovery Castle*, and the murder of the survivors, mainly Canadian wounded and medical personnel, are cited to this day as precedents on the scope of the defence of superior orders.[11]

The Treaty of Sèvres of 1920, which governed the peace with Turkey, also provided for war crimes trials.[12] The proposed prosecutions against the Turks were even more radical, going beyond the trial of suspects whose victims were either Allied soldiers or civilians in occupied territories to include subjects of the Ottoman Empire. This was the embryo of what would later be called crimes against humanity. However, the Treaty of Sèvres was never ratified by Turkey, and the trials were never held. The Treaty of Sèvres was replaced by the Treaty of Lausanne of 1923 which contained a 'Declaration of Amnesty' for all offences committed between 1 August 1914 and 20 November 1922.[13]

Although these initial efforts to create an international criminal court were unsuccessful, they stimulated many international lawyers to devote their attention to the matter during the years that followed. Baron Descamps of Belgium, a member of the Advisory Committee of Jurists appointed by the Council of the League of Nations, urged the establish-

---

[10] *Ibid.*, Arts 228–230.
[11] *German War Trials, Report of Proceedings Before the Supreme Court in Leipzig*, London: His Majesty's Stationery Office, 1921. See also James F. Willis, *Prologue to Nuremberg: The Politics and Diplomacy of Punishing War Criminals of the First World War*, Westport, CT: Greenwood Press, 1982.
[12] (1920) UKTS 11; (1929) 99 (3rd Series), DeMartens, Recueil général des traités, No. 12, p. 720 (French version).
[13] Treaty of Lausanne Between Principal Allied and Associated Powers and Turkey, (1923) 28 LNTS 11.

ment of a 'high court of international justice'. Using language borrowed from the Martens clause in the preamble to the Hague Conventions, Descamps recommended that the jurisdiction of the court include offences 'recognized by the civilized nations but also by the demands of public conscience [and] the dictates of the legal conscience of civilized nations'. The Third Committee of the Assembly of the League declared that Descamps' ideas were 'premature'. Efforts by expert bodies, such as the International Law Association and the International Association of Penal Law, culminated, in 1937, in the adoption of a treaty by the League of Nations that contemplated the establishment of an international criminal court.[14] But, failing a sufficient number of ratifying States, that treaty never came into force.

The Nuremberg and Tokyo trials

In the Moscow Declaration of 1 November 1943, the Allies affirmed their determination to prosecute the Nazis for war crimes. The United Nations Commission for the Investigation of War Crimes, composed of representatives of most of the Allies, and chaired by Sir Cecil Hurst of the United Kingdom, was established to set the stage for post-war prosecution. The Commission prepared a 'Draft Convention for the Establishment of a United Nations War Crimes Court', basing its text largely on the 1937 treaty of the League of Nations.[15] But it was the work of the London Conference, convened at the close of the war and limited to the four major powers, the United Kingdom, France, the United States and the Soviet Union, that laid the groundwork for the prosecutions at Nuremberg. The Agreement for the Prosecution and Punishment of Major War Criminals of the European Axis, and Establishing the Charter of the International Military Tribunal (IMT) was formally adopted on 8 August 1945, and was promptly signed by representatives of the four powers. The Charter of the International Military Tribunal was annexed to the Agreement.[16] This

[14] Convention for the Creation of an International Criminal Court, League of Nations OJ Spec. Supp. No. 156 (1936), LN Doc. C.547(I).M.384(I).1937.V (1938).

[15] 'Draft Convention for the Establishment of a United Nations War Crimes Court', UN War Crimes Commission, Doc. C.50(1), 30 September 1944.

[16] Agreement for the Prosecution and Punishment of Major War Criminals of the European Axis, and Establishing the Charter of the International Military Tribunal (IMT), Annex, (1951) 82 UNTS 279. See Arieh J. Kochavi, *Prelude to Nuremberg, Allied War Crimes Policy and the Question of Punishment*, Chapel Hill and London: University of North Carolina Press, 1998; *Report of Robert H. Jackson, United States Representative to the International Conference on Military Trials*, Washington: US Government Printing Office, 1949.

treaty was eventually adhered to by nineteen other States who, although they played no active role in the Tribunal's activities or the negotiation of its statute, sought to express their support for the concept.

In October 1945, indictments were served on twenty-four Nazi leaders, and their trial – known as the Trial of the Major War Criminals – began the following month. It concluded nearly a year later, with the conviction of nineteen defendants and the imposition of sentence of death in twelve cases. The Tribunal's jurisdiction was confined to three categories of offence: crimes against peace, war crimes and crimes against humanity. The Charter of the International Military Tribunal had been adopted after the crimes had been committed, and for this reason it was attacked as constituting *ex post facto* criminalization. Rejecting such arguments, the Tribunal referred to the Hague Conventions, for the war crimes, and to the 1928 Kellogg–Briand Pact, for crimes against peace.[17] It also answered that the prohibition of retroactive crimes was a principle of justice, and that it would fly in the face of justice to leave the Nazi crimes unpunished. This argument was particularly important with respect to the category of crimes against humanity, for which there was little real precedent. In the case of some war crimes charges, the Tribunal refused to convict after hearing evidence of similar behaviour by British and American soldiers.[18]

In December 1945, the four Allied powers enacted a somewhat modified version of the Charter of the International Military Tribunal, known as Control Council Law No. 10.[19] It provided the legal basis for a series of trials before military tribunals that were run by the victorious Allies, as well as for subsequent prosecutions by German courts that continued for several decades. Control Council Law No. 10, which was really a form of domestic legislation because it applied to prosecution of Germans by courts of the civil authorities, largely borrowed the definition of crimes

---

[17] The Kellogg–Briand Pact was an international treaty that renounced the use of war as a means to settle international disputes. Previously, war as such was not prohibited by international law. States had erected a network of bilateral and multilateral treaties of non-aggression and alliance in order to protect themselves from attack and invasion.

[18] *France et al.* v. *Goering et al.*, (1946) 22 IMT 203; (1946) 13 ILR 203; (1946) 41 *American Journal of International Law* 172. The judgment itself, as well as the transcript of the hearings and the documentary evidence, are reproduced in a forty-volume series published in English and French and available in most major reference libraries. The literature on the Nuremberg trial of the major war criminals is extensive. Probably the best modern account is Telford Taylor, *The Anatomy of the Nuremberg Trials*, New York: Alfred A. Knopf, 1992.

[19] Control Council Law No. 10, Punishment of Persons Guilty of War Crimes, Crimes Against Peace and Against Humanity, 20 December 1945, *Official Gazette of the Control Council for Germany*, No. 3, 31 January 1946, pp. 50–5.

against humanity found in the Charter of the Nuremberg Tribunal, but omitted the latter's insistence on a link between crimes against humanity and the existence of a state of war, thereby facilitating prosecution for pre-1939 crimes committed against German civilians, including persecution of the Jews and euthanasia of the disabled. Several important trials were held pursuant to Control Council Law No. 10 in the period 1946–1948 by American military tribunals. These focused on groups of defendants, such as judges, doctors, bureaucrats and military leaders.[20]

In the Pacific theatre, the victorious Allies established the International Military Tribunal for the Far East. Japanese war criminals were tried under similar provisions to those used at Nuremberg. The bench was more cosmopolitan, consisting of judges from eleven countries, including India, China and the Philippines, whereas the Nuremberg judges were appointed by the four major powers, the United States, the United Kingdom, France and the Soviet Union.

At Nuremberg, Nazi war criminals were charged with what the prosecutor called 'genocide', but the term did not appear in the substantive provisions of the Statute and the Tribunal convicted them of 'crimes against humanity' for the atrocities committed against the Jewish people of Europe. Within weeks of the judgment, efforts began in the General Assembly of the United Nations to push the law further in this area. In December 1946, a resolution was adopted declaring genocide a crime against international law and calling for the preparation of a convention on the subject.[21] Two years later, the General Assembly adopted the Convention for the Prevention and Punishment of the Crime of Genocide.[22] The definition of genocide set out in Article II of the 1948 Convention is incorporated unchanged in the Statute of the International Criminal Court, as Article 6. But, besides defining the crime and setting out a variety of obligations relating to its prosecution, Article VI of the Convention said that trial for genocide was to take place before 'a competent tribunal of the State in the territory of which the act was committed,

---

[20] Frank M. Buscher, *The US War Crimes Trial Program in Germany, 1946–1955*, Westport, CT: Greenwood Press, 1989. The judgments in the cases, as well as much secondary material and documentary evidence, have been published in two series, one by the United States Government titled *Trials of the War Criminals* (15 volumes), the other by the United Kingdom Government titled *Law Reports of the Trials of the War Criminals* (15 volumes). Both series are readily available in reference libraries.　　[21] GA Res. 96(I).

[22] Convention on the Prevention and Punishment of the Crime of Genocide, (1951) 78 UNTS 277.

or by such international penal tribunal as may have jurisdiction with respect to those Contracting Parties which shall have accepted its jurisdiction'. An early draft of the Genocide Convention prepared by the United Nations Secretariat had actually included a model statute for a court, based on the 1937 treaty developed within the League of Nations, but the proposal was too ambitious for the time and the conservative drafters stopped short of establishing such an institution.[23] Instead, a General Assembly resolution adopted the same day as the Convention called upon the International Law Commission to prepare the statute of the court promised by Article VI.[24]

International Law Commission

The International Law Commission is a body of experts named by the United Nations General Assembly and charged with the codification and progressive development of international law. Besides the mandate to draft the statute of an international criminal court derived from Article VI of the Genocide Convention, in the post-war euphoria about war crimes prosecution the General Assembly had also asked the Commission to prepare what are known as the 'Nuremberg Principles', a task it completed in 1950, and the 'Code of Crimes Against the Peace and Security of Mankind', a job that took considerably longer. Indeed, much of the work on the draft statute of an international criminal court and the draft code of crimes went on within the Commission in parallel, almost as if the two tasks were hardly related. The pair of instruments can be understood by analogy with domestic law. They correspond in a general sense to the definitions of crimes and general principles found in criminal or penal codes (the 'code of crimes'), and the institutional and procedural framework found in codes of criminal procedure (the 'statute').

Meanwhile, in parallel with the work of the International Law Commission, the General Assembly also established a committee charged with drafting the statute of an international criminal court. Composed of seventeen States, it submitted its report and draft statute in 1952.[25] A new

---

[23] William A. Schabas, *Genocide in International Law, The Crime of Crimes*, Cambridge: Cambridge University Press, 2000.

[24] 'Study by the International Law Commission of the Question of an International Criminal Jurisdiction', GA Res. 216B(III).

[25] 'Report of the Committee on International Criminal Court Jurisdiction', UN Doc. A/2135 (1952).

committee, created by the General Assembly to review the draft statute in the light of comments by Member States, reported to the General Assembly in 1954.[26] The International Law Commission made considerable progress on its draft code and actually submitted a proposal in 1954.[27] Then, the General Assembly suspended the mandates, ostensibly pending the sensitive task of defining the crime of aggression.[28] In fact, political tensions associated with the Cold War had made progress on the war crimes agenda virtually impossible.

The General Assembly eventually adopted a definition of aggression, in 1974,[29] but the work did not immediately resume on the proposed international criminal court. In 1981, the General Assembly asked the International Law Commission to revive the work on its draft code of crimes.[30] Doudou Thiam was designated the special rapporteur of the Commission, and he produced annual reports on various aspects of the draft code for more than a decade. Thiam's work, and the associated debates in the Commission, addressed a range of questions, including definitions of crimes, criminal participation, defences and penalties.[31] A substantially revised version of the 1954 draft code was provisionally adopted by the Commission in 1991, and then sent to Member States for their reaction.

But the code did not necessarily involve an international jurisdiction. That aspect of the work was only initiated in 1989, the year of the fall of the Berlin Wall. Trinidad and Tobago, one of several Caribbean States plagued by narcotics problems and related transnational crime issues, initiated a resolution in the General Assembly directing the International Law Commission to consider the subject of an international criminal court within the context of its work on the draft code of crimes.[32] Special Rapporteur Doudou Thiam made an initial presentation on the subject in 1992. By 1993, the Commission had prepared a draft statute, this time under the direction of Special Rapporteur James Crawford. The draft statute was examined that year by the General Assembly, which encouraged the Commission to complete its work. The following year, in 1994,

[26] 'Report of the Committee on International Criminal Court Jurisdiction', UN Doc. A/2645 (1954).
[27] *Yearbook . . . 1954*, Vol. I, 267th meeting, para. 39, p. 131 (ten in favour, with one abstention). On the 1954 draft code in general, see D.H.N. Johnson, 'Draft Code of Offences Against the Peace and Security of Mankind', (1955) 4 *International and Comparative Law Quarterly* 445.
[28] GA Res. 897(IX) (1954).   [29] GA Res. 3314(XXIX) (1974).   [30] GA Res. 36/106 (1981).
[31] These materials appear in the annual reports of the International Law Commission.
[32] GA Res. 44/89.

the Commission submitted the final version of its draft statute for an international criminal court to the General Assembly.[33]

The International Law Commission's draft statute of 1994 focused on procedural and organizational matters, leaving the question of defining the crimes and the associated legal principles to the code of crimes, which it had yet to complete. Two years later, at its 1996 session, the Commission adopted the final draft of its 'Code of Crimes Against the Peace and Security of Mankind'.[34] The draft statute of 1994 and the draft code of 1996 played a seminal role in the preparation of the Statute of the International Criminal Court. The International Criminal Tribunal for the Former Yugoslavia has remarked that 'the Draft Code is an authoritative international instrument which, depending upon the specific question at issue, may (i) constitute evidence of customary law, or (ii) shed light on customary rules which are of uncertain content or are in the process of formation, or, at the very least, (iii) be indicative of the legal views of eminently qualified publicists representing the major legal systems of the world'.[35]

The ad hoc tribunals

While the draft statute of an international criminal court was being considered in the International Law Commission, events compelled the creation of a court on an *ad hoc* basis in order to address the atrocities being committed in the former Yugoslavia. In late 1992, as war raged in Bosnia, a Commission of Experts established by the Security Council identified a range of war crimes and crimes against humanity that had been committed and that were continuing. It urged the establishment of an international criminal tribunal, an idea that had originally been recommended by Lord Owen and Cyrus Vance. The proposal was endorsed by the General

---

[33] James Crawford, 'The ILC's Draft Statute for an International Criminal Tribunal', (1994) 88 *American Journal of International Law* 140; James Crawford, 'The ILC Adopts a Statute for an International Criminal Court', (1995) 89 *American Journal of International Law* 404. For the International Law Commission's discussion of the history of the draft statute, see 'Report of the International Law Commission on the Work of its Forty-Sixth Session, 2 May–22 July 1994', UN Doc. A/49/10, chapter II, paras 23–41.

[34] Timothy L. H. McCormack and G. J. Simpson, 'The International Law Commission's Draft Code of Crimes Against the Peace and Security of Mankind: An Appraisal of the Substantive Provisions', (1994) 5 *Criminal Law Forum* 1; John Allain and John R. W. D. Jones, 'A Patchwork of Norms: A Commentary on the 1996 Draft Code of Crimes Against the Peace and Security of Mankind', (1997) 8 *European Journal of International Law* 100.

[35] *Prosecutor* v. *Furundzija* (Case No. IT-95-17/1-T), Judgment, 10 December 1998, para. 227.

Assembly in a December 1992 resolution. The rapporteurs appointed under the Moscow Human Dimension Mechanism of the Conference on Security and Co-operation in Europe, Hans Correll, Gro Hillestad Thune and Helmut Türk, took the initiative to prepare a draft statute. Several governments also submitted draft proposals or otherwise commented upon the creation of a tribunal.[36]

On 22 February 1993, the Security Council decided upon the establishment of a tribunal mandated to prosecute 'persons responsible for serious violations of international humanitarian law committed in the territory of the former Yugoslavia since 1991'.[37] The draft proposed by the Secretary-General was adopted without modification by the Security Council in its Resolution 827 of 8 May 1993. According to the Secretary-General's report, the tribunal was to apply rules of international humanitarian law that are 'beyond any doubt part of the customary law'.[38] The Statute clearly borrowed from the work then underway within the International Law Commission on the statute and the code of crimes, in effect combining the two into an instrument that both defined the crimes and established the procedure before the court. The Tribunal's territorial jurisdiction was confined to the territory of the former Yugoslavia. Temporally, it was entitled to prosecute offences beginning in 1991, leaving its end-point to be established by the Security Council.

In November 1994, acting on a request from Rwanda, the Security Council voted to create a second *ad hoc* tribunal, charged with the prosecution of genocide and other serious violations of international humanitarian law committed in Rwanda and in neighbouring countries during the year 1994.[39] Its Statute closely resembles that of the International Criminal Tribunal for the Former Yugoslavia, although the war crimes provisions reflect the fact that the Rwandan genocide took place within the context of a purely internal armed conflict. The resolution creating the Tribunal expressed the Council's 'grave concern at the reports indicating that genocide and other systematic, widespread and flagrant violations of international humanitarian law have been committed in Rwanda', and referred to the reports of the Special Rapporteur for Rwanda of the United

---

[36] For the documentary history of the Yugoslav Tribunal, see Virginia Morris and Michael P. Scharf, *An Insider's Guide to the International Criminal Tribunal for the Former Yugoslavia: A Documentary History and Analysis*, New York: Transnational Publishers, 1995

[37] SC Res. 808 (1993).

[38] 'Report of the Secretary-General Pursuant to Paragraph 2 of Security Council Resolution 808 (1993)', UN Doc. S/25704.   [39] SC Res. 955 (1994).

Nations Commission on Human Rights, as well as the preliminary report of the Commission of Experts, which the Council had established earlier in the year.

The Yugoslav and Rwanda tribunals are in effect joined at the hip, sharing not only virtually identical statutes but also some of their institutions. The Prosecutor is the same for both tribunals, as is the Appeals Chamber. The consequence, at least in theory, is economy of scale as well as uniformity of both prosecutorial policy and appellate jurisprudence. The first major judgment by the Appeals Chamber of the Yugoslav Tribunal, the *Tadic* jurisdictional decision of 2 October 1995, clarified important legal issues relating to the creation of the body.[40] It also pointed the Tribunal towards an innovative and progressive view of war crimes law, going well beyond the Nuremberg precedents by declaring that crimes against humanity could be committed in peacetime, and by establishing the criminal nature of war crimes during internal armed conflicts.

Subsequent rulings of the *ad hoc* tribunals on a variety of matters fed the debates on the creation of an international criminal court. The findings in *Tadic* with respect to the scope of war crimes were essentially incorporated into the Statute of the International Criminal Court. Other judgments, such as a controversial holding that excluded recourse to a defence of duress,[41] prompted the drafters of the Rome Statute to enact a provision ensuring precisely the opposite.[42] The issue of 'national security' information, ignored by the International Law Commission, was thrust to the forefront of the debates after the Tribunal ordered Croatia to produce government documents,[43] and resulted in one of the lengthiest and most enigmatic provisions in the final Statute.[44] But the Tribunals did more than simply set legal precedent to guide the drafters. They also provided a reassuring model of what an international criminal court might look like. This was particularly important in debates concerning the role of the Prosecutor. The integrity, neutrality and good judgment of Richard

---

[40] *Prosecutor* v. *Tadic* (Case No. IT-94-1-AR72), Decision on the Defence Motion for Interlocutory Appeal on Jurisdiction, 2 October 1995, (1997) 105 ILR 453, (1997) 35 ILM 32.
[41] *Prosecutor* v. *Erdemovic* (Case No. IT-96-22-A), Sentencing Appeal, 7 October 1997, (1998) 111 ILR 298.
[42] Rome Statute of the International Criminal Court, UN Doc. A/CONF.183/9 (hereinafter Rome Statute), Art. 31(1)(d).
[43] *Prosecutor* v. *Blaskic* (Case No. IT-95-14-AR108*bis*), Objection to the Issue of *Subpoenae Duces Tecum*, 29 October1997, (1998) 110 ILR 677.   [44] Rome Statute, Art. 72.

Goldstone and his successor, Louise Arbour, answered those who warned of the dangers of a reckless and irresponsible 'Dr Strangelove prosecutor'.

Drafting of the ICC Statute

In 1994, the United Nations General Assembly decided to pursue work towards the establishment of an international criminal court, taking the International Law Commission's draft statute as a basis.[45] It convened an Ad Hoc Committee, which met twice in 1995.[46] Debates within the Ad Hoc Committee revealed rather profound differences among States about the complexion of the future court, and some delegations continued to contest the overall feasibility of the project, although their voices became more and more subdued as the negotiations pursued. The International Law Commission draft envisaged a court with 'primacy', much like the *ad hoc* tribunals that had been set up by the Security Council for the former Yugoslavia and Rwanda. If the court's prosecutor chose to proceed with a case, domestic courts could not pre-empt this by offering to do the job themselves. In meetings of the Ad Hoc Committee, a new concept reared its head, that of 'complementarity', by which the court could only exercise jurisdiction if domestic courts were unwilling or unable to prosecute. Another departure of the Ad Hoc Committee from the International Law Commission draft was its insistence that the crimes within the court's jurisdiction be defined in some detail and not simply enumerated. The International Law Commission had contented itself with listing the crimes subject to the court's jurisdiction – war crimes, aggression, crimes against humanity and genocide – presumably because the draft code of crimes, on which it was also working, would provide the more comprehensive definitional aspects. Beginning with the Ad Hoc Committee, the nearly fifty-year-old distinction between the 'statute' and the 'code' disappeared. Henceforth, the statute would include detailed definitions of crimes as well as elaborate provisions dealing with general principles of law and

[45] All of the basic documents of the drafting history of the Statute, including the draft statute prepared by the International Law Commission, have been reproduced in M. Cherif Bassiouni, ed., *The Statute of the International Criminal Court: A Documentary History*, Ardsley, NY: Transnational Publishers, 1998.

[46] Generally, on the drafting of the Statute, see M. Cherif Bassiouni, 'Negotiating the Treaty of Rome on the Establishment of an International Criminal Court', (1999) 32 *Cornell International Law Journal* 443.

other substantive matters. The Ad Hoc Committee concluded that the new court was to conform to principles and rules that would ensure the highest standards of justice, and that these should be incorporated in the statute itself rather than being left to the uncertainty of judicial discretion.[47]

It had been hoped that the Ad Hoc Committee's work would set the stage for a diplomatic conference where the statute could be adopted. But it became evident that this was premature. At its 1995 session, the General Assembly decided to convene a 'Preparatory Committee', inviting participation by Member States, non-governmental organizations and international organizations of various sorts. The 'PrepCom', as it became known, held two three-week sessions in 1996, presenting the General Assembly with a voluminous report comprising a hefty list of proposed amendments to the International Law Commission draft.[48] It met again in 1997, this time holding three sessions. These were punctuated by informal intersessional meetings, of which the most important was surely that held in Zutphen, in the Netherlands, in January 1998. The 'Zutphen draft' consolidated the various proposals into a more or less coherent text.[49] The 'Zutphen draft' was reworked somewhat at the final session of the Preparatory Committee, and then submitted for consideration by the Diplomatic Conference.[50] Few provisions of the original International Law Commission proposal had survived intact. Most of the Articles in the final draft were accompanied with an assortment of options and alternatives, surrounded by square brackets to indicate a lack of consensus, foreboding difficult negotiations at the Diplomatic Conference.[51] Some important issues such as 'complementarity' – recognition that cases would only be admissible before the new court when national justice systems were unwilling or unable to try them – were largely resolved during the

[47] 'Report of the Ad Hoc Committee on the Establishment of an International Criminal Court', UN Doc. A/50/22. See Roy Lee, 'The Rome Conference and Its Contributions to International Law', in Roy Lee, ed., *The International Criminal Court, The Making of the Rome Statute, Issues, Negotiations, Results*, The Hague: Kluwer Law International, 1999, pp. 1–39, at p. 7; Tuiloma Neroni Slade and Roger S. Clark, 'Preamble and Final Clauses', in Lee, *ibid.*, pp. 421–50, at pp. 436–7.

[48] 'Report of the Preparatory Committee on the Establishment of an International Criminal Court', UN Doc. A/51/22.

[49] 'Report of the Inter-Sessional Meeting from 19 to 30 January 1998 in Zutphen, The Netherlands', UN Doc. A/AC.249/1998/L.13.

[50] 'Report of the Preparatory Committee on the Establishment of an International Criminal Court, Addendum', UN Doc. A/CONF.183/2/Add.1.

[51] See M. Cherif Bassiouni, 'Observations Concerning the 1997–98 Preparatory Committee's Work', (1997) 25 *Denver Journal of International Law and Policy* 397.

PrepCom process. The challenge to the negotiators at the Diplomatic Conference was to ensure that these issues were not reopened. Other matters, such as the issue of capital punishment, had been studiously avoided during the sessions of the PrepCom, and were to emerge suddenly as impasses in the final negotiations.

Pursuant to General Assembly resolutions adopted in 1996 and 1997, the Diplomatic Conference of Plenipotentiaries on the Establishment of an International Criminal Court convened on 15 June 1998 in Rome, at the headquarters of the Food and Agriculture Organization. More than 160 States sent delegates to the Conference, in addition to a range of international organizations and literally hundreds of non-governmental organizations. The enthusiasm was quite astonishing, with essentially all of the delegations expressing their support for the concept. Driving the dynamism of the Conference were two new constituencies: a geographically heterogeneous caucus of States known as the 'like minded'; and a well-organized coalition of non-governmental organizations.[52] The 'like minded'; initially chaired by Canada, had been active since the early stages of the Preparatory Commission, gradually consolidating its positions while at the same time expanding its membership. By the time the Rome Conference began, the 'like minded caucus' included more than sixty of the 160 participating States.[53] The like-minded were committed to a handful of key propositions that were substantially at odds with the premises of the 1994 International Law Commission draft and, by and large, in conflict with the conception of the court held by the permanent members of the Security Council. The principles of the like-minded were: an inherent jurisdiction of the Court over the 'core crimes' of genocide, crimes against humanity and war crimes (and, perhaps, aggression); elimination of a Security Council veto on prosecutions; an independent prosecutor

---

[52] On the phenomenal and unprecedented contribution of non-governmental organizations, see William R. Pace and Mark Thieroff, 'Participation of Non-Governmental Organizations', in Lee, *The International Criminal Court*, pp. 391–8; William Bourdon, 'Rôle de la société civile et des ONG', in *La Cour pénale internationale*, Paris: La Documentation française, 1999, pp. 89–96.

[53] Andorra, Argentina, Australia, Austria, Belgium, Brunei, Benin, Bosnia-Herzegovina, Bulgaria, Burkina Faso, Burundi, Canada, Chile, Congo (Brazzaville), Costa Rica, Croatia, Czech Republic, Denmark, Egypt, Estonia, Finland, Gabon, Georgia, Germany, Ghana, Greece, Hungary, Ireland, Italy, Jordan, Latvia, Lesotho, Liechtenstein, Lithuania, Luxembourg, Malawi, Malta, Namibia, the Netherlands, New Zealand, Norway, the Philippines, Poland, Portugal, Republic of Korea, Romania, Samoa, Senegal, Sierra Leone, Singapore, Slovakia, Slovenia, Solomon Islands, South Africa, Spain, Swaziland, Sweden, Switzerland, Trinidad and Tobago, United Kingdom, Venezuela and Zambia.

with the power to initiate proceedings *proprio motu*; and the prohibition of reservations to the statute. While operating relatively informally, the like-minded quickly dominated the structure of the Conference. Key functions, including the chairs of most of the working groups, as well as membership in the Bureau, which was the executive body that directed the day-to-day affairs of the Conference, were taken up by its members. Canada relinquished the chair of the like-minded when the legal advisor to its foreign ministry, Philippe Kirsch, was elected president of the Conference's Committee of the Whole.

But there were other caucuses and groupings at work, many of them reflections of existing formations within other international bodies, like the United Nations. The caucus of the Non-Aligned Movement (NAM) was particularly active in its insistence that the crime of aggression be included within the subject matter jurisdiction of the Court. A relatively new force, the Southern African Development Community (SADC), under the dynamic influence of post-*apartheid* South Africa, took important positions on human rights, providing a valuable counter-weight to the Europeans in this field. The caucus of the Arab and Islamic States were active in a number of areas, including a call for prohibition of nuclear weapons, and support for inclusion of the death penalty within the statute. The beauty of the like-minded caucus, indeed the key to its great success, was its ability to cut across the traditional regionalist lines. Following the election of the Labour Government in the United Kingdom, the like-minded caucus even managed to recruit a permanent member of the Security Council to its ranks.

The Rome Conference began with a few days of formal speeches from political figures, United Nations officials and personalities from the growing ranks of those actually involved in international criminal prosecution, including the presidents of the two *ad hoc* tribunals and their Prosecutor.[54] Then the Conference divided into a series of working groups with responsibility for matters such as general principles, procedure and penalties. Much of this involved details, unlikely to create insurmountable difficulties to the extent that the delegates were committed to the success

---

[54] For a detailed discussion of the proceedings at the Rome Conference, see Philippe Kirsch and John T. Holmes, 'The Rome Conference on an International Criminal Court, The Negotiating Process', (1999) 93 *American Journal of International Law* 2; Roy Lee, 'The Rome Conference and Its Contributions to International Law', in Lee, *The International Criminal Court*, pp. 1–39, particularly pp. 21–3; and Philippe Kirsch, 'The Development of the Rome Statute', in Lee, *The International Criminal Court*, pp. 451–61.

of the endeavour. But a handful of core issues – jurisdiction, the 'trigger mechanism' for prosecutions, the role of the Security Council – remained under the wing of the Bureau. These difficult questions were not publicly debated for most of the Conference, although much negotiating took place informally.

One by one, the provisions of the statute were adopted 'by general agreement' in the working groups, that is, without a vote. The process was tedious, in that it allowed a handful of States or even one of them to hold up progress by refusing to join consensus. The chairs of the working groups would patiently negotiate compromises, drawing on comments by States who often expressed their views on a provision but then indicated their willingness to be flexible. Within a week of the beginning of the Conference, the working groups were forwarding progress reports to the Committee of the Whole, indicating the provisions that had already met with agreement. These were subsequently examined by the Drafting Committee, chaired by Professor M. Cherif Bassiouni, for terminological and linguistic coherence in the various official language versions of the statute.

But as the weeks rolled by, the key issues remained to be settled, of which the most important were the role of the Security Council, the list of 'core crimes' over which the court would have inherent jurisdiction and the scope of its jurisdiction over persons who were not nationals of States Parties. These had not been assigned to any of the working groups, and instead were handled personally by the chair of the Committee of the Whole, Philippe Kirsch. With two weeks remaining, Kirsch issued a draft that set out the options on these difficult questions. The problem, though, was that many States belonged to the majority on one question but dissented on others. Finding a common denominator, that is, a workable statute that could reliably obtain the support of two-thirds of the delegates in the event that the draft statute were ever to come to a vote, remained daunting. Suspense mounted in the final week, with Kirsch promising a final proposal that in fact he only issued on the morning of 17 July, the day the Conference was scheduled to conclude. By then it was too late for any changes. Like a skilled blackjack player, Kirsch had carefully counted his cards, yet he had no guarantee that his proposal might meet unexpected opposition and lead, inexorably, to the collapse of the negotiations. Throughout the final day of the Conference delegates expressed their support for the 'package', and resisted any attempts to alter or adjust it out of fear that the entire compromise might unravel. The United States tried unsuccessfully to rally opposition, convening a meeting of what it had assessed as 'waverers'. Indeed, hopes that the draft statute might be adopted by consensus at the final session were dashed when the United States exercised its right to demand that a vote be taken. The result was 120 in favour, with twenty-one abstentions and seven votes against. The vote was not taken by roll call, and only the declarations made by States themselves indicate who voted for what. The United States, Israel and China stated that they had opposed adoption of the statute.[55] Among the abstainers were several Arab and Islamic States, as well as a number of delegations from the Commonwealth Caribbean.

In addition to the Statute of the International Criminal Court,[56] on 17 July, 1998 the Diplomatic Conference also adopted a Final Act,[57] providing for the establishment of a Preparatory Commission. The Commission was assigned a variety of tasks, of which the most important were the drafting of the Rules of Procedure and Evidence,[58] which provide details on a variety of procedural and evidentiary questions, and the Elements of Crimes,[59] which elaborate upon the definitions of offences in Articles 6, 7 and 8 of the Statute. The Commission met the deadline of 30 June 2000 set for it by the Final Act, for the completion of the Rules and the Elements.[60] Other tasks include drafting an agreement with the United Nations on the relationship between the two organizations, and preparation of a host state agreement with the Netherlands, which is to be the seat of the Court. The Preparatory Commission is to operate until the Statute comes into force, at which point the Assembly of States Parties will be convened. The Assembly will elect the judges and prosecutor, and presumably endorse the work of the Preparatory Commission.

[55] Lee, *The International Criminal Court*, at pp. 25–6; and Giovanni Conso, 'Looking to the Future', in Lee, *The International Criminal Court*, pp. 471–7. For the positions of the United States and China, see UN Doc. A/C.6/53/SR.9.

[56] The text of the Statute adopted at the close of the Rome Conference contained a number of minor errors, essentially of a technical nature. There have been two attempts at correction: UN Doc. C.N.577.1998.TREATIES-8 (10 November 1998) and UN Doc. C.N.604.1999. TREATIES-18 (12 July 1999).   [57] UN Doc. A/CONF.183/10.

[58] Provided for in Art. 51 of the Rome Statute.

[59] Provided for in Art. 9 of the Rome Statute.

[60] 'Report of the Preparatory Commission for the International Criminal Court, Addendum, Finalized Draft Text of the Elements of Crimes', UN Doc. PCNICC/2000/INF/3/Add.2; 'Report of the Preparatory Commission for the International Criminal Court, Addendum, Finalized Draft Text of the Rules of Procedure and Evidence', UN Doc. PCNICC/2000/INF/3/Add.3.

The Statute requires sixty ratifications before it can enter into force. States are also invited to sign the Statute, which is a preliminary step indicating their intention to ratify. They were given until the end of 2000 to do so, and some 139, including the United States, Israel and several Arab and Islamic States, availed themselves of the opportunity to do so. Delays between signature and ratification are to be expected, because most States must undertake significant legislative changes in order to comply with the obligations imposed by the Statute, and it is normal that they will want to resolve these issues before formal ratification. Specifically, they must provide for cooperation with the Court in terms of investigation, arrest and transfer of suspects. Many States now prohibit the extradition of their own nationals, a situation incompatible with the requirements of the Statute. In addition, because the Statute is predicated on 'complementarity', by which States themselves are presumed to be responsible for prosecuting suspects found on their own territory, many must also bring their substantive criminal law into line, enacting the offences of genocide, crimes against humanity and war crimes as defined in the Statute and ensuring that their courts can exercise universal jurisdiction over these crimes.[61]

The influence of the Rome Statute will extend deep into domestic criminal law, enriching the jurisprudence of national courts and challenging prosecutors and judges to greater zeal in the repression of serious violations of human rights. National courts have shown, in recent years, a growing enthusiasm for the use of international law materials in the application of their own laws. The Statute itself, and eventually the case law of the International Criminal Court, will no doubt contribute in this area. The International Criminal Tribunal for the Former Yugoslavia, in *Prosecutor v. Furundzija*, described the Statute's current legal significance as follows:

[A]t present it is still a non-binding international treaty (it has not yet entered into force). It was adopted by an overwhelming majority of the States attending the Rome Diplomatic Conference and was substantially endorsed by the General Assembly's Sixth Committee on 26 November

---

[61] William A. Schabas, 'The Follow Up to Rome: Preparing for Entry into Force of the International Criminal Court Statute', (1999) 20 *Human Rights Law Journal* 157; S. Rama Rao, 'Financing of the Court, Assembly of States Parties and the Preparatory Commission', in Lee, *The International Criminal Court*, pp. 399–420, at pp. 414–20; Bruce Broomhall, 'The International Criminal Court: A Checklist for National Implementation', (1999) 13*quater Nouvelles études pénales* 113.

1998. In many areas the Statute may be regarded as indicative of the legal views, i.e. *opinio juris* of a great number of States. Notwithstanding article 10 of the Statute, the purpose of which is to ensure that existing or developing law is not 'limited' or 'prejudiced' by the Statute's provisions, resort may be had *com grano salis* to these provisions to help elucidate customary international law. Depending on the matter at issue, the Rome Statute may be taken to restate, reflect or clarify customary rules or crystallise them, whereas in some areas it creates new law or modifies existing law. At any event, the Rome Statute by and large may be taken as constituting an authoritative expression of the legal views of a great number of States.[62]

The International Criminal Court is perhaps the most innovative and exciting development in international law since the creation of the United Nations. The Statute is one of the most complex international instruments ever negotiated, a sophisticated web of highly technical provisions drawn from comparative criminal law combined with a series of more political propositions that touch the very heart of State concerns with their own sovereignty. Without any doubt its creation is the result of the human rights agenda that has steadily taken centre stage within the United Nations since Article 1 of its Charter proclaimed the promotion of human rights to be one of its purposes. From a hesitant commitment in 1945, to an ambitious Universal Declaration of Human Rights in 1948, we have now reached a point where individual criminal liability is established for those responsible for serious violations of human rights, and where an institution is created to see that this is more than just some pious wish.

---

[62] *Prosecutor v. Furundzija, supra* note 35, para. 227. For an example of the draft statute of the court being cited as a guide to evolving customary international law, see the reasons of Justice Michel Bastarache of the Supreme Court of Canada in *Pushpanathan* v. *Canada (Minister of Citizenship and Immigration)* [1998] 1 SCR 982, at paras 66–8.

2

Crimes prosecuted by the Court

The International Criminal Court has jurisdiction over four categories of crimes: genocide, crimes against humanity, war crimes and aggression. In both the preamble to the Statute and in Article 5, these are variously described as 'the most serious crimes of concern to the international community as a whole'. Elsewhere, the Statute describes them as 'unimaginable atrocities that deeply shock the conscience of humanity' (preamble), 'international crimes' (preamble), and 'the most serious crimes of international concern' (Article 1).

The concept of 'international crimes' has been around for centuries. They were generally considered to be offences whose repression compelled some international dimension. Piracy, for example, was committed on the high seas. This feature of the crime necessitated special jurisdictional rules as well as cooperation between States. Similar requirements obtained with respect to the slave trade, trafficking in women and children, traffic in narcotic drugs, hijacking, terrorism and money laundering. It was indeed this sort of crime that inspired Trinidad and Tobago, in 1989, to reactivate the issue of an international criminal court within the General Assembly of the United Nations.[1] Crimes of this type are already addressed in a rather sophisticated scheme of international treaties, and for this reason the drafters of the Rome Statute referred to them as 'treaty crimes'.

The crimes over which the International Criminal Court has jurisdiction are 'international' not so much because international cooperation is needed for their repression, although this is also true, but because their heinous nature elevates them to a level where they are of 'concern' to the international community. These crimes are somewhat more recent in origin than many of the so-called 'treaty crimes', in that their recognition and subsequent development is closely associated with the human rights movement that arose subsequent to World War II. They dictate

---

[1] GA Res. 44/89.

prosecution because humanity as a whole is the victim. Moreover, humanity as a whole is entitled, indeed required, to prosecute them for essentially the same reasons as we now say that humanity as a whole is concerned by violations of human rights that were once considered to lie within the exclusive prerogatives of State sovereignty.

All four crimes within the jurisdiction of the Court were prosecuted, at least in an earlier and somewhat embryonic form, by the Nuremberg Tribunal and the other post-war courts. At Nuremberg, they were called crimes against peace, war crimes and crimes against humanity.[2] The term 'crimes against peace' is now replaced by 'aggression'; while probably not identical, the two terms largely overlap. Although the term 'genocide' already existed at the time of the Nuremberg trial, and it was used by the prosecutors, the indictments against Nazi criminals for the genocide of European Jews were based on the charge of 'crimes against humanity'. But, in contemporary usage, the crime of 'genocide' is now subsumed within the broader concept of 'crimes against humanity'.

The definitions of crimes within the Nuremberg Charter are relatively laconic, and the scope of the four categories of crimes as they are now conceived has evolved considerably since that time. Since Nuremberg, the concepts of crimes against humanity and war crimes have also undergone considerable development and enlargement. For example, crimes against humanity can now take place in peacetime as well as during armed combat, and war crimes exist in non-international as well as in international armed conflict. The evolution in the definitions is somewhat reflected in the length of the definitions in the Rome Statute. But other factors are also at work. It was easier to define the crimes at Nuremberg because it was the prosecutors who were doing the defining. When States realize they are setting a standard by which they themselves, or their leaders and military personnel, may be judged, they seem to take greater care and insist upon many safeguards. Arguments in favour of more detailed texts also relied upon principles of procedural fairness in criminal law, recognized by contemporary human rights law. At Rome, States argued that the 'principle of legality' dictated detailed and precise provisions setting out the punishable crimes.

The definition of the crimes in the Rome Statute is in some cases the

---

[2] Agreement for the Prosecution and Punishment of Major War Criminals of the European Axis, and Establishing the Charter of the International Military Tribunal (IMT), Annex, (1951) 82 UNTS 279.

result of recent treaties, such as the 1984 Convention Against Torture[3] or the earlier Apartheid Convention.[4] But much of the development in the definition of these crimes is attributed to the evolution of customary law, whose content is not always as easy to identify with clarity. The definitions of crimes set out in Articles 6 to 8, as completed by the Elements of Crimes, correspond in a general sense to the state of customary international law. The three categories of crimes are drawn from existing definitions and use familiar terminology. The drafters might have chosen to dispense with these old terms – crimes against humanity, war crimes – in favour of a genuinely original codification, defining the Court's subject matter jurisdiction as being over 'serious violations of human rights'.[5] But they did not take such a route. Nevertheless, while the correspondence with customary international law is close, it is far from perfect. To answer concerns that the Statute's definitions of crimes be taken as a codification of custom, Article 10 of the Statute declares: 'Nothing in this Part shall be interpreted as limiting or prejudicing in any way existing or developing rules of international law for purposes other than this Statute.' Those who argue that customary law goes beyond the Statute, for example by prohibiting the use of certain weapons that are not listed in Article 8, can rely on this provision.[6] It will become more and more important in the future, because customary law should evolve and the Statute may not be able to keep pace with it. For example, it is foreseeable that international law may raise the age of prohibited military recruitment from fifteen, or consider certain weapons to be prohibited. As a result of Article 10, the Statute cannot provide comfort to those who argue against this evolution of customary law. But, of course, the logic of Article 10 cuts both ways. To those who claim that the Statute sets a new minimum standard, for example in the field of gender crimes, conservative jurists will plead Article 10 and stress the differences between the texts in the Statute and their less prolix ancestors in the Geneva Conventions and related instruments.

There would be little disagreement with the proposition that the Court

---

[3] Convention Against Torture and Other Cruel, Inhuman or Degrading Treatment or Punishment, (1987) 1465 UNTS 85.

[4] International Convention on the Suppression and Punishment of the Crime of Apartheid, (1976) 1015 UNTS 243.

[5] See, on this, L. C. Green, '"Grave Breaches" or Crimes Against Humanity', (1997/98) 8 *United States Air Force Academy Journal of Legal Studies* 19; William J. Fenrick, 'Should Crimes Against Humanity Replace War Crimes?', (1999) 37 *Columbia Journal of Transnational Law* 767.

[6] Note also the definitions of crimes, which begin with the phrase 'For the purpose of this Statute . . .'.

is not designed to try all perpetrators of the four core crimes. It will be concerned not only with 'the most serious crimes' but also with the most serious criminals, generally leaders, organizers and instigators. Lower-level offenders are unlikely to attract the attention of a prosecutor whose energies must be concentrated, if only because of budgetary constraints. Article 17(1)(d) of the Statute says that the Court must declare a case inadmissible if it is not 'of sufficient gravity'. The Prosecutor, in the exercise of his or her discretion as to whether to proceed with a case, is instructed to forego prosecution when '[a] prosecution is not in the interests of justice, taking into account all the circumstances, including the gravity of the crime, the interests of victims and the age or infirmity of the alleged perpetrator, and his or her role in the alleged crime'.[7] In the case of juvenile offenders, the Statute does this explicitly, declaring simply that the Court is without jurisdiction over a person who was under the age of eighteen at the time of the alleged commission of a crime.[8] This does not, of course, mean that a young person of seventeen cannot commit a crime against humanity or a war crime. Rather, it is a policy decision made by the drafters of the Statute that was driven by considerations about the nature of the accused rather than the nature of the crime.

In addition, all of the definitions of crimes within the jurisdiction of the Court have some form of built-in threshold that will help to focus these decisions and limit the discretion of the Prosecutor. In the case of genocide, the result is achieved by the very high level of *dolus specialis* or 'special intent' that is part of the definition of the crime. The offender must intend to destroy the targeted group in whole or in part. Many of those who participate in a genocide may well fall outside this definition. Although they are actively involved, they may lack knowledge of the context of the crime and for that reason lack the requisite intent. In the case of crimes against humanity, this issue is addressed somewhat differently, with a criterion by which the offence must be part of a 'widespread or systematic attack'. Both genocide, by its very nature, and crimes against humanity, by the widespread or systematic qualification, have a quantitative dimension. They are not isolated crimes, and will in practice only be prosecuted when planned or committed on a large scale. In contrast, war crimes do not, in a definitional sense, require the same quantitative scale. A single murder of a prisoner of war or a civilian may constitute a war crime, but it is hard to

---

[7] Rome Statute of the International Criminal Court, UN Doc. A/CONF.183/9 (hereinafter Rome Statute), Art. 53(2)(c).   [8] *Ibid.*, Art. 26.

envisage a single murder constituting genocide or a crime against humanity, at least in the absence of some broader context. For this reason, the
Rome Statute attempts to narrow the scope of war crimes with a short
introductory paragraph or *chapeau* at the beginning of Article 8: 'The
Court shall have jurisdiction in respect of war crimes in particular when
committed as a part of a plan or policy or as part of a large-scale commission of such crimes.' Many States were opposed to any such limitation on
the scope of war crimes, and only agreed to the provision if the words 'in
particular' were included. It should not be taken as any new restriction on
the customary definition of war crimes but rather as a technique to limit
the jurisdiction of the Court.

The Statute does not propose any formal hierarchy among the four categories of crime. There are suggestions, within customary international
law, the case law of international tribunals and the Statute itself, that even
among these 'most serious crimes', some are more serious than others. It
might be argued that war crimes are less important than both genocide
and crimes against humanity because Article 124 of the Statute allows
States to 'opt out' temporarily of jurisdiction for war crimes at the time of
ratification. Also, two of the defences that are codified by the Statute,
superior orders and defence of property,[9] are admissible only in the case of
war crimes, implying that justification may exist for war crimes where it
can never exist for genocide and crimes against humanity. The crime of
'direct and public incitement' exists only in the case of genocide;[10] the
drafters at Rome rejected suggestions that this inchoate form of criminal-
ity, drawn from Article III of the 1948 Genocide Convention, be broad-
ened to encompass crimes against humanity and war crimes. Before the *ad
hoc* tribunals for the former Yugoslavia and Rwanda, the judges appear to
be divided on whether or not there is a hierarchy between the different categories of offences, although a majority seems unfavourable to the
concept.[11]

Article 5 of the Rome Statute declares that the Court's jurisdiction is
limited to 'the most serious crimes of concern to the international community as a whole' and, specifically, to the crime of genocide, crimes

---

[9] *Ibid.*, Arts 33(2) and 31(1)(c) respectively.   [10] *Ibid.*, Art. 25(3)(e).

[11] *Prosecutor* v. *Erdemovic* (Case No. IT-96-22-A), Sentencing Appeal, 7 October 1997, (1998) 111
ILR 298; *Prosecutor* v. *Kupreskić et al.* (Case No. IT-95-16-T), Judgment, 14 January 2000;
Prosecutor v. *Tadić* (Case No. IT-94-1-A and IT-94-1-A*bis*), Judgment in Sentencing Appeals,
26 January 2000; *Prosecutor* v. *Furundzija* (Case No. IT-96-17/1-A), Judgment, 17 July 2000.

against humanity, war crimes and the crime of aggression. A review conference, to be held seven years after the entry into force of the Statute, may consider amendments to the list of crimes contained in Article 5,[12] and it is therefore not inconceivable that new offences may be added. The Statute also contemplates the possibility of amendments to the definitions that were adopted at Rome.[13]

Some offences, while theoretically within the subject matter jurisdiction of the Court, are subject to further decisions and agreements. For example, the war crimes provision dealing with use of weapons and methods of warfare of a nature to cause superfluous injury or unnecessary suffering, or which are inherently indiscriminate, can only become operational when a list of such weapons and methods is included in an annex to the Statute. But the real 'sleeper' in the Court's subject matter jurisdiction is the crime of aggression. While the Rome Conference agreed that aggression should be part of its subject matter jurisdiction, it proved impossible to agree upon either a definition or the appropriate mechanism for judicial determination of whether or not the crime had actually occurred. The definition of aggression and the conditions of its prosecution, as well as the annex enumerating prohibited weapons and methods of warfare, require a formal amendment, in accordance with Articles 121 and 123 of the Statute.

It was largely the non-aligned countries who insisted that aggression remain within the jurisdiction of the Court, and these States pursued a 'compromise on the addition of aggression as a generic crime pending the definition of its elements by a preparatory committee or a review conference at a later stage'.[14] The Bureau of the Rome Conference suggested, on 10 July 1998, that if generally acceptable provisions and definitions were not developed forthwith, aggression would have to be dropped from the Statute.[15] But, literally on the final day of the conference, agreement was reached that gives the Court jurisdiction over aggression once it is defined and its scope designated in a manner consistent with the purposes of the Statute and the ideals of the United Nations. Of course, prosecutions for 'crimes against peace', a more ancient term used to describe the concept of aggression, were undertaken at Nuremberg and Tokyo. During the Rome Conference, both German and Japanese delegations insisted that aggres-

---

[12] Rome Statute, Art. 123.   [13] *Ibid.*, Art. 121(5).
[14] Terraviva, 13 July 1998, No. 21, p. 2; UN Press Release L/ROM/16, 13 July 1998.
[15] UN Doc. A/CONF.183/C.1/L.59.

sion be included, expressing bewilderment over the fact it had been an international crime in 1945 – indeed, the supreme international crime, according to the Nuremberg Tribunal – yet seemed to be one of only secondary importance half a century later.[16] In the early years of the international criminal court project, difficulties in subsequent definition of aggression led to a suspension of the work of the International Law Commission on the Code of Crimes in 1954. A definition was ultimately adopted, by the General Assembly in the early 1970s.[17] Nevertheless, the General Assembly resolution was not designed as an instrument of criminal prosecution, although it will provide a useful basis for a definition.[18]

The reference, in Article 5(2) of the Rome Statute, to the fact that the definition 'shall be consistent with the relevant provisions of the Charter of the United Nations' was a 'carefully constructed phrase' that was 'understood as a reference to the role the Council may or should play'.[19] The underlying issue is the fact that Article 39 of the Charter of the United Nations declares that determining situations of aggression is a prerogative of the Security Council. If the Security Council is the arbiter of situations of aggression, would this mean that the Court can only prosecute aggression once the Council has pronounced on the subject? Such a view seems an incredible encroachment upon the independence of the Court, and would mean, for starters, that no permanent member of the Security Council would ever be subject to prosecution for aggression.[20] Moreover, no Court can leave determination of such a central factual issue to what is essentially a political body. As Judge Schwebel of the International Court of Justice noted, a Security Council determination of aggression is not a legal assessment but is based on political considerations. The Security

---

[16] 'Report of the Ad Hoc Committee on the Establishment of an International Criminal Court', UN Doc. A/50/22, paras 63–71; 'Report of the Preparatory Committee on the Establishment of an International Criminal Court', UN Doc. A/51/22, Vol. I, paras 65–73.

[17] GA Res. 3314. See J. Hogan-Doran and B. T. Van Ginkel, 'Aggression as a Crime under International Law and the Prosecution of Individuals by the Proposed International Criminal Court', (1996) 43 *Netherlands International Law Review* 321.

[18] Lyle S. Sunga, 'The Crimes within the Jurisdiction of the International Criminal Court (Part II, Articles 5–10)', (1998) 6 *European Journal of Crime, Criminal Law and Criminal Justice* 61, at p. 65.

[19] Herman von Hebel and Darryl Robinson, 'Crimes Within the Jurisdiction of the Court', in Roy Lee, ed., *The International Criminal Court, The Making of the Rome Statute, Issues, Negotiations, Results*, The Hague: Kluwer Law International, 1999, pp. 79–126, at p. 85.

[20] Lionel Yee, 'The International Criminal Court and the Security Council: Articles 13(b) and 16', in Lee, *The International Criminal Court*, pp. 143–52, at pp. 144–5. For a discussion of the two views on aggression, see Daniel D. Ntanda Nsereko, 'The International Criminal Court: Jurisdictional and Related Issues', (1999) 10 *Criminal Law Forum* 87, at pp. 94–7.

Council is not acting as a court.[21] At its first session, in February 1999, the Preparatory Commission undertook what was prudently described as 'a preliminary consideration of the modalities of discussion' for a definition of the crime of aggression.[22] But, in August 1999, the Chair of the Commission expressed regret that considerable time had been spent on organizational issues relating to the definition of aggression, to the detriment of substantive discussions, and that there were 'persistent differences' among delegations on the principle and timing of establishing the working group.[23]

Although the original impetus to revive the international criminal court project, in 1989, came from States concerned with matters such as international drug trafficking and terrorism, there was ultimately no consensus on including the 'treaty crimes' within the jurisdiction of the Court and they were excluded at the Rome Conference. These are called 'treaty crimes' because they have been proscribed in a variety of multilateral conventions dealing with terrorist crimes, drug crimes and crimes against United Nations personnel.[24] Proposals at the Rome Conference to include drug trafficking[25] and terrorism[26] did not meet with sufficient consensus. Some considered they should be excluded because they are not 'as serious' as genocide, crimes against humanity and war crimes.[27] In the final version of the Statute, certain crimes against United Nations personnel were incorporated within the definition of war crimes, but that is about all.[28] The Final Act of the Rome Conference, adopted at the same time as the Statute, includes a resolution on treaty crimes recommending that the Review Conference consider means to enable the inclusion of crimes of terrorism and drug crimes.[29] Trinidad and Tobago and other Caribbean

[21] *Military and Paramilitary Activities in and Against Nicaragua (Nicaragua v. United States)*, Merits, [1986] ICJ Reports 14, at 290.

[22] 'Proceedings of the Preparatory Commission at Its First Session (16–26 February 1999), Summary', UN Doc. PCNICC/1999/L.3/Rev.1, para. 11.

[23] UN Press Release L/2932, 9 August 1999.

[24] See especially 'Report of the Preparatory Committee on the Establishment of an International Criminal Court, Addendum', UN Doc. A/CONF.183/2/Add.1 (1998), Art. 5.

[25] 'Proposal Submitted by Barbados, Dominica, Jamaica, and Trinidad and Tobago on Article 5', UN Doc. A/CONF.183/C.1/L.48.

[26] 'Proposal Submitted by Algeria, India, Sri Lanka and Turkey on Article 5', UN Doc. A/CONF.183/C.1/L.27/Corr.1.

[27] Nsereko, 'The International Criminal Court', at pp. 91–2. See also Neil Boister, 'The Exclusion of Treaty Crimes from the Jurisdiction of the Proposed International Criminal Court: Law, Pragmatism, Politics', (1998) 3 *Journal of Armed Conflict Law* 27.

[28] Rome Statute, Arts. 8(2)(b)(iii), 8(2)(b)(vii) and 8(2)(3)(iii).

[29] UN Doc. A/CONF.183/C.1/L.76/Add.14, at p. 8.

Community (Caricom) Member States expressed disappointment at the exclusion of trafficking in narcotic drugs from the Court's subject matter jurisdiction.[30]

For the purposes of interpreting and applying the definitions of crimes found in Articles 6, 7 and 8 of the Rome Statute, reference must also be made to the Elements of Crimes, a fifty-page document adopted in June 2000 by the Preparatory Commission, subject to eventual endorsement by the Assembly of States Parties once the Statute comes into force.[31] The Elements of Crimes are a source of applicable law for the Court,[32] but as a form of subordinate legislation they must also be consistent with the Statute itself. The whole concept originated with the United States delegation, and, while at Rome many met it with some suspicion, the idea seemed rather less harmful than many other Washington-based initiatives and it was incorporated in the Statute without great opposition. Fundamentally, the Elements reflect the continuing suspicion among States of any degree of judicial discretion. Thus, in addition to prolix definitions of crimes, the Elements further fetter the possibilities of judicial interpretation. On a more positive note, they are somewhat easier to amend than the Statute itself, thereby allowing the Assembly of States Parties the possibility of 'tweaking' the definitions of crimes when this seems desirable.

Genocide

The word 'genocide' was coined in 1944 by Raphael Lemkin in his book on Nazi crimes in occupied Europe.[33] Lemkin felt that the treaty regime aimed at protection of national minorities established between the two world wars had important shortcomings, amongst them the failure to provide for prosecution of crimes against groups. The term 'genocide' was adopted the following year by the prosecutors at Nuremberg (although not by the judges), and in 1946 genocide was declared an international crime by the General Assembly of the United Nations.[34] The Assembly also decided to proceed with the drafting of a treaty on genocide.

---

[30] UN Doc. A/C.6/53/SR.9.

[31] Pursuant to Art. 9 of the Rome Statute. For the draft Elements of Crimes, see 'Report of the Preparatory Commission for the International Criminal Court, Addendum, Finalized Draft Text of the Elements of Crimes', UN Doc. PCNICC/2000/INF/3/Add.2.

[32] Rome Statute, Art. 21(1)(a).

[33] Raphael Lemkin, *Axis Rule in Occupied Europe: Laws of Occupation, Analysis of Government, Proposals for Redress*, Washington: Carnegie Endowment for World Peace, 1944.

[34] GA Res. 96(I).

At the time, it was considered important to define genocide as a separate crime in order to distinguish it from crimes against humanity. The latter term referred to a rather wider range of atrocities, but it also had a narrow aspect, in that the prevailing view was that crimes against humanity could only be committed in association with an international armed conflict. The General Assembly wanted to go a step further, recognizing that one atrocity, namely genocide, would constitute an international crime even if it were committed in time of peace. The price to pay, however, was an exceedingly narrow definition of the mental and material elements of the crime. This was set out in the Convention on the Prevention and Punishment of the Crime of Genocide, adopted by the General Assembly of the United Nations on 9 December 1948.[35] The Convention entered into force two years later after obtaining twenty ratifications. The Convention itself has been described as the quintessential human rights treaty.[36]

The distinction between genocide and crimes against humanity is less significant today, because the recognized definition of crimes against humanity has evolved and now unquestionably refers to atrocities committed in peacetime as well as in wartime. Today, genocide constitutes the most aggravated form of crime against humanity.[37] The International Criminal Tribunal for Rwanda has labelled it 'the crime of crimes'.[38] Not surprisingly, then, it is the first crime set out in the Rome Statute and the only one to be adopted by the drafters with virtually no controversy. Genocide is defined in Article 6 of the Rome Statute.[39] The provision is

[35] Convention on the Prevention and Punishment of the Crime of Genocide, (1951) 78 UNTS 277.

[36] 'Report of the International Law Commission on the Work of its Forty-Ninth Session 12 May–18 July 1997', UN Doc. A/52/10, para. 76. See also *Prosecutor* v. *Kayishema and Ruzindana* (Case No. ICTR-95-1-T), Judgment, 21 May 1999, para. 88.

[37] On the crime of genocide, see Nehemiah Robinson, *The Genocide Convention: A Commentary*, New York: Institute of Jewish Affairs, 1960; Pieter Nicolaas Drost, *Genocide, United Nations Legislation on International Criminal Law*, Leyden: A. W. Sithoff, 1959; William A. Schabas, *Genocide in International Law, The Crime of Crimes*, Cambridge: Cambridge University Press, 2000.

[38] *Prosecutor* v. *Kambanda* (Case No. ICTR-97-23-S), Judgment and Sentence, 4 September 1998, para. 16; *Prosecutor* v. *Serashugo* (Case No. ICTR-98-39-S), Sentence, 2 February 1999, para. 15.

[39] Sunga, 'Crimes Within the Jurisdiction', at pp. 66–8; von Hebel and Robinson, 'Crimes Within the Jurisdiction', at pp. 89–90; William A. Schabas, 'Article 6', in Otto Triffterer, ed., *Commentary on the Rome Statute of the International Criminal Court, Observers' Notes, Article by Article*, Baden-Baden: Nomos Verlagsgesellschaft, 1999, pp. 107–16; Emanuela Fronza, 'Genocide in the Rome Statute', in Flavia Lattanzi and William A. Schabas, eds, *Essays on the Rome Statute of the ICC*, Rome: Editrice il Sirente, 2000, pp. 105–38.

essentially a copy of Article II of the 1948 Convention. The definition set out in Article II, although often criticized for being overly restrictive and difficult to apply to many cases of mass killing and atrocity, has stood the test of time. The decision of the Rome Conference to maintain a fifty-year-old text is convincing evidence that Article 6 of the Statute constitutes a codification of a customary international norm.

Article 6 of the Rome Statute, and Article II of the Genocide Convention, define genocide as five specific acts committed with the intent to destroy a national, ethnical, racial or religious group as such. The five acts are: killing members of the group; causing serious bodily or mental harm to members of the group; imposing conditions on the group calculated to destroy it; preventing births within the group; and forcibly transferring children from the group to another group. The definition has been incorporated in the penal codes of many countries, although actual prosecutions have been rare. The 1961 trial of Adolf Eichmann in Israel was conducted under a legal provision modelled on Article II of the Convention. Only in late 1998, after the adoption of the Rome Statute, were the first significant judgments of the *ad hoc* tribunals issued dealing with interpretation of the norm.

It is often said that what distinguishes genocide from all other crimes is its *dolus specialis* or 'special intent'. In effect, all three crimes that are defined by the Rome Statute provide for prosecution for killing or murder. What sets genocide apart from crimes against humanity and war crimes is that the act, whether killing or one of the other four acts defined in Article 6, must be committed with the specific intent to destroy in whole or in part a national, ethnical, racial or religious group as such. As can be seen, this 'special intent' has several components.

The perpetrator's intent must be 'to destroy' the group. During the debates surrounding the adoption of the Genocide Convention, the forms of destruction were grouped into three categories: physical, biological and cultural. Cultural genocide was the most troublesome of the three, because it could well be interpreted in such a way as to include the suppression of national languages and similar measures. The drafters of the Convention considered that such matters were better left to human rights declarations on the rights of minorities and they actually voted to exclude cultural genocide from the scope of the definition. However, it can be argued that a contemporary interpreter of the definition of genocide should not be bound by the intent of the drafters back in 1948. The words 'to destroy' can readily bear the concept of cultural as well as physical and biological genocide, and bold judges might be tempted to adopt such progressive constructions. In any event, evidence of 'cultural genocide' has already proven to be an important indicator of the intent to perpetrate physical genocide.[40]

The definition of genocide contains no formal requirement that the punishable acts be committed as part of a widespread or systematic attack, or as part of a general or organized plan to destroy the group. This would seem, however, to be an implicit characteristic of the crime of genocide, although in the *Jelesic* case a Trial Chamber of the International Criminal Tribunal for the Former Yugoslavia entertained the hypothesis of the lone genocidal maniac.[41] The Elements of Crimes adopted by the Preparatory Commission require that an act of genocide 'took place in the context of a manifest pattern of similar conduct directed against that group or was conduct that could itself effect such destruction'.[42]

With the words 'in whole or in part' the definition indicates a quantitative dimension. The quantity contemplated must be significant, and an intent to kill only a few members of a group cannot be genocide. The prevailing view is that where only part of a group is destroyed, it must be a 'substantial' part.[43] There is much confusion about this, because it is often thought that there is some precise numerical threshold of real victims before genocide can take place. But the reference to quantity is in the description of the mental element of the crime, and what is important is not the actual number of victims, rather that the perpetrator intended to destroy a large number of members of the group. Where the number of victims becomes genuinely significant is in the proof of such a genocidal intent. The greater the number of real victims, the more logical the conclusion that the intent was to destroy the group 'in whole or in part'.

The destruction must be directed at one of the four groups listed in the definition: national, ethnical, racial or religious. The enumeration has often been criticized because of its limited scope. In effect, proposals to include political and social groups within the definition were rejected in 1948 and, again, during the drafting of the Rome Statute. But dissatisfac-

---

[40] *Prosecutor v. Karadzic and Mladic* (Case No. IT-95-5-R61, IT-95-18-R61), Consideration of the Indictment Within the Framework of Rule 61 of the Rules of Procedure and Evidence, 11 July 1996, para. 94.
[41] *Prosecutor v. Jelesic* (Case No. IT-95-10-T), Judgment, 14 December 1999, para. 100.
[42] Elements of Crimes, UN Doc. PCNICC/2000/INF/3/Add.2, Art. 6(a)(4).
[43] *Prosecutor v. Jelesic, supra* note 41, para. 82.

tion with the narrowness of the four terms was reflected in the first conviction for genocide by the International Criminal Tribunal for Rwanda. It
stated that the drafters of the Genocide Convention meant for the definition to apply to all 'permanent and stable' groups, a questionable interpretation because it so clearly goes beyond the text.[44] The four terms
themselves are not easy to define. Moreover, the common meaning of such
concepts as 'racial groups' has changed considerably since 1948. Taken as a
whole, the four terms correspond closely to what human rights law refers
to as ethnic or national minorities, expressions that themselves have
eluded precise definition.

The description of the crime of genocide concludes with the puzzling
words 'as such'. These were added in 1948 as a compromise between States
that felt genocide required not only an intentional element but also a
motive. The two concepts are not equivalent. Individuals may commit
crimes intentionally, but for a variety of motives: greed, jealousy, hatred
and so on. Proof of motive creates an additional obstacle to effective prosecution, and it is for this reason that several delegations opposed requiring
it as an element of the crime. To date, courts interpreting the definition
have simply avoided the question.

The definition of the mental element or *mens rea* of the crime of genocide, found in the *chapeau* of the provision, is followed by five paragraphs
listing the punishable acts of genocide. The list is an exhaustive one, and
cannot properly be extended to other acts of persecution directed against
ethnic minorities. Such atrocities – for example 'ethnic cleansing', as it is
now known – will for this reason probably be prosecuted as crimes against
humanity rather than as genocide.[45]

Killing is at the core of the definition and is without doubt the most
important of the five acts of genocide. The term killing is synonymous
with murder or intentional homicide (although the Elements of Crimes
say that the term killing is 'interchangeable' with 'causing death'). The
second act of genocide, causing serious bodily or mental harm, refers to

---

[44] *Prosecutor* v. *Akayesu* (Case No. ICTR-96-4-T), Judgment, 2 September 1998, (1998) 37 ILM
1399, para. 515. But in other cases this approach has not been adopted: *Prosecutor* v. *Kayishema
and Ruzindana, supra* note 36, para. 94. See also *Prosecutor* v. *Rutaganda* (Case No. ICTR-96-3-
T), Judgment, 6 December 1999.

[45] Note, for example, that the Prosecutor of the International Criminal Tribunal for the Former
Yugoslavia indicted Slobodan Milosevic for crimes against humanity and not genocide with
respect to allegations of 'ethnic cleansing' in Kosovo during 1999: *Prosecutor* v. *Milosevic et al.*
(Case No. IT-99-37-I), Indictment, 22 May 1999.

acts of major violence falling short of homicide. In the *Akayesu* decision, the Rwanda Tribunal gave rape as an example of such acts. The Elements are even more detailed, stating that such conduct may include 'acts of torture, rape, sexual violence or inhuman or degrading treatment'.[46] The third act of genocide, imposing conditions of life calculated to destroy the group, applies to cases like the forced marches of the Armenian minority in Turkey in 1915. But none of the acts defined in Article 6 consists of genocide if they are not accompanied by the specific genocidal intent. In cases where the intent falls short of the definition, prosecution may still lie for crimes against humanity or war crimes.

Crimes against humanity

Although occasional references to the expression 'crimes against humanity' can be found dating back several centuries, the term was first used in its contemporary context in 1915. The massacres of Turkey's Armenian population were denounced as a crime against humanity in a declaration of three Allied powers pledging that those responsible would be held personally accountable.[47] But, in the post-war peace negotiations, there were objections that this was a form of retroactive criminal legislation and no prosecutions were ever undertaken on an international level for the genocide of the Armenians. The term 'crimes against humanity' reappeared in 1945 as one of three categories of offence within the jurisdiction of the Nuremberg Tribunal. Once again, the arguments about retroactivity resurfaced, but they were successfully rebuffed.

In 1945, there was far less legal difficulty with prosecution of Nazi war criminals for acts committed against civilians in occupied territories. International law already proscribed persecution of civilians within occupied territories, and it was a short step to define these as international crimes. But when Allied lawyers met in 1943 and 1944 to prepare the post-war prosecutions, many of them considered it legally unsound to hold the Nazis responsible for crimes committed against Germans within the borders of Germany. Not without considerable pressure from Jewish non-governmental organizations, there was an important change in thinking

---

[46] Elements of Crimes, Art. 6(b), para. 1, n. 3.
[47] United Nations War Crimes Commission, *History of the United Nations War Crimes Commission and the Development of the Laws of War*, London: His Majesty's Stationery Office, 1948, p. 35.

and it was agreed to extend the criminal responsibility of the Nazis to internal atrocities under the rubric 'crimes against humanity'. But even the Allies were uncomfortable with the ramifications that this might have with respect to treatment of minorities within their own countries, not to mention their colonies. For this reason, they insisted that crimes against humanity could only be committed if they were associated with one of the other crimes within the Nuremberg Tribunal's jurisdiction, that is, war crimes and crimes against peace.[48] In effect, they had imposed a requirement or *nexus*, as it is known, between crimes against humanity and international armed conflict. Lyle Sunga describes the Nuremberg Charter's approach to crimes against humanity as the Siamese twin of war crimes, unnaturally joined.[49] Indeed, we refer to the Nuremberg prosecutions as 'war crimes trials', and the restrictive terminology requiring a *nexus* with armed conflict continues to haunt international prosecution of human rights atrocities, many of which are actually committed during peacetime.

Dissatisfaction with such a limitation emerged within weeks of the Nuremberg judgment. The United Nations General Assembly decided to define the most egregious form of crime against humanity, namely genocide, as a distinct offence that could be committed in time of peace as well as in wartime. Over the years since 1945, there were several variants on the definition of crimes against humanity, some of them eliminating the *nexus* with armed conflict.[50] This led many to suggest that, from the standpoint of customary law, the definition had evolved to cover atrocities committed in peacetime. Elimination of the link with armed conflict was clarified by the Security Council when it established the International Criminal Tribunal for Rwanda,[51] and further recognized by the Appeals Chamber of

---

[48] *Report of Robert H. Jackson, United States Representative to the International Conference on Military Trials*, Washington: US Government Printing Office, 1949; Egon Schwelb, 'Crimes Against Humanity', (1946) 23 *British Yearbook of International Law* 178; Roger S. Clark, 'Crimes Against Humanity at Nuremberg', in G. Ginsburgs and V. N. Kudriavstsev, eds, *The Nuremberg Trial and International Law*, Dordrecht and Boston: Martinus Nijhoff, 1990, pp. 177–212.   [49] Sunga, 'Crimes Within the Jurisdiction', p. 68.

[50] Agreement for the Prosecution and Punishment of Major War Criminals, *supra* note 2, Art. 6(c); International Military Tribunal for the Far East, TIAS No. 1589, Annex, Charter of the International Military Tribunal for the Far East, Art. 5(c); Control Council Law No. 10, Punishment of Persons Guilty of War Crimes, Crimes Against Peace and Against Humanity, 20 December 1945, *Official Gazette of the Control Council for Germany*, No. 3, 31 January 1946, pp. 50–5, Art. II(1)(c); Statute of the International Criminal Tribunal for the Former Yugoslavia, UN Doc. S/RES/827, Annex, Art. 5; Statute of the International Criminal Tribunal for Rwanda, UN Doc. S/RES/955, Annex, Art. 4.

[51] Statute of the International Criminal Tribunal for Rwanda, *supra* note 50, Art. 3.

the International Criminal Tribunal for the Former Yugoslavia in its cele-
brated *Tadic* jurisdictional decision.[52]

Article 7 of the Rome Statute codifies this evolution in the definition of
crimes against humanity, although an argument that customary international law still requires the *nexus* is not inconceivable, based upon the fact
that at Rome 'a significant number of delegations argued vigorously that
crimes against humanity could only be committed during an armed
conflict'.[53] As with genocide, there is nothing specific to indicate that the
crime can be committed in the absence of international armed conflict,
but this is undoubtedly implicit. Article 7 begins with an introductory
paragraph or *chapeau* stating: 'For the purpose of this Statute, "crime
against humanity" means any of the following acts when committed as
part of a widespread or systematic attack directed against any civilian population, with knowledge of the attack.' Like genocide, then, there is an
important threshold that elevates the 'acts' set out later in the provision to
the level of crimes against humanity.

First among them, and the subject of great controversy at the Rome
Conference, is the requirement that these acts be part of a 'widespread or
systematic attack'. Some of the earlier proposals had required that the
attack be widespread *and* systematic. But the apparent broadening of the
threshold may be a deception, because further in Article 8 the term attack
is defined as 'a course of conduct involving the multiple commission of
acts referred to in paragraph 1 against any civilian population, pursuant to
or in furtherance of a State or organizational policy to commit such
attack'. It seems, therefore, that the term attack has both widespread and
systematic aspects. In addition, the attack must be directed against a civilian population, distinguishing it from many war crimes, which may be
targeted at combatants or at civilians. The attack need not be a military
attack.[54] The attack must also be carried out 'pursuant to or in furtherance
of a State or organizational policy to commit such attack'. This phrase

[52] *Prosecutor* v. *Tadic* (Case No. IT-94-1-AR72), Decision on the Defence Motion for
Interlocutory Appeal on Jurisdiction, 2 October 1995, (1997) 105 ILR 453, (1997) 35 ILM 32.
[53] Von Hebel and Robinson, 'Crimes Within the Jurisdiction', at p. 92. See also, on Art. 7 of the
Rome Statute: Darryl Robinson, 'Crimes Against Humanity: Reflections on State Sovereignty,
Legal Precision and the Dictates of the Public Conscience', in Lattanzi and Schabas, *Essays on
the Rome Statute*, pp. 139–70; Machteld Boot, Rodney Dixon and Christopher K. Hall, 'Article
7', in Triffterer, *Commentary*, pp. 117–72; M. Cherif Bassiouni, *Crimes Against Humanity in
International Law*, 2nd edn, The Hague: Kluwer Law International, 1999; Darryl Robinson,
'Defining "Crimes Against Humanity" at the Rome Conference', (1999) 93 *American Journal of
International Law* 43.   [54] Elements of Crimes, Art. 7, Introduction, para. 3.

indicates that crimes against humanity may in some circumstances be committed by non-State actors. Finally, the perpetrator must have 'knowledge of the attack'. This amounts to a form of specific intent, although one that is less demanding than the specific intent required by the definition of genocide. An individual who participates in crimes against humanity but who is unaware that they are part of a widespread or systematic attack on a civilian population may be guilty of murder and perhaps even war crimes but cannot be convicted by the International Criminal Court for crimes against humanity. However, according to the Elements of Crimes, this does not require 'that the perpetrator had knowledge of all characteristics of the attack or the precise details of the plan or policy of the State or organization'.[55]

The definition of crimes against humanity makes no mention of the motive for such crimes, unlike some earlier models for the definition that imply such a requirement. Some States had argued for the contrary view, insisting that they were supported by customary international law, but they gave way to the majority on this point.[56] This issue, too, remained controversial until a 1999 judgment of the Appeals Chamber of the ICTY declared that there was no particular motive requirement for crimes against humanity in general (the act of 'persecution' has a motive requirement built into its definition).[57] This does not mean, of course, that motive is never relevant to prosecution of crimes against humanity. Where it can be shown that an accused had a motive to commit the crime, this may be a compelling indicator of guilt, just as the absence of any motive may raise a doubt about innocence. Motive is also germane to the establishment of an appropriate sentence for the crime.[58]

The *chapeau* of paragraph 1 of Article 7 is followed by a list of eleven acts of crimes against humanity. At Nuremberg, the list was considerably shorter. It has been enriched principally by developments in international human rights law. Accordingly, there are subparagraphs dealing with specific types of crimes against humanity that have already been the subject of prohibitions in international law, namely, apartheid, torture and enforced disappearance. Some terms that were recognized at the time of Nuremberg have also been developed and expanded. For example, to

---

[55] *Ibid.*, para. 2.
[56] Von Hebel and Robinson, 'Crimes Within the Jurisdiction', at pp. 93–4.
[57] *Prosecutor v. Tadic* (Case No. IT-94-1-A), Judgment, 15 July 1999.
[58] For example, Rules of Procedure and Evidence, UN Doc. PCNICC/2000/INF/3/Add.1, Rule 145(2)(v).

'deportation' is now added the words 'forcible transfer of population', recognizing our condemnation of what in recent years has been known as 'ethnic cleansing', particularly when this takes place within a country's own borders. However, proposals to include other new acts of crimes against humanity, including economic embargo, terrorism and mass starvation, did not rally sufficient support.

The most dramatic example of enlarging the scope of the crime is found in the very substantial list of 'gender crimes'. The Nuremberg Charter did not even recognize rape as a form of crime against humanity, at least explicitly, although this was corrected by judicial interpretation as well as in the texts of subsequent definitions. The Rome Statute goes much further, referring to '[r]ape, sexual slavery, enforced prostitution, forced pregnancy, enforced sterilization, or any other form of sexual violence of comparable gravity'.[59] The term 'forced pregnancy' was the most problematic, because some believed it might be construed as creating an obligation upon States to provide women who had been forcibly impregnated with access to abortion.[60] A definition of the term was agreed to: '"Forced pregnancy" means the unlawful confinement, of a woman forcibly made pregnant, with the intent of affecting the ethnic composition of any population or carrying out other grave violations of international law. This definition shall not in any way be interpreted as affecting national laws relating to pregnancy.'[61] The second sentence was added to reassure some States that the Rome Statute would not conflict with anti-abortion laws.[62]

Although Article 7 expands the scope of crimes against humanity, in some respects it may also limit it. For example, the Statute defines persecution as a punishable act: 'Persecution against any identifiable group or col-

---

[59] For detailed analysis of the gender crime provisions in crimes against humanity, see Kelly Dawn Askin, 'Crimes Within the Jurisdiction of the International Criminal Court', (1999) 10 *Criminal Law Forum* 33; Cate Steains, 'Gender Issues', in Lee, *The International Criminal Court*, pp. 357–90; Barbara C. Bedont, 'Gender-Specific Provisions in the Statute of the ICC', in Lattanzi and Schabas, *Essays on the Rome Statute*, pp. 183–210. See also Nicole Eva Erb, 'Gender-Based Crimes under the Draft Statute for the Permanent International Criminal Court', (1998) 29 *Columbia Human Rights Law Review* 401; Patricia Viseur Sellers and Kaoru Okuizuma, 'International Prosecution of Sexual Assaults', (1997) 7 *Transnational Law and Contemporary Problems* 45.
[60] The Holy See attempted to introduce a reference to 'human beings' in the preamble that was widely viewed as an attempt to raise the abortion issue, and was rejected for this reason: Tuiloma Neroni Slade and Roger S. Clark, 'Preamble and Final Clauses', in Lee, *The International Criminal Court*, pp. 421–50, at p. 426.   [61] Rome Statute, Art. 7(2)(f).
[62] Steains, 'Gender Issues', at p. 368. But for a somewhat different view, that seems to allow a contrary interpretation of the text, see Bedont, 'Gender-Specific Provisions', at pp. 198–9.

lectivity on political, racial, national, ethnic, cultural, religious, gender as defined in paragraph 3, or other grounds that are universally recognized as impermissible under international law, in connection with any act referred to in this paragraph or any crime within the jurisdiction of the Court.' The list of groups or collectivities is considerably larger than anything previous. However, the words 'in connection with any act referred to in this paragraph or any crime within the jurisdiction of the Court' narrows its scope considerably and is a departure from previous definitions. Defining 'persecution' perplexed the Rome drafters, with many judging it to be ambiguous and vague. The result is a compromise. The Elements of Crimes explain that in the act of persecution, the perpetrator 'severely deprived, contrary to international law, one or more persons of fundamental rights'.[63]

Where the Statute leaves the door open for some evolution is in the final paragraph of the list of crimes against humanity, dealing with 'other inhumane acts'. In the *Akayesu* decision, the *ad hoc* Tribunal for Rwanda used 'other inhumane acts' to encompass such behaviour as forced nakedness of Tutsi women.[64] But, under the Rome Statute, the concept of 'other inhumane acts' is actually narrowed by appending the words 'of a similar character intentionally causing great suffering, or serious injury to body or to mental or physical health'. It is open to question whether the acts of sexual indignity condemned by the Rwanda Tribunal would now fit within the restrictive language of the Rome Statute. Human rights treaties and declarations to be adopted in the future should assist the Court in determining the extent of 'other inhumane acts'.

Article 7 concludes with two further paragraphs that endeavour to define some of the more difficult terms of paragraph 1. Accordingly, the term 'attack' is defined, as explained above, as well as 'extermination', 'enslavement', 'deportation or forcible transfer of population', 'torture', 'forced pregnancy', 'persecution', 'the crime of apartheid' and 'enforced disappearance of persons'. A special provision defines 'gender', not only for the purposes of crimes against humanity but as it may be used elsewhere in the Statute as well. In a formulation borrowed from the 1995 Beijing Conference, Article 7 states that 'it is understood that the term 'gender' refers to the two sexes, male and female, within the context of society'.[65]

---

[63] Elements of Crimes, Art. 7(1)(h), para. 1.   [64] *Prosecutor* v. *Akayesu*, *supra* note 44.
[65] On the debate surrounding the term 'gender', see Steains, 'Gender Issues', at pp. 371–5. But, for a somewhat different view, that seems to allow a contrary interpretation of the text, see Bedont, 'Gender-Specific Provisions', at pp. 198–9.

War crimes

The lengthiest provision defining offences within the jurisdiction of the International Criminal Court is Article 8, entitled 'War crimes'.[66] This is certainly the oldest of the four categories. War crimes have been punished as domestic offences probably since the beginning of criminal law.[67] Moreover, they were the first to be prosecuted pursuant to international law. The trials conducted at Leipzig in the early 1920s, as a consequence of Articles 228 to 230 of the Treaty of Versailles, convicted a handful of German soldiers of 'acts in violation of the laws and customs of war'. The basis in international law for these offences was the Regulations annexed to the 1907 Hague Convention IV.[68] And while that instrument had not originally been conceived of as a source of individual criminal responsibility, its terms had been the basis of the definitions of war crimes by the 1919 Commission on Responsibilities. Certainly, from that point on, there is little argument about the existence of war crimes under international law.

War crimes were subsequently codified in the Nuremberg Charter, where they are defined in a succinct provision:

> violations of the laws or customs of war. Such violations shall include, but not be limited to, murder, ill-treatment or deportation to slave labour or for any other purpose of civilian population of or in occupied territory, murder or ill-treatment of prisoners of war or persons on the seas, killing of hostages, plunder of public or private property, wanton destruction of cities, towns or villages, or devastation not justified by military necessity.[69]

Four years later, in the 'grave breaches' provisions of the four Geneva Conventions of 1949,[70] a second codification was advanced:

---

[66] Von Hebel and Robinson, 'Crimes Within the Jurisdiction', at pp. 103–22; Gabriella Venturini, 'War Crimes', in Lattanzi and Schabas, *Essays on the Rome Statute*, pp. 171–82; Michael Cottier, William J. Fenrick, Patricia Viseur Sellers and Andreas Zimmermann, 'Article 8', in Triffterer, *Commentary*, pp. 173–288.

[67] Leslie C. Green, 'International Regulation of Armed Conflict', in M. Cherif Bassiouni, ed., *International Criminal Law*, 2nd edn, Vol. I, pp. 355–91.

[68] Convention Concerning the Laws and Customs of War on Land (Hague IV), 18 October 1907, 3 *Martens Nouveau Recueil* (3d) 461.

[69] Agreement for the Prosecution and Punishment of Major War Criminals, *supra* note 2, Art. 6(c).

[70] Convention (I) for the Amelioration of the Condition of the Wounded and Sick in Armed Forces in the Field, (1949) 75 UNTS 31; Convention (II) for the Amelioration of the Condition of Wounded, Sick and Shipwrecked Members of Armed Forces at Sea, (1950) 75 UNTS 85; Convention (III) Relative to the Treatment of Prisoners of War, (1950) 75 UNTS 135; Convention (IV) Relative to the Protection of Civilian Persons in Time of War, (1950) 75 UNTS 287.

wilful killing, torture or inhuman treatment, including biological experiments, wilfully causing great suffering or serious injury to body or health,
unlawful deportation or transfer or unlawful confinement of a protected
person, compelling a protected person to serve in the forces of a hostile
Power, or wilfully depriving a protected person of the rights of fair and
regular trial prescribed in the present Convention, taking of hostages and
extensive destruction and appropriation of property, not justified by military necessity and carried out unlawfully and wantonly.

Both of these provisions do not by any extent cover the entire range
of serious violations of the laws of war. They extend only to the most
severe atrocities, and their victims must be, by and large, civilians or non-
combatants. Moreover, these provisions only contemplate armed conflicts
of an international nature.

Until the mid-1990s, there was considerable confusion about the scope
of international criminal responsibility for war crimes. Some considered
that the law of war crimes had been codified and that consequently, since
1949, the concept was limited to grave breaches of the Geneva
Conventions. But the Conventions only covered what is known as 'Geneva
law', addressing the protection of the victims of armed conflict. War
crimes as conceived at Nuremberg were derived from 'Hague law', which
focused on the methods and materials of warfare. In any case, beyond
these two categories there seemed to be little doubt that international
criminal responsibility did not extend to internal armed conflicts. Indeed,
when the 1949 Geneva Conventions were updated with two additional
protocols in 1977, the drafters quite explicitly excluded any suggestion
that there could be 'grave breaches' during a non-international armed
conflict.

This conception of the law of international criminal responsibility was
reflected in the Statute of the International Criminal Tribunal for the
Former Yugoslavia, adopted in May 1993.[71] At the time, the Secretary-
General made it clear that the Statute would not innovate and that it
would confine itself to crimes generally recognized by customary international law. Accordingly, there were two separate provisions, Article 2, cov-
ering 'grave breaches' of the Geneva Conventions, and Article 3,
addressing the 'Hague law' violations of the 'laws and customs of war'. But
movement was afoot, and a year later, when it adopted the Statute of the

---

[71] Statute of the International Criminal Tribunal for the Former Yugoslavia, UN Doc. S/RES/827,
Annex.

International Criminal Tribunal for Rwanda, the Security Council recognized the punishability of war crimes in internal armed conflict.[72] A year later, in its first major judgment, the Appeals Chamber of the ICTY stunned international lawyers by issuing a broad and innovative reading of the two war crimes of the ICTY Statute, confirming the fact that international criminal responsibility included acts committed during internal armed conflict.[73] In *Tadic*, the judges in effect read this in as a component of the rather archaic term 'laws and customs of war'. These developments were on the ground that this was dictated by the evolution of customary law. Their interpretation was open to criticism as a form of retroactive legislation. Yet doubts about the broadening of the scope of war crimes were laid to rest at the Rome Conference in 1998, when States confirmed that they were prepared to recognize responsibility for war crimes in non-international armed conflict.

Article 8 of the Rome Statute is one of the longest provisions in the Statute, a striking observation when compared with the relatively laconic provisions of the Nuremberg Charter and the Geneva Conventions. To some extent it represents a progressive development over these antecedents, because it expressly covers non-international armed conflicts. Furthermore, some war crimes are defined in considerable detail, focusing attention on their forms and variations. Yet such detailed definition may also serve to narrow the scope of war crimes in some cases. In the future, judges will have greater difficulty undertaking the kind of judicial lawmaking that the *ad hoc* Tribunal for Yugoslavia performed in the *Tadic* case, and this will make it harder for justice to keep up with the imagination and inventiveness of war criminals. Indeed, the *Tadic* Appeals Chamber may well have frightened States with its bold judicial lawmaking, who then resolved that they would leave far less room for such developments in any statute of an international criminal court. Of course, the definitions in the Statute can always be amended, but the process is cumbersome.

The drafters of the Rome Statute drew upon the existing sources of war crimes law and these are reflected in the structure of Article 8, although the law would have been considerably more accessible and coherent had they attempted to rewrite this complex body of norms in a more simple form. As it now stands, Article 8 consists of four categories of war crimes,

---

[72] Statute of the International Criminal Tribunal for Rwanda, UN Doc. S/RES/955, Annex, Art. 4.
[73] *Prosecutor v. Tadic, supra* note 52.

two of them addressing international armed conflict and two of them non-international armed conflict. Not only are the specific acts set out in excruciating detail, the actual categories impose a difficult exercise of assessment of the type of armed conflict. Courts will be required to distinguish between international and non-international conflicts, complicated by the fact that within the subset of non-international conflicts there are two distinct categories. The judgments of the *ad hoc* Tribunal for the Former Yugoslavia have already shown just how difficult this task of qualification can be.

This is notably the case with so-called 'gender crimes'. Rape has always been considered a war crime, although it was not mentioned as such in either the Nuremberg Charter or the Geneva Conventions,[74] which probably reflects the fact that it was not always prosecuted with great diligence. The Rome Statute provides a detailed enumeration of rape and similar crimes, the result of vigorous lobbying by women's groups prior to and during the Rome Conference. The real question is whether this rather prolix provision actually offers women better protection than the rather archaic yet potentially large terms of Geneva Convention IV: 'Women shall be especially protected against any attack on their honour, in particular against rape, enforced prostitution, or any form of indecent assault.'[75]

As all criminal lawyers know, there is a dark side to detailed codification. The greater the detail in the provisions, the more loopholes exist for able defence arguments. It may well be wrong to interpret the lengthy text of Article 8 as an enlargement of the concept of war crimes. The extremely precise and complex provisions of Article 8 are mainly due to the nervousness of States about the scope of war crimes prosecutions, and arguably have the effect of narrowing the potential scope of prosecutions. Much of this was cloaked in rhetoric about the need for precision in legal texts and the sanctity of the principle of legality.

In customary law, a major distinction between war crimes and the other two categories, crimes against humanity and genocide, is that the latter two have jurisdictional thresholds while the former does not. Crimes against humanity must be 'widespread' or 'systematic', and genocide requires a very high level of specific intent. War crimes, on the other hand,

---

[74] See, for example, the 'Leiber Code', Instructions for the Government of Armies of the United States in the Field, General Orders No. 100, 24 April 1863, Arts 44 and 47. See also Theodor Meron, 'Rape as a Crime Under International Humanitarian Law', (1993) 87 *American Journal of International Law* 424.   [75] Convention (IV), *supra* note 70, Art. 27.

can in principle cover even isolated acts committed by individual soldiers acting without direction or guidance from higher up. While genocide and crimes against humanity would seem to be *prima facie* serious enough to warrant intervention by the Court, this will not always be the case for war crimes. As a result, Article 8 begins with what has been called a 'non-threshold threshold'.[76] The Court has jurisdiction over war crimes 'in particular when committed as a part of a plan or policy or as part of a large-scale commission of such crimes'. The language brings war crimes closer to crimes against humanity. The Rome Conference found middle ground with the words 'in particular', thereby compromising between those favouring a rigid threshold and those opposed to any such limitation on jurisdiction.[77]

The preliminary issue to be determined in charges under Article 8 is the existence of an armed conflict, be it international or non-international. In terms of time, some war crimes can be committed after the conclusion of overt hostilities, particularly those relating to the repatriation of prisoners of war. Therefore, war crimes can actually be committed when there is no armed conflict or, in other words, after the conclusion of the conflict. From the standpoint of territory, war crimes law applies in some cases to the entire territory of a State, and not just the region where hostilities have been committed. The International Criminal Tribunal for the Former Yugoslavia has written that 'an armed conflict exists whenever there is a resort to armed force between States or protracted armed violence between governmental authorities and organized armed groups or between such groups within a State'.[78] However, the Rwanda Tribunal has refused to convict local officials of war crimes, despite accepting the existence of an internal armed conflict within Rwanda in 1994. For the Trial Chambers of the Rwanda Tribunal, even proof that an accused wore military clothing, carried a rifle, and assisted the military is insufficient to establish that he or she 'acted for either the Government or the [Rwandese Patriotic Front] in the execution of their respective conflict objectives'.[79] This very conservative reading of the application of war crimes is under appeal.

[76] Von Hebel and Robinson, 'Crimes Within the Jurisdiction', at p. 124.
[77] *Ibid.*, pp. 107–8.
[78] *Prosecutor* v. *Tadic, supra* note 52, para. 70. See also *Prosecutor* v. *Tadic* (Case No. IT-94-1-T), Opinion and Judgment, 7 May 1997, (1997) 36 ILM 908; (1997) 112 ILR 1, para. 561; *Prosecutor* v. *Aleksovski* (Case No. IT-95-14/1-T), Judgment, 25 June 1999, para. 43.
[79] *Prosecutor* v. *Akayesu, supra* note 44, paras 640–3.

The Elements clarify that while the Prosecutor must establish these threshold elements of war crimes, he or she need not prove that the perpetrator had knowledge of whether or not there was an armed conflict, or whether it was international or non-international. According to the Elements, '[t]here is only a requirement for the awareness of the factual circumstances that established the existence of an armed conflict that is implicit in the terms "took place in the context of and was associated with"'.[80]

The first category of war crimes enumerated in Article 8 is that of 'grave breaches' of the Geneva Conventions. The four Geneva Conventions were adopted on 12 August 1949, replacing an earlier and rather more summary protection contained in the two Geneva Conventions of 1929. The four Conventions are distinguished by the group of persons being protected: Convention I protects wounded and sick in land warfare; Convention II protects wounded, sick and shipwrecked in sea warfare; Convention III protects prisoners of war; and Convention IV protects civilians. Probably the most significant difference between the two generations of treaties is that the 1949 Conventions finally provided a detailed protection of civilian non-combatants. But another very important development in the 1949 treaties was the recognition of individual criminal responsibility for certain particularly severe violations of the treaties, known as 'grave breaches'. This was an incredible innovation at the time, the recognition by States that they were obliged to investigate, prosecute or extradite persons suspected of committing 'grave breaches', irrespective of their nationality or the place where the crime was committed. This obligation is often characterized by the Latin phrase *aut dedere aut judicare*, meaning 'extradite or prosecute'.

The 'grave breaches' of the 1949 Conventions are limited in scope. According to the fourth or 'civilian' Convention, grave breaches consist of:

wilful killing, torture or inhuman treatment, including biological experiments, wilfully causing great suffering or serious injury to body or health, unlawful deportation or transfer or unlawful confinement of a protected person, compelling a protected person to serve in the forces of a hostile Power, or wilfully depriving a protected person of the rights of fair and regular trial prescribed in the present Convention, taking of hostages and extensive destruction and appropriation of property, not justified by military necessity and carried out unlawfully and wantonly.[81]

---

[80] Elements of Crimes, Art. 8, Introduction. [81] Convention (IV), *supra* note 70, Art. 147.

The other three Conventions contain somewhat shorter enumerations, but the fundamentals remain the same. In terms of application, however, what was in 1949 a very radical step of defining international crimes and responsibilities was accompanied by a narrowness in application: 'grave breaches' could only be committed in the course of international armed conflict.

The 'grave breaches' of the Geneva Conventions are set out in Article 8(2)(a) of the Rome Statute. Nothing in paragraph (a) insists that these apply only to international armed conflict, although the context suggests that this must necessarily be the case.[82] The *chapeau* describes grave breaches as acts committed 'against persons or property protected under the provisions of the relevant Geneva Convention'. There are no significant changes in the wording between the provisions of the four Conventions and the Rome Statute. In the *Tadic* decision, the International Criminal Tribunal for the Former Yugoslavia held that the grave breaches regime applied only to international armed conflict, even though this was not stated in the Tribunal's Statute.[83]

Victims of 'grave breaches' must be 'protected persons'. In the case of the first three Conventions, this means members of the armed forces of a party to the international armed conflict. With respect to the fourth Convention, protected persons must be 'in the hands of a Party to the conflict or Occupying Power of which they are not nationals'. The Yugoslav Tribunal has declared that even 'nationals', in the traditional international law sense, are protected if they cannot rely upon the protection of the State of which they are citizens because, for example, they belong to a national minority.[84] According to the Elements, the perpetrator need not know the nationality of the offender, it being sufficient that he or she knew that the victim belonged to an adverse party to the conflict.[85]

Because there is so little case law in the application of the Geneva Conventions, many of the terms used in the Statute (and the Conventions) still await judicial interpretation. For example, what is the difference

[82] The international armed conflict is made explicit in the Elements of Crimes. The Elements also specify that 'the term "international armed conflict" includes military occupation' (at p. 19, n. 34).

[83] *Prosecutor v. Tadic, supra* note 52, para. 80. But see the dissenting opinion of Judge Abi-Saab in *Prosecutor v. Tadic, ibid.; Prosecutor v. Delalic et al.* (Case No. IT-96-21-T), Judgment, 16 November 1998, (1999) 38 ILM 57, para. 202; Dissenting Opinion of Judge Rodrigues in *Prosecutor v. Aleksovski, supra* note 78, paras 29–49.

[84] *Prosecutor v. Tadic, supra* note 57, paras 164–6.

[85] Elements of Crimes, Art. 8(2)(a)(i), para. 3, n. 33.

between ordinary 'killing', a familiar expression in national criminal law systems, and 'wilful killing', the term used in the Conventions? Most legal systems would consider 'killing' to be intentional murder, and therefore 'wilful', and so the adjective is really rather superfluous. Indeed, this is the solution adopted by the Preparatory Commission in the Elements of Crimes.[86] And what of 'appropriation of property', which must be carried out not only 'unlawfully' but also 'wantonly'? Subsequent to the adoption of the Statute, participants in the Preparatory Commission devoted a great deal of attention to specifying the scope of these provisions. In their work, they were guided mainly by the Commentaries to the Geneva Conventions, prepared by the International Committee of the Red Cross during the 1950s. The Commentaries are based largely on the *travaux préparatoires* of the Conventions and constitute the principal interpretative source thereof.

In addition to the requirement that they be committed during international armed conflict, grave breaches must also be committed against 'protected persons'. These are, according to the Conventions, combatants who are *hors de combat* because of injury, shipwreck or illness, prisoners of war, and civilians. Persons who might otherwise be 'protected' can be excluded if they themselves are responsible for war crimes, or if they commit certain acts, such as espionage, or act as mercenaries.

The second category of war crimes that is listed in Article 8 of the Rome Statute is '[o]ther serious violations of the laws and customs applicable in international armed conflict, within the established framework of international law'. The wording makes it quite explicit that this category, found in paragraph (b), is, like the crimes in paragraph (a), confined to international armed conflict. The list consists of crimes generally defined as 'Hague law', because these are principally drawn from the regulations annexed to the 1907 Hague Convention IV.[87] There is no requirement, unlike the situation for 'grave breaches', that the victims be 'protected persons'. Indeed, the overall focus of Hague law is on combatants themselves as victims. Hague law is concerned not so much with the innocent victims of war as with its very authors, the combatants. More than Geneva law, then, it is the continuation of ancient rules of chivalry and similar systems reflecting a code of conduct among warriors. In fact, some of the language sounds positively anachronistic. In the past, this was also the

---

[86] *Ibid.*, Art. 8(2)(a)(i), para. 1.
[87] Convention Concerning the Laws and Customs of War on Land (Hague IV), *supra* note 68.

source used by the Commission on Responsibilities that explored the notion of war crimes following World War I, as well as of the post-World War II tribunals at Nuremberg, Tokyo and elsewhere. Unlike the Geneva Conventions, which have a rigorous codification of 'grave breaches', the notion of 'serious violations of the laws and customs of war' is rather malleable and has evolved over the years.

In addition to those provisions reflecting the terms of the 1907 instru- ment, there are also some 'new' crimes in paragraph (b). These were in a sense codified by the drafters at Rome and it is not improbable that those accused in the future will argue that they were not part of customary law applicable at the time the Statute was adopted. Among the new provisions included in Article 8(2)(b) are those concerning the protection of human- itarian or peacekeeping missions[88] and prohibiting environmental damage.[89] Probably the most controversial provision was sub-paragraph (viii), defining as a war crime 'the transfer, directly or indirectly, by the Occupying Power of parts of its own civilian population into the territory it occupies, or the deportation or transfer of all or parts of the population of the occupied territory within or outside this territory'. The provision governs not only population transfer within the occupied territory, but also the transfer by an occupying power of parts of its own civilian popu- lation into the occupied territory.[90] Israel felt itself particularly targeted by the provision, and in a speech delivered on the evening of 17 July at the close of the Rome Conference, it announced it would vote against the Statute because of its irritation that a crime not previously considered to be part of customary international law had been included in the instru- ment because of political exigencies.[91]

Several of the provisions of paragraph (b) deal with prohibited weapons. These include poison or poisoned weapons, asphyxiating, poi- sonous or other gases and bullets that expand or flatten easily in the

---

[88] Rome Statute, Art. 8(b)(iii).   [89] *Ibid.*, Art. 8(b)(iv).
[90] Von Hebel and Robinson, 'Crimes Within the Jurisdiction', at p. 112.
[91] This provision caused Israel to vote against the ICC Statute, stating: 'Israel has reluctantly cast a negative vote. It fails to comprehend why it has been considered necessary to insert into the list of the most heinous and grievous war crimes the action of transferring [a] population into occupied territory. The exigencies of lack of time and intense political and public pressure have obliged the Conference to by-pass very basic sovereign prerogatives to which we are entitled.' 'UN Diplomatic Conference Concludes in Rome with Decision to Establish Permanent International Criminal Court', UN Press Release L/ROM/22, 17 July 1998, at Explanations of Vote.

human body.[92] The casual reader of the Statute might get the impression that it was drafted in the nineteenth century, as these horrific weapons seem rather obsolete alongside modern-day weapons, including those of mass destruction, like land mines, chemical and biological weapons, and nuclear weapons. Such, however, are the consequences of diplomatic negotiations, especially in the context of an international system where a handful of States monopolize the production and control of the most nefarious weapons. The nuclear powers resisted any language that might impact upon their own prerogatives, such as a reference to weapons that might in the future be deemed contrary to customary international law. They had already had a close scrape in the International Court of Justice in 1996, which came near to an outright prohibition of nuclear weapons.[93] As a result, they insisted upon specifying that 'material and methods of warfare which are of a nature to cause superfluous injury or unnecessary suffering or which are inherently indiscriminate' also be the subject of a comprehensive prohibition included in an annex to the Statute, yet to be prepared.[94] With the exclusion of nuclear weapons, some of the non-nuclear States in the developing world objected to language that would explicitly prohibit the 'poor man's atomic bomb', that is, chemical and biological weapons. The result, then, is a situation where poisoned arrows and hollow bullets are forbidden yet nuclear, biological and chemical weapons, as well as anti-personnel land mines, are not.[95]

As with crimes against humanity, the 'laws and customs of war' provision significantly develops the area of sexual offences. The text is essentially new law.[96] It prohibits rape, sexual slavery, enforced prostitution, forced pregnancy, enforced sterilization or any other form of sexual violence also constituting a grave breach of the Geneva Conventions. Another provision consisting of new law makes it a crime to conscript or enlist children under the age of fifteen into the national armed forces or to use them to participate actively in hostilities. This wording is drawn from the 1989

---

[92] Roger S. Clark, 'Methods of Warfare That Cause Unnecessary Suffering or Are Inherently Indiscriminate: A Memorial Tribute to Howard Berman', (1998) 28 *California Western International Law Journal* 379.

[93] *Legality of the Threat or Use of Nuclear Weapons (Request by the United Nations General Assembly for an Advisory Opinion)*, [1996] ICJ Reports 226.

[94] Rome Statute, Art. 8(b)(xx).

[95] Von Hebel and Robinson, 'Crimes Within the Jurisdiction', at pp. 113–16.

[96] Rome Statute, Art. 8(b)(xxii).

Convention on the Rights of the Child[97] as well as Additional Protocol I to the Geneva Conventions.[98] The term 'recruiting' appeared in an earlier draft, but was replaced with 'conscripting or enlisting' to suggest something more passive, such as putting the name of a person on a list. Secondly, the word 'national' was added before 'armed forces' to allay concerns of several Arab States who feared that the term might cover young Palestinians joining the *intifadah* revolt.[99] Interestingly, the latter provision was deemed too moderate by many States and has resulted in an optional protocol, adopted by the General Assembly in May 2000, aimed at increasing the age to eighteen.

The category of 'serious violations of the laws and customs of war' also contains several offences drawn from Protocol Additional I to the Geneva Conventions of 1949. Protocol Additional I, adopted in 1977, expanded somewhat upon the definition of grave breaches in the 1949 Conventions, although it also slightly watered down the obligations upon States that flow from them. Interestingly, the Rome Statute includes some of these new 'grave breaches' within paragraph (b) rather than in paragraph (a), but it does not include them all.[100] Unlike the four Conventions, which have enjoyed near-universal ratification, Protocol Additional I still enjoys far less unanimity, and its reflection in Article 8 of the Rome Statute testifies to the ongoing uncertainty with respect to its definitions of 'grave breaches'. Protocol Additional I applies to a somewhat broader range of conflicts than the four Geneva Conventions, and the Prosecutor might well argue before the International Criminal Court that the specific provisions in Article 8 derived from Protocol Additional I can be committed in 'armed conflicts which peoples are fighting against colonial domination and alien occupation and against racist regimes in the exercise of their right of self-determination'.[101]

The two succeeding categories of war crimes in Article 8 apply to non-international armed conflict, a far more controversial area of international law, at least in an historical sense. As early as 1949, and even before, States were prepared to recognize international legal obligations, including

---

[97] Convention on the Rights of the Child, GA Res. 44/25, Annex, Art. 38.
[98] Protocol Additional to the 1949 Geneva Conventions of 12 August 1949, and Relating to the Protection of Victims of International Armed Conflicts, (1979) 1125 UNTS 3, Art. 77(2).
[99] Von Hebel and Robinson, 'Crimes Within the Jurisdiction', at p. 118.
[100] E.g., unjustifiable delay in repatriation of prisoners of war or civilians (Protocol Additional I, Art. 85(4)(b)) or apartheid (Protocol Additional I, Art. 85(4)(c)).
[101] Protocol Additional I, Art. 1(4).

international criminal responsibility, arising between them. However, they were far more hesitant when it came to internal conflict or civil war, which many considered to be nobody's business but their own. The 1949 Geneva Conventions refer to non-international armed conflict in only one provision, known as 'common Article 3'; Article 3 is 'common' because it is identical in all four Conventions. Attempts to expand the scope of Article 3 in 1977, in the adoption of Protocol Additional II, were only moderately successful.[102] The Protocol elaborates somewhat on the laconic terms of common Article 3, but does not extend the concept of 'grave breaches' to non-international armed conflict, nor does it recognize prisoner of war status in such wars.

Therefore, subject to a few minor exceptions, paragraphs (c) and (d) of Article 8 apply to non-international armed conflicts contemplated by common Article 3 of the four Geneva Conventions, while paragraphs (e) and (f) apply to non-international armed conflicts within the scope of Protocol Additional II. The threshold of application of Article 3 is somewhat lower. The scope of both provisions is limited in a negative sense, it being stated that they apply to armed conflicts not of an international character, but not 'to situations of internal disturbances and tensions, such as riots, isolated and sporadic acts of violence or other acts of a similar nature'. But the Protocol Additional II crimes listed in paragraph (e) apply to 'armed conflicts that take place in the territory of a State when there is protracted armed conflict between governmental authorities and organized armed groups or between such groups'.[103] There is a further limitation on the common Article 3 crimes: 'Nothing in paragraphs 2(c) and (d) shall affect the responsibility of a Government to maintain or re-establish law and order in the State or to defend the unity and territorial integrity of the State, by all legitimate means.' These thresholds, drawn from the Geneva Conventions and Protocol Additional II, have been constantly criticized for their narrow scope. In effect, in cases of internal disturbances and tensions, atrocities may be punishable as crimes against humanity but they will not be punishable, at least by the International Criminal Court, as war crimes.

The common Article 3 crimes listed in paragraph (c), like the 'grave

[102] Protocol Additional II to the 1949 Geneva Conventions and Relating to the Protection of Victims of Non-International Armed Conflicts, (1979) 1125 UNTS 3.

[103] In fact, Art. 8(2)(e) of the Rome Statute is slightly broader than Protocol Additional II, in requiring that the conflict be 'protracted', whereas the Protocol requires rebels to control territory.

breaches' in paragraph (a), must be committed against 'protected persons'. The latter are defined, for the purposes of common Article 3, as 'persons taking no active part in the hostilities, including members of armed forces who have laid down their arms and those placed *hors de combat* by sickness, wounds, detention or any other cause'. The punishable acts consist of murder, mutilation, cruel treatment and torture, outrages upon personal dignity, taking of hostages and summary executions. They represent, in reality, a common denominator of core human rights. The International Committee of the Red Cross has often described common Article 3 as a 'mini-convention' of the laws applicable to non-international armed conflict.

The crimes listed in paragraph (e) are largely drawn from Protocol Additional II, and address attacks that are intentionally directed against civilians, culturally significant buildings, hospitals and Red Cross and Red Crescent units and other humanitarian workers such as peacekeeping missions. Nevertheless, not all serious violations of Protocol II are included in Article 8 of the Statute.[104] A detailed codification of sexual or gender crimes, similar to the one in paragraph (b), is also included. There is a prohibition on child soldiers under the age of fifteen. A number of offences concern the conduct of belligerents amongst themselves that echo the provisions applicable to international armed conflict.

Other offences

The Court is also given jurisdiction over what are called 'offences against the administration of justice', when these relate to proceedings before the Court.[105] The Statute specifies that such offences must be committed intentionally. These are: perjury or the presentation of evidence known to be false or forged, influencing or interfering with witnesses, corrupting or bribing officials of the Court or retaliating against them, and, in the case of officials of the Court, soliciting or accepting bribes. The Court can impose a term of imprisonment of up to five years or a fine upon conviction.

---

[104] For a discussion on these omissions in the sessions of the Preparatory Committee, see Christopher Keith Hall, 'The Fifth Session of the UN Preparatory Committee on the Establishment of an International Criminal Court', (1998) 92 *American Journal of International Law* 331, at p. 336; Christopher Keith Hall, 'The Third and Fourth Sessions of the UN Preparatory Committee on the Establishment of an International Criminal Court', (1998) 92 *American Journal of International Law* 124.

[105] Rome Statute, Art. 70; Rules of Procedure and Evidence, Rules 162–169 and 172.

States Parties are obliged to provide for criminal offences of the same nature with respect to offences against the administration of justice that are committed on their territory or by their nationals.

The Court can also 'sanction' misconduct before the Court, such as disruption of its proceedings or deliberate refusal to comply with its directions. But, unlike the case of 'offences against the administration of justice', available measures are limited to temporary or permanent removal from the courtroom and a fine of up to 2,000 euros.[106]

---

[106] Rome Statute, Art. 71; Rules of Procedure and Evidence, Rules 170–172.

3

Jurisdiction and admissibility

One of the most delicate issues in the creation of the International Criminal Court was the determination of its territorial and personal jurisdiction. Although there were useful models for many aspects of international justice, never before had the international community attempted to create a court with such general scope and application. The Nuremberg Tribunal had exercised jurisdiction 'to try and punish persons who, acting in the interests of the European Axis countries, whether as individuals or as members of organizations' had committed one of the crimes within the court's subject matter jurisdiction.[1] Thus, its jurisdiction was personal in nature; defendants had to have acted in the interests of the European Axis countries. The jurisdiction of the International Criminal Tribunal for the Former Yugoslavia is confined to crimes committed on the territory of the former Yugoslavia, subsequent to 1991.[2] The jurisdiction is therefore territorial in nature. The International Criminal Tribunal for Rwanda has jurisdiction over crimes committed in Rwanda during 1994, and over crimes committed by Rwandan nationals in neighbouring countries in the same period.[3] Accordingly, its jurisdiction is both territorial and personal.

The basic difference with these precedents is that the International Criminal Court is being created with the consent of those who will themselves be subject to its jurisdiction. They have agreed that it is crimes committed on their territory, or by their nationals, that may be prosecuted. These are the fundamentals of the Court's jurisdiction. The jurisdiction that the international community has accepted for its new Court is narrower than the jurisdiction that individual States are entitled to exercise with respect to the same crimes. Moreover, the drafters of the Rome

[1] Agreement for the Prosecution and Punishment of Major War Criminals of the European Axis, and Establishing the Charter of the International Military Tribunal (IMT), Annex, (1951) 82 UNTS 279, Art. 6.
[2] Statute of the International Criminal Tribunal for the Former Yugoslavia, UN Doc. S/RES/827, Annex.
[3] Statute of the International Criminal Tribunal for Rwanda, UN Doc. S/RES/955, Annex.

Statute sought to limit the ability of the Court to try cases over which it has, at least in theory, jurisdiction. Consequently, they have required that the State's own courts get the first bite at the apple. Only when the domestic justice system is 'unwilling' or 'unable' to prosecute can the International Criminal Court take over. This is what the Statute refers to as admissibility.

The Rome Statute distinguishes between these two related concepts, jurisdiction and admissibility. Jurisdiction refers to the legal parameters of the Court's operations, in terms of subject matter (jurisdiction *ratione materiae*), time (jurisdiction *ratione temporis*), space (jurisdiction *ratione loci*) as well as over individuals (jurisdiction *ratione personae*). The question of admissibility arises at a subsequent stage, and seeks to establish whether matters over which the Court properly has jurisdiction should be litigated before it. To a large extent, the question of jurisdiction concerns the Court's consideration of a 'situation' in which a crime has been committed, whereas by the time the issue of admissibility is being examined, prosecution will necessarily have progressed to the identification of a 'case'.[4] The Court may have jurisdiction over a 'situation', because it arises within the territory of a State party or involves its nationals as perpetrators, yet a specific 'case' will be inadmissible because the individual suspect is being prosecuted by a national legal system. 'Admissibility' seems to suggest a degree of discretion, whereas the rules of jurisdiction are strict and brook no exception. The Court must always satisfy itself that it has jurisdiction over a case, whether or not the parties raise the issue, whereas its consideration of admissibility is only permissive.[5] According to John Holmes, '[a]dmissibility, on the other hand, was less the duty of the Court to establish than a bar to the Court's consideration of a case'.[6]

But the line between jurisdiction and admissibility is not always easy to discern, and provisions in the Statute that seem to address one or the other concept appear to overlap. For example, in a clearly jurisdictional provision, the Statute declares that the Court has jurisdiction over war crimes 'in particular when committed as a part of a plan or policy or as part of a

---

[4] Ruth B. Philips, 'The International Criminal Court Statute: Jurisdiction and Admissibility', (1999) 10 *Criminal Law Forum* 61, at p. 77.

[5] Rome Statute of the International Criminal Court, UN Doc. A/CONF.183/9 (hereinafter Rome Statute), Art. 19(1).

[6] John T. Holmes, 'The Principle of Complementarity', in Roy Lee, ed., *The International Criminal Court, The Making of the Rome Statute, Issues, Negotiations, Results*, The Hague: Kluwer Law International, 1999, pp. 41–78, at p. 61.

large-scale commission of such crimes'.[7] Yet in a provision dealing with admissibility, the Court is empowered to refuse to hear a case that 'is not of sufficient gravity'.[8] In practice, the implications of the two provisions, one addressing jurisdiction while the other addresses admissibility, may be rather comparable, in that the Court will decline to prosecute less serious or relatively minor crimes.

Subject matter (ratione materiae) jurisdiction

Subject matter jurisdiction refers to the crimes which the Court may prosecute: genocide, crimes against humanity, war crimes, aggression and offences against the administration of justice. This matter has been addressed in chapter 2 under the heading 'Crimes prosecuted by the Court'.

Temporal (ratione temporis) jurisdiction

The Court is a prospective institution in that it cannot exercise jurisdiction over crimes committed prior to the entry into force of the Statute.[9] In the case of States that become parties to the Statute subsequent to its entry into force, the Court has jurisdiction over crimes committed after the entry into force of the Statute with respect to that State.[10] The Statute seems to return to this issue in Article 24, which declares that no person shall be criminally responsible for conduct prior to the entry into force of the Statute. Articles 24 and 11 are in fact quite closely related, and at one point during drafting the chair of the Working Group on General Principles proposed that they be merged.[11] There is an exception to the general rule concerning temporal application of the Statute, because it is possible for a State to make an *ad hoc* declaration recognizing the Court's jurisdiction over specific crimes, even if the State is not a party to the Statute.[12] But, even in such a case, the Court would obviously be without jurisdiction to prosecute a crime committed prior to the entry into force of the Statute.

The provisions dealing with temporal jurisdiction have to be read in conjunction with Article 126 which governs the entry into force of the

---

[7] Rome Statute, Art. 8(1).   [8] *Ibid.*, Art. 17(4).   [9] *Ibid.*, Art. 11(1).
[10] *Ibid.*, Art. 11(2).
[11] Per Saland, 'International Criminal Law Principles', in Lee, *The International Criminal Court*, pp. 189–216, at p. 197.   [12] Rome Statute, Art. 12(3).

Statute. It declares that the Statute enters into force on the first day of the month after the sixtieth day following the deposit of the sixtieth instrument of ratification. With respect to States that ratify after the entry into force of the Statute, it enters into force for those States on the first day of the month after the sixtieth day following the deposit of that State's instrument of ratification.

The Statute has been criticized for its inability to reach into the past and prosecute atrocities committed prior to its coming into force. The answer to this objection is entirely pragmatic. Few States – even those who were the Court's most fervent advocates – would have been prepared to recognize a Court with such an ambit. The idea was unmarketable and was never seriously entertained during the drafting. But the failure to prosecute retroactively does not wipe the slate clean and grant a form of impunity to previous offenders. Those responsible for atrocities committed prior to entry into force of the Rome Statute may and should be punished by national courts. Where the State of nationality or the territorial State refuse to act, an increasing number of States now provide for universal jurisdiction over such offences.[13]

The issue of jurisdiction *ratione temporis* should not be confused with the question of retroactive crimes. International human rights law considers the prohibition of retroactive crimes and punishments to be one of its most fundamental principles. Known by the Latin expression *nullum crimen nulla poena sine lege*, this norm forbids prosecution of crimes that were not recognized as such at the time they were committed. There are, of course, varying interpretations as to the scope of the principle. The Nuremberg Tribunal could point to existing legal texts, such as the Hague Convention IV of 1907, in the case of war crimes, and the Kellogg–Briand Pact, in the case of crimes against peace. But while these described certain acts as being contrary to international law, they did not define them as generating individual criminal liability. Inspired by the writings of Hans Kelsen, the Nuremberg Tribunal answered the charge only indirectly, noting that *nullum crimen* was a principle of justice, and that it would be unjust to let the Nazi leaders go unpunished.[14] Since then, similar

---

[13] On this subject generally, see Naomi Roht-Arriaza, ed., *Impunity and Human Rights in International Law and Practice*, New York and London: Oxford University Press, 1995; Steven R. Ratner and Jason S. Abrams, *Accountability for Human Rights Atrocities in International Law, Beyond the Nuremberg Legacy*, Oxford: Clarendon Press, 1997.

[14] Hans Kelsen, 'Will the Judgment in the Nuremberg Trial Constitute a Precedent in International Law?', (1947) 1 *International Law Quarterly* 153, at p. 165.

pronouncements can be found in the *Eichmann* case of 1961 and even recently in the *Erdemovic* judgment of the International Criminal Tribunal for the Former Yugoslavia.[15]

In any event, *nullum crimen* is set out in Articles 22 and 23. Specifically, Article 22(1) declares: 'A person shall not be criminally responsible under this Statute unless the conduct in question constitutes, at the time it takes place, a crime within the jurisdiction of the Court.' Why Article 22(1) is necessary may initially seem puzzling, given the general jurisdictional prohibition on crimes committed prior to the entry into force of the Statute. After all, this is not a court like those at Nuremberg or Tokyo, or the *ad hoc* tribunals established for Yugoslavia and Rwanda, all of them established with a view to judging crimes already committed. But where a State has made an *ad hoc* declaration recognizing the jurisdiction of the Court, with respect to a crime committed in the past, a defendant might argue that one or another of the provisions of Articles 6, 7 and 8 are not recognized as norms of customary international law and are therefore not punishable by the Court. Likewise, this question may be raised where the Security Council gives jurisdiction to the Court,[16] just as it has been raised by defendants in The Hague and Arusha.[17] But the argument, though not totally frivolous, has never really succeeded before international courts in the past and is unlikely to cut much ice with the Court in the future. The standard adopted by the European Court of Human Rights with respect to retroactive crimes is that they must be foreseeable by an offender.[18] Inevitably, the Prosecutor will adopt this reasoning, and argue that from the moment the Statute was adopted, or at the very least from the moment it enters into force, individuals have received sufficient warning that they risk being prosecuted for such offences, and that the Statute itself (in Article 12(3)) contemplates such prosecution even with respect to States that are not yet parties to the Statute.

The question of 'continuous crimes' arose during the Rome Conference. This might present itself, for example, in the case of an 'enforced disappearance', which is a crime against humanity punishable

---

[15] *Prosecutor v. Erdemovic* (Case No. IT-96-22-T), Sentencing Judgment, 29 November 1996, (1998) 108 ILR 180, para. 35.   [16] Rome Statute, Art. 13(b).
[17] *Prosecutor v. Tadic* (Case No. IT-94-1-AR72), Decision on the Defence Motion for Interlocutory Appeal on Jurisdiction, 2 October 1995, (1997) 105 ILR 453.
[18] *SW v. United Kingdom*, Series A, No. 335-B, 22 November 1995, paras 35–6. See also *CR v. United Kingdom*, Series A, No. 335-B, 22 November 1995, paras 33–4.

under Article 7. Someone might have disappeared prior to entry into force of the Statute but the crime would continue after entry into force to the extent that the disappearance persisted. It might also be argued that this is the case where a population had been forcibly transferred or deported, and was being prohibited from returning home. Verbs such as 'committed', 'occurred', 'commenced' or 'completed', in Article 24, were ways in which the problem might have been addressed, but this proved difficult to cope with in all six working languages in an appropriate manner. Eventually the 'unresolvable matter' was resolved by the chair of the Working Group on General Principles, who proposed simply avoiding the troublesome verb in the English version. Thus, the issue of 'continuous crimes' remains undecided and it will be for the Court to determine how it should be handled.[19] The Drafting Committee appended an intriguing footnote to paragraph 1, reading: 'The question has been raised as regards a conduct which started before the entry into force and continues after the entry into force.'[20] It is an extremely unusual step for the Drafting Committee to insert a footnote. This may well have been a late-night compromise aimed at appeasing a handful of delegates who were obsessed with the question of continuous offences.

Bases of jurisdiction

States exercise jurisdiction in the field of criminal law on five bases: territory, protection, nationality of offender (active personality), nationality of victim (passive personality), and universality.[21] Territory is the most common, if for no other reason than that it is the only form of jurisdiction where the State can be reasonably sure of actually executing the process of its courts. In the *Lotus* case, Judge Moore of the Permanent Court of International Justice indicated a presumption favouring the *forum delicti commissi*.[22] One of the earliest criminal law treaties, the Treaty of International Penal Law, signed at Montevideo on 23 January 1889, stated

---

[19] Saland, 'International Criminal Law Principles', pp. 196–7; Raul Pangalangan, 'Article 24', in Otto Triffterer, ed., *Commentary on the Rome Statute of the International Criminal Court, Observers' Notes, Article by Article*, Baden-Baden: Nomos, 1999, pp. 467–73, at pp. 471–2.

[20] UN Doc. A/CONF.183/C.1/L.65/Rev.1, p. 2. There was no footnote in the final version adopted by the Conference: UN Doc. A/CONF.183/C.1/L.76/Add.3, pp. 1–2.

[21] *United States* v. *Yunis*, 681 F. Supp. 896, 900–1 (DDC 1988). See Yoram Dinstein, 'The Universality Principle and War Crimes', in Michael N. Schmitt and Leslie C. Green, eds, *The Law of Armed Conflict: Into the Next Millennium*, Newport, RI: Naval War College, 1998, pp. 17–37. [22] *SS Lotus (France* v. *Turkey)*, PCIJ, 1927, Series A, No. 10, p. 70.

that: 'Crimes are tried by the Courts and punished by the laws of the nation on whose territory they are perpetrated, whatever may be the nationality of the actor, or of the injured.'[23] Sometimes territory may be given a rather broad scope, so as to encompass acts which take place outside the State's territory but which have a direct effect upon it.[24] Jurisdiction based on nationality of the victim or the offender, as well as on the right of a State to protect its interests, is somewhat rarer. The Permanent Court of International Justice, in the *Lotus* case, left unresolved the right of States to exercise jurisdiction based on the nationality of the victim (passive personality jurisdiction) rather than that of the offender (active personality jurisdiction),[25] which is well established.

Universal jurisdiction – *quasi delicta juris gentium* – applies to a limited number of crimes for which any State, even absent a personal or territorial link with the offence, is entitled to try the offender. In customary international law, these crimes are piracy,[26] the slave trade, and traffic in children and women. Recognition of universal jurisdiction for these crimes was largely predicated on the grounds that they were often committed in *terra nullius*, where no State could exercise territorial jurisdiction. More recently, some multilateral treaties have also recognized universal jurisdiction for particular offences such as hijacking and other threats to air travel,[27] piracy,[28] attacks upon diplomats,[29] nuclear safety,[30] terrorism,[31] apartheid[32] and torture.[33] The application of universal jurisdiction is also widely recognized for genocide, crimes against humanity and war crimes, that is, for the core crimes of the Rome Statute.

---

[23] (1935) 29 *American Journal of International Law* 638.
[24] *United States* v. *Noriega*, 746 F. Supp. 1506 (SD Fla. 1990). See Lynden Hall, '"Territorial" Jurisdiction and the Criminal Law', (1972) *Criminal Law Review* 276.
[25] *SS Lotus (France* v. *Turkey), supra* note 22.
[26] *United States* v. *Smith*, 18 US (5 Wheat.) 153, 161–2 (1820).
[27] Convention for the Suppression of Unlawful Seizure of Aircraft, (1971) 860 UNTS 105; Montreal Convention for the Suppression of Unlawful Acts Against the Safety of Civil Aviation, (1976) 974 UNTS 177.
[28] Convention on the Law of the Sea, (1994) 1833 UNTS 3, Art. 105.
[29] Convention on the Prevention and Punishment of Crimes Against Internationally Protected Persons Including Diplomatic Agents, (1977) 1035 UNTS 167.
[30] Vienna Convention of 1980, (1984) 1456 UNTS 101.
[31] European Convention on the Suppression of Terrorism, (1978) 1137 UNTS 99; International Convention Against the Taking of Hostages, (1983) 1316 UNTS 205.
[32] International Convention on the Suppression and Punishment of the Crime of Apartheid, (1976) 1015 UNTS 243, Art. IV(b).
[33] Convention Against Torture and Other Cruel, Inhuman or Degrading Treatment or Punishment, (1987) 1465 UNTS 85, Art. 10.

During the drafting of the Statute, some argued that what States could do individually in their own national justice systems they could also do collectively in an international body.[34] Consequently, if they have the right to exercise universal jurisdiction over the core crimes of genocide, crimes against humanity and war crimes, they ought also to be able to create an international court that can do the same. If the statute were to provide for universal jurisdiction in such a way, it was asserted, then the new international court would have the authority to try anybody found on the territory of a State party, even if the crime had been committed elsewhere and if the accused was not a national of the State party. But such an approach met with two objections.[35] First, some States felt the solution too ambitious and likely to discourage ratifications. It is true that, in practice, universal jurisdiction is rarely exercised by States, and many would probably prefer not to be pushed into matters that in the past, for diplomatic or other reasons, they have sought to avoid. Secondly, a few States quarrelled with the legality of an international court that could exercise universal jurisdiction. The United States in particular argued that there was no rationale in law for such a court, and insisted that the only legal basis would be active personal jurisdiction, that is, the court would only be entitled to try nationals of a State party. Thereby, a State could shield its nationals from the jurisdiction of the Court, even for crimes committed abroad, by simply withholding ratification. The United States threatened that, if universal jurisdiction were to be incorporated in the Statute, it would have to oppose the Court actively. Indeed, the United States remains extremely unhappy with the compromise reached at Rome whereby the Court may exercise jurisdiction over crimes committed within the territory of a State party or by a national of a State party.[36]

This debate about jurisdiction of the Court was labelled the 'State consent' issue during the drafting process. The International Law Commission had adopted an approach to jurisdiction whereby States would have to 'opt-in' to jurisdiction on specific crimes. Jurisdiction was not to be conferred automatically simply because a State ratified the future

---

[34] Daniel D. Ntanda Nsereko, 'The International Criminal Court: Jurisdictional and Related Issues', (1999) 10 *Criminal Law Forum* 87, at p. 101.

[35] Morten Bergsmo, 'The Jurisdictional Regime of the International Criminal Court (Part II, Articles 11–19)', (1998) 6 *European Journal of Crime, Criminal Law and Criminal Justice* 29; Philips, 'The ICC Statute'.

[36] David Scheffer, 'The United States and the International Criminal Court', (1999) 93 *American Journal of International Law* 12.

Statute.[37] This was not unlike the Statute of the International Court of Justice, whereby States belong to the Court and are parties to the Statute but must make additional declarations in order to accept jurisdiction. The International Law Commission draft allowed for one exception, in the case of genocide, at least for parties to the 1948 Genocide Convention. This was predicated on the fact that the 1948 Genocide Convention specifically contemplated an international criminal court with jurisdiction over the crime.[38]

As debate unfolded in the *ad hoc* Committee, in 1995, and later in the Preparatory Committee, there was a trend towards enlarging the scope of the 'inherent jurisdiction' of the court from genocide to crimes against humanity and war crimes. Accompanying this development, and contributing to it, was a tendency to move away from including 'treaty crimes', such as terrorism and drug trafficking, in the subject matter jurisdiction of the court. Thus, as the scope of the crimes narrowed to those upon which there was genuine consensus as to their severity and significance, the argument that the court should have automatic jurisdiction over all crimes within its subject matter jurisdiction became more compelling.[39] Article 12, entitled 'Preconditions to the exercise of jurisdiction', was the result of this difficult debate.[40]

Territorial (ratione loci) jurisdiction

The Court will have jurisdiction over crimes committed on the territory of States parties, regardless of the nationality of the offender. This general principle is set out in Article 12(2)(a). It will also have jurisdiction over crimes committed on the territory of States that accept its jurisdiction on an *ad hoc* basis and on territory so designated by the Security Council. The

---

[37] 'Report of the International Law Commission on the Work of Its Forty-Sixth Session, 2 May–22 July 1994', UN Doc. A/49/10, Art. 22(1).

[38] Convention on the Prevention and Punishment of the Crime of Genocide, (1951) 78 UNTS 277, Art. VI.

[39] Elizabeth Wilmshurst, 'Jurisdiction of the Court', in Lee, *The International Criminal Court*, pp. 127–41.

[40] Hans-Peter Kaul, 'Special Note: The Struggle for the International Criminal Courts Jurisdiction', (1998) 6 *European Journal of Crime, Criminal Law and Criminal Justice* 48. See also Vera Gowlland-Debbas, 'The Relationship Between the Security Council and the Projected International Criminal Court', (1998) 3 *Journal of Armed Conflict Law* 97; Pietro Gargiulo, 'The Controversial Relationship Between the International Criminal Court and the Security Council', in Flavia Lattanzi and William A. Schabas, eds, *Essays on the Rome Statute of the ICC*, Rome: Editrice il Sirente, 2000, pp. 67–104.

1948 Genocide Convention provides some precedent for the idea that an international criminal court will have jurisdiction over crimes committed on the territory of a State party. Article VI of the Convention envisages just such an eventuality.

Territory, for the purposes of criminal law jurisdiction, is a term that needs to be defined. Obviously it will extend to the land territory of the State. The Statute also extends the concept of territory to include crimes committed onboard vessels or aircraft registered in the State party.[41] This is a rather common and widely accepted extension of the concept of territorial jurisdiction. Logically, territorial jurisdiction should extend to the air above the State, and to its territorial waters. But the actual scope of these grey areas remains to be determined. There are really no useful precedents from the case law of previous international criminal tribunals. Solutions to these issues will be sought in the practice of national justice systems, although this varies considerably and it is difficult to establish any common rules that are generally accepted.

Many national jurisdictions extend the concept of territorial jurisdiction to include crimes that create effects upon the territory of a State. For example, it could be argued that, in the case of a conspiracy to commit genocide,[42] the Court might have jurisdiction even if the conspirators actually hatched their plan outside the territory where the crime was to take place. Similarly, an order to take no prisoners, which is a crime in and of itself even if nobody acts upon the order,[43] could be committed outside the territory of a State but might be deemed to fall within the jurisdiction of the Court if its effects were felt on the territory. The case becomes somewhat clearer in cases of incitement and abetting. Nevertheless, given the silence of the Statute about effects jurisdiction, there are compelling arguments in favour of a strict construction of Article 12 and the exclusion of such a concept.

Personal (ratione personae) jurisdiction

The International Criminal Court will also have jurisdiction over nationals of a State party who are accused of a crime, in accordance with Article 12(2)(b). Again, the Court can also prosecute nationals of non-party States that accept its jurisdiction on an *ad hoc* basis,[44] or pursuant to a decision of

---

[41] Rome Statute, Art. 12(2)(a).   [42] *Ibid.*, Arts 6 and 25(d).

[43] *Ibid.*, Arts. 8(2)(b)(xii) and 8(2)(e)(x).

[44] *Ibid.*, Art. 12(3); and Rules of Procedure and Evidence, UN Doc. PCNICC/2000/INF/3/Add.1, Rule 44.

the Security Council.[45] Creating jurisdiction based on nationality of the offender is the least controversial form of jurisdiction and was the absolute minimum proposed by some States at the Rome Conference. Cases may arise where the concept of nationality has to be considered by the Court. In accordance with general principles of public international law, the International Criminal Court should look at whether a person's links with a given State are genuine and substantial, rather than it being governed by some formal and perhaps even fraudulent grant of citizenship.[46]

The Court is prevented from exercising its jurisdiction in the case of defendants who are immune to prosecution. In domestic legal systems, immunity in the case of diplomats and sometimes in the case of senior officials or heads of State is not at all uncommon. The Statute is rather more strict on this subject, however. Although Article 98 prevents the Court from proceeding with a request for surrender or assistance where this requires a State to violate other international legal agreements concerning immunity, the Statute provides no immunity as such. Once an individual is in its custody, there would seem to be no room for an immunity-based argument. The suggestion that a head of State can invoke some argument of immunity was laid to rest at Nuremberg, the principle repeated in Article IV of the Genocide Convention, and once again reaffirmed in Article 27 of the Rome Statute, not to mention its rejection by important national courts.[47]

The Rome Statute also declares that the Court has no jurisdiction over a person under the age of eighteen at the time of the infraction.[48] The solution is disarmingly simple, but much energy was expended on the issue in tedious debates during the sessions of the Preparatory Committee and the Diplomatic Conference.[49] The Working Group on General Principles agreed to impose a 'jurisdictional solution' and to provide that the Court would simply be unable to prosecute persons who were under eighteen at the time of the commission of the crime.[50]

[45] In Resolution 955, the Security Council established an *ad hoc* tribunal with jurisdiction over Rwandan nationals.
[46] *Nottebohm Case (Second Phase)*, Judgment of 6 April 1955, [1955] ICJ Reports 24; *Proposed Amendments to the Naturalization Provisions of the Constitution of Costa Rica*, Advisory Opinion OC-4/84, 19 January 1984, Series A, No. 4, para. 35.
[47] *R. v. Bow Street Stipendiary Magistrate and others, ex parte Pinochet Ugarte* [1998] 4 All ER 897, [1998] 3 WLR 1456 (House of Lords).
[48] UN Doc. A/CONF.183/C.1/L.76/Add.3, p. 3.
[49] Saland, 'International Criminal Law Principles', pp. 200–2.
[50] UN Doc. A/CONF.183/C.1/WGGP/L.1, p. 2.

Security Council veto of prosecution

The Court may be prevented from exercising its jurisdiction when so directed by the Security Council, according to Article 16. This is called 'deferral'. It seems that the measure can be permanent. The Statute says that the Security Council may adopt a resolution under Chapter VII of the Charter of the United Nations requesting the Court to suspend prosecution, and that in such a case the Court may not proceed. This highly controversial provision is, however, a rather significant improvement upon a text in the original draft statute prepared by the International Law Commission. In that document, the Court was prohibited from prosecuting a case 'being dealt with by the Security Council as a threat to or breach of the peace or an act of aggression under Chapter VII of the Charter, unless the Security Council otherwise decides'.[51] Such a provision would have allowed a single State that was a member of the Council to obstruct prosecution by placing a matter on the agenda, something that could only be overridden by a decision of the Council itself. And a decision of the Council itself can be blocked at any time by one of the five permanent members – the United States, the United Kingdom, China, France and the Russian Federation – exercising its veto.

The International Law Commission proposal met with sharp criticism as an interference in the independence and impartiality of the future court. By allowing political considerations to influence prosecution, many felt that the entire process could be discredited.[52] At the same time, it must be recognized that there may be times when difficult decisions must be taken about the wisdom of criminal prosecution when sensitive political negotiations are underway. Should the Court be in a position to trump the Security Council and possibly sabotage measures aimed at promoting international peace and security?

The debate in the Preparatory Committee and the Rome Conference itself about the International Law Commission proposal was in many respects a confrontation between the five permanent members and all other countries. The uninformed observer might have been given the

---

[51] 'Report of the International Law Commission on the Work of Its Forty-Sixth Session, 2 May–22 July 1994', *supra* note 37, Art. 23(3).

[52] For the debates, see 'Report of the Ad Hoc Committee on the Establishment of an International Criminal Court', UN Doc. A/50/22, paras 124–5; 'Report of the Preparatory Committee on the Establishment of an International Criminal Court', UN Doc. A/51/22, paras 140–4.

impression that United Nations reform was being accomplished indirectly, in the creation of a new institution – the International Criminal
Court – which would be involved in many of the same issues as the
Security Council but where there would be no veto. A compromise,
inspired by a draft submitted by Singapore, was ultimately worked out,
allowing for the Council to suspend prosecution but only by positive resolution, subject to annual renewal.[53] In practice, this should make it
extremely difficult for the Council to obstruct prosecutions. But even the
compromise was bitterly opposed by some delegates who saw it as a
blemish on the independence and impartiality of the Court. In a statement
issued on the night of the final vote in Rome, India said it was hard to
understand or accept any power of the Security Council to block prosecution:

> On the one hand, it is argued that the ICC is being set up to try crimes of the
> gravest magnitude. On the other, it is argued that the maintenance of inter-
> national peace and security might require that those who have committed
> these crimes should be permitted to escape justice, if the Council so decrees.
> The moment this argument is conceded, the Conference accepts the propo-
> sition that justice could undermine international peace and security.[54]

The Statute imposes the requirement that in seeking a deferral or stay of
proceedings, the Council act pursuant to Chapter VII of the Charter. This
means that the Council must determine the existence of a 'threat to the
peace', a 'breach of the peace' or an 'act of aggression', in the words of
Article 39 of the Charter. Conceivably, the Court could assess whether or
not the Council was validly acting pursuant to Chapter VII. In the past,
international courts have been extremely reluctant to second-guess the
Security Council in such matters.[55]

Admissibility

Under the rubric of 'admissibility', in Article 17, the Statute addresses the
complex relationship between national legal systems and the International

---

[53] See Lionel Yee, 'The International Criminal Court and the Security Council: Articles 13(b) and
16', in Lee, *The International Criminal Court*, pp. 143–52, at pp. 149–52.
[54] 'Explanation of vote by India on the Adoption of the Statute of the International Criminal
Court, Rome, July 17, 1998', p. 3.
[55] *Prosecutor* v. *Tadic* (Case No. IT-94-1-AR72), Decision on the Defence Motion for
Interlocutory Appeal on Jurisdiction, 2 October 1995, (1997) 105 ILR 453; (1997) 35 ILM 32.

Criminal Court. The Court is required to rule a case inadmissible when it is being appropriately dealt with by a national justice system. The key word here is 'complementarity', a term that does not in fact appear anywhere in the Statute. However, paragraph 10 of the preamble says that 'the International Criminal Court established under this Statute shall be complementary to national criminal jurisdictions', and Article 1 reiterates this. Article 17(1) makes an explicit reference to paragraph 10 of the preamble and to Article 1.[56] The term 'complementarity' may be somewhat of a misnomer, because what is established is a relationship between international justice and national justice that is far from 'complementary'. Rather, the two systems function in opposition and to some extent hostility with respect to each other. The concept is very much the contrary of the scheme established for the *ad hoc* tribunals, referred to as 'primacy', whereby the international court can assume jurisdiction as of right, without having to demonstrate the failure or inadequacy of the domestic system.[57]

Several aspects of 'complementarity' are addressed in specific provisions. Article 17(1) states that a case is inadmissible when it is being investigated or prosecuted by a State that has jurisdiction over it, or when the case has already been investigated and the State has decided not to prosecute. In such circumstances, the Court may only proceed where the State 'is unwilling or unable genuinely' to investigate or prosecute the case. The terms 'unwilling' and 'unable' are explained in some detail in Article 17, although the enigmatic adjective 'genuinely' is left entirely to the appreciation of the Court.

The issue of unwillingness will arise where a national justice system is 'going through the motions' in order to make it look as if investigation and prosecution is underway although it may lack the resolve to see them through, or may even be indulging in a sham trial held so that in any subsequent proceedings an accused can argue that he or she had already been

---

[56] See John T. Holmes, 'The Principle of Complementarity', in Lee, *The International Criminal Court*, pp. 41–78.

[57] Bartram S. Brown, 'Primacy or Complementarity: Reconciling the Jurisdiction of National Courts and International Criminal Tribunals', (1998) 23 *Yale Journal of International Law* 383; Adolphus G. Karibi-Whyte, 'The Twin *Ad Hoc* Tribunals and Primacy over National Courts', (1998–1999) 9 *Criminal Law Forum* 55; Flavia Lattanzi, 'The Complementary Character of the Jurisdiction of the Court with Respect to National Jurisdictions', in Flavia Lattanzi, ed., *The International Criminal Court, Comments on the Draft Statute*, Naples: Editoriale Scientifica, 1998, pp. 1–18; Paolo Benvenuti, 'Complementarity of the International Criminal Court to National Criminal Jurisdictions', in Lattanzi and Schabas, *Essays on the Rome Statute*, pp. 21–50.

tried and convicted and that any new trial is blocked by application of the rule against double jeopardy. The Statute requires the Court to consider these issues 'having regard to the principles of due process recognized by international law', suggesting an assessment of the quality of justice from the standpoint of procedural and perhaps even substantive fairness. The issue of inability will arise when a State cannot obtain the accused or necessary evidence and testimony or is otherwise unable to carry out its proceedings. The Statute makes this conditional on 'a total or substantial collapse or unavailability of its national judicial system' (an early draft used the word 'partial' in place of 'substantial', a less demanding standard).[58] Thus, a developed and functional justice system that is unable to obtain custody of an offender because of a lack of extradition treaties, for example, would still be able to resist prosecution by the Court on the ground of complementarity.

The concept of complementarity emerged as early as the International Law Commission draft in 1994.[59] But, in the debates that followed, the proposed complementarity mechanism was harshly criticized by such experienced international criminal law personalities as the Prosecutor of the *ad hoc* tribunals. Louise Arbour argued essentially that the regime would work in favour of rich, developed countries and against poor countries. Although the Court's Prosecutor might easily make the claim that a justice system in an underdeveloped country was ineffective and therefore 'unable' to proceed, essentially for reasons of poverty, the difficulties involved in challenging a State with a sophisticated and functional justice system would be virtually insurmountable. Certainly there is a danger that the provisions of Article 17 will become a tool for overly harsh assessments of the judicial machinery in developing countries.

During the drafting of the Statute there was also great debate about the attitude that the Court should take to alternative methods of accountability. The South Africans were the most insistent on this point, concerned that approaches like their Truth and Reconciliation Commission, which offer amnesty in return for truthful confession, would be dismissed as evidence of a State's unwillingness to prosecute. While there was widespread sympathy with the South African model, many delegations recalled the disgraceful amnesties accorded by South American dictators to them-

---

[58] Holmes, 'Principle of Complementarity', at pp. 75–6.
[59] 'Report of the International Law Commission on the Work of Its Forty-Sixth Session, 2 May–22 July 1994', *supra* note 37, Art. 35.

selves, the most poignant being that of former Chilean president Augusto Pinochet. But drafting a provision that would legitimize the South African experiment yet condemn the Chilean one proved elusive. It has been suggested that genuine but non-judicial efforts at accountability that fall short of criminal prosecution would have the practical effect of convincing the Prosecutor to set priorities elsewhere.

Judges of the Court might well consider that a sincere truth commission project amounts to a form of investigation that does not suggest 'genuine unwillingness' on the part of the State to administer justice, thereby meeting the terms of Article 17(1)(a) and (b). Should that not be enough, the Statute also declares inadmissible a case that is not 'of sufficient gravity to justify further action by the Court'.[60] Moreover, the Prosecutor is invited to consider, in determining whether or not to investigate a case, whether '[t]aking into account the gravity of the crime and the interests of victims, there are nonetheless substantial reasons to believe that an investigation would not serve the interests of justice'.[61] Yet judicial attitudes are impossible to predict, and judges or prosecutors might well decide that it is precisely in cases like the South African one where a line must be drawn establishing that amnesty for such crimes is unacceptable.[62]

When a case has already been tried by a domestic justice system, the complementarity article in the Statute points to another provision, the prohibition of double jeopardy or *ne bis in idem*, set out in Article 20 and codified in important human rights treaties such as the International Covenant on Civil and Political Rights.[63] The test as to whether the national trial proceedings were legitimate is slightly different from the 'unable or unwilling genuinely' standard of Article 17, which applies with respect to pending or completed investigations and pending prosecutions. If a domestic trial has already been completed, the judgment is a bar to prosecution by the Court except in the case of sham proceedings. These are defined as trials held to shield an offender from criminal responsibility, or that were otherwise not conducted independently or impartially and were held in a manner which 'in the circumstances, was inconsistent with an intent to bring the person concerned to justice'.[64]

---

[60] Rome Statute, Art. 17(1)(d).   [61] *Ibid.*, Art. 53(1)(c).

[62] Nsereko, 'The International Criminal Court', at pp. 119–20; Michael P. Scharf, 'The Amnesty Exception to the Jurisdiction of the International Criminal Court', (1999) 32 *Cornell International Law Journal* 507.

[63] International Covenant on Civil and Political Rights, (1976) UNTS 171, Art. 14(7).

[64] Rome Statute, Art. 20(3).

In a case where an individual is properly tried, but then is subsequently pardoned, the Court would seem to be permanently barred from intervening. The case is far from hypothetical. In the early 1970s, William Calley was convicted of war crimes for an atrocious massacre in My Lai village in Vietnam. Justice had done its job and he was duly sentenced to a term of life imprisonment. Then the United States President, Richard Nixon, intervened and granted him a pardon after only a brief term of detention had been served.

There is some doubt about the application of complementarity and the *ne bis in idem* rule to situations where an individual has already been tried by a national justice system, but for a crime under ordinary criminal law such as murder, rather than for the truly international offences of genocide, crimes against humanity and war crimes. It will be argued that trial for an underlying offence tends to trivialize the crime and contribute to revisionism or negationism. Many who violate human rights may be willing to accept the fact that they have committed murder or assault, but will refuse to admit the more grievous crimes of genocide or crimes against humanity. Yet murder is a very serious crime in all justice systems and is generally sanctioned by the most severe penalties. Article 20(3) seems to suggest this, when it declares that such subsequent proceedings before the International Criminal Court when there has already been a trial 'for conduct also proscribed under Articles 6, 7 and 8' is prohibited. In the alternative, the Statute ought to have said 'for a crime referred to in Article 5', as it does in Article 20(2).

The Statute also prohibits domestic justice systems from trying an individual for one of the crimes listed in the Statute if that person has already been convicted or acquitted by the Court. This rule is somewhat narrower, in that it only excludes prosecution before national courts for genocide, crimes against humanity and war crimes. Accordingly, someone acquitted of genocide by the International Criminal Court, for lack of evidence of intent, could subsequently be tried by national courts for the crime of murder without violating the Statute. This rule in the Statute goes somewhat further than the prohibition of double jeopardy in international human rights law, because international courts and tribunals have generally considered that the norm only applies within the same jurisdiction, and does not prevent a subsequent trial in another jurisdiction.[65]

---

[65]   *AP* v. *Italy* (no. 204/1986), para. 7.3.

4

General principles of criminal law

The statutes of the Nuremberg and Tokyo tribunals, as well as those of the *ad hoc* tribunals for the former Yugoslavia and Rwanda, are very thin when it comes to what criminal lawyers call 'general principles'. Once the crimes were defined, the drafters of these earlier models left issues like the appreciation of the evidence or the assessment of responsibility for accomplices and other 'secondary' offenders to the discretion of the judges. After all, those appointed to preside over these tribunals were eminent jurists in their own countries and could draw on a rich, multicultural resource of domestic criminal law practice. The Rome Statute is far less generous with judges. It seeks to delimit in great detail any possible exercise of judicial discretion. Part 3 of the Statute, consisting of Articles 22 to 33, is entitled 'General principles of criminal law'.[1] It directs the Court on such issues as criminal participation, the mental element of crimes and the availability of various defences. But elsewhere in the Statute can be found other provisions that are also germane to the issue of general principles. They present a fascinating experiment in comparative criminal law, drawing upon elements from the common law, the Romano-Germanic system, *Sharia* law and other regimes of penal justice.

Sources of law

Article 21 of the Rome Statute, entitled 'Applicable law', sets out the legal sources upon which the International Criminal Court may draw. The Statute itself cannot provide answers to every question likely to arise before the Court and judges will have to seek guidance elsewhere, just as

---

[1] On the general principles, see Per Saland, 'International Criminal Law Principles', in Roy Lee, ed., *The International Criminal Court, The Making of the Rome Statute, Issues, Negotiations, Results*, The Hague: Kluwer Law International, 1999, pp. 189–216; William A. Schabas, 'General Principles of Criminal Law in the International Criminal Court Statute (Part III)', (1998) 6 *European Journal of Crime, Criminal Law and Criminal Justice* 84; Kai Ambos, 'General Principles of Law in the Rome Statute', (1999) 10 *Criminal Law Forum* 1.

they do under domestic law when criminal codes leave questions ambiguous or simply unanswered.[2]

International law already has a general response to this problem in Article 38 of the Statute of the International Court of Justice, the international judicial organ created as part of the United Nations in 1945 with jurisdiction over disputes between sovereign States. The ICJ's Statute defines three primary sources of international law: international treaties; international custom; and general principles of law recognized by civilized nations. It is recognized that the three sources are of equal value and that there is no hierarchy among them, although case law has tended to give the third source, general principles of law, a rather marginal significance. According to the Statute of the ICJ, subsidiary means for determining the rules of law are judicial decisions and academic writings. Besides these enumerated sources, international legal rules can also be created by unilateral acts, such as a declaration or a reservation.

The Rome Statute creates a special regime as far as sources of law are concerned. The Statute proposes a three-tiered hierarchy. At the top is the Statute itself, accompanied by the Elements of Crimes and the Rules of Procedure and Evidence. The Rome Statute was adopted at the 1998 Rome Diplomatic Conference, whereas the Elements and the Rules were drafted by the subsequent Preparatory Commission sessions, in 1999 and 2000, and are to be confirmed by the Assembly of States Parties once the Statute enters into force.[3] Although Article 21 suggests that the Statute, the Elements and the Rules are all of equal importance, provisions elsewhere in the Statute make it clear that, in case of conflict, the Elements (Article 9) and the Rules (Article 51) are overridden by the Statute itself.[4]

The second tier in the hierarchy of sources consists of 'applicable treaties and the principles and rules of international law, including the established principles of the international law of armed conflict'. This category rather generally corresponds to the sources of international law set out in Article 38 of the Statute of the ICJ, although the wording is quite original.

---

[2] Ida Caracciolo, 'Applicable Law', in Flavia Lattanzi and William A. Schabas, eds, *Essays on the Rome Statute of the ICC*, Rome: Editrice il Sirente, 2000, pp. 211–32.

[3] 'Report of the Preparatory Commission for the International Criminal Court, Addendum, Finalized Draft Text of the Elements of Crimes', UN Doc. PCNICC/2000/INF/3/Add.2; 'Report of the Preparatory Commission for the International Criminal Court, Addendum, Finalized Draft Text of the Rules of Procedure and Evidence', UN Doc. PCNICC/2000/INF/3/Add.3.

[4] Herman von Hebel and Darryl Robinson, 'Crimes Within the Jurisdiction of the Court', in Lee, *The International Criminal Court*, pp. 79–126, at p. 88.

There is no express mention of customary internationally law, but it is surely covered by the reference to 'principles and rules of international law'. Moreover, the third source in the enumeration of the Statute of the ICJ, general principles of law, is excluded from this second tier of sources. The reference to the 'international law of armed conflict' provides an opening for a detailed and increasingly sophisticated body of law of which the Hague Conventions of 1899 and 1907, together with the Geneva Conventions of 1949 and their two Protocols of 1977, are the centrepiece. It may, for example, invite recognition by the Court of certain defences, such as reprisal and military necessity, not codified elsewhere in the Statute. But it is perhaps significant that the Rome Conference referred to the 'international law of armed conflict' rather than to 'international humanitarian law'. The Appeals Chamber of the International Criminal Tribunal for the Former Yugoslavia has suggested that 'international humanitarian law' is a more modern terminology than the more archaic 'laws of armed conflict', one that has emerged as a result of the influence of human rights doctrines.[5]

The third tier in the hierarchy is pointed towards domestic law. Article 21 invites the Court, should it fail to resolve questions applying the first two sources, to resort to general principles of law derived from national laws of legal systems of the world including, as appropriate, 'the national laws of States that would normally exercise jurisdiction over the crime'. The reference to general principles enhances the role of comparative criminal law and corresponds, in practice, to what international judges do already before the *ad hoc* tribunals. The special attention given to national laws of States that would normally exercise jurisdiction is intriguing because it suggests that the law applied by the Court might vary slightly depending on the place of the crime or the nationality of the offender. As Per Saland has noted, '[t]here is of course a certain contradiction between the idea of deriving general principles, which indicates that this process could take place before a certain case is adjudicated, and that of looking also to particular national laws of relevance to a certain case; but that price had to be paid in order to reach a compromise'.[6]

---

[5] *Prosecutor* v. *Tadic* (Case No. IT-94-1-AR72), Decision on the Defence Motion for Interlocutory Appeal on Jurisdiction, 2 October 1995, (1997) 105 ILR 453; (1997) 35 ILM 32, para. 87.

[6] Saland, 'International Criminal Law Principles', p. 215. See also Margaret McAuliffe de Guzman, 'Article 21', in Otto Triffterer, ed., *Commentary on the Rome Statute of the International Criminal Court, Observers' Notes, Article by Article*, Baden-Baden: Nomos, 1999, pp. 435–46.

As sources of law, the Statute does not formally recognize the important body of international human rights treaties and declarations that has developed since the Universal Declaration of Human Rights in 1948, although arguably this is included in the general reference to applicable treaties and principles and rules found in Article 21(1)(b). However, Article 21(3) states that the application and interpretation of law 'must be consistent with internationally recognized human rights'. There are obvious implications of this principle with respect to the rights of the accused. But it may well extend into other areas, such as the rights of victims. The provision also means that the Statute is not locked into the prevailing values at the time of its adoption. International human rights law continues to evolve inexorably, and the reference to it in the Statute is full of promise for innovative interpretation in future years.

The reference to internationally recognized human rights was only won after considerable controversy. Ostensibly, the debate focused on use of the word 'gender' instead of 'sex' as a prohibited ground for discrimination. Several States, led by the Holy See, were opposed to such contemporary terminology, apparently out of concerns that it somehow condoned homosexuality, although the word was never mentioned in the discussion.[7] But underlying the dispute was also a malaise with the reference to human rights, and for a time at Rome the entire provision seemed in jeopardy. There was a proposal to truncate the text after the words 'human rights', thereby eliminating the troublesome term 'gender'. Another attempt at compromise envisaged a statement by the President of the Conference referring to the use of the term 'gender' in the 1995 Beijing Declaration. Ultimately, the term 'gender' survived, but accompanied by a definition: 'For the purpose of this Statute it is understood that the term 'gender' refers to the two sexes, male and female, within the context of society. The term "gender" does not indicate any meaning different from the above.'[8]

Interpreting the Rome Statute

The Rome Statute provides little in the way of guidance as to the rules of legal interpretation that ought to be followed. As an international treaty, the governing principles are those contained in Articles 31 and 32 of the

[7] Saland, 'International Criminal Law Principles', p. 216.
[8] See Barbara C. Bedont, 'Gender-Specific Provisions in the Statute of the ICC', in Lattanzi and Schabas, eds, *Essays on the Rome Statute*, pp. 183–210, at pp. 186–8.

1969 Vienna Convention on the Laws of Treaties. They establish, as a general rule of interpretation, that a treaty is to be interpreted in good faith in accordance with the ordinary meaning to be given to the terms of the treaty in their context and in the light of its object and purpose. Article 31 of the Vienna Convention indicates that the context should include the preamble of the Rome Statute, as well as the Final Act adopted on 17 July 1998. In addition, subsequent agreements, such as the Rules of Procedure and Evidence and the Elements of Crimes are germane to interpretation. As supplementary means of interpretation, the Vienna Convention points to the drafting history or *travaux préparatoires* of the Statute, but only when the meaning is ambiguous or obscure, or the general rule of interpretation leads to an absurd or unreasonable result.[9]

But, as a source of criminal law, there will be those who argue that the Rome Statute should be subject to the rule of 'strict construction', or that, in the event of ambiguity or uncertainty, the result more favourable to the accused should be endorsed. Such a rule is drawn from national criminal law practice. It is confirmed, at least with respect to the definitions of crimes, in Article 22(2) of the Rome Statute: 'The definition of a crime shall be strictly construed and shall not be extended by analogy. In case of ambiguity, the definition shall be interpreted in favour of the person being investigated, prosecuted or convicted.' But the wording of this provision is precise enough to leave open the question of whether or not strict construction applies to provisions of the Statute other than those that define the offences themselves. When problems of interpretation arise, the 'contextual rule' of the Vienna Convention and the principle of strict construction drawn from national legal practice, as well as from Article 22, may lead to very different results. The judges of the Court will have to resolve this without any substantial assistance from the Statute. Perhaps the judges recruited from the public international law field will lean towards the Vienna Convention while those who are criminal law practitioners in national legal systems will favour strict construction.

Presumption of innocence

The presumption of innocence, recognized in Article 66 of the Statute, imposes the burden upon the prosecution to prove guilt beyond a reasonable doubt, a specialized application in criminal law of a general rule

---

[9] Vienna Convention on the Law of Treaties, (1979) 1155 UNTS 331.

common to most forms of litigation, namely, that the plaintiff has the burden of proof. But the presumption of innocence has other manifestations, for example in the right of an accused person to interim release pending trial, subject to exceptional circumstances in which preventive detention may be ordered, the right of the accused person to be detained separately from those who have been convicted, and the right of the accused to remain silent during the investigation and during trial. Several of the rules that reflect the presumption of innocence are incorporated within the Statute. For example, during an investigation, there is a right '[t]o remain silent, without such silence being a consideration in the determination of guilt or innocence';[10] there is a right to interim release;[11] and there are grounds for appeal which are wider in scope for the defence than for the prosecution.[12] Nevertheless, it was also felt necessary to affirm the principle generally and explicitly.

The European Court of Human Rights has defined the presumption of innocence as follows:

> It requires, *inter alia*, that when carrying out their duties, the members of a court should not start with the preconceived idea that the accused has committed the offence charged; the burden of proof is on the prosecution, and any doubt should benefit the accused. It also follows that it is for the prosecution to inform the accused of the case that will be made against him, so that he may prepare and present his defence accordingly, and to adduce evidence sufficient to convict him.[13]

In its 'General Comment' on Article 14 of the International Covenant on Civil and Political Rights, the Human Rights Committee has insisted that the presumption of innocence imposes a duty on all public authorities to 'refrain from prejudging the outcome of a trial'.[14] According to the European Commission of Human Rights:

> It is a fundamental principle embodied in [the presumption of innocence] which protects everybody against being treated by public officials as being

---

[10] Rome Statute of the International Criminal Court, UN Doc. A/CONF.183/9 (hereinafter Rome Statute), Art. 56.   [11] *Ibid.*, Arts 59(3)–(6) and 60(2)–(4).

[12] *Ibid.*, Art. 81(1). See M. Cherif Bassiouni and Peter Manikas, *The Law of the International Criminal Tribunal for the Former Yugoslavia,* New York: Transnational Publishers, 1995, p. 961, for a similar observation on the Statute of the International Criminal Tribunal of the Former Yugoslavia, UN Doc. S/RES/827, Annex, and its 'Rules of Procedure and Evidence', UN Doc. IT/32.

[13] *Barberà, Messegué and Jabardo* v. *Spain,* Series A, No. 146, 6 December 1988, para. 77.

[14] 'General Comment 13/21', UN Doc. A/39/40, pp. 143–7.

guilty of an offence before this is established according to law by a competent court. Article 6, paragraph 2 [of the *European Convention on Human Rights*], therefore, may be violated by public officials if they declare that somebody is responsible for criminal acts without a court having found so. This does not mean, of course, that the authorities may not inform the public about criminal investigations. They do not violate Article 6, paragraph 2, if they state that a suspicion exists, that people have been arrested, that they have confessed, etc. What is excluded, however, is a formal declaration that somebody is guilty.[15]

Transposing these notions, derived from domestic prosecutions, to the international context gives some intriguing results. The 'authorities' on the international scene will be such bodies as the Commission on Human Rights, the High Commissioner for Human Rights, the Security Council, the General Assembly and the Secretary-General. If, for example, the General Assembly charges that genocide has been committed by the leaders of a given regime, can the latter invoke this essentially political accusation before the ICC in claiming that the presumption of innocence has been denied?[16] One answer is that there may well be a denial of the presumption of innocence but that it will not have been committed by the Court itself. But the Appeals Chamber of the *ad hoc* Tribunal for Rwanda has already judged it appropriate to grant a stay of proceedings in a case where rights of an accused were violated by a national justice system and not by the authorities of the tribunals themselves.[17]

Arguably, the presumption of innocence may require that decisions by the Court, particularly given the seriousness of the charges and of the available sentences, be unanimous. Certainly where questions of fact are at issue, is it not logical to conclude that, where one member of the Court has a reasonable doubt, this should be enough to create a reasonable doubt in

---

[15] *Krause* v. *Switzerland* (App. No. 7986/77), (1978) 13 DR 73. Also, from the Court, see *Allenet de Ribemont* v. *France*, Series A, No. 308, 10 February 1995, paras 37 and 41. See Francis G. Jacobs and Robin C. A. White, *The European Convention on Human Rights*, 2nd edn, Oxford: Clarendon Press, 1996, p. 150.

[16] A Security Council resolution denouncing the atrocities in Srebrenica, UN Doc. S/RES/1034 (1995), singled out for special mention the Bosnian Serb leaders Radovan Karadzic and Ratko Mladic, noting that they had been indicted by the International Criminal Tribunal for their responsibilities in the massacre. The word 'alleged' did not accompany the reference to their responsibilities. The resolution '[c]ondemn[ed] in particular in the strongest possible terms the violations of international humanitarian law and of human rights by Bosnian Serb and paramilitary forces in the areas of Srebrenica'.

[17] *Barayagwiza* v. *Prosecutor* (Case No. ICTR-97-19-AR72), Decision of 3 November 1999.

the minds of the tribunal as a whole?[18] Compelling as the suggestion may be – and it was argued by some delegates at the Rome Conference – the Statute provides clearly that in case of division, a majority of the Court will suffice for a finding of guilt.[19]

Rights of the accused

During World War II, Churchill and other Allied leaders flirted with the idea of some form of summary justice for major war criminals.[20] But, speaking of the Nuremberg trial, prosecutor Robert Jackson said that history would assess the proceedings in light of the fairness with which the defendants were treated. Only a few years later, one of the Nuremberg tribunals held that Nazi prosecutors and judges involved in a trial lacking the fundamental guarantees of fairness could be held responsible for crimes against humanity. Such guarantees include the presumption of innocence, the right of the accused to introduce evidence, to confront witnesses, to present evidence, to be tried in public, to have counsel of choice, and to be informed of the nature of the charges.[21] And, more recently, the judges of the International Criminal Tribunal for the Former Yugoslavia, in the first major ruling of the Appeals Chamber, said: 'For a Tribunal such as this one to be established according to the rule of law, it must be established in accordance with the proper international standards; it must provide all the guarantees of fairness, justice and even-handedness, in full conformity with internationally recognized human rights instruments.'[22] As if there could be any doubt, the Rome Statute ensures the protection of the rights of the accused with a detailed codification of procedural guarantees.

Article 67 of the Rome Statute, entitled 'Rights of the accused', is modelled on Article 14(3) of the International Covenant on Civil and Political Rights, one of the principal human rights treaties.[23] The right to a fair trial

---

[18] For such a suggestion, see Lawyers Committee for Human Rights, 'Fairness to Defendants at the International Criminal Court', August 1996, pp. 12–13.

[19] Rome Statute, Art. 74(3).

[20] Arieh J. Kochavi, *Prelude to Nuremberg, Allied War Crimes Policy and the Question of Punishment*, Chapel Hill and London: University of North Carolina Press, 1998, pp. 63–91.

[21] *United States of America* v. *Alstötter et al.* ('Justice trial'), (1948) 3 TWC 1, 6 LRTWC 1, 14 ILR 278.

[22] *Prosecutor* v. *Tadic* (Case No. IT-94-1-AR72), Decision on the Defence Motion for Interlocutory Appeal on Jurisdiction, 2 October 1995, (1997) 105 ILR 453, 35 ILM 32, para. 45.

[23] International Covenant on Civil and Political Rights, (1976) UNTS 171.

is also enshrined in the Universal Declaration of Human Rights,[24] the regional human rights conventions,[25] as well as in humanitarian law instruments.[26] The general right to a 'fair hearing' established in the *chapeau* of Article 67 provides defendants with a powerful tool to go beyond the text of the Statute, and to require that the Court's respect for the rights of an accused keep pace with the progressive development of human rights law. The case law of the Strasbourg organs, established to implement the European Convention on Human Rights, has used this residual right to a fair hearing to fill in some of the gaps in the more specific provisions.[27] That the term 'fair hearing' invites the Court to exceed the precise terms of Article 67 in appropriate circumstances is confirmed by the reference within the *chapeau* to 'minimum guarantees'. The term 'fair hearing' also suggests that, where individual problems with specific rights set out in Article 67 do not, on their own, amount to a violation, the requirement of a fair hearing may allow a cumulative view and lead to the conclusion that there is a breach where there have been a number of apparently minor or less significant encroachments on Article 67.[28] International case law has developed the notion of 'equality of arms' within the concept of the right to a fair trial.[29]

The Statute also states that the hearing must be 'conducted impartially'. According to the European Court of Human Rights, 'impartiality' means

[24] GA Res. 217A(III), UN Doc. A/810 (1948). Art. 10: 'Everyone is entitled in full equality to a fair and public hearing by an independent and impartial tribunal, in the determination of his rights and obligations and of any criminal charge against him.' Art. 11(3): 'Everyone charged with a penal offence has the right to be presumed innocent until proved guilty according to law in a public trial at which he has had all the guarantees necessary for his defence.'

[25] American Convention on Human Rights, (1978) 1144 UNTS 123, Art. 8; European Convention on Human Rights, (1955) 213 UNTS 221, Art. 6; African Charter on Human and People's Rights, OAU Doc. CAB/LEG/67/3 rev. 5, Art. 7; Convention on the Rights of the Child, GA Res. 44/25, Annex, Art. 40, para. 2.

[26] Geneva Convention (III) Relative to the Treatment of Prisoners of War, (1950) 75 UNTS 135, Arts 84–87 and 99–108; Geneva Convention (IV) Relative to the Protection of Civilians, (1950) 75 UNTS 287, Arts 5 and 64–76; Protocol Additional I to the 1949 Geneva Conventions and Relating to the Protection of Victims of International Armed Conflicts, (1979) 1125 UNTS 3, Art. 75; Protocol Additional II to the 1949 Geneva Conventions and Relating to the Protection of Victims of Non-International Armed Conflicts, (1979) 1125 UNTS 3, Art. 6.

[27] D. J. Harris, M. O'Boyle and C. Warbrick, *Law of the European Convention on Human Rights*, London; Butterworths, 1995, pp. 202–3.

[28] *Stanford* v. *United Kingdom*, Series A, No. 182-A, 30 August 1990, para. 24.

[29] *Neumeister* v. *Austria*, Series A, No. 8, 11 Yearbook 822, 27 June 1968; Manfred Novak, *CCPR Commentary*, Kehl, Germany: N. P. Engel, 1993. For recognition of the principle of 'equality of arms' by the International Criminal Tribunal for the Former Yugoslavia, see *Prosecutor* v. *Tadic* (Case No. IT-94-1-T), Separate Opinion of Judge Vohrah on Prosecution Motion for Production of Defence Witness Statements, 27 November 1996, pp. 4 and 7.

lack of 'prejudice or bias'.[30] It comprises both a subjective and an objective dimension: '[t]he existence of impartiality . . . must be determined according to a subjective test, that is, on the basis of the personal conviction of a particular judge in a given case, and also according to an objective test, namely, ascertaining whether the judge offered guarantees sufficient to exclude any legitimate doubt in this respect'.[31]

Among the guarantees to the defendant set out in Article 67 are the right to be informed in detail of the nature, cause and content of the charge, to have adequate time and facilities for the preparation of the defence, to communicate freely with counsel of one's choosing, to be tried without undue delay, to be present at trial, to examine witnesses, and to benefit from the services of an interpreter if required. The International Covenant on Civil and Political Rights is more than thirty years old and, reflecting evolving contemporary standards of procedural fairness, the Rome Statute goes somewhat beyond the minimum basis found in Article 14(3) of the Covenant. Thus, Article 67 of the Statute ensures the right to silence, the right to make an unsworn statement, and a protection against any reversal of the burden of proof or an onus of rebuttal. In addition to persons charged with an offence, the Statute also enumerates rights that accrue to 'persons during an investigation'[32] and to persons about to be questioned by the Prosecutor or even national authorities for crimes within the jurisdiction of the Court.[33]

Individual criminal responsibility

The International Criminal Court is concerned with trying and punishing individuals, not States. 'Crimes against international law are committed by men, not by abstract entities, and only by punishing individuals who commit such crimes can the provisions of international law be enforced', wrote the Nuremberg Tribunal in 1946. This philosophy is reflected in Article 25 of the Rome Statute. Proposals that the Court also exercise jurisdiction over corporate bodies in addition to individuals were seriously considered at the Rome Conference. While all national legal systems provide for individual criminal responsibility, their approaches to corporate criminal liability vary considerably. With a Court predicated on the

---

[30] *Piersack* v. *Belgium*, Series A, No. 53, 1 October 1982.
[31] *Hauschildt* v. *Denmark*, Series A, No. 154, 24 December 1989, para. 46.
[32] Rome Statute, Art. 55(1).   [33] *Ibid.*, Art. 55(2).

principle of complementarity, it would have been unfair to establish a form of jurisdiction that would in effect be inapplicable to those States that do not punish corporate bodies under criminal law. During negotiations, attempts at encompassing some form of corporate liability made considerable progress. But time was simply too short for the delegates to reach a consensus and ultimately the concept had to be abandoned.[34]

The International Criminal Court, like its earlier models at Nuremberg, The Hague and Arusha, is targeted at the major criminals responsible for large-scale atrocities. Most of its 'clientele' will not be the actual perpetrators of the crimes, soiling their hands with flesh and blood. Rather, they will be 'accomplices', those who organize, plan and incite genocide, crimes against humanity and war crimes. The Court can approach this issue in two different ways. The first is to consider the planners and organizers as principal offenders. The District Court of Jerusalem held Adolf Eichmann to be a principal offender 'in the same way as two or more persons who collaborate in forging a document are all principal offenders'.[35] Alternatively, they may be tried as accomplices, who aid or abet the principal offenders. The Trial Chamber of the International Criminal Tribunal for the Former Yugoslavia has stated that there is a customary law basis for the criminalization of accessories or participants.[36] Either approach will work under the Rome Statute, which in Article 25 sets out rather elaborate texts dealing with complicity or secondary liability.

Complicity is specifically addressed in the Rome Statute in two provisions, sub-paragraphs (b) and (c) of Article 25(3). The former covers the individual who 'orders, solicits or induces' the crime, while the latter deals with the person who 'aids, abets or otherwise assists'. There is a certain redundancy about these two paragraphs, perhaps because of an unfamiliarity of the drafters with the common law term 'abets' which, while it appears in paragraph (c), in reality covers everything described in paragraph (b). The Rome Statute does not indicate whether there is some quantitative degree of aiding and abetting required to constitute the material acts involved in complicity. Here, it departs from a model that was familiar to the drafters, the 1996 'Code of Crimes' of the International Law Commission, which specifies that complicity must be 'direct and

---

[34] Saland, 'International Criminal Law Principles', p. 199; Ambos, 'General Principles', p. 7.
[35] *A-G Israel* v. *Eichmann*, (1968) 36 ILR 18 (District Court, Jerusalem), para. 194.
[36] *Prosecutor* v. *Tadic* (Case No. IT-94-1-T), Opinion and Judgment, 7 May 1997, paras 666 and 669.

substantial'.[37] The judges of the *ad hoc* tribunals have read this requirement into the complicity provisions of their statutes, despite the silence of
their statutes. The absence of words like 'substantial' in the Rome Statute,
and the failure to follow the International Law Commission draft, may
suggest that the Diplomatic Conference meant to reject the higher threshold of the recent case law of The Hague and Arusha.[38] It is clear that mere
presence at the scene of a crime, in the absence of a material act or omission, does not constitute complicity. But, where the accused has a legal
duty to intervene, because of a hierarchically superior position for
example, presence without any other overt act may amount to a form of
participation; the failure to intervene constitutes encouragement or
incitement.[39] However, aside from the specific provision dealing with
responsibility of commanders and other superiors, there is no criminal
liability established in the Statute for mere failure to act.

The Rome Statute also specifically provides for the incomplete or
'inchoate' crime of direct and public incitement to commit genocide, an
offence that takes place even if there is no result.[40] The text is derived from
Article III(c) of the Genocide Convention, a provision which was controversial in 1948 and which remains so today.[41] When the Genocide
Convention was being drafted, the terms 'direct and public' were added,
mainly at the request of the United States, in order to limit the scope of the
provision. The United States was concerned that this might encroach
upon the right of free speech. There were unsuccessful efforts during the
drafting of the Rome Statute to enlarge the inchoate offence of incitement
so as to cover the other core crimes but the same arguments that had been
made in 1948, essentially based on freedom of expression, resurfaced.[42]

The issue of conspiracy has vexed international criminal law since
Nuremberg. Under the common law system, a conspiracy is committed
once two or more persons agree to commit a crime, whether or not the

---

[37] 'Report of the International Law Commission on the Work of Its Forty-Eighth Session, 6
    May–26 July 1996', UN Doc. A/51/10, p. 24.
[38] *Prosecutor* v. *Tadic* (Case No. IT-94-1-T), Opinion and Judgment, 7 May 1997, paras 691 and
    692. See also *Prosecutor* v. *Aleksovski* (Case No. IT-95-14/1-T), Judgment, 25 June 1999, para.
    61.
[39] *Prosecutor* v. *Tadic* (Case No. IT-94-1-T), Opinion and Judgment, 7 May 1997, paras 678 and
    691.   [40] Rome Statute, Art. 25(3)(e).
[41] See William A. Schabas, *Genocide in International Law, The Crime of Crimes*, Cambridge:
    Cambridge University Press, 2000, pp. 266–80.
[42] Saland, 'International Criminal Law Principles', p. 200; Ambos, 'General Principles', pp.
    13–14.

crime itself is committed, whereas in continental systems inspired from the Napoleonic tradition, conspiracy is generally viewed as a form of complicity or participation in an actual crime or attempt. Here, the Rome Statute strikes a compromise, requiring the commission of some overt act as evidence of the conspiracy but imposing no requirement that the crime itself actually be committed. The solution was borrowed from the 1997 Convention for the Suppression of Terrorist Bombings, where an acceptable formula had been adopted by consensus.[43] One unfortunate consequence is that the Rome Statute does not fully reflect the provisions of the Genocide Convention which, in Article III(b), defines 'conspiracy' as an act of genocide. The drafting history of the Genocide Convention indicates the intent to cover the common law notion of conspiracy, that is, a truly inchoate offence.[44]

The Rome Statute provisions on criminal participation also contemplate liability in the case of an attempted crime.[45] If the ultimate goal of the Court is to prevent human rights abuses and atrocities, prosecution for attempts ought to be of considerable significance. But the history of war crimes prosecutions yields few examples, probably because the very idea of criminal repression has arisen after the commission of the crimes. Starting from the premise that guilty thoughts, in and of themselves, should not be subject to criminal liability, the theoretical problem with attempts is determining at what point prior to committing the actual act should prosecution be permitted. Domestic justice systems have devised a variety of tests to distinguish between genuine attempts and 'mere preparatory acts'. The Rome Statute speaks of 'action that commences [the crime's] execution by means of a substantial step', a hybrid and internally contradictory formulation drawn from French and American law that sets a relatively low threshold. The Statute allows a defendant to plead that an attempt was voluntarily abandoned.[46]

Responsibility of commanders and other superiors

One of the dilemmas of war crimes prosecution is the difficulty linking commanders to the crimes committed by their subordinates. The Statute

---

[43] GA Res. 52/164, Annex. See also Saland, 'International Criminal Law Principles', pp. 199–200.
[44] Schabas, *Genocide in International Law*, pp. 260–1.   [45] Rome Statute, Art. 25(3)(f).
[46] Ambos, 'General Principles', pp. 12–13; Kai Ambos, 'Article 25', in Triffterer, *Commentary*, pp. 475–92.

requires proof of guilt beyond a reasonable doubt. In cases where this is forthcoming, the commanding superior's guilt sits on a plane that is much higher than that of the underling who follows orders. As a Trial Chamber of the Yugoslav Tribunal has noted, '[t]he Tribunal has particularly valid grounds for exercising its jurisdiction over persons who, through their position of political or military authority, are able to order the commission of crimes falling within its competence *ratione materiae* or who knowingly refrain from preventing or punishing the perpetrators of such crimes'.[47] But, while responsibility of a commander, in the absence of actual proof that orders were given, might seem probable, judges may be reluctant to convict based solely on such circumstantial evidence. This probably explains why Louise Arbour, Prosecutor of the Yugoslav Tribunal, waited for many weeks before indicting President Milosevic for crimes against humanity. She was unsatisfied with the circumstantial evidence of atrocities in Kosovo for which he had been condemned in the international press and was awaiting more concrete evidence that he had ordered them before proceeding.

There are two possible solutions to the dilemma of prosecuting commanders when direct evidence is lacking that they ordered crimes or knowingly ignored their perpetration. The first is to create a presumption by which commanders are deemed to have ordered the crimes committed by their subordinates, leaving it to the commander to answer the charges by establishing that no such orders were given. This technique is common in domestic criminal systems where it is difficult to prove that certain crimes were committed knowingly, such as environmental damage, false advertising and driving while intoxicated. This simplifies considerably the task of prosecutors, but it runs up against the principle of the presumption of innocence.[48] Moreover, Article 67 of the Rome Statute expressly excludes any mechanism by which the burden of proof is shifted onto the accused. The other solution is to prosecute the commander not for ordering the crime itself, but for being negligent in preventing it. This second approach has some precedents to support it and is enshrined in Article 28 of the Rome Statute.

The notion that military commanders are criminally liable for the acts of

---

[47] *Prosecutor v. Martic* (Case No. IT-85–11), Rule 61 Decision, 6 March 1996, para. 21.
[48] Nevertheless, the European Court of Human Rights has tolerated such provisions in some circumstances: *Salabiaku v. France*, Series A, No. 141-A, 7 October 1988, para. 28; *Pham Hoang v. France*, Series A, No. 243, 25 September 1992.

their subordinates, even where it cannot be proven that they had knowledge of these acts, was established in controversial rulings in post-Second World War trials.[49] The concept of command responsibility was later recognized as a positive legal norm in the case of prosecutions for grave breaches of Protocol Additional I to the Geneva Conventions, adopted in 1977.[50] In the case of the Yugoslav and Rwanda Tribunals, the fact that a crime within the jurisdiction of the Tribunal was committed by a subordinate 'does not relieve his or her superior of criminal responsibility if he or she knew or had reason to know that the subordinate was about to commit such acts or had done so and the superior failed to take the necessary and reasonable measures to prevent such acts or to punish the perpetrators thereof'.[51]

There was no real controversy about including the concept of command responsibility within the Statute. Extending it to include civilian superiors gained widespread support, although China continued to oppose such a development.[52] The compromise, brokered by the United States, was to adopt different rules on command responsibility depending on whether military commanders or civilian superiors are involved.[53] In order to incur liability, a military commander must know or 'should have known', whilst a civilian superior must either have known or 'consciously disregarded information which clearly indicated' that subordinates were committing or about to commit crimes. The military commander can be prosecuted for what amounts to negligence ('should have known'). Guilt of a civilian superior under this provision, however, must meet a higher standard. It is necessary to establish that the civilian superior had actual or 'constructive' knowledge of the crimes being committed.[54]

Mens rea or mental element

Criminal law sets itself apart from other areas of law in that, as a general rule, it is concerned with intentional and knowing behaviour. An

---

[49] *United States of America* v. *Yamashita*, (1948) 4 LRTWC 1, pp. 36–7; *In re Yamashita*, 327 US 1 (1945); *Canada* v. *Meyer*, (1948) 4 LRTWC 98 (Canadian Military Court).

[50] Protocol Additional I, Art. 86(2).

[51] Statute of the International Criminal Tribunal for the Former Yugoslavia, UN Doc. S/RES/827, Annex, Art. 7(3); Statute of the International Criminal Tribunal for Rwanda, UN Doc. S/RES/955, Annex, Art. 6(3).

[52] Civilian responsibility on this basis is now recognized at customary law: *Prosecutor* v. *Delalic et al.* (Case No. IT-96-21-T), Judgment, 16 November 1998, (1999) 38 ILM 57, paras 355–63.

[53] Saland, 'International Criminal Law Principles', pp. 202–3.

[54] William J. Fenrick, 'Article 28', in Triffterer, *Commentary*, pp. 16–20.

individual who causes accidental harm to another may be liable before some other body but will by and large not be held responsible before the criminal courts. Intent is often described using the Latin expression *mens rea* ('guilty mind'), taken from the phrase *actus non facit reum nisi mens sit rea*. But even if it is understood that a *criminal* act must be intentional and knowing, there are degrees of intention ranging from mere negligence to recklessness and full-blown intent with premeditation.[55] In keeping with the seriousness of the offences over which the Court has jurisdiction, the Rome Statute sets a high standard for the mental element, requiring in paragraph (1) of Article 30 that '[u]nless otherwise provided' the material elements of the offence must be committed 'with intent and knowledge'.[56] In two subsequent paragraphs, the Statute defines these concepts. A person has intent with respect to conduct when that person means to engage in the conduct. A person has intent with respect to a consequence when that person means to cause that consequence or is aware that it will occur in the ordinary course of events. Knowledge is defined as 'awareness that a circumstance exists or a consequence will occur in the ordinary course of events'. Article 30 defines 'knowledge', adding that 'know and knowingly' shall be construed accordingly.[57]

The general rule requiring intent or knowledge is hardly necessary for most of the crimes listed in the Rome Statute, because the definitions have their own built-in *mens rea* requirement. Thus, genocide is defined as a punishable act committed 'with the intent to destroy' a protected group.[58] Crimes against humanity involve a widespread or systematic attack directed against a civilian population 'with knowledge of the attack'.[59] Many of the war crimes listed in Article 8 include the adjectives 'wilfully', 'wantonly' or 'treacherously'. Indeed, it is at least partly for this reason that Article 30 begins with the words '[u]nless otherwise provided'.[60] During drafting of the Statute, difficulties arose when attempting to lower the *mens rea* threshold to such concepts as recklessness and gross negligence.[61] A square bracketed text on recklessness[62] was ultimately dropped by the

---

[55] Jean Pradel, *Droit pénal comparé*, Paris: Dalloz, 1995, p. 251.
[56] UN Doc. A/CONF.183/C.1/L.76/Add.3, p. 4.
[57] But 'know' and 'knowingly' are not used in either Art. 30 or, for that matter, elsewhere in the Rome Statute. The word 'known' appears in the command responsibility provision (Art. 28). The word 'knowledge' is in the *chapeau* of Art. 7, crimes against humanity.
[58] Rome Statute, Art. 6.   [59] *Ibid.*, Art. 7.
[60] Donald K. Piragoff, 'Article 30', in Triffterer, *Commentary*, pp. 527–35, at pp. 531–2.
[61] Saland, 'International Criminal Law Principles', pp. 205–6.
[62] UN Doc. A/CONF.183/C.1/WGGP/L.4, p. 1.

Working Group.[63] There was really little reason to define recklessness as it is not an element in the definition of any of the offences within the jurisdiction of the Court.[64]

The words '[u]nless otherwise provided' also protect Article 28, which sets a negligence standard for guilt by command responsibility that clearly falls below the knowledge and intent requirements of Article 30. Whether these words mean, in practice, '[u]nless otherwise provided *by the Statute*' is somewhat of an open question. It would seem to be going too far to suggest that the Article 30 standard in the Statute could be amended if an exception is provided for in the Elements, yet this is precisely what is done when the Elements refer to a crime committed against a person who the offender 'should have known' was under age,[65] or in cases where he or she 'should have known' of the prohibited use of a flag of truce or the Red Cross emblem and similar insignia.[66] The general introduction to the Elements states that they include exceptions to Article 30 that are based on both the Article 30 standard and 'applicable law'.

There is no equivalent provision for the material element of the offence, the *actus reus*.[67] The final Preparatory Committee draft contained an *actus reus* article, but the Working Group was unable to reach consensus on its content,[68] essentially because of problems in defining the notion of omission. During the debates, the Chair of the Working Group noted that Article 22(2) prohibiting analogies would ensure that judicial discretion on the subject of omissions was never abusive. A footnote to the Working Group's report stated: 'Some delegations were of the view that the deletion of article 28 [on omission] required further consideration and reserved their right to reopen the issue at an appropriate time.'[69] However, nothing more was heard of the subject.

[63] UN Doc. A/CONF.183/C.1/WGGP/L.4/Corr.1; UN Doc. A/CONF.183/C.1/L.76/Add.3, p. 4.
[64] 'Commentary on Parts 2 and 3 of the Zutphen Intersessional Draft: General Principles of Criminal Law', (1998) 13*bis Nouvelles études pénales* 43, p. 52.
[65] Elements of Crimes, Art. 6(e), para. 6 and Arts. 8(2)(b)(xxvi), para. 3 and 8(2)(e)(vii), para. 3. Note, also, in the Introduction to the Elements for genocide, the words '[n]otwithstanding the normal requirement for a mental element provided for in article 30 . . .', suggesting that the drafters of the Elements believed they could modify the Art. 30 *mens rea* requirement.
[66] Elements of Crimes, Art. 8(2)(b)(vii).
[67] Saland, 'International Criminal Law Principles', pp. 212–13.
[68] 'Report of the Ad Hoc Committee on the Establishment of an International Criminal Court', UN Doc. A/50/22, Annex II, p. 58; 'Report of the Preparatory Committee on the Establishment of an International Criminal Court', UN Doc. A/51/22, Vol. I, p. 45; 'Report of the Preparatory Committee on the Establishment of an International Criminal Court', UN Doc. A/51/22, Vol. II, pp. 90–1; UN Doc. A/AC.249/1997/L.5, pp. 26–7; UN Doc. A/AC.249/1997/WG.2/CRP.5; UN Doc. A/AC.249/1998/L.13, pp. 58–9; UN Doc. A/CONF.183/2/Add.1, pp. 54–5.
[69] UN Doc. A/CONF.183/C.1/WGGP/L.4/Add.1/Rev.1, p. 3, n. 3.

Defences

A defence is an answer to a criminal charge. It is used to denote 'all grounds which, for one reason or another, hinder the sanctioning of an offence – despite the fact that the offence has fulfilled all definitional elements of a crime'.[70] Previous international criminal law instruments have made no real attempt at even a partial codification of defences, confining themselves to rather limited issues such as the inadmissibility of the defence of superior orders. Case law on war crimes prosecutions suggests that, aside from superior orders and command of the law, the main pleas invoked by the accused are acting in an official capacity, duress, military necessity, self-defence, reprisal, mistake of law or fact, and insanity.

The Rome Statute partially codifies available defences in Articles 31, 32 and 33. Article 31, entitled 'grounds for excluding criminal responsibility',[71] deals specifically with insanity, intoxication, self-defence, duress and necessity. Article 32 addresses mistake, and Article 33 concerns superior orders and prescription of law. The Statute allows the Court to accept other defences,[72] relying on the sources set out in Article 21(1). Indeed, it affirms a general right of the accused to raise defences.[73] Obvious candidates for uncodified defences would include alibi, military necessity, abuse of process, consent and reprisal.[74] Nevertheless, where the defence intends to raise an uncodified defence, it is required by the Rules of Procedure and Evidence to give notice to the Prosecutor prior to trial, and to obtain a preliminary ruling on the admissibility of the defence from the Trial Chamber.[75] Other defences are formally excluded, either by the terms of the Statute itself – defence of official capacity,[76] lack of knowledge (in the case of command responsibility)[77] and superior orders (in cases of genocide and crimes against humanity)[78] – or by international case law – for example, tu quoque (literally I can do to you what you have done to me).[79]

---

[70] Albin Eser, '"Defences" in War Crime Trials', in Yoram Dinstein and Mala Tabory, eds, *War Crimes in International Law*, The Hague, Boston and London: Kluwer Law International, 1996, pp. 251–73, at p. 251.   [71] Albin Eser, 'Article 31', in Triffterer, *Commentary*, pp. 537–54.

[72] Rome Statute, Art. 31(3).   [73] *Ibid.*, Art. 67(1)(e).

[74] Eser, '"Defences"', pp. 643–4. Note, however, attempts in the Elements of Crimes, Arts 8(2)(b)(x), n. 46, 8(2)(e)(xi), n. 68, and the Rules of Procedure and Evidence, Rule 70, to limit the defence of consent.   [75] Rules of Procedure and Evidence, Rule 80.

[76] Rome Statute, Art. 27.   [77] *Ibid.*, Art. 28.   [78] *Ibid.*, Art. 33.

[79] *Prosecutor* v. *Kupreskic et al.* (Case No. IT-95–16), Decision on Defence Motion to Summon Witness, 3 February 1999; *Prosecutor* v. *Kupreskic et al.* (Case No. IT-95–16), Decision on Evidence of the Good Character of the Accused and the Defence of Tu Quoque, 17 February 1999.

Insanity as a defence has arisen only rarely in the case law of major war crimes prosecutions. Rudolf Hess unsuccessfully raised it at Nuremberg. The text of Article 31(1)(a) echoes the so-called *M'Naghten* rules derived from the common law,[80] but would also seem to be generally consistent with the approach taken in Romano-Germanic and *Sharia* systems. An individual who succeeds with a plea of insanity is entitled to a declaration that he or she is not criminally responsible. The Statute does not speak directly to the burden of proof in cases of the defence of insanity. Is a defendant required only to raise a doubt about mental capacity, or must he or she actually prove such an exception based on a preponderance of evidence? Domestic justice systems take different views of this matter. The *ad hoc* Tribunal for the Former Yugoslavia has opted for the preponderance of evidence standard, making proof of insanity more difficult for the accused.[81] Yet Article 67 of the Statute, which shields the accused from 'any reversal of the burden of proof or any onus of rebuttal', may compel the less onerous requirement that the accused only raise a reasonable doubt.

If the codification of an uncontroversial definition of the insanity defence seems somewhat unnecessary, given the rare cases where this will arise in practice, the provision that follows, concerning intoxication, seems to go from the sublime to the ridiculous. Drafting of the provision was troublesome, and the final result 'had the benefit of not satisfying anyone'.[82] Many individual war crimes may be committed by soldiers and thugs under the influence of drugs and alcohol, but the Court is surely not intended to deal with such 'small fry'. This is a Court established for 'big fish', a relatively small number of leaders, organizers and planners, in cases of genocide, crimes against humanity and large-scale war crimes. The nature of such crimes, involving planning and preparation, is virtually inconsistent with a plea of voluntary intoxication. In practice, examples in case law, even for mere war crimes, are as infrequent as in the case of insanity. The Rome Statute admits the defence of intoxication if it has destroyed the accused's capacity to appreciate the unlawfulness or nature of his or her conduct, or the capacity to control his or her conduct to conform to

---

[80] *M'Naghten's Case* (1843) 10 Cl. & Fin. 200, 8 ER 718.
[81] *Prosecutor* v. *Delalic et al.* (Case No. IT-96-21-T), Order on Esad Landzo's Submission Regarding Diminished or Lack of Mental Capacity, 18 June 1998; *Prosecutor* v. *Delalic et al.* (Case No. IT-96-21-T), Order on Landzo's Request for Definition of Diminished or Lack of Mental Capacity, 15 July 1998; *Prosecutor* v. *Delalic et al.* (Case No. IT-96-21-T), Judgment, 16 November 1998, (1999) 38 ILM 57, para. 1160.
[82] Saland, 'International Criminal Law Principles', p. 207.

the requirements of law. But the defence cannot be invoked if the person became voluntarily intoxicated knowing of the likelihood that he or she would engage in such terrible crimes. This is the case of somebody who drinks in order to get up courage to commit an atrocity.

The Statute allows a defence of self-defence or defence of another person where an accused acts 'reasonably' and in a manner that is 'proportionate' to the degree of danger. These terms are common in national legal norms that deal with the use of force, and there will be no shortage of authority to guide the Court.[83] But a disturbing compromise during the Rome Conference resulted in recognition of the defence of property, although it is confined to cases of war crimes. The property defended must be 'essential for the survival of the person or another person' or 'essential for accomplishing a military mission, against an imminent and unlawful use of force'. In practice, these terms are narrow enough that the troublesome recognition of defence of property in the Statute is unlikely to have much in the way of practical consequences. But they have provoked sharp criticism from some quarters. The Belgian scholar Eric David calls the exception 'a Pandora's box that is rigorously incompatible with the law of armed conflict'. Professor David goes as far as to call this provision a violation of *jus cogens*, concluding that it is, consequently, null and void pursuant to the Vienna Convention on the Law of Treaties.[84]

Article 31 also codifies the defences of duress and necessity. The defence of duress is often confounded with that of superior orders, but the two are quite distinct. A person acting under duress is someone who is compelled to commit the crime by a threat to his or her life, or to that of another person. In the related defence of necessity, this inexorable threat is the result of natural circumstances rather than that of other persons. But, in either case, the defendant is deemed to have no viable moral choice in the matter. An exhaustive judgment of the Appeals Chamber of the International Criminal Tribunal for the Former Yugoslavia, in 1997, determined, by a majority of three to two, that duress is not admissible as a defence to crimes against humanity.[85] The consequence of the provision in

---

[83] One interesting source may be the case law of the European Court of Human Rights in the interpretation of Art. 2(2) of the European Convention on Human Rights, allowing for self-defence as an exception to the right to life.

[84] Eric David, *Principes de droit des conflits armés*, 2nd edn, Brussels: Bruylant, 1999, p. 693.

[85] *Prosecutor v. Erdemovic* (Case No. IT-96-22-A), Sentencing Appeal, 7 October 1997, (1998) 111 ILR 298.

the Rome Statute is to set aside the precedent established by the Yugoslav Tribunal and to reinstate the defence of duress.

The defences of mistake of fact and mistake of law are defined in a distinct provision.[86] An offender who lacks knowledge of an essential fact does not possess the guilty mind or *mens rea* necessary for conviction. This is in fact what the Rome Statute declares, admitting mistake only if it 'negates the mental element'. Mistake of fact as a defence is not controversial, and it is a simple matter to conceive of examples where it might be invoked. A military recruiter charged with conscripting children under fifteen might argue a mistaken belief that the victim was older than he or she appeared. Of course, the Court will need to assess the credibility of such a claim in the light of the circumstances, and would be unlikely even to consider a defence of mistake of fact that did not have an air of reality to it.

Most national legal systems refuse to admit the defence of mistake of law on public policy grounds, although war crimes jurisprudence has tended to be more flexible, probably because international humanitarian law is considered to be quite specialized and rather technical. This is not always easy to understand, however, given that most basic norms of humanitarian law constitute a common denominator of humane behaviour, and ought to be within the grasp of everyone. Mistake of law is particularly relevant to the final defence set out in the Rome Statute, that of superior orders and prescription of law. Indeed, the relationship is provided for in the text itself, which admits the defence of mistake of law 'as provided for in article 33'. Although the defence of superior orders is ruled out in some international criminal law instruments, such as the Charter of the Nuremberg Tribunal and the statutes of the *ad hoc* tribunals, other treaties such as the Genocide Convention stopped short of proscribing it entirely, and the same is the case for the Rome Statute. Article 33 allows the defence under three conditions: the accused must be under a legal obligation to obey orders; the accused must not know that the order was unlawful; and the order must not be manifestly unlawful. The text corresponds to international case law on the subject.[87] With respect, then, to mistake of law, the accused may be excused for ignorance of the illegality of the order but not for ignorance of the manifest illegality of the order. But the Rome Statute subjects this to an exception: 'For the purposes of this article,

---

[86] Rome Statute, Art. 32. See Otto Triffterer, 'Article 32', in Triffterer, *Commentary*, pp. 555–71.

[87] *Llandovery Castle Case* (1923–1924) 2 Ann. Dig. 436 (German Reichsgericht of Leipzig); *United States* v. *Calley*, 22 USMCA 534 (1973).

orders to commit genocide or crimes against humanity are manifestly unlawful.'[88]

The Rome Statute also declares official capacity as Head of State or Government or some other form to be irrelevant to the issue of criminal responsibility and, furthermore, to the issue of mitigation of sentence.[89] The issue was uncontested during negotiations and there were no problems reaching agreement on an acceptable text.[90] Immunities or special procedural rules that may attach to a person's capacity are also no impediment to the exercise by the Court of its jurisdiction. Nevertheless, Article 98(2) of the Statute states that the Court may not proceed with requests for surrender or assistance which would require the requested State to act inconsistently with its obligations under international law with respect to the State or diplomatic immunity of a person, unless the Court can first obtain the cooperation of that third State for the waiver of the immunity. This suggests that a national of a State Party properly before the Court cannot invoke a plea of Head of State or diplomatic immunity, but that the answer may not be the same in the case of a national of a non-State party.

Statutory limitation

The Rome Statute declares that crimes within the jurisdiction of the Court shall not be subject to any statute of limitations.[91] Because there is no statutory limitation provided within the Statute itself, it seems that Article 29 is directed more at national legislation. Many domestic criminal law systems provide for the statutory limitation of crimes, even the most serious.[92] Under French law, for example, prosecutions for murder are time barred after ten years.[93] Codes derived from the Napoleonic model generally have similar provisions. At his trial in Israel in 1961, Nazi war criminal Adolf Eichmann invoked a fifteen-year limitation period in force in Argentina, from where he had been kidnapped. The District Court of Jerusalem ruled that Argentine norms could not apply, adding a reference

---

[88] Paola Gaeta, 'The Defence of Superior Orders: The Statute of the International Criminal Court Versus Customary International Law', (1999) 10 *European Journal of International Law* 172.

[89] Rome Statute, Art. 27.

[90] Saland, 'International Criminal Law Principles', p. 202; Otto Triffterer, 'Article 28', in Triffterer, *Commentary*, pp. 501–14.   [91] Rome Statute, Art. 29.

[92] See Anne-Marie Larosa, *Dictionnaire de droit international pénal, Termes choisis*, Paris: Presses universitaires de France, 1998, pp. 50–2.   [93] Penal Code (France), Art. 7.

to applicable Israeli legislation declaring that 'the rules of prescription . . . shall not apply to offences under this Law'.[94]

International opposition to statutory limitation for war crimes, crimes against humanity and genocide has taken the form of General Assembly resolutions,[95] and treaties within both the United Nations system[96] and that of the Council of Europe.[97] But the treaties have not been a great success in terms of signature and ratification; the United Nations instrument still has only forty-three States parties. The low rate of adhesion to the United Nations Convention has led some academics to contest the suggestion that this is a customary norm.[98] Nevertheless, in the *Barbie* case, the French *Cour de cassation* ruled that the prohibition on statutory limitations for crimes against humanity is now part of customary law.[99]

Article 29's role in the Statute would appear to be part of the complex relationship between national and international judicial systems. It acts as a bar to States who might refuse to surrender offenders on the grounds that the offence was time barred under national legislation. More than that, Article 29 may effect the prohibition on statutory limitation that the international treaties have failed to do.[100]

---

[94] *A-G Israel* v. *Eichmann*, (1968) 36 ILR 18 (District Court, Jerusalem), para. 53.

[95] GA Res. 3(I); GA Res. 170(II); GA Res. 2583(XXIV); GA Res. 2712(XXV); GA Res. 2840(XXVI); GA Res. 3020(XXVII); GA Res. 3074(XXVIII).

[96] Convention on the Nonapplicability of Statutory Limitations to War Crimes and Crimes Against Humanity, (1970) 754 UNTS 73. See Robert H. Miller, 'The Convention on the Non-Applicability of Statutory Limitations to War Crimes and Crimes Against Humanity', (1971) 65 *American Journal of International Law* 476.

[97] European Convention on the Non-Applicability of Statutory Limitation to Crimes Against Humanity and War Crimes of January 25, 1974, ETS 82.

[98] Steven R. Ratner and Jason S. Abrams, *Accountability for Human Rights Atrocities in International Law, Beyond the Nuremberg Legacy*, Oxford: Clarendon Press, 1997, p. 126.

[99] *Fédération nationale des déportés et internés résistants et patriotes et al.* v. *Barbie*, (1984) 78 ILR 125, p. 135.   [100] William A. Schabas, 'Article 29', in Triffterer, *Commentary*, pp. 204–5.

5

Investigation and pre-trial procedure

Many of the States involved in drafting the Rome Statute initially treated debates about the procedural regime to be followed by the Court as an opportunity to affirm the merits of their own justice systems within an international forum. Often, they were simply unable, because of training or prejudice, to conceive of the possibility that other judicial models from different cultures could offer alternative and perhaps better solutions to procedural issues. Describing debates in the International Law Commission, James Crawford noted 'the tendency of each duly socialized lawyer to prefer his own criminal justice system's values and institutions'.[1] But, over time, the drafters came to appreciate that there was much to be learned from different legal systems. Of course, they also recognized that compromise was essential if agreement was to be reached. As one observer of the Rome Conference said so eloquently: 'the fight between common law and civil law has been replaced by an agreement on common principles and civil behaviour'.[2] In this regard, the ongoing work of the *ad hoc* international criminal tribunals was of great value. Since their establishment in 1993 and 1994, the courts in The Hague and Arusha have been engaged in a fascinating exercise in comparative criminal procedure, borrowing the best from different national legal systems and in some cases simply devising innovative and original rules.

The procedural regime of the International Criminal Court is largely a hybrid of two different systems: the adversarial approach of the English common law and the inquisitorial approach of the Napoleonic code and other European legislations of the Romano-Germanic tradition (often described as the 'civil law' system). This is perhaps an oversimplification, because, within the English and continental models, there is enormous

---

[1] James Crawford, 'The ILC Adopts a Statute for an International Criminal Court', (1995) 89 *American Journal of International Law* 404.
[2] Hans-Jörg Behrens, 'Investigation, Trial and Appeal in the International Criminal Court Statute (Parts V, VI, VIII)', (1998) 6 *European Journal of Crime, Criminal Law and Criminal Justice* 113, at p. 113, n. 2.

variation from one country to another. Particularly in Europe, States have recently begun rethinking their approach to criminal procedure, largely in reaction to judgments of the European Court of Human Rights.[3]

Under the adversarial procedure, which is the general rule in common law countries, the authorities responsible for prosecution prepare a criminal charge inspired either by a private complaint or on their own initiative. Although generally bound to respect standards of fairness and the presumption of innocence, their efforts focus on building a case against the accused. When the trial begins, there is no evidence before the judge. Evidence is admitted in accordance with specific and often quite restrictive rules, and its admission may be contested by the defence. Many of these strict rules exist because questions of fact will be decided by lay jurors who lack the training and instincts of professional judges in the assessment of the probity of different types of evidence. For example, the lay juror may have difficulty determining the value of indirect or 'hearsay' evidence, whereas the professional judge knows that it is often quite unreliable. At trial, the prosecution will attempt to lead incriminating evidence, and will simply ignore exculpatory evidence, as this is counterproductive to its own case. Under certain national systems, the prosecution must provide the defence with any favourable evidence that is in its possession, but the obligation rarely goes any further. When the prosecution's case is complete, if the evidence is insufficient to establish guilt, the defence may move to dismiss the charges. Where the evidence appears sufficient, the defence may then decide to reply with its own evidence, whose admissibility is subject to the same rules as for the prosecution.

Under the inquisitorial system, instructing magistrates prepare the case by collecting evidence and interviewing witnesses, often unbeknownst to the accused. The instructing magistrate is a judicial official, who is bound to complete the job with neutrality and impartiality, and who must collect evidence of both guilt and of innocence. The evidence compiled, including witness statements, is then filed in court preliminary to the start of the trial itself. Usually the trial becomes more adversarial at this point, because prosecution and defence each participate in the judicial debates. The trial judges may then assess the evidence in the case file, or, at the request of one or other of the parties or on their own initiative, require that additional evidence be presented. Rules of evidence are not nearly as

---

[3] Mireille Delmas-Marty, *Pour un droit commun*, Paris: Editions du Seuil, 1994.

technical under the inquisitorial as under the adversarial system, mainly because the evidence is being assessed exclusively by professional judges rather than, in the case of the common law system, by lay jurors.

Trials under the inquisitorial system are generally much shorter than their common law counterparts because most of the evidence has already been produced in the court record before the trial begins. Common law trials tend to be much longer and probably more thorough, although there are fewer of them. Because common law proceedings are so complex, only a minority of cases actually get to trial. Most are resolved by agreement between prosecutor and defence counsel, who can usually reach a reasonable compromise as to the likely outcome of a trial based on their own experience with similar cases. The accused pleads guilty to a charge that is agreed to by both lawyers, and after a summary verification the plea is simply endorsed by a trial judge who imposes a sentence, again usually following a recommendation from both counsel. The inquisitorial system does not allow for such 'plea bargaining', and a conviction is impossible until the instructing magistrate has prepared evidence that satisfies the trial judges of guilt.

Drawing on both systems, the Rome Statute provides for an adversarial approach, but one where the Court has dramatic powers to intervene and control the procedure. Although the inquisitorial system is often criticized by lawyers of the common law for its inadequate protection of the rights of the defence, in an international context, where the defence may have insurmountable obstacles to obtaining evidence and interviewing witnesses within uncooperative States, the inquisitorial system may ultimately prove the better approach. Accordingly, the International Criminal Court has wide authority under the Statute to supervise matters at the investigation stage. Both the Prosecutor and the Pre-Trial Chamber are particularly important in this respect, and they have special responsibilities in terms of identifying and securing exculpatory evidence to assist in preparation of the defence.[4]

Initiation of prosecution

The initiative to prosecute a case may come from three sources: a State party, the Security Council or the Prosecutor.[5] In the jargon of the negoti-

---

[4] Leila Nadya Sadat and S. Richard Carden, 'The New International Criminal Court: An Uneasy Revolution', (2000) 88 *Georgetown Law Journal* 381, at pp. 399–400.
[5] Rome Statute of the International Criminal Court, UN Doc. A/CONF.183/9 (hereinafter Rome Statute), Art. 13.

ations, this was known as the 'trigger mechanism'. International organizations, individuals, non-governmental organizations and States that are not parties to the Statute are given no formal recognition with respect to initiating proceedings. However, in practice all of them are likely to establish contact with the Prosecutor and attempt to persuade him or her to take action.

Giving the Prosecutor the power to initiate prosecution is the mechanism most analogous with domestic justice systems but it was also the most controversial. The International Law Commission draft statute denied the Prosecutor any such power. The Commission conceived of the court as 'a facility available to States Parties to its Statute, and in certain cases to the Security Council' who alone were empowered to initiate a case.[6] During the drafting process, the 'like-minded countries' as well as the non-governmental organizations made the *proprio motu* prosecutor one of their battle cries. The concept of an independent prosecutor was an idea whose time had come, and it gained inexorable momentum as the drafting process unfolded.[7] The case for independent prosecutorial powers was immensely strengthened by the extremely positive model of responsible officials presented by Richard Goldstone and Louise Arbour, the *ad hoc* tribunals' prosecutors who held office while the Statute was being drafted.

Some powerful States vigorously opposed the idea, fearful that the position might be occupied by an NGO-friendly litigator with an attitude. They used the expression 'Doctor Strangelove prosecutor', referring to a classic film in which a nutty American nuclear scientist loses his grip and personally initiates a nuclear war. During the Rome Conference, the United States declared that an independent prosecutor 'not only offers little by way of advancing the mandate of the Court and the principles of prosecutorial independence and effectiveness, but also will make much more difficult the Prosecutor's central task of thoroughly and fairly investigating the most egregious of crimes'.[8] In any case, as Morten Bergsmo has written, '[t]he Prosecutor still needs the Security Council to be able to

---

[6] 'Report of the International Law Commission on the Work of Its Forty-Sixth Session, 2 May–22 July 1994', UN Doc. A/49/10, at pp. 89–90.

[7] Silvia A. Fernández de Gurmendi, 'The Role of the International Prosecutor', in Roy Lee, ed., *The International Criminal Court, The Making of the Rome Statute, Issues, Negotiations, Results*, The Hague: Kluwer Law International, 1999, pp. 175–88.

[8] 'The Concerns of the United States Regarding the Proposal for a Proprio Motu Prosecutor', 22 June 1998, p. 1.

work *effectively*[9] because the Security Council has coercive powers that are simply unavailable to the Prosecutor.

The fears of the conservatives have been given some recognition in provisions by which the Court's judges may supervise prosecutorial discretion. In the result, the Prosecutor's decision to undertake investigation of a case *proprio motu* is subject to endorsement by the Pre-Trial Chamber, which is composed of three judges. When the Prosecutor concludes that there is a 'reasonable basis' for proceeding with an investigation, the Prosecutor must submit a request for authorization of an investigation to the Pre-Trial Chamber.[10] Supporting material is to be provided to the judges at this stage. Victims are specifically entitled to 'make representations' during this proceeding, presumably in support of a request for authorization to investigate. The Pre-Trial Chamber must confirm that a 'reasonable basis' for investigation exists, in addition to making a preliminary determination that the case falls within the jurisdiction of the Court.[11] This does not mean that issues of jurisdiction and admissibility are definitively settled, and the Court is not prevented from reversing its initial assessment at some subsequent stage. Should the Pre-Trial Chamber reject the Prosecutor's request, he or she can always return with a subsequent application for authorization based on new facts or evidence.

The Statute says the Prosecutor is to take action *proprio motu* (legal Latin for acting on his or her own initiative) 'on the basis of information'. Such information has to come from somewhere.[12] In fact, the Statute invites the Prosecutor to seek 'information' from States (it does not specify whether they must be parties or not), United Nations organs, intergovernmental or non-governmental organizations, 'and other reliable sources that he or she deems appropriate'.[13] The Prosecutor may well determine that the information provided does not justify proceeding, but in such a case he or she is required to inform those who provided the information of the decision. An unsatisfied informant is without any further recourse and may not challenge or appeal the Prosecutor's decision, although the Statute explicitly contemplates the possibility of new facts being submitted.[14]

[9] Morten Bergsmo, 'The Jurisdictional Regime of the International Criminal Court (Part II, Articles 11–19)', (1998) 6 *European Journal of Crime, Criminal Law and Criminal Justice* 29, p. 41 (italics in the original).
[10] Rules of Procedure and Evidence, UN Doc. PCNICC/2000/INF/3/Add.3, Rule 50.
[11] Rome Statute, Art. 15(4).   [12] *Ibid.*, Art. 15(1).   [13] *Ibid.*, Art. 15(2).
[14] *Ibid.*, Art. 15(6).

The Prosecutor will have to pick and choose appropriate cases to investigate and prosecute. As Louise Arbour, Prosecutor of the ICTY, noted in a statement to the December 1997 session of the Preparatory Committee, there is a major distinction between domestic and international prosecution and it lies in the unfettered discretion of the prosecutor. In a domestic context, there is an assumption that all crimes that go beyond the trivial or *de minimis* range are to be prosecuted. But before an international tribunal, particularly one based on complementarity, 'the discretion to prosecute is considerably larger, and the criteria upon which such Prosecutorial discretion is to be exercised are ill-defined, and complex. In my experience, based on the work of the two Tribunals to date, I believe that the real challenge posed to a Prosecutor is to choose from many meritorious complaints the appropriate ones for international intervention, rather than to weed out weak or frivolous ones.'[15]

The second 'trigger mechanism' in the Statute is State party referral. A State party to the Statute may refer 'a situation in which one or more crimes within the jurisdiction of the Court appear to have been committed requesting the Prosecutor to investigate the situation for the purpose of determining whether one or more specific persons should be charged with the commission of such crimes'.[16] The State party does not actually denounce an individual but simply a 'situation', in much the same way as in a domestic justice system where responsible citizens may inform police or prosecutors that they think a crime has taken place, but without necessarily identifying the person responsible. States may be motivated by altruistic considerations in unleashing the jurisdiction of the Court, but they are also likely to be driven by political agendas. There are many doubts about how often this mechanism will actually be used. Somewhat analogous schemes permitting States to denounce human rights violations in other States exist under several international treaties but in only one of them, the European Convention on Human Rights, has it ever actually been invoked, and then only rarely.[17] In the original International Law Commission draft, the State party referral was the only way to bring a case before the Court, excluding of course the special situation of Security Council action. It may well turn out to be a drafting anachronism, because

---

[15] 'Statement by Justice Louise Arbour to the Preparatory Committee on the Establishment of an International Criminal Court, December 8, 1997', pp. 7–8.

[16] Rome Statute, Arts 13(a) and 14.

[17] Daniel D. Ntanda Nsereko, 'The International Criminal Court: Jurisdictional and Related Issues', (1999) 10 *Criminal Law Forum* 87, at p. 109.

States that desire the Court to take up a matter are more likely to lobby with the Prosecutor. The result will be the same, but they will save the diplomatic discomforts that accompany public denunciation.

Finally, prosecution may be undertaken at the request of the Security Council.[18] The Statute furnishes no additional details or requirements with respect to Security Council referral, except to specify that the Council must be acting under Chapter VII of the Charter of the United Nations. What is envisaged is the use of the Court as a kind of standing *ad hoc* tribunal, should the Security Council resolve to pursue prosecution along the lines of the tribunals for the former Yugoslavia and Rwanda. An important question of funding arises here. In the case of tribunals formally created by the Council, it is normal that they be financed out of United Nations resources. But the International Criminal Court is not a United Nations organ, and it seems unreasonable that its facilities be offered to the United Nations free of charge, so to speak. If it triggers the Court, the Council would have to be prepared to live within the parameters of the Statute with respect to such matters as jurisdiction. For example, it could not request that the Court consider the atrocities committed by the Khmer Rouge in Cambodia during the late 1970s because Article 11 of the Statute clearly declares that the Court cannot judge crimes committed prior to the entry into force of the Statute. In such cases, the Council would be required to set up an additional *ad hoc* tribunal. For the same reason, the Council could not transfer the powers of the existing *ad hoc* tribunals to the new Court once it is created. It remains uncertain whether the Security Council must also meet the other admissibility criteria and respect the principle of complementarity, a matter that seems to have been intentionally left unresolved at the Rome Conference.[19]

When prosecution is initiated by referral of a State party or at the request of the Security Council, it would seem that the Prosecutor has no discretion as to whether or not to proceed. However, the Statute recognizes that in such cases the Prosecutor may, after launching an investigation, quickly conclude that further investigation should be halted. The standard to be applied by the Prosecutor is that of a 'sufficient basis' for prosecution. When the Prosecutor concludes that there is no sufficient basis for prosecution, he or she must inform the Pre-Trial Chamber as well

---

[18] Rome Statute, Art. 13(b).
[19] Ruth B. Philips, 'The International Criminal Court Statute: Jurisdiction and Admissibility', (1999) 10 *Criminal Law Forum* 61, at p. 73; see also *ibid.*, p. 81.

as the referring State or the Security Council, as the case may be. Reasons must be provided by the Prosecutor for the decision not to proceed. The Statute says the Prosecutor may conclude that there is not a 'sufficient basis' because there is an insufficient legal or factual basis to obtain an arrest warrant or summons, because the case is inadmissible according to the terms of Article 17, or because it is 'not in the interests of justice, taking into account all the circumstances, including the gravity of the crime, the interests of victims and the age or infirmity of the alleged perpetrator, and his or her role in the alleged crime'.[20] The State party or the Security Council, depending on the originator of the case, may apply to the Pre-Trial Chamber for review of the Prosecutor's decision not to proceed.[21] The Statute says that the Pre-Trial Chamber may 'request' the Prosecutor to reconsider the decision. The language is lukewarm, implying that ultimately the discretion to investigate or not to investigate resides with the Prosecutor.

Rulings on jurisdiction and admissibility

The principle of complementarity, which is discussed at length in chapter 4, prevents the Court from investigating or trying cases that are already being addressed by national legal systems. In order to protect State sovereignty and ensure that the principle of complementarity is effectively applied, the Statute saddles the Prosecutor with an onerous procedure that must be fulfilled before investigation can proceed. Two distinct preliminary proceedings are set out in the Statute allowing for contestation on either jurisdictional or admissibility grounds. The first, set out in Article 18, is entitled 'Preliminary rulings regarding admissibility', and applies only to investigations initiated by a State party referral or at the initiative of the Prosecutor. The second, described in Article 19, is described as 'challenges to the jurisdiction of the Court or the admissibility of a case', and applies generally to cases before the Court.

Pursuant to Article 18, which applies to all but cases referred by the Security Council, the Prosecutor is required to publicize his or her intention to proceed with an investigation. Notice must be sent to all States parties to the Statute as well as any and all States that would normally exercise jurisdiction over the crimes concerned. In practice, this means that the State

---

[20] Rome Statute, Art. 53(2).
[21] Ibid., Art. 53(3); Rules of Procedure and Evidence, Rules 107–110.

where the crime has been committed as well as the State of nationality of the alleged offender will normally be informed. Indeed, on a generous interpretation of the requirement, it could be argued that all States in the world be informed as they may normally exercise jurisdiction over the crimes pursuant to the concept of universal jurisdiction. The Statute entitles the Prosecutor to give such notice on a confidential basis, and to limit the scope of information provided so as to protect persons, prevent destruction of evidence or prevent absconding of suspects.[22] But because at least one State with jurisdiction over the offence will almost invariably be complicit with the suspects, the Prosecutor will probably lose all element of surprise. Perhaps it is too soon, however, to be overly pessimistic about the consequences of this requirement. The *ad hoc* tribunals have, after all, been able to arrest suspects, obtain evidence and protect witnesses despite the fact that the same kind of information as that which must be communicated by the International Criminal Court's prosecutor is common knowledge.

States have one month from receipt of the notice of the Prosecutor in which to inform the Prosecutor that they are investigating or have investigated the crimes in question. In effect, they are putting the Prosecutor on notice that they consider the case to be inadmissible under the principles of complementarity, as set out in Article 17. Upon receipt of such notice, the Prosecutor cannot proceed further until further authorization from the Pre-Trial Chamber has been obtained.[23] Thus, it is the Prosecutor who applies to the Pre-Trial Chamber for a 'preliminary ruling on admissibility'. The Pre-Trial Chamber is to assess whether there is a 'reasonable basis' to proceed with the investigation. If authorization is refused by the Pre-Trial Chamber, the Prosecutor can return subsequently with new facts or evidence. Both sides can appeal a determination by the Pre-Trial Chamber. The Prosecutor can apply for provisional measures in order to preserve evidence while the Article 18 proceedings are underway.

A second assessment of the admissibility of cases is envisaged by Article 19. The Article 19 procedure applies to all cases before the Court, even those resulting from a situation referred by the Security Council. In the first place, the Court is required to satisfy itself that it has jurisdiction over a case, a power that is inherent in any event.[24] In addition, it *may* deter-

---

[22] Rome Statute, Art. 19(1).   [23] *Ibid.*, Art. 19(3).

[24] Christopher K. Hall, 'Article 19', in Otto Triffterer, ed., *Commentary on the Rome Statute of the International Criminal Court, Observers' Notes, Article by Article*, Baden-Baden: Nomos, 1999, pp. 403–18, at p. 407.

mine the admissibility of a case according to the criteria of Article 17. Whatever the result of the Court's own assessment, Article 19 also allows challenges to the Court's jurisdiction or to the admissibility of a case by the accused, or by a State with jurisdiction over the case, and even by the Prosecutor. These issues of jurisdiction and admissibility may be raised before confirmation of the charges, in which case they are heard by the Pre-Trial Chamber, or later, before the Trial Chamber.

The Statute clearly envisages a hearing before the Court in which Prosecutor and State participate, along with the accused, and all sides are entitled to appeal the decision to the Appeals Chamber. Fears, no doubt well-founded, that precious time would elapse during this tedious procedure led the drafters of the Rome Statute to make special allowance for interim investigative steps being authorized by the Court. Thus, pending a ruling by the Pre-Trial Chamber, the Prosecutor may seek 'on an exceptional basis' authorization to investigate with a view to preserving evidence 'where there is a unique opportunity to obtain important evidence or there is a significant risk that such evidence may not be subsequently available'.[25] If the Prosecutor decides not to challenge the State's claim that it is investigating the matter, he or she may review this determination six months later, or at any time when there has been a significant change of circumstances with respect to the State's unwillingness or inability to investigate. The Prosecutor is entitled to request the State to provide periodic updates on the progress of investigations and subsequent prosecutions with a view to ongoing monitoring of the State's 'willingness'.[26]

Investigation

The Prosecutor is required 'to cover all facts and evidence relevant to an assessment of whether there is criminal responsibility under this Statute, and, in doing so, investigate incriminating and exonerating circumstances equally'.[27] The wording suggests a Prosecutor with a high level of neutrality and impartiality. Such a Prosecutor is rather more like the investigating magistrate or *juge d'instruction* of the continental legal system than the adversarial prosecuting attorney of the common law. This provision is one of many examples of the efforts of the drafters to seek some balance between common law and Romano-Germanic procedural models.[28]

---

[25] Rome Statute, Art. 19(6). See also Art. 95.   [26] *Ibid.*, Art. 18(5).   [27] *Ibid.*, Art. 54(1).
[28] Morten Bergsmo and Pieter Kruger, 'Article 54', in Triffterer, *Commentary*, pp. 715–25, at p. 716.

Other language in the same provision recalls the often delicate and highly sensitive nature of investigations into war crimes, crimes against humanity and genocide. The Prosecutor is to respect the interests and personal circumstances of victims and witnesses, and to be especially thoughtful in matters involving sexual violence, gender violence or violence against children.[29]

It is at the investigation stage that major differences between national and international justice are highlighted. Under a national justice system, the prosecuting authority has more or less unfettered access to witnesses and material evidence, subject to judicial authorization where search or seizure are involved. The matter is not nearly as simple for an international court, because the Prosecutor must conduct investigations on the territory of sovereign States. The investigation depends on the receptivity of the domestic legal system to initiatives from the Prosecutor's office. This will be especially difficult in the case of States that are not parties to the Statute or States that find themselves threatened by such an investigation, both of them rather probable scenarios.

The Prosecutor's powers during an investigation consist of collection and examination of evidence and attendance and questioning of suspects, victims and witnesses. Here, the Prosecutor may seek the cooperation of States or intergovernmental organizations, and even enter into arrangements or agreements necessary to facilitate such cooperation. He or she may also agree to the non-disclosure of materials that are obtained under the condition of confidentiality and solely for the purpose of generating new evidence.[30] The effect of such a provision is to shelter such information from any requirement of disclosure to the defence.

The Prosecutor's ability to conduct 'on site investigations', as they were referred to during the drafting, was highly controversial. Some delegations were unambiguously opposed, taking the view that investigation was solely the prerogative of the State in question, as it would be in the case of inter-State judicial cooperation. Ultimately, the Prosecutor is allowed under the Statute to undertake specific investigative steps in the territory of a State *without* having previously obtained its consent and cooperation. But any such investigation is contingent upon judicial leave. Thus, the Pre-Trial Chamber must authorize any such measures, and it can only do so after determining that the State is clearly unable to execute a request for

---

[29] Rome Statute, Art. 54(1)(b).   [30] *Ibid.*, Art. 54.

cooperation due to the unavailability of any appropriate authority within its judicial system.[31] In practice, such a power 'is not practicable and cannot be effectively utilized', as Fabricio Guariglia has pointed out.[32] Elsewhere, the Statute allows the Prosecutor to take evidence and interview witnesses within a State and without its consent, but all of this must be carried out on a voluntary basis and after seeking permission from the State.[33]

Cases may arise where a State party is 'clearly unable to execute a request for cooperation due to the unavailability of any authority or any component of its judicial system competent to execute the request for cooperation'. In such situations, the Pre-Trial Chamber may authorize the Prosecutor to take specific investigative steps within that State's territory without its consent, although the Statute urges that this be done 'whenever possible having regard to the views of the State concerned'.[34]

States are under a general obligation to cooperate with the Court in its investigation of crimes.[35] They must ensure that they have domestic legal provisions in effect in order to provide such cooperation.[36] But the formulation of this obligation, which would seem obvious enough for States parties to the Statute, proved difficult at Rome. According to Phakiso Mochochoko, '[d]elegations were divided on the issue of whether cooperation should be defined as a matter of legal obligation that the Court can rely upon, or whether such cooperation should remain an uncertain variable, subject to the will or circumstances of a particular State'.[37] The resulting compromise specifies precise obligations with respect to cooperation, but also requires more generally that States parties 'cooperate fully' with the Court.

The mechanisms established by the Court will be largely familiar to States, in that they closely resemble those that already exist in the form of bilateral or multilateral treaties on judicial assistance. Requests for cooperation are to be transmitted through the diplomatic channel or any other appropriate mechanism designated by each State party.[38] The request is to

---

[31] Ibid., Art. 57(3)(d).

[32] Fabricio Guariglia, 'Investigation and Prosecution', in Lee, The International Criminal Court, pp. 227–38.

[33] Rome Statute, Art. 99(4). See Kimberly Prost and Angelika Schlunck, 'Article 99', in Triffterer, Commentary, pp. 1135–42.   [34] Rome Statute, Art. 57(1)(d).   [35] Ibid., Art. 86.

[36] Ibid., Art. 88.

[37] Phakiso Mochochoko, 'International Cooperation and Judicial Assistance', in Lee, The International Criminal Court, pp. 305–17, at p. 306.

[38] Rome Statute, Art. 87(1)(a); Rules of Procedure and Evidence, Rules 176–180.

be formulated in an official language of the State, or in a language designated by the State. States are required to safeguard the confidentiality of the
request, except to the extent necessary for its fulfilment.[39] Requests may
also be transmitted through Interpol or an appropriate regional police
organization. Applications for assistance are to be made in writing, as a
general rule, and are to include a concise statement of the purpose of the
request, including the legal basis and the grounds of the request.[40]

The specific forms of cooperation to which the Court is entitled are
listed in Article 93 of the Statute, although there is a more general obligation to provide any type of assistance not prohibited by the law of the
requested State, with a view to facilitating investigation. States parties are
required to provide assistance in: identification of and determining the
whereabouts of persons or the location of items; taking of evidence,
including testimony under oath, and the production of evidence, including expert opinions and reports necessary to the Court; questioning of
suspects; service of documents; facilitating the voluntary appearance of
persons as witnesses or experts before the Court; examination of places or
sites, including the exhumation and examination of grave sites; execution
of searches and seizures; provision of records and documents, including
official records and documents; protection of victims and witnesses and
the preservation of evidence; and identification, tracing and freezing or
seizure of proceeds, property and assets and instrumentalities of crimes
for the purpose of eventual forfeiture.[41] States are only entitled to deny
requests for production of documents or disclosure of evidence relating to
'national security', a matter of which they seem to be the sole arbiter.[42]
Incidentally, there is a certain reciprocity to the cooperation procedures,
in that the Court may also provide assistance to States parties that are conducting their own investigations into serious crimes.[43]

But what can be done when States parties, who are bound by the Statute
to cooperate with the Court, refuse perfectly legal requests for assistance?
Article 87(7) states that the Court may make a finding of non-compliance
and then refer the matter to the Assembly of States Parties. Where the
Security Council has referred the matter to the Court, the Court may refer
the matter to the Security Council, although this would hardly seem necessary as the Security Council could certainly take action in any case, pur-

---

[39] Rome Statute, Art. 87(3).   [40] *Ibid.*, Art. 96(2).
[41] *Ibid.*, Art. 93(1). See also *ibid.*, Art. 72.   [42] *Ibid.*, Arts 93(4) and 72.
[43] *Ibid.*, Art. 93(10).

suant to its powers under the Charter of the United Nations. As for the Assembly of States Parties, its powers, in the case of non-compliance, would seem to be limited to 'naming and shaming'.

Although most of the investigation will take place in practice under the provisions of a State's national law, with respect to questioning, search, seizure and similar processes, the rights of individuals during investigations are subject to special protection by the Statute. National law varies considerably in this area, and it would be unconscionable for the Court to implicate itself in domestic judicial proceedings that breach fundamental rights. In fact, the Statute almost seems to be saying that it cannot trust domestic justice systems to provide adequate respect for the rights of the individual. The provisions in the Statute set a high standard and offer a good model for national systems. According to Article 55, during investigation a person shall not be compelled to incriminate himself or herself or to confess guilt; shall not be subjected to any form of coercion, duress or threat, to torture or to any other form of cruel, inhuman or degrading treatment or punishment; shall, if questioned in a language other than a language the person fully understands and speaks, have, free of any cost, the assistance of a competent interpreter and such translations as are necessary to meet the requirements of fairness; shall not be subjected to arbitrary arrest or detention; and shall not be deprived of his or her liberty except on such grounds and in accordance with such procedures as are established in the Statute. If such standards were universally respected, there would probably be no need for an international criminal court!

A person suspected of having committed a crime subject to the jurisdiction of the Court is entitled to be informed of other specific rights prior to being questioned.[44] The person shall be informed that he or she is indeed suspected of having committed a crime, that he or she may remain silent without such silence being a consideration in determining guilt or innocence at trial, to have legal assistance, if necessary provided for them in cases of indigence and where the interest of justice so require, and to be questioned in the presence of counsel unless this right has been voluntarily waived. These rights go well beyond the requirements of international human rights norms set out in such instruments as the International Covenant on Civil and Political Rights,[45] and as a general rule surpass the

---

[44] See on this point *Prosecutor* v. *Music* (Case No. IT 96-21-T), Decision on Music's Motion for Exclusion of Evidence, 2 September 1997.

[45] International Covenant on Civil and Political Rights, (1976) UNTS 171, Art. 9.

rights recognized in even the most advanced and progressive justice systems.[46] But the Statute insists that these norms be honoured, even if the questioning is being carried out by officials of national justice systems pursuant to a request from the Court. If these rules are violated, the Court is entitled to exclude any evidence obtained, such as a confession.[47] However, before excluding evidence the Court must also satisfy itself that the violation 'raises substantial doubt on the reliability of the evidence' or that 'the admission of the evidence would be antithetical to and would seriously damage the integrity of the proceedings'. In any event, given these elaborate provisions, it is hard to imagine why any suspect would ever agree to talk to investigators from the office of the Prosecutor. Certainly competent defence counsel will almost invariably advise against any cooperation, except in exceptional circumstances, such as a declaration that an alibi defence will be invoked at trial.

The Statute makes special provision for testimony or evidence that may not be available at trial. An example would be testimony of a victim who will die before trial. While the interests of justice require that special provision be made to allow for the admissibility of such evidence, or rather a record of it, there is also the need to protect the rights of the defence. Article 56 entitles the Prosecutor, when there is a 'unique investigative opportunity' with respect to testimony or evidence that may subsequently be unavailable, to request authorization to record the testimony or to collect and test the evidence. The Pre-Trial Chamber is to ensure that measures are taken to guarantee the efficiency and integrity of the proceedings and, in particular, that the rights of the defence are protected. The Pre-Trial Chamber is to name one of its judges to attend proceedings in this respect. The Prosecutor is expected to seek such measures, even when the evidence is favourable to the defence, in keeping with the duty of neutrality and impartiality.[48] The Pre-Trial Chamber has a certain role in supervising the Prosecutor, and may challenge the latter if measures to preserve testimony or evidence in such cases are not sought. If the Prosecutor's failure to do so is deemed unjustifiable, the Pre-Trial Chamber may take such measures on its own initiative. Here too, the Statute departs from a purely adversarial model in favour of the more neutral prosecution of the continental or Romano-Germanic system of criminal procedure.

---

[46] Rome Statute, Art. 55(2).   [47] *Ibid.*, Art. 67(7).
[48] Behrens, 'Investigation, Trial and Appeal', at pp. 122–3.

Arrest and surrender

At any time after the initiation of an investigation, the Prosecutor may seek a warrant of arrest from the Pre-Trial Chamber. The Chamber must be satisfied that there are reasonable grounds to believe the person has committed a crime within the Court's jurisdiction, and that the arrest of the person is necessary. Arrest is considered necessary in order to ensure appearance at trial, to prevent obstruction of the investigation, or to prevent the person from undertaking any further activity prohibited by the Statute.[49] The Prosecutor must include a concise statement of the relevant facts and a summary of the evidence in order to justify the existence of reasonable grounds, as well as supporting materials to account for the need for arrest. The warrant of arrest, if issued, should contain a concise statement of the facts but does not need to indicate the evidence that supports this. Summons is offered as an alternative to arrest, where it will be sufficient to ensure a person's appearance before the Court.[50]

The Court communicates its request for arrest to the State concerned, which is then required to take immediate steps to arrest the person.[51] The State is called the 'custodial State' in the Statute. The arrested person is to be brought promptly before the competent judicial authority in the custodial State which is to determine that the warrant applies to that person, that proper process has been followed and that the person's rights have been respected. In urgent cases, the Court may request the provisional arrest of the person, pending presentation of the request for surrender together with the supporting documents.[52] The request for provisional arrest may be delivered 'by any medium capable of delivering a written record'. A person arrested provisionally is entitled to be released if the formal request for surrender and the supporting documents are not produced within sixty days.[53] However, a suspect may consent to surrender even prior to the expiry of the period if the laws of the custodial State permit this.

The arrested person is entitled to apply to the authorities of the custodial State for interim release pending surrender. However, the Statute creates a presumption in favour of detention.[54] The authorities of the

---

[49] Rome Statute, Art. 58(1); Rules of Procedure and Evidence, Rule 117.
[50] Rome Statute, Art. 58(7).   [51] *Ibid.*, Art. 89(1).
[52] *Ibid.*, Art. 92; Rules of Procedure and Evidence, Rule 119.
[53] Rules of Procedure and Evidence, Rule 188.
[54] The International Covenant on Civil and Political Rights, (1976) UNTS 171, Art. 9(3), states that '[i]t shall not be the general rule that persons awaiting trial shall be detained in custody'.

custodial State are to grant judicial release only when justified by 'urgent and exceptional circumstances' and where the necessary safeguards exist to ensure the surrender of the person to the Court. The Pre-Trial Chamber has a supervisory role in the area of interim release. It is to be informed by the custodial State of any application for interim release, and may make recommendations to the competent authorities of the custodial State. These recommendations are to be given 'full consideration'. If interim release is authorized, the Pre-Trial Chamber may request periodic reports on its status.

The competent authorities of the custodial State are expressly forbidden by the Statute from questioning whether the warrant was properly issued by the Pre-Trial Chamber. However, the Statute unequivocally envisages other forms of contestation by the accused. For example, an accused may challenge arrest on the grounds of double jeopardy, in which case the custodial State is to consult with the Court to determine whether there has been a ruling on admissibility.[55] If the Court is considering the issue of admissibility, then the custodial State may postpone execution of the request for surrender.

The Statute does not use the term 'extradition' to describe the rendition of a suspect from a State party to the Court. This is consistent with an approach to this issue already adopted in the statutes of the *ad hoc* tribunals, which speak of 'surrender or transfer' (*le transfert ou la traduction*).[56] So that there is no doubt about the point, the Rome Statute includes a rather exceptional definitional provision that declares extradition to be 'the delivering up of a person by one State to another as provided by treaty, convention or national legislation' and surrender to be 'the delivering up of a person by a State to the Court, pursuant to this Statute'.[57] But the international court is really only the sum of its parts, and 'transfer' or 'surrender' is in a sense the 'extradition' to an ensemble of States, acting together. The reason for what at first blush seems obtuse terminology is to respond to objections from States that have legislation, and sometimes even constitutional provisions, prohibiting the *extradition* of their own nationals.[58] Obviously a refusal to extradite citizens would be totally

[55] Rome Statute, Art. 89(2).
[56] Statute of the International Criminal Tribunal for the Former Yugoslavia, UN Doc. S/RES/827, Annex, Art. 29(2)(e); Statute of the International Criminal Tribunal for Rwanda, UN Doc. S/RES/955, Annex, Art. 28(2)(e). See also 'Rules of Procedure and Evidence', UN Doc. IT/32, Rule 58.   [57] Rome Statute, Art. 102.
[58] Claus Kress, 'Investigation, Trial and Appeal in the International Criminal Court Statute (Parts

incompatible with a State's obligations under the Statute. But early drafts of the Statute had allowed States to refuse surrender of their nationals, and the matter remained controversial through to the final days of the Rome Conference.[59]

It is difficult to predict how national courts will take to these distinctions, and there are few precedents. Three rationales have been advanced by academic writers for the prohibitions on extradition of nationals that are relatively common in domestic laws: national judges are the natural judges of the offence; a State must protect its own nationals; a foreigner would be subject to prejudice.[60] None of these apply to the International Criminal Court, especially given that States parties have the first bite at the apple, in accordance with the principle of complementarity. Yet some national judges seem to have a visceral hostility to international justice, as can be seen in the embarrassingly tardy efforts of the United States to secure the transfer of a Rwandan suspect to the Arusha tribunal.[61] Accordingly, that a national judge would consider a distinction between 'transfer or surrender' and 'extradition' to be little more than legal sophistry cannot be ruled out, despite the clear words of Article 102.[62]

Penalties may also pose problems for some States with regard to transfer and surrender. The issue was raised at Rome during the debates on the death penalty and life imprisonment, with some delegations noting their constitutional prohibition on extradition in the case of such severe penalties. For example, the Colombian Constitution forbids life imprisonment. Presumably, a Colombian accused could argue before domestic courts in proceedings to effect transfer to the International Criminal Court that eligibility for parole, as set out in Article 77 of the Statute, does not exclude the possibility of such a sentence.[63] Colombian courts might hold, by

V, VI, VIII)', (1998) 6 *European Journal of Crime, Criminal Law and Criminal Justice* 126, at p. 136.

[59] Phakiso Mochochoko, 'International Cooperation and Judicial Assistance', in Lee, *The International Criminal Court*, pp. 305–17, at pp. 311–12.

[60] Geoff Gilbert, *Aspects of Extradition Law*, Boston, Dordrecht and London: Martinus Nijhoff, 1991, p. 96.

[61] Robert Kushen and Kenneth J. Harris, 'Surrender of Fugitives by the United States to the War Crimes Tribunals for Yugoslavia and Rwanda', (1996) 90 *American Journal of International Law* 254.

[62] According to Cherif Bassiouni, '[I]n most States, surrender is equivalent to extradition': M. Cherif Bassiouni and Peter Manikas, *The Law of the International Criminal Tribunal for the Former Yugoslavia*, Irvington-on-Hudson, NY: Transnational Publishers, 1995, p. 787.

[63] Gisbert H. Flanz, 'Colombia', translated by Peter B. Heller and Marcia W. Coward, in Gisbert H. Flanz, ed., *Constitutions of the Countries of the World*, Dobbs Ferry, NY: Oceana Publications, 1995, Art. 34.

analogy with a recent decision of the Italian Constitutional Court,[64] that because they cannot or should not speculate upon whether parole might be granted, transfer or surrender must be denied. Nor should the prospect be gainsaid that sometime in the future, regional or universal human rights bodies might determine that the sentences allowed by the Rome Statute, specifically life imprisonment without the possibility of parole before twenty-five years, are in breach of international human rights norms.[65] States preoccupied by their compliance with the Rome Statute might be led to contemplate reservations to human rights treaties on this basis, although the compatibility of such reservations with the object and purpose of human rights instruments would be debatable.

There may be competing requests for the same individual, one from the Court and the other from another State seeking extradition. This of course raises the issue of complementarity, because the application by the State for extradition indicates that there is in fact a national justice system seeking to exercise its jurisdiction over the offender and the offence. In such cases, the custodial State may not extradite the person until the Court has ruled that the case is inadmissible.[66] It may also confront a State with two incompatible legal obligations, that of extradition pursuant to the applicable extradition treaty and that of surrender in accordance with the Statute. Here, the Statute does not impose a firm duty on the custodial State to proceed with surrender to the Court. Rather, the custodial State is entitled to assess a number of relevant factors, including the respective dates of the requests, whether the requesting State may have territorial or personal jurisdiction over the offender, and the possibility of subsequent surrender from the Court to the requesting State.[67]

A person who has been unlawfully arrested or detained is entitled to compensation.[68] This right goes beyond existing international human rights obligations, which generally provide for some form of indemnification only when there has been a genuine miscarriage of justice. The Appeals Chamber of the International Criminal Tribunal for Rwanda has ruled that a person unlawfully detained may be entitled to a stay of proceedings and release, in extreme cases. Alternatively, in less severe situa-

---

[64] *Venezia* v. *United States of America*, Decision No. 223, 25 June 1996 (Constitutional Court of Italy).

[65] See, for example, Dirk Van Zyl Smit, 'Life Imprisonment as the Ultimate Penalty in International Law: A Human Rights Perspective', (1998) 9 *Criminal Law Forum* 1.

[66] Rome Statute, Art. 90.   [67] *Ibid.*, Art. 90(6).

[68] Rome Statute, Art. 85(1); Rules of Procedure and Evidence, Rules 173–175.

tions, if the individual is acquitted then financial compensation is in order, and if the individual is convicted he or she should receive a reduction in sentence.[69]

Appearance before the Court and interim release

An accused may appear before the Court in one of two ways: by surrender from a State where he or she has been apprehended; or by voluntarily presenting him or herself pursuant to a summons. A hearing is to be held before the Pre-Trial Chamber, which is to satisfy itself that the accused has been informed of the crimes alleged and of his or her rights under the Statute, including the right to apply for interim release pending trial.[70]

In the case of individuals who present themselves pursuant to a summons, the Statute presumes that they will be allowed to remain at liberty during trial. For those arrested and surrendered, detention would seem to be the rule. Basically, the Prosecutor must satisfy the Pre-Trial Chamber that the same reasons that justified arrest continue to exist, namely that this is necessary to ensure attendance at trial, to prevent obstruction of the investigation or court proceedings, or to prevent continued criminal behaviour.[71] International human rights law favours release during trial, a corollary of the presumption of innocence. But it seems appropriate that the rule be somewhat attenuated in the case of the International Criminal Court. Two reasons justify this. First, because the crimes – and the penalties – are so serious, it seems logical to expect an accused to try to avoid trial by any means possible. Secondly, release during trial as a general rule might well trivialize the role of the Court in the public eye and, more particularly, outrage victims of the crimes in question.

The Pre-Trial Chamber is to ensure that individuals are not detained 'for an unreasonable period' prior to trial where this is due to 'inexcusable delay' by the Prosecutor. In such cases, the Court is to consider releasing the person, with or without conditions. The Appeals Chamber of the International Criminal Tribunal for Rwanda has considered that inexcusable delay attributable to the Prosecutor, in extreme circumstances, entitles the accused to have the charges dropped 'with prejudice' to the Prosecutor, that is, without the possibility of retrial.[72] But the Statute of

[69] *Barayagwiza* v. *Prosecutor* (Case No. ICTR-97-19-AR72), Decisions of 3 November 1999 and 31 March 2000.   [70] Rome Statute, Art. 60(1).   [71] *Ibid.*, Art. 60.

[72] *Barayagwiza* v. *Prosecutor, supra* note 69.

the Rwanda Tribunal is silent as to an appropriate remedy in such cases. That the Rome Statute establishes a specific remedy, namely, release from custody (but not a stay of the proceedings) would seem to rule out the more radical solution adopted recently by the Appeals Chamber of the Rwanda Tribunal.

The issue of interim release can be revisited by both Prosecutor and defendant at any time on the basis of changed circumstances. In the case of a person who is at liberty, the Pre-Trial Chamber may issue an arrest warrant.

Confirmation hearing

The Pre-Trial Chamber is to hold a hearing to confirm the charges on which the Prosecutor intends to go to trial. Normally, the hearing is to be held in the presence of the accused as well as his or her counsel. Exceptionally, however, the Pre-Trial Chamber may hold this confirmation hearing in the absence of the accused, either at the Prosecutor's request or at its own initiative. Such an *ex parte* hearing will be justified where the accused has waived the right to be present, or where the accused has fled or cannot be found. In such cases, the Chamber is to satisfy itself that all reasonable steps have been taken to secure the person's appearance and to inform him or her of the charges and the fact that such a confirmation hearing is to be held. The Pre-Trial Chamber may allow an absent accused to be represented by counsel when this is in 'the interests of justice'.[73]

The pre-trial confirmation hearing resembles in some ways the 'Rule 61 Procedure' adopted by the *ad hoc* tribunals. In the early days, when there was little real trial work because few accused had been apprehended, the judges of the International Criminal Tribunal for the Former Yugoslavia developed an original technique of *ex parte* hearings, pursuant to Rule 61 of their Rules of Proecdure and Evidence, at which prosecution evidence was led and the Tribunal ruled on the sufficiency of the evidence.[74] Despite

---

[73] Rome Statute, Art. 61(2); Rules of Procedure and Evidence, Rules 121–126.

[74] Pursuant to Rule 61, 'Rules of Procedure and Evidence', UN Doc. IT/32. See Faiza Patel King, 'Public Disclosure in Rule 61 Proceedings Before the International Criminal Tribunal for the Former Yugoslavia', (1997) 29 *New York University Journal of International Law and Policy* 523; Mark Thieroff and Edward A. Amley Jr, 'Proceeding to Justice and Accountability in the Balkans: The International Criminal Tribunal for the Former Yugoslavia and Rule 61', (1998) 23 *Yale Journal of International Law* 231.

persistent denials,[75] it had many similarities with an *in absentia* procedure and was, in many respects, an honourable compromise between the different views of the Romano-Germanic and common law systems with respect to such proceedings. The Tribunal has used the *ex parte* hearing procedure when frustrated with attempts to arrest a defendant. The situation is rather different with the pre-trial confirmation hearing of the International Criminal Court, as this will only take place with an absent accused in the case of an individual who was arrested or summoned, who appeared before the Pre-Trial Chamber and was granted interim release, and who subsequently absconded.

Prior to the confirmation hearing, the accused is to be provided with a copy of the document containing the charges, and to be informed of the evidence on which the Prosecutor intends to rely at the hearing. The Pre-Trial Chamber may make orders concerning disclosure of information for the purposes of the hearing. The Statute does not specify whether such orders can only be directed against the Prosecutor, although it seems that this flows logically from the nature of such a hearing. At the hearing itself, the Prosecutor is required to support each specific charge with 'sufficient evidence to establish substantial grounds to believe that the person committed the crime charged'.[76] The Prosecutor can do this by means of documentary or summary evidence, and is not required to call the witnesses expected to testify at the trial itself. The accused may challenge the Prosecutor's evidence and present evidence.

The confirmation hearing seems to resemble preliminary hearings held under common law procedure. It allows the Court to ensure that a prosecution is not frivolous and that there is sufficient evidence for a finding of guilt, thereby protecting the accused from prosecutorial abuse. From the standpoint of the defendant, it also provides a useful opportunity to be informed of important evidence in the possession of the prosecution and even to test the value of such evidence, at least in a superficial way, during a judicial proceeding. Where the Statute is not clear is in the usefulness of submitting defence evidence during the confirmation hearing. While the

---

[75] *Prosecutor* v. *Rajic* (IT-95-12-R61), Review of the Indictment Pursuant to Rule 61 of the Rules of Procedure and Evidence, 13 September 1996: 'A Rule 61 proceeding is not a trial in absentia. There is no finding of guilt in this proceeding.' *Prosecutor* v. *Nikolic* (Case No. IT-95-2-R61), Review of Indictment Pursuant to Rule 61, 20 October 1995, (1998) 108 ILR 21: 'The Rule 61 procedure . . . cannot be considered a trial in absentia: it does not culminate in a verdict nor does it deprive the accused of the right to contest in person the charges brought against him before the Tribunal.'   [76] Rome Statute, Art. 61(5).

Statute invites the defence to present evidence at this stage, it is not obvious that contradictory evidence adduced by the defence can have any effect upon the determination of the existence of 'sufficient evidence'. The Pre-Trial Chamber may well decide that whether or not defence evidence raises doubts about the validity of Prosecution evidence is a matter for the trial court and not a pre-trial issue.

At the close of the confirmation hearing, the Pre-Trial Chamber may conclude that there is sufficient evidence and commit the person for trial. Upon confirmation, the Presidency of the Court is to constitute a Trial Chamber responsible for subsequent proceedings.[77] The Trial Chamber is to confer with the parties and address a number of preliminary matters, including the language or languages to be used at trial. Its powers also include provision 'for disclosure of documents or information not previously disclosed, sufficiently in advance of the commencement of the trial to enable adequate preparation for trial'.[78] Finally, the Trial Chamber may make orders for joinder or severance of charges against more than one accused.

But the Pre-Trial Chamber may also decline to confirm the charges, a decision that does not prevent the Prosecutor from returning with a subsequent request on the basis of additional evidence. There is also a third option: the Pre-Trial Chamber may adjourn the hearing and ask the Prosecutor to provide further evidence or to pursue further investigation or, alternatively, to amend the charges because the available evidence shows a crime different from the one charged.

International human rights law is somewhat uncertain as to the scope of the obligation on the prosecution to disclose evidence to the defence prior to trial. Although the instruments impose no clear duty in this respect,[79] recently, the European Court of Human Rights declared 'that it is a requirement of fairness . . . that the prosecution authorities disclose to the defence all material evidence for or against the accused'.[80] The Rules of the *ad hoc* tribunals make detailed provision for disclosure of the prosecution case and, according to recent amendments, for the defence case as well.[81] A duty

---

[77] *Ibid.*, Art. 61(11).   [78] *Ibid.*, Art. 65(3)(c).

[79] The closest is Principle 21 of the United Nations Basic Principles on the Role of Lawyers, UN Doc. A/CONF.144/28/Rev.1 (1990): 'It is the duty of the competent authorities to ensure lawyers access to appropriate information, files and documents in their possession or control in sufficient time to enable lawyers to provide effective legal assistance to their clients.'

[80] *Edwards v. United Kingdom*, Series A, No. 247B, 16 December 1992.

[81] 'Rules of Procedure and Evidence', UN Doc. IT/32, Rules 65*ter*, 66, 67 and 68. See Anne-Marie La Rosa, 'Réflexions sur l'apport du Tribunal pénal international pour l'ex-Yougoslavie au droit à un procès équitable', (1997) *Revue générale de droit international public* 945, p. 974.

on the prosecution to disclose its evidence, both exculpatory and inculpatory, is now recognized in many legal systems.[82] The existence of a reciprocal duty on the defence is less common although in some cases, such as a defence of alibi, the credibility of the defence will depend on prompt disclosure of material facts.[83] In an interlocutory decision in the *Tadic* case, Judge Stephen of the Yugoslav Tribunal said the defence has 'no disclosure obligation at all unless an alibi or a special defence is sought to be relied upon and then only to a quite limited extent'.[84]

The Rules of Procedure and Evidence adopted by the Preparatory Commission establish a far more thorough regime of disclosure, applicable to both Prosecutor and defence. The prosecution is required to provide the defence with the names of witnesses it intends to call at trial together with copies of their statements, subject to certain exceptions relating to the protection of the witnesses themselves.[85] The defence has a corresponding obligation with respect to witnesses, although this is worded slightly more narrowly, applying only to those expected to support specific defences.[86] Both sides are required to allow the other to inspect books, documents, photographs and other tangible objects in their possession or control which they intend to use as evidence. The Prosecutor must also disclose any such items that may assist the defence, although a comparable duty is not imposed upon the defence to disclose items that might assist the prosecution.[87] These provisions should have the effect of reducing cases of 'trial by ambush', enhancing fairness and also contributing to expeditious hearings.

---

[82] Jean Pradel, *Droit pénal comparé*, Paris: Dalloz, 1995, pp. 414–20.

[83] *Williams* v. *Florida*, 399 US 78 (1970).

[84] *Prosecutor* v. *Tadic* (Case No. IT-94-1-T), Separate Opinion of Judge Stephen on Prosecution Motion for Production of Defence Witness Statements, 27 November 1996.

[85] Rules of Procedure and Evidence, Rule 76.   [86] *Ibid.*, Rule 79.   [87] *Ibid.*, Rules 77–78.

6

Trial and appeal

Although much of the procedure of the Court is a hybrid of different judicial systems, it seems clear that there is a definite tilt towards the common law approach of an adversarial trial hearing. However, the exact colouring that the Court may take will ultimately be determined by its judges. The terms of the Statute are large enough to provide for considerable divergence in judicial approaches. For example, Article 63(6)(d) entitles the Trial Chamber to '[o]rder the production of evidence in addition to that already collected prior to the trial or presented during the trial by the parties'. A traditional common law judge would view this as a power to be exercised only rarely, because an aggressively interventionist approach might distort the balance between the two adversaries at trial. A judge favouring the continental system could interpret the provision as a licence for major judicial involvement in the production of evidence, something that would seem most normal under his or her system.

Judges in the continental system expect most of the evidence to form part of the court record even prior to trial. The evidence already on the record will have been prepared beforehand by the investigating magistrate as part of the pre-trial proceedings. Common law judges, on the other hand, consider that they begin the trial as a blank sheet; indeed they believe that any prior knowledge of the facts is likely to prejudice their judgment. Under the common law system, prosecutor and defence submit the evidence that makes up the record in accordance with strict technical rules. Here too, the Statute leaves considerable ambiguity on this point. Nothing, for example, would seem to prevent a judge from ordering the production of the Prosecutor's record as evidence at the outset of the trial, in much the same way as an investigating magistrate's file would be used by the trial court. The International Criminal Tribunal for Rwanda, under the presidency of a judge trained in the Romano-Germanic system, took this approach in the *Akayesu* case, requiring that the prosecutor's file be submitted as part of the record.

The trial is to take place at the seat of the Court, in The Hague, unless otherwise decided.[1] The trial shall be held in public, something that is expressed both as a duty of the Trial Chamber and as a right of the accused. Nevertheless, the Trial Chamber may depart from the general principle of a public hearing. A detailed enumeration of exceptions to the public hearing principle had been proposed but was rejected by the Preparatory Committee. Article 64(7) explicitly allows *in camera* proceedings for the protection of victims and witnesses, or to protect confidential or sensitive information to be given in evidence. Furthermore, Article 68(2) provides:

> As an exception to the principle of public hearings provided for in article 67, the Chambers of the Court may, to protect victims and witnesses or an accused, conduct any part of the proceedings *in camera* or allow the presentation of evidence by electronic or other special means. In particular, such measures shall be implemented in the case of a victim of sexual violence or a child who is a victim or a witness, unless otherwise ordered by the Court, having regard to all the circumstances, particularly the views of the victim or witness.

The already elaborate case law of the *ad hoc* tribunals in this matter should guide the Court in this difficult area.[2] Confidential or sensitive information may have several sources. There may be claims to confidentiality based on privilege, and the Court is to respect this pursuant to Article 69(5), as provided for in the Rules of Procedure and Evidence. But the major source of problems with this exception will be information derived from sovereign States. The Statute allows a State to apply 'for necessary measures' to respect 'confidential or sensitive information'.[3]

The accused must be present at trial,[4] even those parts of it that are held *in camera*.[5] During the drafting of the Statute, there was considerable

---

[1] Rome Statute of the International Criminal Court, UN Doc. A/CONF.183/9 (hereinafter Rome Statute), Art. 62; Rules of Procedure and Evidence, UN Doc. PCNICC/2000/INF/3/Add.3, Rule 100.

[2] For example *Prosecutor* v. *Tadic* (Case No. IT-94-1-T), Decision on the Prosecutor's Motion Requesting Protective Measures for Victims and Witnesses, 10 August 1995; *Prosecutor* v. *Rutaganda* (Case No. ICTR-96-3-T), Decision on the Preliminary Motion Submitted by the Prosecutor for Protective Measures for Witnesses, 26 September 1996. See Anne-Marie La Rosa, 'Réflexions sur l'apport du Tribunal pénal international pour l'ex-Yougoslavie au droit à un procès équitable', (1997) *Revue générale de droit international public* 945, pp. 962–70.

[3] Rome Statute, Art. 68(6).

[4] *Ibid.*, Art. 63. Art. 67(1)(d), concerning the rights of the accused, also declares: 'Subject to article 63, paragraph 2, [the accused has the right] to be present at the trial.'

[5] Rome Statute, Art. 72(7) allows for a hearing concerning the protection of national security information to take place *ex parte*, that is, in the absence of one or both of the parties.

debate about whether or not to permit *in absentia* trials,[6] which are widely held under the continental procedural model. It was argued that *in absentia* trials were particularly important in the context of international justice because of its didactic effect as well as the extreme practical difficulties involved in compelling attendance at trial.[7] The accused's right to be present at trial is recognized in the principal international human rights instruments,[8] but international tribunals and monitoring bodies have not viewed presence at trial as indispensable. The practice of domestic justice systems that derive from the Romano-Germanic models, where *in absentia* proceedings are well accepted, is considered compatible with the right to presence at trial, as long as the accused has been duly served with appropriate notice of the hearing.[9] During the drafting of the Rome Statute, the issue was often presented, erroneously, as one of principled difference with the common law system, which does not allow for *in absentia* trials as a general rule. But the fact that common law jurisdictions make a number of exceptions, and allow for such proceedings where appropriate, shows that this is not an issue of fundamental values so much as one of different practice. At Nuremberg, one of the major war criminals, Martin Bormann, was tried in his absence, pursuant to Article 12 of the Statute of the International Military Tribunal.[10] Because of the devotion of negotiators to their own domestic models, it proved impossible to reach consensus on this question. As one observer has noted, '[n]o compromise could

---

[6] Daniel J. Brown, 'The International Criminal Court and Trial in Absentia', (1999) 24 *Brooklyn Journal of International Law* 763; Hans-Jörg Behrens, 'Investigation, Trial and Appeal in the International Criminal Court Statute (Parts V, VI, VIII)', (1998) 6 *European Journal of Crime, Criminal Law and Criminal Justice* 113, at p. 123; Hakan Friman, 'Rights of Persons Suspected or Accused of a Crime', in Roy Lee, ed., *The International Criminal Court, The Making of the Rome Statute, Issues, Negotiations, Results*, The Hague: Kluwer Law International, 1999, pp. 247–62, at pp. 255–61.

[7] 'Report of the Preparatory Committee on the Establishment of an International Criminal Court', UN Doc. A/51/10, Vol. I, para. 254, pp. 54–5; also para. 259, p. 55. See also Eric David, 'Le tribunal international pénal pour l'ex-Yougoslavie', (1992) 25 *Revue belge de droit international* 565; Alain Pellet, 'Le tribunal criminel international pour l'ex-Yougoslavie. Poudre aux yeux ou avancée décisive?', (1994) 98 *Revue générale de droit international public* 7.

[8] *France et al. v. Goering et al.*, (1946) 22 IMT 203, 13 ILR 203, 41 *American Journal of International Law* 172. It has since been established that Bormann was already dead when the trial took place.

[9] *Mbenge v. Zaire* (No. 16/1977), UN Doc. A/34/40, p. 134; 'General Comment No. 13 (21)', UN Doc. A/36/40, para. 11; *Colozza and Rubinat v. Italy*, Series A, No. 89, 12 February 1985, para. 29; *Stamoulakatos v. Greece*, Series A, No. 271, 26 October 1993.

[10] Agreement for the Prosecution and Punishment of Major War Criminals of the European Axis, and Establishing the Charter of the International Military Tribunal (IMT), Annex, (1951) 82 UNTS 279.

be found and the time constraint ruled in favour of a straightforward solution – trials *in absentia* are not provided for under any circumstances in the Statute'.[11]

Presence at trial should imply more than mere physical presence. The accused should be in a position to understand the proceedings, and this may require interpretation in cases where the two official languages of the Court are not available to the accused.[12] The Statute is silent with respect to cases of an accused who is unfit to stand trial because of mental disorder, although this lacuna is corrected in the Rules, which direct the Trial Chamber to adjourn the proceedings when it 'is satisfied that the accused is unfit to stand trial'.[13] The problem of fitness to stand trial should not be confused with the defence of insanity, allowed by Article 31(1)(a) of the Statute, where the issue is the accused's mental condition at the time of the crime. An accused who is unfit to stand trial is not 'present' within the meaning of Article 63 and therefore the hearing cannot proceed. In many national justice systems, an accused may be held in detention pending a change in his or her condition permitting the court to determine fitness. The suggestion in the International Law Commission draft statute that the court be permitted to continue proceedings in the case of 'ill health' of an accused, a provision that might possibly have allowed the Court to address such situations, was rejected by the Diplomatic Conference.

The situation of an accused who is unfit to stand trial is far from an idle hypothesis. In the *Erdemovic* case, the ICTY remanded the accused for psychiatric examination so as to determine whether the plea of guilty had been made by a man who was 'present' in all senses of the word. A panel of experts concluded that he was suffering from post-traumatic stress disorder and that his mental condition at the time did not permit his trial before the Trial Chamber.[14] The Trial Chamber postponed the pre-sentencing hearing and ordered a second evaluation of the appellant to be submitted in three months' time.[15] A subsequent report concluded that Erdemovic's condition had improved such that he was 'sufficiently able to stand trial'.[16] At Nuremberg, the International Military Tribunal rejected

[11] Friman, 'Rights of Persons', at pp. 255–61, at p. 262.
[12] See also: Rome Statute, Art. 67(1)(f).   [13] Rules of Procedure and Evidence, Rule 135(4).
[14] *Prosecutor v. Erdemovic* (Case No. IT-96-22-T), Sentencing Judgment, 29 November 1996, para. 5.
[15] *Prosecutor v. Erdemovic* (Case No. IT-96-22-A), Appeal Judgment, 7 October 1997, para. 5.
[16] *Ibid.*, para. 8.

suggestions that defendants Rudolf Hess and Julius Streicher were not fit to stand trial.[17]

The trial may proceed in the absence of the accused where he or she disrupts the proceedings. The Statute indicates that the accused must 'continue' to disrupt the trial, indicating that the trouble must be repetitive and persistent.[18] It is, of course, difficult to codify in any detail how judges are to administer such a power. The problem is a familiar one in domestic justice systems, and the Court will surely rely on national practices in developing its own jurisprudence on this point. It must bear in mind, however, that its case load will be, by its very nature, quite politicized, and that this will increase the likelihood that defendants mount vigorous, energetic and original challenges to the charges. The Court's definition of 'disruption' should not become a tool to muzzle defendants in such circumstances. This is why the Statute also specifies that such measures shall be taken only in exceptional circumstances, after other reasonable alternatives have proved inadequate. Also, exclusion from the hearing is only allowed for such duration as is strictly required. The Court must review periodically whether the accused may be permitted to return to the hearing. Where the accused has been excluded from the hearing, the Statute requires the Trial Chamber to make provision for the accused to observe the trial and instruct counsel from outside the courtroom, through the use of communications technology, if required.

The Statute recognizes a right to an interpreter. An accused who does not understand the proceedings is not 'present' at trial. Thus, the right to an interpreter seems axiomatic. Although the requirement that documents be translated may be cumbersome, time-consuming and costly, it has been recognized by the European Court of Human Rights as a corollary of the right to an interpreter.[19] The provision does not require interpretation into the accused's mother tongue, or into a language of the accused's choice.[20] In an interlocutory ruling, the International Criminal Tribunal for the Former Yugoslavia denied an accused's request for a 'Croatian' interpreter, given that there was regular translation of Serbo-Croatian, a sufficiently similar language.[21]

---

[17] *France et al.* v. *Goering et al.*, *supra* note 8.

[18] Rome Statute, Art. 63(2); Rules of Procedure and Evidence, Rule 170.

[19] *Luedicke, Belkacem and Koc* v. *Germany*, Series A, No. 29, 28 November 1978, para. 48; *Kamasinski* v. *Federal Republic of Germany*, Series A, No. 168, 19 December 1989, para. 74.

[20] *Guesdon* v. *France* (No. 219/1986), UN Doc. A/44/40, p. 222, paras 10.2, and 10.3.

[21] *Prosecutor* v. *Delalic et al.* (Case No. IT-96-21-T), Order on Zdravko Mucic's Oral Request for Croatian Interpretation, 23 June 1997.

The accused is entitled to defend himself or herself in person. There is at least one precedent, the case of Jean-Paul Akayesu before the International Criminal Tribunal for Rwanda, who fired his counsel after being convicted and acted on his own at the sentencing phase of his trial, in September and October 1998. According to the Strasbourg jurisprudence, the accused may be required to be assisted by a lawyer under certain circumstances, where this may affect the fairness of the trial.[22] Furthermore, a defendant who acts without legal assistance may be held responsible for a lack of due diligence in the proceedings, and may not always be able to rely on claims of inexperience, although he or she is entitled to some degree of indulgence.[23] In rare cases of a stubborn defendant who refuses all assistance by counsel, the Court might opt to appoint an *amicus curiae* (literally, 'friend of the court') in order to ensure that justice is not offended.[24]

Although the accused is entitled to choice of counsel, this right cannot be unlimited. The *ad hoc* tribunals have adopted a rule requiring that counsel be either admitted to the practice of law in a State or be a university professor of law.[25] The Rules of Procedure and Evidence are somewhat different, and focus on substance rather than form, requiring that 'counsel for the defence shall have established competence in international or criminal law and procedure, as well as the necessary relevant experience, whether as judge, prosecutor, advocate or in other similar capacity, in criminal proceedings'. Defence counsel must also have 'an excellent knowledge of and be fluent in at least one of the working languages of the Court'.[26] The European Commission on Human Rights has dismissed claims alleging a violation of the right to counsel on the basis of failure to respect professional ethics,[27] where counsel was also a defence witness,[28] and even for a refusal to wear a gown.[29] But it is unclear who is to evaluate whether in fact counsel meet these requirements. Moreover, there is a potential conflict between these rather rigorous requirements in the Rules and Article 67(1)(d) of the Statute itself, which recognizes the defendant's right 'to conduct the defence in person or through legal assistance of the accused's choosing'.

[22] *Croissant* v. *Germany*, Series A, No. 237-B, 25 September 1992; *Philis* v. *Greece* (App. No. 16598/90), (1990) 66 DR 260.

[23] *Melin* v. *France*, Series A, No. 261-A, 22 June 1993, para. 25.

[24] Rules of Procedure and Evidence, Rule 103. However, Rule 103 seems to limit the role of *amici curiae* to the submission of observations rather than an active participation in proceedings.

[25] 'Rules of Procedure and Evidence', UN Doc. IT/32, Rule 44.

[26] Rules of Procedure and Evidence, Rule 22.

[27] *Ensslin, Baader and Raspe* v. *Federal Republic of Germany* (App. Nos 7572/76, 7586/76 and 7587/76), (1978) 14 DR 64.   [28] *K* v. *Denmark* (no. 19524/92), unreported.

[29] *X and Y* v. *Federal Republic of Germany* (App. Nos 5217/71 and 5367/72), (1972) 42 Coll. 139.

In the International Covenant on Civil and Political Rights, the right to funded counsel for indigent defendants is subject to the requirement that this be in cases 'where the interests of justice so require',[30] a provision that is echoed in Article 67 of the Rome Statute. Arguably, this will be the situation in all cases before the International Criminal Court. Probably for this reason, the International Law Commission removed the 'interests of justice' condition in its draft statute,[31] only to have it introduced again by the Preparatory Committee.[32] Administration of the system of legal aid to indigent defendants is the responsibility of the Registrar.[33]

The trial is to begin with the accused being read all charges previously confirmed by the Pre-Trial Chamber. The Trial Chamber is to satisfy itself that the accused understands the nature of the charges. The accused will be asked to plead guilty or not guilty.[34] The practice of the ad hoc tribunals has shown that it is not at all unusual for an accused to offer to plead guilty.[35] This may be motivated by a number of factors, including a genuine feeling of remorse and contrition in the more sincere cases, and a hope that admission of guilt when conviction seems certain may result in a diminished sentence and better treatment in the more cynical cases. There were difficulties in circumscribing the rules applicable to guilty pleas because of differing philosophical approaches to the matter in the main judicial systems of national law. Under common law, a guilty plea is often the norm, obtained from an accused in exchange for commitments from the prosecutor as to the severity of the sentence and the nature of the charges. Under continental law, confession of guilt is viewed with deep suspicion and courts are expected to rule on guilt and innocence based on the evidence, irrespective of such a plea. But on a practical level, the differences may not be so great, although there are many misconceptions on both sides about the other system's approach to admissions of guilt. At common law, undertakings by the prosecutor do not bind the judge, who

---

[30] International Covenant on Civil and Political Rights, (1976) UNTS 171, Art. 14(3)(d).

[31] 'Report of the International Law Commission on the Work of Its Forty-Sixth Session, 2 May–22 July 1994', UN Doc. A/49/10, p. 116. See also: 'Code of Crimes Against the Peace and Security of Mankind', UN Doc. A/51/332, Art. 11(e).

[32] 'Decisions Taken by the Preparatory Committee at Its Session Held 4 to 15 August 1997', UN Doc. A/AC.249/1997/L.8/Rev.1.   [33] Rules of Procedure and Evidence, Rule 21.

[34] Rome Statute, Art. 64(8)(a).

[35] Prosecutor v. Erdemovic (Case No. IT-96-22-S), Sentencing Judgment, 5 March 1998, (1998) 37 ILM 1182; Prosecutor v. Kambanda (Case No. ICTR-97-23-S), Judgment and Sentence, 4 September 1998, (1998) 37 ILM 1411; Prosecutor v. Serushago (Case No. ICTR-98-39-S), Sentence, 2 February 1999; Prosecutor v. Jelesic (Case No. IT-95-10-T), Judgment, 14 December 1999; Prosecutor v. Ruggiu (Case No. ICTR-97-32-I), Judgment and Sentence, 1 June 2000.

must be satisfied that there is sufficient evidence and that there is no charade or fraud on the court. But erroneous notions by some European lawyers about common law procedure resulted in the addition of a totally superfluous provision, Article 65(5), to reassure them that plea negotiations could not bind the Court. In continental systems, an admission of guilt will be a compelling factor and will almost certainly simplify the process.[36] Thus, it is not correct to say that continental judges are indifferent to admissions of guilt and that this does not accelerate the trial.

Under the Rome Statute, a 'healthy balance' has been struck between the two approaches.[37] When an accused makes an admission of guilt, the Trial Chamber is to ensure that he or she understands its nature and consequences, that the admission has been made voluntarily after sufficient consultation with counsel, and that it is supported by the facts of the case.[38] If the Trial Chamber is not satisfied that these conditions have been met, it deems the admission not to have been made and orders that the trial proceed. It may even order that the trial take place before another Trial Chamber. Alternatively, the Trial Chamber may consider that 'a more complete presentation of the facts of the case is required in the interests of justice, in particular the interests of the victims', and request additional evidence to be adduced.

Evidence

Unlike the common law system, with its complex and technical rules of evidence, the Statute follows the tradition of international criminal tribunals by allowing the admission of all relevant and necessary evidence. Probably the biggest surprise here, for lawyers trained in common law systems, is that there is no general rule excluding hearsay or indirect evidence,[39] although it seems likely that in ruling on the admissibility of such evidence the future Court may be guided by 'hearsay exceptions generally recognized by some national legal systems, as well as the truthfulness, voluntariness and trustworthiness of the evidence, as appropriate'.[40] As

---

[36] Behrens, 'Investigation, Trial and Appeal', pp. 123–4.

[37] Silvia A. Fernández de Gurmendi, 'International Criminal Law Procedures', in Lee, *The International Criminal Court*, pp. 217–27, at p. 223.   [38] Rome Statute, Art. 65(1).

[39] See *Prosecutor* v. *Tadic* (Case No. IT-94-1-T), Opinion and Judgment, 7 May 1997, (1997) 36 ILM 908, 112 ILR 1, para. 555.

[40] *Prosecutor* v. *Tadic* (Case No. IT-94-1-T), Decision on Defence Motion on Hearsay, 5 August 1996, paras 7–19.

Helen Brady has explained, '[d]ebates in the *Ad Hoc* Committee and the Preparatory Committee revealed a deep chasm between the civil law and the common law traditions on the scope and nature of the ICC's rules of evidence. However, a compromise was finally attained [that] is a delicate combination of civil and common-law concepts of fair trial and due process.'[41]

To be admissible, evidence must be relevant and necessary.[42] This general rule is similar to a provision in the Rules of Procedure and Evidence adopted by the International Criminal Tribunal for the Former Yugoslavia.[43] Interpreting the provision, the *ad hoc* Tribunal has considered whether or not to read into the text a requirement of reliability. National practice on this point varies considerably. The Trial Chamber described reliability as 'the invisible golden thread which runs through all the components of admissibility', but stopped short of adding it as a requirement to the extent that it was not specifically set out in the provision.[44] Thus, points out Helen Brady, although Article 69 does not actually refer to reliability as a condition of admissibility of evidence, it would seem that reliability is an implicit component of relevance and probative value. 'Any assessment of relevance and probative value must involve some consideration of the reliability of the evidence – it must be *prima facie* credible. Evidence which does not have sufficient indicia of reliability cannot be said to be either relevant or probative to the issues to be decided.'[45]

The defence has the right to examine witnesses on the same basis as the Prosecutor.[46] This does not explicitly provide for a full right to cross-examination, as it is understood in the common law. Under continental or Romano-Germanic legal systems, questions may be posed by the judge at the request of counsel. At trial, the presiding judge may issue directions as to the conduct of the proceedings,[47] failing which the Prosecutor and the defence are to agree on the order and the manner in which evidence is to be presented.[48] Witnesses are questioned by the party that presents them, fol-

---

[41] Helen Brady, 'The System of Evidence in the Statute of the International Criminal Court', in Flavia Lattanzi and William A. Schabas, eds, *Essays on the Rome Statute of the ICC*, Rome: Editrice il Sirente, 2000, pp. 279–302, at p. 286.   [42] Rome Statute, Art. 69(3).

[43] 'Rules of Procedure and Evidence', UN Doc. IT/32, Rule 89(C).

[44] *Prosecutor v. Delalic et al.* (Case No. IT-98-21-T), Decision on the Admissibility of Exhibit 155, 19 January 1998, para. 32.   [45] Brady, 'The System of Evidence', at p. 290.

[46] Rome Statute, Art. 67(1)(e).   [47] *Ibid.*, Art. 64(8)(b).

[48] Rules of Procedure and Evidence, Rule 140(1).

lowed by questioning by the other party and by the Court. The defence has the right to be the last to examine a witness.[49] The defence is also the last to make closing arguments.[50]

There are limits to the right to examine witnesses. The formal provisions governing testimony of victims of sexual crimes is an example. The Statute authorizes the Court to allow the presentation of evidence by electronic or other special means.[51] Some questions are out of bounds: the Rules of Procedure and Evidence state that evidence of the prior or subsequent sexual conduct of a victim or witness is not to be admitted.[52] It may also disallow questions because they are abusive or repetitive. What is important is that the parties, prosecution and defence, be treated equally and that the trial be fundamentally fair. The Statute also allows the Court to recognize witness privileges. The Preparatory Commission agreed to confirm, in draft Rule 73, a principle already recognized by the International Criminal Tribunal for the Former Yugoslavia, by which the International Committee of the Red Cross has a right to non-disclosure of evidence obtained by a former employee in the course of official duties. The Tribunal relied on customary international law in reaching its decision.[53] Witnesses may also refuse to make statements that might tend to incriminate a spouse, child or parent.[54]

Nothing in the Statute provides for compellability of witnesses, for example by issuance of *subpoenae* or similar orders to appear before the Court. Witnesses are to appear voluntarily. Once a person is before the Court, however, then Article 71 gives the Court a degree of control over the recalcitrant witness, and allows for the imposition of a fine.[55] Testimony given by witnesses must be accompanied by an undertaking: 'I solemnly declare that I will speak the truth, the whole truth and nothing but the truth.'[56] Witnesses must testify before the Court in person, subject to the possibility of testimony being delivered by electronic or other special means in order to protect victims, witnesses or an accused. Such measures should particularly be considered in the case of victims of sexual violence or children.[57] There is one witness who can never be compelled to

---

[49] *Ibid.*, Rule 140(2).   [50] *Ibid.*, Rule 141.   [51] Rome Statute, Art. 68(2).
[52] Rules of Procedure and Evidence, Rule 71.
[53] *Prosecutor* v. *Simic et al.* (Case No. IT-95–9–PT), Decision on the Prosecution Motion Under Rule 73 for a Ruling Concerning the Testimony of a Witness, 27 July 1999.
[54] Rules of Procedure and Evidence, Rule 75.   [55] *Ibid.*, Rules 65 and 171(1).
[56] Rome Statute, Art. 69(1); Rules of Procedure and Evidence, Rule 66(1).
[57] Rome Statute, Art. 68(2).

testify, however: the defendant. The right to silence provision in the Statute is based on the International Covenant on Civil and Political Rights, but goes considerably further. The Covenant says that an accused has the right '[n]ot to be compelled to testify against himself or to confess guilt'.[58] The Statute removes the qualification 'against himself', and adds an additional norm that is not at all implicit in the Covenant, namely, that the silence of an accused cannot be a consideration in the determination of guilt or innocence. The text clarifies the fact that an accused may refuse to testify altogether, and not merely to testify when the evidence is 'against himself'. The provision reflects concerns with encroachments upon the right to silence in some national justice systems. Specifically, English common law has always prevented any adverse inference being drawn from an accused's failure to testify.[59]

While the accused cannot be compelled to 'testify', he or she may make an unsworn oral or written statement in his or her defence.[60] This is a practice recognized under many criminal codes throughout the world. In fact, continental European jurists are 'astonished' that it could be otherwise, as in their jurisdictions the accused is never sworn.[61] Under common law systems, an unsworn statement would in principle be inadmissible as evidence. The 'unsworn statement' seems to present itself as an exception to the general rule requiring that testimony be accompanied by an undertaking as to truthfulness.[62]

Evidence obtained in violation of the Statute or in a manner contrary to internationally recognized human rights shall be inadmissible if it 'casts substantial doubt on the reliability of the evidence' or if its admission 'would be antithetical to and would seriously damage the integrity of the proceedings'.[63] In the case of the former, it hardly seems necessary to make a special rule dealing with unreliable evidence, as it should not be admitted in any case.

A distinct regime operates in the case of what is known as 'national security information'.[64] In national legal systems, special rules apply for the production of evidence deemed to raise major concerns of State secur-

---

[58] International Covenant on Civil and Political Rights, (1976) UNTS 171, Art. 14(3)(g).
[59] But, in recent years, legislation adopted within the United Kingdom now allows prosecutors to propose such conclusions: Criminal Justice and Public Order Act 1994, s. 4(3).
[60] Rome Statute, Art. 67(1)(h).
[61] Jean Pradel, *Droit pénal comparé*, Paris: Dalloz, 1995, p. 449, n. 1.
[62] Rome Statute, Art. 69(1).   [63] *Ibid.*, Art. 69(7).   [64] *Ibid.*, Art. 72.

ity.[65] In some countries, the evidence is allowed but subject to a mechanism that protects its confidential nature. In others, it is prohibited altogether. Although generalizations are always hazardous, it is probably fair to say that the heart of litigation on this subject under domestic legal systems concerns attempts by the defence to have access to information in the possession of State authorities. Prosecutors are less likely to find themselves in such an antagonistic relationship with State authorities.

The drafters of the Rome Statute began with much the same orientation. Thus, the initial concerns in this area, which first arose in the Ad Hoc Committee of the General Assembly in 1995 and continued during the work of the Preparatory Committee in 1996 and 1997, were directed to denying access by the defence to confidential information in the possession of the Prosecutor and, ordinarily, subject to disclosure as part of the preparation for a fair trial.[66] A decision by the Appeals Chamber of the International Criminal Tribunal for the Former Yugoslavia in October 1997[67] seems to have redirected the attention of the drafters, who realized that, given the nature of the crimes to be tried by the Court, the heart of the problem was likely to lie with conflict between the Prosecutor and State authorities.

The provision that ultimately resulted, Article 72, is lengthy and confusing. Its complexity is exacerbated by the fact that much of its language was concocted during the Rome Conference itself, and did not benefit from the years of reflection provided by the Preparatory Committee process. The final version differs substantially from the various models considered during the Preparatory Committee phase. As a result, language is employed whose consequences are uncertain. Donald K. Piragoff, one of the experts involved in its drafting, speaking of 'the ambiguities of some of the provisions',[68] has certainly understated the matter. Basically, Article 72 leaves determination of whether or not matters affect national security to the State itself. The provision would seem to make things rather

---

[65] *Prosecutor* v. *Blaskic* (Case No. IT-95-14-AR108*bis*), Objection to the Issue of Subpoenae Duces Tecum, 29 October 1997, (1998) 110 ILR 677, paras 109, 124–6 and 141–6.

[66] Donald K. Piragoff, 'Protection of National Security Information', in Lee, *The International Criminal Court*, pp. 270–94, at p. 274.

[67] *Prosecutor* v. *Blaskic* (Case No. IT-95-14-AR108*bis*), Objection to the Issue of Subpoenae Duces Tecum, 29 October 1997, (1998) 110 ILR 677.

[68] Piragoff, 'Protection of National Security Information', p. 294. See also Rodney Dixon and Helen Duffy, 'Article 72', in Otto Triffterer, ed., *Commentary on the Rome Statute of the International Criminal Court, Observers' Notes, Article by Article*, Baden-Baden: Nomos, 1999, pp. 937–46.

straightforward for a State that wishes to stonewall the Court. Where a State refuses a request for information in its possession, the Court may not order production.[69] It can only refer the non-compliance of the State concerned to the Assembly of States Parties or the Security Council although it can also draw 'evidentiary inferences'.

The Statute does not indicate what standard of proof is to be applied. Romano-Germanic systems require guilt to be proven to a degree that satisfies the *intime conviction* of the trier of fact, whereas the common law speaks of proof 'beyond a reasonable doubt'. The European Commission and Court of Human Rights have no clear pronouncement on which standard is preferable in light of human rights norms.[70] An amendment specifying the 'reasonable doubt' standard of proof was defeated during the drafting of Article 14 of the International Covenant on Civil and Political Rights but was never adopted.[71] However, the Human Rights Committee has been less circumspect, clarifying that the prosecution must establish proof of guilt beyond reasonable doubt.[72] The International Military Tribunal at Nuremberg applied the standard of reasonable doubt, stating explicitly in its judgment that Schacht and von Papen were to be acquitted because of failure to meet that burden of proof.[73] As for the *ad hoc* tribunals, they seem to have had no difficulty with the issue, and there are frequent statements in their initial judgments to the effect that the reasonable doubt standard applies.[74] In the *Celebici* case, the Trial Chamber said that 'the Prosecution is bound in law to prove the case alleged against the accused beyond a reasonable doubt. At the conclusion of the case the accused is entitled to the benefit of the doubt as to whether the offence has been proved.'[75]

Common law judges have devoted considerable effort to defining the notion of reasonable doubt, generally in an attempt to provide clear instructions for lay jurors. This is surely less important for experienced judges such as those likely to be elected to the Court. In *Celebici*, the Trial Chamber of the ICTY adopted a common law definition:

---

[69] Rome Statute, Art. 72(7)(a).   [70] *Austria v. Italy*, (1962) 9 Yearbook 740, at p. 784.

[71] UN Doc. E/CN.4/365, UN Doc. E/CN.4/SR.156.

[72] 'General Comment 13/21', UN Doc. A/39/40, pp. 143–7, para. 7.

[73] *France et al. v. Goering et al., supra* note 8.

[74] See the numerous references to the reasonable doubt standard in, for example, *Prosecutor v. Tadic, supra* note 39; *Prosecutor v. Akayesu* (Case No. ICTR-96-4-T), Judgment, 2 September 1998, (1998) 37 ILM 1399; *Prosecutor v. Delalic et al.* (Case No. IT-96-21-T), Judgment, 16 November 1998, (1999) 38 ILM 57.   [75] *Prosecutor v. Delalic et al., supra* note 74, para. 601.

A reasonable doubt is a doubt which the particular jury entertain in the circumstances. Jurymen themselves set the standard of what is reasonable in the circumstances. It is that ability which is attributed to them which is one of the virtues of our mode of trial: to their task of deciding facts they bring to bear their experience and judgment.[76]

But the Court's judges are not lay jurors, and the reference of the Tribunal in *Celebici* is puzzling. Simply put, 'reasonable doubt' means a doubt that is founded in reason. It does not mean 'any doubt', 'beyond a shadow of a doubt', 'absolute certainty' or 'moral certainty'.[77] Nor, on the other end of the scale, does it imply 'an actual substantive doubt' or 'such doubt as would give rise to a grave uncertainty'.[78]

Judgment of the Trial Chamber must be reached by a majority of the three judges present, although the Statute encourages unanimity.[79] This is similar to the situation before the *ad hoc* tribunals. The *ad hoc* tribunals have established a tradition of dissent, with both majority and minority penning lengthy reasons. The Statute requires the Trial Chamber to deliver written reasons containing 'a full and reasoned statement' of its findings on the evidence and conclusions. Of course, all judges of the Court's Trial Chamber assigned to a case must be present at all stages of the trial and during the deliberations. The Statute allows the Presidency to appoint an alternate judge who can be present in order to replace a member who is unable to continue attending.

Sentencing procedure

Upon determination of guilt, the Trial Chamber is to establish the 'appropriate sentence' in a distinct phase of the trial.[80] In so doing, the Statute instructs the Trial Chamber to consider the evidence presented and submissions made during the trial that are relevant to the sentence. Mitigating and aggravating factors relating to the commission of the crime itself, such as the individual role of the offender in the treatment of the victims, will form part of the evidence germane to guilt or innocence and thus appear as part of the record of the trial. There is a strong presumption in favour of a distinct sentencing hearing following conviction. Though not

---

[76] *Ibid.*, para. 600; citing *Green* v. *R.* (1972) 46 ALJR 545.
[77] *Victor* v. *Nebraska*, 127 L. Ed. 2d 583 (1994).
[78] *Cage* v. *Louisiana*, 498 US 39 (1990); *Sullivan* v. *Louisiana*, 113 S. Ct. 2078 (1993).
[79] Rome Statute, Art. 74.   [80] *Ibid.*, Art. 76; Rules of Procedure and Evidence, Rule 143.

mandatory, it must be held upon the request of either the Prosecutor or the accused, and, failing application from either party, the Court may decide to hold such a hearing.[81] The *ad hoc* tribunals held separate sentencing hearings and issued distinct sentencing decisions in their initial cases, although this was not mandated either by their statutes or their rules.[82] Later, the rules of the two *ad hoc* tribunals were amended in order to eliminate any suggestion of a separate sentencing phase. In the *Celebici* judgment, rendered in November 1998, those accused who were found guilty were sentenced immediately; before rendering its verdict, the Tribunal held a special hearing on sentencing matters.[83]

Failure to hold a separate sentencing hearing after conviction may put the accused at a real disadvantage during the trial. He or she may be in a position to submit relevant evidence in mitigation of sentence, for example concerning the individual's specific role in the crimes *vis-à-vis* accomplices, or efforts by the offender to reduce the suffering of the victim. The only way to introduce such evidence may be for the accused to renounce the right to silence and the protection against self-incrimination. Providing the accused with the right to a post-conviction sentencing hearing, where new evidence and submissions may be presented, thus enhances the right to silence of the accused at trial. From the Prosecutor's standpoint, there are also advantages to a sentencing hearing. Aggravating evidence, such as proof of bad character or prior convictions, might well be deemed inadmissible at trial, yet it would possibly pass the relevance test once guilt had been established and the only remaining issue is the determination of a fit penalty.

The purpose of the sentencing hearing is to provide for the submission of additional evidence or submissions relevant to the sentence. The *ad hoc*

---

[81] Before the international and the United States military tribunals, there appears to have been no practice of holding distinct hearings to address matters concerning the sanction, once guilt had been established, although the British military tribunals seem to have followed this procedure in some cases: *United Kingdom* v. *Eck et al.* ('Peleus Trial'), (1947) 1 LRTWC 1, 13; *United Kingdom* v. *Grumfelt* ('Scuttled U-Boats Case'), (1947) 1 LRTWC 55, 65; *United Kingdom* v. *Kramer et al.* ('Belsen Trial'), (1947) 2 LRTWC 1, 122–5. See William A. Schabas, 'Sentencing and the International Tribunals: For a Human Rights Approach', (1997) 7 *Duke Journal of Comparative and International Law* 461.

[82] *Prosecutor* v. *Tadic* (Case No. IT-94-1-S), Sentencing Judgment, 14 July 1997; *Prosecutor* v. *Akayesu* (Case No. ICTR-96-4-T), Sentencing Judgment, 2 October 1998. The original Rule 100 ('Rules of Procedure and Evidence', UN Doc. IT/32), entitled 'Pre-Sentencing Procedure', stated: 'If a Trial Chamber finds the accused guilty of a crime, the Prosecutor and the defence may submit any relevant information that may assist the Trial Chamber in determining an appropriate sentence.' The Tribunal later amended Rule 100, eliminating this text. Sentencing is now governed by Rule 98*ter*, which applies to the judgment on the merits of the case.

[83] *Prosecutor* v. *Delalic*, *supra* note 74, para. 83.

tribunals have considered such relevant information to include psychiatric and psychological reports, as well as testimony by the convicted person. In the *Erdemovic* case, a commission of three experts was designated, two named by the Tribunal, a third from a list submitted by the defence.[84] The *Erdemovic* sentencing court also heard character witnesses, two of whom were granted protective measures by the Trial Chamber.[85] Erdemovic testified in the course of his own sentencing hearing. In *Tadic*, the Trial Chamber considered oral and written reports, including 'victim impact' statements. The Trial Chamber insisted that 'it will receive only reports, written statements and oral statements which provide relevant information that may assist the Trial Chamber in determining an appropriate sentence and that it will reject any material relating to the guilt or innocence of Dusko Tadic'.[86]

Appeal and revision

Judgments of the Trial Chambers of the International Criminal Court are subject to appeal. The Prosecutor may appeal an acquittal on grounds of procedural error, error of fact or error of law. There was difficulty with this provision at the Rome Conference, because some common law jurisdictions prohibit any prosecution appeal of an acquittal.[87] The defendant may appeal a conviction on grounds of procedural error, error of fact, error of law or '[a]ny other ground that affects the fairness or reliability of the proceedings or decision'. The Prosecutor is also entitled to appeal a conviction on behalf of the defendant.[88] Sentences may be appealed by both Prosecutor and convicted person 'on the ground of disproportion between the crime and the sentence'. If, during an appeal against sentence, the Court considers there are grounds to set aside a conviction, it may intervene to quash the judgment. Similarly, it may also intervene on sentence during an appeal taken against the conviction only.

In addition to final judgments of the Trial Chamber on questions of guilt or innocence, and on the sentence, appeals regarding specific or

[84] *Prosecutor* v. *Erdemovic, supra* note 14.
[85] *Prosecutor* v. *Erdemovic* (Case No. IT-96-22-T), Order for Protective Measures for Witness X, 18 October 1996.
[86] *Prosecutor* v. *Tadic* (Case No. IT-94-1-T), Scheduling Order, 27 May 1997, and *Prosecutor* v. *Tadic* (Case No. IT-94-1-T), Scheduling Order, 12 June 1997.
[87] Helen Brady and Mark Jennings, 'Appeal and Revision', in Lee, *The International Criminal Court*, pp. 294–304.   [88] Rome Statute, Art. 81.

interlocutory issues that are decided in the course of prosecution are allowed in certain cases.[89] Appeal is also permitted regarding decisions dealing with admissibility and jurisdiction, those granting or denying release of a person being investigated or prosecuted, certain decisions of the Pre-Trial Chamber, and any ruling 'that would significantly affect the fair and expeditious conduct of the proceedings or the outcome of the trial'. An example of such an appeal, drawn from the case law of the *ad hoc* Tribunal for the Former Yugoslavia, is the jurisdictional appeal raised by Dusko Tadic. It resulted in a seminal ruling of the Appeals Chamber issued prior to the beginning of the trial itself that pronounced on such matters as the legality of the creation of the Tribunal by decision of the Security Council and the scope of its subject matter jurisdiction, especially with respect to war crimes committed in non-international armed conflict.[90]

During an appeal of a conviction or sentence, the execution of the decision or sentence is suspended, although the convicted person should remain in custody. Given the conviction, it can no longer be said that the person benefits from the presumption of innocence and as a result the same entitlement to provisional release does not exist. However, if an appellant is detained during the appeal and if the full sentence is served during that time, he or she must be released. In the event of acquittal, an accused is normally to be released immediately, although the Prosecution may apply to the Trial Chamber for an order imposing continued detention pending its appeal of the verdict. Interlocutory appeals are potentially disruptive of the normal course of trial, and afford the defence an opportunity to generate considerable delays in the proceedings. For that reason, such appeals do not normally suspend the ordinary trial proceedings.

Where the Appeals Chamber grants the appeal on a point of law or fact that materially influenced the decision, or because of unfairness at the trial proceedings affecting the reliability of the decision or sentence, it may reverse or amend the decision or sentence, or order a new trial before a different Trial Chamber. It may vary a sentence if it finds it is 'disproportionate to the crime'. In a defence appeal, the Appeals Chamber cannot modify a decision to the detriment of the convicted person, for example by increasing a sentence beyond that imposed at trial or by adding convic-

---

[89] *Ibid.*, Art. 83.
[90] *Prosecutor* v. *Tadic* (Case No. IT-94-1-AR72), Decision on the Defence Motion for Interlocutory Appeal on Jurisdiction, 2 October 1995, (1997) 105 ILR 453, (1997) 35 ILM 32.

tions under additional counts. It is possible for the Appeals Chamber to remand a factual issue back to the original Trial Chamber. The Appeals Chamber can also call evidence itself in order to determine an issue.[91]

Like the judgment and sentence, an appeal is settled by a majority of the judges. Members of the Appeals Chamber may register their dissent, and if the experience of the *ad hoc* tribunals is any guide, dissenting judgments will be frequent and they will be long. Some delegations at the Rome Conference believed that appeals decisions should be unanimous. But, here again, the practice of the *ad hoc* tribunals provided a compelling model. Delegates pointed to the *Erdemovic* decision of the Appeals Chamber of the International Criminal Tribunal for the Former Yugoslavia, where the court split three to two.[92] But it was the dissenting judgments penned by Judges Cassese and Stephen that ultimately prevailed, because their conclusions were incorporated into the Rome Statute.

It is also possible to seek revision of a conviction or sentence. Revision involves intervention at the appellate level that does not call into question findings of the Trial Chamber. It is based on the discovery of new evidence, the discovery that decisive evidence at trial was false, forged or falsified, or a realization that a judge of the Trial Chamber participating in the trial was guilty of serious misconduct or breach of duty sufficient to justify removal from the bench.[93] When it grants review, the Trial Chamber may reconvene the original Trial Chamber, constitute a new Trial Chamber or dispose of the matter itself.

The Statute is silent on the subject of reconsideration of decisions of the Appeal Chamber. But there should be a remedy if it is established that the Appeals Chamber was in error on a point of law or fact, or if the proceedings were unfair. Nor is there any reason to deny review if a judge who sits on the Appeals Chamber is subsequently found guilty of misconduct, in the same way as for the Trial Chamber. But, in the absence of a specific provision, the Appeals Chamber would have to craft its own remedy in the exercise of its inherent powers.

In the event of discovery of a miscarriage of justice as a result of new facts where a person has already suffered punishment, that person is

[91] On standards to be used in admitting new evidence upon appeal, see *Barayagwiza* v. *Prosecutor* (Case No. ICTR-97-19-AR72), Decision of 3 November 1999. The ICTR Appeals Chamber's standard seems to be extraordinarily broad.
[92] *Prosecutor* v. *Erdemovic, supra* note 15.   [93] Rome Statute, Art. 84.

entitled to compensation, unless he or she was responsible for the non-disclosure of the fact or facts in question.[94] The applicable procedure for compensation in such circumstances is set out in the Rules of Procedure and Evidence.[95]

---

[94] *Ibid.*, Art. 85.
[95] Rules of Procedure and Evidence, Rules 173–175.

7

Punishment and the rights of victims

Criminal law, in all domestic systems, culminates in a penalty phase. This is what principally distinguishes it from other forms of judicial and quasi-judicial accountability, be they traditional mechanisms like civil lawsuits or innovative contemporary experiments like truth commissions. And the International Criminal Court is no different. According to the Rome Statute, the basic penalty to be imposed by the Court is one of imprisonment, up to and including life imprisonment in extreme cases. Reflecting developments in international human rights law, the Court excludes any possibility of capital punishment, despite the seriousness of the offences that it will judge.

Most domestic criminal codes set out a precise and detailed range of sentencing options. Often, each specific offence is accompanied by the applicable penalty, including references to maximum and minimum terms. Whether international justice should follow this pattern has been debated for decades, dating back to the sessions of the International Law Commission in the 1950s. The final result in the Rome Statute, however, is a few laconic provisions establishing the maximum available sentence and, by and large, leaving determination in specific cases to the judges. This constitutes, incidentally, a rather dramatic exception to the general policy of the drafters of the Statute and the Rules, which was to define and delimit judicial discretion as much as possible. In determining the appropriate sentence, the judges have been given a very free hand.[1]

The reference point for drafting of the Statute was usually 'customary international law', with particular attention to the case law of the *ad hoc* tribunals. To that extent, much of the exercise was one of codification. But, in

---

[1] See Claus Kress, 'Investigation, Trial and Appeal in the International Criminal Court Statute (Parts V, VI, VIII)', (1998) 6 *European Journal of Crime, Criminal Law and Criminal Justice* 126; Rolf E. Fife, 'Penalties', in Roy Lee, ed., *The International Criminal Court, The Making of the Rome Statute*, The Hague: Kluwer Law, 1999, pp. 319–44; Faiza P. King, Anne-Marie La Rosa, 'Penalties under the ICC Statute', in Flavia Lattanzi and William A. Schabas, eds, *Essays on the Rome Statute of the ICC*, Rome: Editrice il Sirente, 2000, pp. 311–38.

the area of punishment, it seems appropriate to speak of progressive development rather than mere codification. After all, in the first great experiment in international justice, at Nuremberg and Tokyo, the maximum available penalty was death. In the late 1940s, capital punishment was imposed with unhesitating enthusiasm. There is in fact some old precedent for the notion that international law has recognized the death penalty as a maximum sentence in the case of war crimes.[2] As for the *ad hoc* tribunals for the former Yugoslavia and Rwanda, they are entitled to impose life imprisonment, but without any statutory qualification as to the appropriate circumstances. In several cases, the Rwanda Tribunal has sentenced offenders to life terms, noting that had the offenders been judged in the corresponding domestic courts, the sentence would have been one of death.[3] The Rome Statute allows for a maximum sentence of life imprisonment, but subjects this to a limitation, namely, that it be 'justified by the extreme gravity of the crime and the individual circumstances of the convicted person'.[4] It constitutes, therefore, from the standpoint of public international law, the most advanced and progressive text on the subject of sentencing.

The great Italian penal reformer of the eighteenth century, Cesare Beccaria, said that 'punishment should not be harsh, but must be inevitable'.[5] According to the International Criminal Tribunal for the Former Yugoslavia:

> It is the infallibility of punishment, rather than the severity of the sanction, which is the tool for retribution, stigmatisation and deterrence. This is particularly the case for the International Tribunal; penalties are made more onerous by its international stature, moral authority and impact upon world public opinion, and this punitive effect must be borne in mind when assessing the suitable length of sentence.[6]

Yet the Rome Statute has virtually nothing to say about the purposes of sentencing, as if this question is so obvious as to require no comment or

---

[2] On sentencing for international crimes, see William A. Schabas, 'War Crimes, Crimes Against Humanity and the Death Penalty', (1997) 60 *Albany Law Journal* 736; William A. Schabas, 'International Sentencing: From Leipzig (1923) to Arusha (1996)', in M. Cherif Bassiouni, *International Criminal Law*, 2nd edn, New York: Transnational Publishers, 1999, pp. 171–93.

[3] *Prosecutor v. Serushago* (Case No. ICTR-98-39-S), Sentence, 2 February 1999, para. 17; *Prosecutor v. Kayishema and Ruzindana* (Case No. ICTR-95-1-T), Judgment, 21 May 1999, para. 6.

[4] Rome Statute of the International Criminal Court, UN Doc. A/CONF.183/9 (hereinafter Rome Statute), Art. 77(1).

[5] Cited in *Prosecutor v. Furundzija* (Case No. IT-95-17/1-T), Judgment, 10 December 1998, (1999) 38 ILM 317, para. 290.   [6] *Ibid.*

direction. The only real reference is in the preamble, which declares that putting an end to impunity for serious international crimes will 'contribute to the prevention of such crimes'.[7] But recognizing that the Court has a deterrent effect is not entirely the same as the suggestion that sentencing policy as such is a genuine deterrent.

There has been some comment from the *ad hoc* tribunals on the purposes of international sentencing. In the *Tadic* sentence, Judge McDonald said that 'retribution and deterrence serve as a primary purposes of sentence'.[8] According to the International Criminal Tribunal for Rwanda:

> It is clear that the penalties imposed on accused persons found guilty by the Tribunal must be directed, on the one hand, at retribution of the said accused, who must see their crimes punished, and over and above that, on other hand, at deterrence, namely to dissuade for good, others who may be tempted in the future to perpetrate such atrocities by showing them that the international community shall not tolerate the serious violations of international humanitarian law and human rights.[9]

Some pronouncements have taken a broader approach. In one sentencing decision, the International Criminal Tribunal for the Former Yugoslavia said that the purposes of criminal law sanctions 'include such aims as just punishment, deterrence, incapacitation of the dangerous and rehabilitation'.[10] In another, it noted that retribution was 'an inheritance of the primitive theory of revenge', adding that it was at cross-purposes with the stated goal of international justice which is reconciliation:

> A consideration of retribution as the only factor in sentencing is likely to be counter-productive and disruptive of the entire purpose of the Security Council, which is the restoration and maintenance of peace in the territory of the former Yugoslavia. Retributive punishment by itself does not bring justice.[11]

[7] Tuiloma Neroni Slade and Roger S. Clark, 'Preamble and Final Clauses', in Lee, *The International Criminal Court*, pp. 421–50, at p. 427.

[8] *Prosecutor* v. *Tadic* (Case No. IT-94-1-S), Sentencing Judgment, 14 July 1997, (1999) 112 ILR 286. See also *Prosecutor* v. *Delalic et al.* (Case No. IT-96-21-T), Judgment, 16 November 1998, (1999) 38 ILM 57, para. 1235; *Prosecutor* v. *Erdemovic* (Case No. IT-96-22-T), Sentencing Judgment, 29 November 1996, para. 64; *Prosecutor* v. *Kupreskic et al.* (Case No. IT-96-16-T), Judgment, 14 January 2000, para. 838.

[9] *Prosecutor* v. *Rutaganda* (Case No. ICTR-96-3), Judgment and Sentence, 6 December 1999. See also *Prosecutor* v. *Serushago* (Case No. ICTR-98-39-S), Sentence, 2 February 1999, para. 20.

[10] *Prosecutor* v. *Tadic* (Case No. IT-94-1-T), Sentencing Judgment, 14 July 1997, para. 61. See also *Prosecutor* v. *Erdemovic, supra* note 8, paras 58 and 60.

[11] *Prosecutor* v. *Delalic, supra* note 8, para. 1231.

The debate about capital punishment threatened to undo the Rome Conference. Unlike many other difficult issues, which had been widely debated and, in some cases, resolved during the Preparatory Committee sessions, the question of the death penalty had been studiously avoided throughout the pre-Rome process. At the December 1997 session of the PrepCom, Norwegian diplomat Rolf Einer Fife, who directed the negotiations on sentencing, simply refused to entertain debate on the matter, saying this would be addressed at Rome. Capital punishment might not have been such an issue were it not for sharp debates that took place in another forum, the United Nations Commission on Human Rights. Beginning in 1997, progressive States had pushed through resolutions on abolition of the death penalty. A particularly difficult exchange took place in March and April 1998 and, although the abolitionists won the day, it appears that a handful of retentionist States decided that they would counterattack.[12]

The campaign was led by a persistent group of Arab and Islamic States, together with English-speaking Caribbean States, and a few others such as Singapore, Rwanda, Ethiopia and Nigeria. The Rome negotiations were a perfect occasion for them to attempt to promote their position, because adoption of the statute would require consensus. A small but well-organized minority searching for a degree of recognition of the legitimacy of capital punishment was in a position to extort concessions, and to an extent they were successful. Desperate to resolve the issue and ensure support for the draft Statute as a whole, the majority of delegates agreed to include a new Article stating that the penalties provisions in the Statute are without prejudice to domestic criminal law sanctions,[13] as well as to authorize a declaration by the President at the conclusion of the Conference pandering to the sensitivity of the death penalty States on the issue.[14] Nevertheless, the exclusion of the death penalty from the Rome

---

[12] CHR Res. 1998/8. See Ilias Bantekas and Peter Hodgkinson, 'Capital Punishment at the United Nations: Recent Developments', (2000) 11 *Criminal Law Forum* 23.

[13] Rome Statute, Art. 80.

[14] 'The debate at this Conference on the issue of which penalties should be applied by the Court has shown that there is no international consensus on the inclusion or non-inclusion of the death penalty. However, in accordance with the principles of complementarity between the Court and national jurisdictions, national justice systems have the primary responsibility for investigating, prosecuting and punishing individuals, in accordance with their national laws, for crimes falling under the jurisdiction of the International Criminal Court. In this regard, the Court would clearly not be able to affect national policies in this field. It should be noted that not including the death penalty in the Statute would not in any way have a legal bearing on

Statute can be nothing but an important benchmark in an unquestionable trend towards universal abolition of capital punishment.[15]

Available penalties

The basic sentencing provision in the Rome Statute declares that the Court may impose imprisonment 'for a specified number of years, which may not exceed a maximum of 30 years',[16] and that it may impose '[a] term of life imprisonment when justified by the extreme gravity of the crime and the individual circumstances of the convicted person'.[17] But there were widely varying views about life imprisonment at Rome. States favourable to the death penalty argued that life imprisonment was too timid a penalty, of course, and they used the lever of capital punishment in order to obtain as harsh a provision as possible for custodial sentences. Several European and Latin American States, on the other hand, were in principle opposed to life imprisonment, and at any event to its imposition without the possibility of parole or conditional release at some future date. In the debate, many States called life imprisonment a cruel, inhuman and degrading form of punishment, prohibited by international human rights norms.[18] The compromise was to allow life imprisonment, but with the proviso of mandatory parole review after a certain period of time, as well as the qualification that life imprisonment be imposed only 'when justified by the extreme gravity of the crime and the individual circumstances of the convicted person'. As a final gesture of respect for the feelings of the more liberal States, the report of the Working Group contained a footnote stating that '[s]ome delegations expressed concerns about an explicit reference to life imprisonment'.[19] The curious reference to 'extreme gravity of the crime' may seem out of place, since the Court is designed to try nothing but crimes of extreme gravity and, moreover, the most heinous offenders.[20] It must be viewed as a signal from the Rome Conference

national legislations and practices with regard to the death penalty. Nor shall it be considered as influencing, in the development of customary international law or in any other way, the legality of penalties imposed by national systems for serious crimes.'

[15] 'Question of the Death Penalty', CHR Res. 1999/61, preamble. See William A. Schabas, *The Abolition of the Death Penalty in International Law*, 2nd edn, Cambridge: Cambridge University Press, 1997.   [16] Rome Statute, Art. 77(1)(a).   [17] *Ibid.*, Art. 77(1)(b).

[18] Dirk Van Zyl Smit, 'Life Imprisonment as the Ultimate Penalty in International Law: A Human Rights Perspective', (1998) 9 *Criminal Law Forum* 1.   [19] *Ibid.*, p. 2, n. 2.

[20] During drafting of the Rules of Procedure and Evidence, Spain proposed that life imprisonment be imposed only if one or more aggravating circumstance had been established and if

favourable to clemency in sentencing practice. The Rules declare that 'extreme gravity and the individual circumstances' are to be assessed with reference to 'the existence of one or more aggravating circumstances'.[21]

The Court is empowered to authorize release after part of the sentence has been served. But this is not strictly speaking conditional release or parole, in the sense this has in most national legal systems, because the decision to free the prisoner is final and irreversible. Article 110 authorizes the Court to reduce the sentence if it finds that one or more of the following factors are present: the early and continuing willingness of the person to cooperate with the Court in its investigations and prosecutions; the voluntary assistance of the person in enabling the enforcement of the judgments and orders of the Court in other cases, and in particular providing assistance in locating assets subject to orders of fine, forfeiture or reparation which may be used for the benefit of victims; and other factors establishing a clear and significant change of circumstances sufficient to justify the reduction of sentence.

The Rome Statute also enables the Court to impose a fine, but only '[i]n addition to imprisonment',[22] and 'forfeiture of proceeds, property and assets derived directly or indirectly from that crime, without prejudice to the rights of bona fide third parties'.[23] There had been proposals to include forfeiture of 'instrumentalities' of crime as well as proceeds, but they were dropped. In the context of war crimes, 'instrumentalities' might include aircraft carriers and similar hardware, and this possibility seemed just a bit too awesome for any consensus to be reached!

In determining the sentence, the Court is to consider such mitigating and aggravating factors as the gravity of the crime and the individual circumstances of the offender.[24] The Statute also declares, in Article 27, that official capacity shall not, 'in and of itself, constitute a ground for reduction of sentence'. In reality, the fact that a convicted person held a senior government position will usually be an aggravating factor, as is confirmed by a number of sentencing rulings of the *ad hoc* tribunals.[25] When a

footnote 20 (*cont.*)
there was a total absence of mitigating factors: 'Proposal Submitted by Spain on the Rules of Procedure and Evidence Relating to Part 7 of the Rome Statute of the International Criminal Court (Penalties)', UN Doc. PCNICC/1999/WGRPE(7)/DP.2, p. 2, para. 7.
[21] Rules of Procedure and Evidence, UN Doc. PCNICC/2000/INF/3/Add.3, Rule 145(3).
[22] Rome Statute, Art. 77(2)(a); Rules of Procedure and Evidence, Rule 146.
[23] Rome Statute, Art. 77(2)(b); Rules of Procedure and Evidence, Rules 147 and 218.
[24] Rome Statute, Art. 78(1).
[25] *Prosecutor* v. *Serushago, supra* note 9, para. 28; *Prosecutor* v. *Kambanda* (Case No. ICTR-97-23-

superior is being prosecuted on the basis of command responsibility, the level of culpability is closer to negligence than real intent and premeditation, and the Court will presumably temper justice with clemency. But 'calculated dereliction of an essential duty cannot operate as a factor in mitigation of criminal responsibility'.[26] In the past, international criminal law instruments dismissed the defence of superior orders, but said the fact a person was acting under orders ought to be a mitigating factor in imposing sentence.[27] Although the Rome Statute is silent on this point, the Rules suggest that most if not all unsuccessful defences, to the extent the grounds invoked have any resonance, will encourage a degree of mitigation.[28] The post-World War II tribunals recognized a wide range of mitigating factors, including superior orders, age, position in the military hierarchy, suffering of the victims, efforts by the criminal to reduce suffering, and duress.[29] The Rules of Procedure and Evidence adopted by the Preparatory Commission list a range of mitigating and aggravating factors, including damage caused, harm caused to victims and their families, the nature of the unlawful behaviour and the means employed to execute the crime, the degree of participation, the degree of intent, the age, education and social and economic condition of the convicted person, conduct after the act, efforts to compensate victims, prior convictions for similar crimes, abuse of power and particular cruelty in commission of the crime.[30]

The relevance of motive in terms of the actual elements of the crimes remains somewhat controversial. But in the area of sentencing, there can be no doubt that it is germane. According to the International Criminal Tribunal for the Former Yugoslavia:

S), Judgment and Sentence, 4 September 1998, paras 44 and 60.viii; *Prosecutor v. Akayesu* (Case No. ICTR-96-4-T), Judgment, 2 September 1998, (1998) 37 ILM 1399, para. 36.ii; *Prosecutor v. Delalic, supra* note 8, para. 1220; *Prosecutor v. Kayishema and Ruzindana* (Case No. ICTR-95-1-T), Judgment, 21 May 1999, para. 15; *Prosecutor v. Rutaganda* (Case No. ICTR-96-3), *supra* note 9; *Prosecutor v. Blaskic* (Case No. IT-95-14), Judgment, 3 March 2000, para. 788.

[26] *Prosecutor v. Delalic, supra* note 8 para. 1250.

[27] Agreement for the Prosecution and Punishment of Major War Criminals of the European Axis, and Establishing the Charter of the International Military Tribunal (IMT), Annex, (1951) 82 UNTS 279, Art. 8; Statute of the International Criminal Tribunal for the Former Yugoslavia, UN Doc. S/RES/827, Annex, Art. 7(4). See *Prosecutor v. Erdemovic, supra* note 8, paras 21, 54 and 89–91; *Prosecutor v. Delalic, supra* note 8, n. 1091.

[28] Rules of Procedure and Evidence, Rule 145(2)(a)(i).

[29] William A. Schabas, 'Sentencing and the International Tribunals: For a Human Rights Approach', (1997) 7 *Duke Journal of Comparative and International Law* 461.

[30] Rules of Procedure and Evidence, Rule 145(1)(c) and (2).

where the accused is found to have committed the offence charged with cold, calculated premeditation, suggestive of revenge against the individual victim or group to which the victim belongs, such circumstances necessitate the imposition of aggravated punishment. On the other hand, if the accused is found to have committed the offence charged reluctantly and under the influence of group pressure and, in addition, demonstrated compassion towards the victim or the group to which the victim belongs, these are certainly mitigating factors which the Trial Chamber will take into consideration in the determination of the appropriate sentence.[31]

In imposing sentence of imprisonment, the International Criminal Court is to 'deduct the time, if any, previously spent in detention in accordance with an order of the Court. The Court may deduct any time otherwise spent in detention in connection with conduct underlying the crime.'[32] This seems only fair, although it was opposed by some delegations at the Rome Conference.

When sentence is pronounced for more than one offence, the Court must specify the sentence for each offence as well as a total period of imprisonment. The total period cannot be less than the highest individual sentence pronounced, nor may it exceed the total set out in Article 77(1)(b), that is, life imprisonment or a fixed term of thirty years. In effect, the *Statute* leaves to the judges of the Court the criteria to be applied in imposition of multiple sentences. It imposes a ceiling, and from a practical standpoint in cases of the most serious crimes there will be little discretion to exercise, because individual offences will deserve the maximum available sentence.

Enforcement

The Court will have no prison, and must rely upon States parties for the enforcement of sentences of imprisonment.[33] States are to volunteer their services, indicating their own willingness to allow convicted prisoners to serve the sentence within their own prison institutions. The Statute explicitly refers to 'the principle that States Parties should share the responsibility for enforcing sentences of imprisonment, in accordance with

---

[31] *Prosecutor* v. *Delalic, supra* note 8, para. 1235.   [32] Rome Statute, Art. 78(2).
[33] Antonio Marchesi, 'The Enforcement of Sentences of the International Criminal Court', in Flavia Lattanzi and William A. Schabas, eds, *Essays on the Rome Statute of the ICC*, Rome: Editrice il Sirente, 2000, pp. 427–46.

principles of equitable distribution'.[34] Failing an offer from a State party, the host State – the Netherlands – is saddled with this responsibility. A somewhat similar mechanism exists for the *ad hoc* tribunals.[35]

After sentencing an offender, the Court will designate the State where the term is to be served,[36] and it may change this determination at any time.[37] In choosing a State of detention, the Court must take into account the views of the sentenced person, his or her nationality, and 'widely accepted international treaty standards governing the treatment of prisoners'. Furthermore, conditions of detention must be neither more nor less favourable than those available to prisoners convicted of similar offences in the State where the sentence is being enforced.[38] There can obviously be no question of sending a prisoner to a State with prison conditions that do not meet international standards. However, the reference to 'international treaty standards' is in fact rather vague, and would seem to exclude application of the rigorous and quite precise Standard Minimum Rules for the Treatment of Prisoners,[39] as these are not a treaty but only a 'soft law' resolution of the Economic and Social Council.

The Court's sentence is binding upon the State of enforcement, and the latter is without any discretion whatsoever to modify it.[40] The Court is required to review a sentence after two-thirds of the term have been served or, in the case of life imprisonment, after twenty-five years.[41] In deciding whether to shorten the term of imprisonment at this stage, the Court is to take into account the prisoner's willingness to cooperate with the Court, his or her assistance in enforcing an order of the Court such as in locating assets subject to fine, forfeiture or reparation, and any other factors 'establishing a clear and significant change of circumstances sufficient to justify the reduction of sentence'.[42]

When sentence is completed, if the prisoner is not a national of the State where the penalty is being enforced, he or she may be transferred to a State 'obliged to receive him or her', or to any other State that agrees.[43] It may

---

[34] Rome Statute, Art. 103(3)(a); Rules of Procedure and Evidence, Rule 201. See Trevor Pascal Chimimba, 'Establishing an Enforcement Regime', in Lee, *The International Criminal Court*, pp. 343–56, at pp. 348–50.

[35] David Tolbert, 'The International Tribunal for the Former Yugoslavia and the Enforcement of Sentences', (1998) 11 *Leiden Journal of International Law* 655.

[36] Rome Statute, Art. 103(1)(a).   [37] *Ibid.*, Art. 104.   [38] *Ibid.*, Art. 106(2).

[39] ECOSOC Res. 663C(XXIV); as amended, ECOSOC Res. 2076(LXII). See Chimimba, 'Establishing an Enforcement Regime', at p. 353.   [40] Rome Statute, Art. 105.

[41] *Ibid.*, Art. 110(3).   [42] *Ibid.*, Art. 110(5)(c); Rules of Procedure and Evidence, Rules 223–224.

[43] Rome Statute, Art. 107(1).

well happen that such individual is wanted elsewhere for criminal prosecution. The Statute bars prosecution for the same crimes, of course, according to the *ne bis in idem* principle.[44] But, where extradition is sought for other crimes, States may extradite a prisoner after release pursuant to their own laws and treaties. In this respect, however, the Statute imposes a rule of 'specialty' similar to that in effect in most bilateral extradition matters. The State where the sentence is served cannot prosecute or extradite for a crime committed prior to delivery of the prisoner for service of sentence, unless this has been authorized by the Court.[45] Thus, a prisoner could be prosecuted for a crime committed while serving the sentence, such as escaping lawful custody or assault on a prison guard.[46]

Victims of crimes and their concerns

The preamble of the Statute recognizes that 'during this century millions of children, women and men have been victims of unimaginable atrocities that deeply shock the conscience of humanity'. While this affirmation is unchallengeable, there were widely varying views about the role of victims in the international criminal process itself. As in many other aspects of the procedure of the Court, different justice systems take very different approaches to the participation of victims. Some recognize an active role for victims, who may initiate criminal trials or intervene in them, and even obtain judgments that effect compensation or indemnification in a civil sense as well as criminal conviction and sentence. Other systems are more cautious about the role of victims, fearful that this may distort the social goals of criminal justice and also uncomfortable with an unbalanced procedure where the accused confronts two adversaries, the prosecutor and the victim, instead of one.[47] Nevertheless, the debate took place in the context of a growing emphasis on the importance of victims in international human rights law[48] and in international humanitarian

---

[44] *Ibid.*, Art. 20(2).
[45] Rome Statute, Art. 108. The principle of complementarity would appear to impose, but indirectly, a rule of specialty on the Tribunal itself. It probably should not be able to prosecute for a crime for which surrender was not sought. But the International Criminal Tribunal for the Former Yugoslavia has not considered itself bound by a rule of specialty: *Prosecutor v. Kovacevic* (Case No. IT-97-24-AR73), Decision Stating Reasons for Appeals Chamber's Order of 29 May 1998, 2 July 1998, para. 37.   [46] Escape is dealt with in Art. 111.
[47] Christopher Muttukumaru, 'Reparation to Victims', in Lee, *The International Criminal Court*, pp. 262–70, at pp. 263–4.
[48] 'Basic Principles and Guidelines on the Right to Reparation for Victims of [Gross] Violations

law.[49] Furthermore, there is an important trend in criminal justice towards what is called 'restorative justice', an approach that is victim-oriented.

Victim-related issues are addressed in various provisions of the Statute. To further emphasis this matter, the Preparatory Commission drafted a 'General principle' as part of the Rules:

> A Chamber in making any direction or order, and other organs of the Court in performing their functions under the Statute or the Rules, shall take into account the needs of all victims and witnesses in accordance with Article 68, in particular children, elderly persons, persons with disabilities and victims of sexual or gender violence.[50]

From the standpoint of procedure, victims may participate in the activity of the International Criminal Court in a number of ways.[51] First, they may intervene before the Pre-Trial Chamber when the Prosecutor is seeking authorization to proceed with an investigation at his or her own initiative.[52] Presumably, victims will tend to support the Prosecutor. To this extent, the right to participate is not too far removed from the situation of the *partie civile* (literally, civil party – a private complainant) in Romano-Germanic legal systems, who may attempt to initiate prosecution. In a more general sense, victims may also participate in the course of challenges to jurisdiction or admissibility, even in cases that have been initiated by States parties or by the Security Council.[53] Victims may, however, also find themselves at cross-purposes with the Prosecutor, when he or she decides not to proceed because there are 'substantial reasons to believe that an investigation would not serve the interests of justice'. The Prosecutor is required to take into account 'the gravity of the crime and the interests of victims' in making such a determination.[54] The presence of victims before the Pre-Trial Chamber should ensure that the Prosecutor does this in a genuine manner.

Even if victims do not participate actively in the trial process, as parties or interveners, their presence is virtually indispensable as witnesses. Here

---

of Human Rights and International Humanitarian Law', UN Doc. E/CN.4/1997/104. See also: 'Declaration on Basic Principles of Justice for Victims of Crimes and Abuse of Power', GA Res. 40/34, Annex.

[49] Convention on the Prohibition of the Use, Stockpiling, Production and Transfer of Anti-Personnel Mines and on Their Destruction (the 'Ottawa Treaty'), Art. 6(3).

[50] Rules of Procedure and Evidence, Rule 86.

[51] See generally David Donat-Cattin, 'The Role of Victims in ICC Proceedings', in Lattanzi and Schabas, *Essays on the Rome Statute*, pp. 251–78.   [52] Rome Statute, Art. 15(3).

[53] *Ibid.*, Art. 19(3).   [54] *Ibid.*, Art. 53(1)(c). See also *ibid.*, Art. 53(2)(c).

there are a number of particular concerns, such as protection of witnesses from reprisals, and ensuring that the investigation and trial themselves do not constitute further victimization of those who have already suffered terribly. At the investigation stage, the Prosecutor is required to 'respect the interests and personal circumstances of victims and witnesses, including age, gender as defined in Article 7, paragraph 3, and health, and take into account the nature of the crime, in particular where it involves sexual violence, gender violence or violence against children'.[55] The Prosecutor is also entitled to withhold disclosure of evidence if this may lead to the 'grave endangerment' of a witness or his or her family.[56] Finally, the Pre-Trial Chamber is to ensure 'the protection and privacy of victims and witnesses'.[57]

Similar responsibilities are imposed upon the Trial Chamber.[58] Specifically, it is to take 'appropriate measures to protect the safety, physical and psychological well-being, dignity and privacy of victims and witnesses'. The Court is to have regard to all relevant factors, including age, gender, health, and the nature of the crime, 'in particular, but not limited to, where the crime involves sexual or gender violence or violence against children'.[59] With this in mind, the Court may derogate from the principle of public hearings.[60] It may hold proceedings *in camera*, or permit evidence to be presented 'by electronic means'. Presumably, this refers to testimony where the witness testifies by video and cannot see the alleged perpetrator, a practice that is widely used in national justice systems involving children. The views of the victim or witness are to be canvassed by the Court in making such a determination.[61]

Victims are entitled to intervene at the trial stage, when their 'personal interests' are affected. The 'views and concerns' of witnesses may be presented at any stage of the proceedings, but in a manner which is not prejudicial to or inconsistent with the rights of the accused and a fair and impartial trial. It appears that victims may be represented by counsel in the presentation of their 'views and concerns'.[62] Special rules exist when an accused enters a guilty plea. In such cases, the Trial Chamber is empowered to require the production of additional evidence where it considers 'that a more complete presentation of the facts of the case is required in the

---

[55] *Ibid.*, Art. 54(1)(b).   [56] *Ibid.*, Art. 68(5).
[57] *Ibid.*, Art. 57(3)(c); see also *ibid.*, Art. 57(3)(e).
[58] *Maryland* v. *Craig*, 497 US 836 (1990); Rome Statute, Art. 64(6)(e).
[59] *Ibid.*, Art. 68(1).   [60] *Ibid.*, Art. 68(2). See also *ibid.*, Art. 69(1).   [61] *Ibid.*, Art. 68(2).
[62] *Ibid.*, Art. 68(3).

interests of justice, in particular the interests of the victims'.[63] This seems to be aimed at situations where a 'deal' is struck between Prosecutor and defence and where sentencing may not fully take into account the rights and interests of victims.

The Rome Statute allows the Court to address the issue of reparations to victims, establishing general principles for 'restitution, compensation and rehabilitation'.[64] The Court is empowered to 'determine the scope and extent of any damage, loss and injury to, or in respect of, victims', acting on its own initiative in cases where there is no specific request from the victims themselves.[65] The purpose of this 'determination', it appears, is to enable enforcement of the rights of victims before national courts. According to Christopher Muttukumaru, Court rulings concerning reparations 'must be sufficiently practicable, clear and precise to be capable of enforcement in the courts of, or by the other relevant national authorities of, the States Parties'.[66] More specifically, the Court may 'make an order directly against a convicted person' specifying reparations, although it may not make an order against a State as such.[67] To some extent the Court can control enforcement of the order, but only if there are resources in the trust fund for victims.[68] It may also, in this context, request States to proceed with seizure of proceeds, property and assets, with a view to forfeiture and ultimate restitution.[69] States are required to give effect to such forfeiture orders.[70]

Two distinct institutions are contemplated by the Statute with a view to enhancing the role and the rights of victims. A Victims and Witnesses Unit is to be established by the Registrar.[71] Its responsibilities include the provision of protective measures and security arrangements, counselling and other appropriate assistance for witnesses, victims who appear before the Court and others who are at risk on account of testimony given by such witnesses. The Unit is to include staff 'with expertise in trauma, including

---

[63] *Ibid.*, Art. 66(4)(a).
[64] Christopher Muttukumaru, 'Reparation to Victims', in Lattanzi and Schabas, *Essays on the Rome Statute*, pp. 303–10.
[65] Rome Statute, Art. 75(1). See also Rules of Procedure and Evidence, Rules 94–99. The idea that the Court could act on its own initiative was very controversial. Those favouring this argued that victims in underdeveloped parts of the world were unlikely to be in a position to exercise the right on their own.
[66] Christopher Muttukumaru, 'Reparation to Victims', in Lee, *The International Ciminal Court*, pp. 262–70, at p. 267.   [67] *Ibid.*, pp. 267–9.   [68] Rome Statute, Art. 75(2).
[69] *Ibid.*, Arts 75(4) and 93(1)(k).   [70] *Ibid.*, Art. 109.
[71] See particularly Rules of Procedure and Evidence, Rules 16–19.

trauma related to crimes of sexual violence'.[72] The drafters did not, however, specifically provide for the creation of other units, such as a unit responsible for legal assistance to defendants.

The Rome Statute also provides for creation of a Trust Fund which will hold fines and assets, and dispose of them. The Fund is to be used 'for the benefit of victims of crimes within the jurisdiction of the Court, and of the families of such victims'.[73] The Fund is to be established by decision of the Assembly of States Parties. The Assembly is also charged with fixing the criteria for the Fund's operation. There were far more ambitious proposals for compensation of victims, but these fell by the wayside during the negotiations. The concept of international compensation is seductive, but it is not without many practical obstacles. Experience of the *ad hoc* tribunals suggests that by and large most defendants succeed in claiming indigence. For example, they are almost invariably represented by tribunal-funded counsel after making perfunctory demonstrations that they are without means to pay for their own defence. The irony is that these are the very people who are widely believed to have looted the countries where they once ruled. It may simply be unrealistic to expect the new Court to be able to locate and seize substantial assets of its prisoners.

---

[72] Rome Statute, Art. 43(6). See also *ibid.*, Art. 68(4).
[73] *Ibid.*, Art. 79.

8

Structure and administration of the Court

The seat of the Court is The Hague,[1] but it may sit elsewhere if it considers this desirable. The Netherlands was the only State to offer its services, despite rumours that circulated before and during the Diplomatic Conference about Rome, Lyon and Nuremberg as possible candidates.[2] The Hague is already the seat of the International Court of Justice as well as of the *ad hoc* Tribunal for the Former Yugoslavia and other international judicial organizations. Its candidacy must have seemed so unbeatable to possible competitors that they declined even to throw their hats into the ring. As part of the preparatory process for coming into force of the Rome Statute, a 'headquarters agreement' is to be negotiated with the Netherlands.[3]

The International Criminal Court is a new and independent international organization. The Court is formally distinct from the United Nations. Nevertheless, the United Nations has played a seminal role in its creation, and continues to fund the process of establishment of the Court. Its Security Council has the right to refer cases to the Court. The precise relationship between the two organizations is to be defined in an agreement that must also be finalized before the Rome Statute comes into force.[4]

The International Criminal Court is composed of four 'organs': the Presidency, the Divisions, the Office of the Prosecutor and the Registry.[5] There are three Divisions, the Appeals Division, the Trial Division and the Pre-Trial Division. The term 'Divisions' rather than 'Chambers' was used in order to resolve a dispute about whether there should be one or several pre-trial chambers.[6]

---

[1] Rome Statute of the International Criminal Court, UN Doc. A/CONF.183/9 (hereinafter Rome Statute), Art. 3.
[2] Frank Jarasch, 'Establishment, Organization and Financing of the International Criminal Court (Parts I, IV, XI–XIII)', (1998) 6 *European Journal of Crime, Criminal Law and Criminal Justice* 9, at pp. 18–19.   [3] Rome Statute, Art. 3(2).   [4] *Ibid.*, Art. 2.
[5] *Ibid.*, Art. 34.   [6] Jarasch, 'Establishment, Organization and Financing', p. 20.

The judges of the Court

Eighteen judges are to be elected by the Assembly of States Parties, of whom three make up the Presidency. Any State party may propose one candidate for the Court in any given election. That candidate need not be a national of the nominating State but must be a national of a State party. But there can be only one judge of any given nationality at any one time. Judges are to be of 'high moral character, impartiality and integrity', a phraseology that is rather typical of international instruments.[7] They must also be qualified for appointment to the highest judicial offices in their respective States,[8] and are to have an excellent knowledge of and be fluent in at least one of the working languages of the Court, namely, English or French. The Statute allows for an 'advisory committee' on nominations.[9] But this is a timid affair indeed compared with a thoroughgoing screening procedure to ensure qualifications that was originally mooted by the United Kingdom, somewhat along the lines of the procedure in force for appointments to the European Court of Human Rights. However, many States resented any attempt to limit their right to designate their own candidates.[10]

The Statute requires a degree of expertise in the subject matter of the Court. Here it creates two categories of candidates, those with criminal law experience and those with international law experience. Specific reference is made to international humanitarian law and the law of human rights. During an election there are to be two lists of candidates, one with the criminal law profile, the other with the international law profile. A nominee for the Court who meets both requirements may choose the list on which he or she will appear. At the first election, a minimum of nine judges must come from the criminal law profile and a minimum of five from the international law profile. Subsequent elections are to be organized so as to maintain the same proportion of judges. Although no specific percentages are set out, Article 36(8) commits the States parties to 'take into account' the need to ensure representation of the principal legal systems of the world, equitable geographic representation, 'a fair representation of female and male judges', and legal expertise on specific issues

---

[7] Art. 2 of the Statute of the International Court of Justice speaks of 'a body of independent judges elected regardless of their nationality from among persons of high moral character'.

[8] Rome Statute, Art. 36(3).   [9] *Ibid.*, Art. 36(4)(c).

[10] Jarasch, 'Establishment, Organization and Financing', p. 21.

such as violence against women or children. The wording is a watered-down version of draft provisions that spoke bluntly of 'gender balance'.[11] The requirement of fair gender representation reflects concerns that the new Court might resemble its close relation, the International Court of Justice, a fifteen-member body to which only one woman has ever been elected in its entire eighty-year history. The *ad hoc* tribunals, whose judges are elected by the Security Council, have shown some modest improvement in this respect. To their credit, both have elected women to the Presidency of the Tribunals.

The term for each judge is nine years and, with a couple of minor and transitional exceptions, they are not eligible for re-election.[12] This should help to ensure both genuine and perceived impartiality, because sitting judges who must campaign with their own governments, as well as others, to be re-elected, might find it difficult to exercise their functions in a dynamic and vigorous manner. International judges are an expensive proposition. They draw high salaries and incur other significant expenses. It seemed unnecessary to employ all eighteen on a full-time basis until more is known about the real workload of the Court. As a result, at least during the Court's early stages, only the three judges making up the Presidency will actually serve full-time from the beginning of their mandates.

Judges who are required to serve on a full-time basis at the seat of the Court are not allowed to engage in any other occupation of a professional nature. All judges, including those who do not work full-time, are forbidden from activities 'likely to interfere with their judicial functions or to affect confidence in their independence'.[13] Given these requirements, it would seem hazardous to allow senior civil servants or diplomats to stand for election to part-time positions, a practice that is tolerated in the case of some other international tribunals that sit on a part-time basis.

The Presidency is responsible for the administration of the Court and a variety of specialized functions set out in the Statute. The Presidency of the Court is elected by the judges. The President and the First and Second Vice-Presidents make up the Presidency. The Presidency is to decide upon the appropriate workload of the other fifteen judges.[14] The Presidency may

---

[11] *Ibid.*, p. 21; Medard R. Rwelamira, 'Composition and Administration of the Court', in Roy Lee, ed., *The International Criminal Court, The Making of the Rome Statute, Issues, Negotiations, Results*, The Hague: Kluwer Law International, 1999, pp. 153–73, at pp. 166–7; Cate Steains, 'Gender Issues', in Lee, *ibid.*, pp. 357–90, at pp. 376–7.
[12] Rome Statute, Art. 36(9). [13] *Ibid.*, Art. 40. [14] *Ibid.*, Art. 35.

also propose that the number of judges be increased, where this is considered necessary and appropriate, although any increase has to be authorized by the Assembly of States Parties. The *ad hoc* tribunals began with only six trial judges, but the number was soon found to be insufficient. Initially, the Yugoslav Tribunal drew upon the five Appeals Chamber judges to assist with some trial work. Then, the Security Council agreed to add a three-judge chamber to each of the tribunals. There are at present twenty-three international judges working full-time on the Rwanda and Yugoslav Tribunals. It would seem likely, then, that the eighteen judges envisaged in the Rome Statute will quickly prove to be inadequate if the Court fulfils even the most modest of expectations.

The Appeals Division is composed of the President and four other judges. Members of the Appeals Division are to serve their entire nine-year term in the Division, reflecting widespread dissatisfaction with practice at the ICTY where judges move from one chamber to another during their terms. The Trial Division and Pre-Trial Division are composed of not less than six judges. Judges in each of these divisions are to serve for at least three years within their division. Judges are to be assigned to the various divisions based on their qualifications and experience, and so as to ensure an appropriate combination of expertise in criminal and international law.[15] The Trial and Pre-Trial Divisions are to contain judges with primarily criminal law experience and, though not stated as such in the Statute, there is the suggestion that the international law judges will gravitate towards the Appeals Division. Reading between the lines, the Statute seems to be saying that the more practically oriented criminal law specialists should focus on trials, while their more professorial brethren in the international law field should focus on appeals.

The Appeals Chamber is to sit as a full bench of the five judges belonging to the Appeals Division. The Trial Chamber is to sit in benches of three judges of the Trial Division. The Pre-Trial Chamber may sit as either a three-judge panel or as a single judge, belonging to the Pre-Trial Division. Judges of the other Trial and Pre-Trial Division may temporarily be assigned to the other, although no judge who has participated in the pre-trial phase of a case may sit on the Trial Chamber of the same case.

Judges may be excused from their functions by the Presidency. They may also be disqualified from sitting in cases in which there can be reason-

---

[15] *Ibid.*, Art. 39(1).

able doubts about their impartiality.[16] That they cannot sit in matters in which they have previously been involved at the national level would seem obvious, but to avoid any doubt this rule is spelled out in the Statute. A Code of Professional Conduct for defence counsel is to be drafted by the Presidency of the Court.[17]

Office of the Prosecutor

The prosecutorial arm of the Court is a separate and independent organ. The Office of the Prosecutor is headed by the Prosecutor, who is assisted by one or more Deputy Prosecutors. The Prosecutor and the Deputy Prosecutors are to be of different nationalities.[18] Both the Prosecutor and the Deputy Prosecutors are to be persons 'of high moral character' with 'extensive, practical experience' in criminal prosecutions. They must be fluent in at least one of the working languages of the Court.

The Prosecutor is elected by secret ballot of an absolute majority of the Assembly of States Parties. The Deputy Prosecutors must also be elected by the Assembly of States Parties, but from a list of candidates proposed by the Prosecutor. The Prosecutor is to submit a list of three candidates for each position of Deputy Prosecutor to be filled. The term of both Prosecutor and Deputy Prosecutors is nine years.

The Prosecutor is to appoint legal experts as advisers on specific issues, such as sexual and gender violence and violence against children. The Prosecutor is also to hire investigators and other staff members. The same requirements as for judges, that is, experience with various judicial systems, geographic representativity and gender balance are to be sought.

The Statute allows persons being investigated or prosecuted to request the disqualification of the Prosecutor or of a Deputy Prosecutor.

The Registry

The Registry is responsible for the non-judicial aspects of the administration and servicing of the Court. The principal administrative officer of the Court is the Registrar, and he or she heads the Registry.[19] The Registrar is to be elected by the judges to a five-year term. If required, the judges may also elect a Deputy Registrar to a five-year term or to such shorter term as they may decide.

---

[16] *Ibid.*, Art. 41. See Rules of Procedure and Evidence, Rules 23–39.
[17] Rules of Procedure and Evidence, Rule 8.   [18] Rome Statute, Art. 42.   [19] *Ibid.*, Art. 43.

The Registrar's staff is to demonstrate experience with various judicial systems, in addition to geographic representativity and gender balance. The Statute specifically provides for the use of 'gratis personnel' offered by States parties, intergovernmental and non-governmental organizations to assist with the work of any of the organs of the Court. Gratis personnel are to be employed only 'in exceptional circumstances'.[20]

Ethical matters

Judges, Prosecutor, Deputy Prosecutors, Registrar and Deputy Registrar are all required to make a solemn undertaking in open court to exercise their functions impartially and conscientiously.[21] Any of them may be removed from office on grounds of serious misconduct, a serious breach of duties, or inability to exercise the functions required by the Statute. In the event of misconduct of a less serious nature, disciplinary measures may be imposed.[22]

Removal is the result of a decision taken by the Assembly of States Parties.[23] Removal of a judge first requires a recommendation to this effect by a two-thirds majority of the other judges. Then, a two-thirds majority of the States parties must agree. The Prosecutor is more vulnerable, and can be removed by a majority of the States parties. The Deputy Prosecutor's removal must be recommended by the Prosecutor and then authorized by a majority of the States parties. The Registrar and Deputy Registrar may be removed by a majority of the judges.[24]

Salaries of the Judges, the Prosecutor and Deputy Prosecutors, and the Registrar and Deputy Registrar, are set by the Assembly of States Parties and may not be reduced during their terms of office.[25]

Languages

The Court has two working languages, English and French, although it may designate other working languages on a case-by-case basis.[26] Judges, the Prosecutor, the Registrar and their deputies, as well as defence counsel, are all required to have fluency in one or the other of these languages.[27]

---

[20] *Ibid.*, Art. 44(4).   [21] *Ibid.*, Art. 45.   [22] *Ibid.*, Art. 47.   [23] *Ibid.*, Art. 46.
[24] On removal and related matters, see Rules of Procedure and Evidence, Rules 23–39.
[25] Rome Statute, Art. 49.   [26] *Ibid.*, Art. 50(2); and Rules of Procedure and Evidence, Rule 41.
[27] Rome Statute, Art. 50.

The Court has six official languages: Arabic, Chinese, English, French, Russian and Spanish. Judgments of the Court, as well as other decisions 'resolving fundamental issues before the Court' are to be published in the official languages.[28] The requirement is consistent with United Nations practice, but may prove cumbersome in the case of judgments running into several hundreds of pages, as has been the custom at the *ad hoc* tribunals. Although the *ad hoc* tribunals have only two official languages, as a general rule they have proven to be unable to issue judgments in both languages simultaneously.[29]

Assembly of States Parties

The Assembly of States Parties is responsible for a wide range of administrative matters, including providing the officers of the Court with general guidelines, adoption of the budget, increases in the number of judges, and similar matters. The Assembly is also the forum for adoption of amendments to the Statute. To some extent, it is also charged with completing the unfinished work of the Rome Conference, in that it must adopt the Elements of Crimes, the Rules of Procedure and Evidence, and other instruments necessary for the operation of the Court. These instruments are being prepared by the Preparatory Commission, which was set up by the Final Act, but subject to formal adoption by the Assembly. The Assembly will be convened as soon as the Statute enters into force.

Each State party has one representative in the Assembly of States Parties.[30] Signatories of the Final Act can be observers in the Assembly. This 'generous' approach prevailed over those who wanted to confine attendance in the Assembly to signatories of the Statute itself.[31] The Assembly is to establish a Bureau as well as subsidiary bodies.[32] Both the Bureau and the Assembly are to meet once a year, although they can be convened more frequently if necessary.

---

[28] Rules of Procedure and Evidence, Rules 40 and 43.
[29] The first major judgment of the International Criminal Tribunal for the Former Yugoslavia, the Tadic jurisdictional decision, was initially issued in English only, prompting a harsh declaration by French-Canadian judge Jules Deschênes. Many months later, a French version of the judgment became available. Less frequently, judgments have been issued in French first with an English language judgment following weeks or months later.
[30] Rome Statute, Art. 112(1).   [31] Jarasch, 'Establishment, Organization and Financing', p. 23.
[32] S. Rama Rao, 'Financing of the Court, Assembly of States Parties and the Preparatory Commission', in Lee, *The International Criminal Court*, pp. 399–420.

Funding

One of the unpleasant consequences of the fact that the Court is not a United Nations body is that it is responsible for its own funding. The Statute allows the Court to take money based on assessed contributions upon States parties, following the basic scale already in use in the United Nations, a calculation that considers population and relative wealth.[33] In addition, the Court may take any funds provided by the United Nations. Specific mention is made of expenses that may be incurred in the case of Security Council referrals, for which it seems only natural that the United Nations must be responsible.[34] The wording suggests this form of mixed financing, but tilts towards the idea that United Nations contributions are to be based principally upon cases involving Security Council referral. Proposals that the Court should be funded strictly by the United Nations were resisted, principally by the three biggest contributors to the United Nations budget, the United States, Germany and Japan.[35]

In addition, the Court is entitled to receive and use any voluntary contributions from governments, international organizations, individuals, corporations and other entities.[36] The practice of receiving voluntary contributions is already well entrenched within the United Nations and other international organizations, and many important programmes would be eliminated without this source of financing. Some important functions of the *ad hoc* tribunals have only been fulfilled as a result of voluntary contributions.

Settlement of disputes

The Rome Statute is an international treaty subject to many general legal rules developed by custom over the centuries and partially codified in the 1969 Vienna Convention on the Law of Treaties.[37] A multilateral treaty is, in effect, a form of contract between the States that adhere to it. Disputes may arise between two or more States as to the interpretation or application of the Statute. Such cases are to be submitted to the Assembly of States Parties, which may attempt to settle the case or propose alternative means of settlement, including referring the case to the International Court of

---

[33] Rome Statute, Art. 117.   [34] *Ibid.*, Art. 115.
[35] Jarasch, 'Establishment, Organization and Financing', p. 23. See also Rao, 'Financing of the Court'.   [36] Rome Statute, Art. 116.
[37] Vienna Convention on the Law of Treaties, (1979) 1155 UNTS 331.

Justice.[38] However, such a procedure can only work with States that have also accepted the jurisdiction of the International Court of Justice, or that agree to its jurisdiction in a specific case.

Reservations

It is not at all uncommon for States to formulate reservations or interpretative declarations at the time they sign or ratify international treaties. In the absence of any special rules in the treaty itself, such reservations are permissible providing they do not violate the 'object and purpose' of the treaty. Complex questions have arisen in recent years with respect to the legality of reservations to certain treaties, and the legal consequences of invalid reservations.[39] All of this is avoided by Article 120, which states simply: 'No reservations may be made to this Statute.'[40] But the provision is unlikely to prevent some States from making interpretative declarations at the time of ratification. To the extent such declarations do not seek to limit the State's obligations under the Statute, they would seem to be permissible. In practice, it is not always easy to distinguish between a reservation and an interpretative declaration.[41] France formulated an interpretative declaration with respect to Article 8 at the time of its ratification of the Statute.

The Statute makes its own exception to the rule by allowing States to formulate a kind of reservation to Article 8. For a seven-year period, States may ratify the Statute but escape jurisdiction over war crimes.[42] The text is all that remains of an early scheme by which States parties would be able to pick and choose the crimes over which the Statute would apply to them. The existing provision was inserted in the final draft of the Statute as a compromise aimed at garnering the support of France and perhaps a few other States.[43] It was resoundingly criticized by human rights non-governmental organizations at the close of the Rome Conference, although these concerns

---

[38] Rome Statute, Art. 119.

[39] The matter is currently being studied by the International Law Commission, under the direction of rapporteur Alain Pellet: 'Report of the International Law Commission on the Work of its Fiftieth Session, 20 April–12 June 1998, 27 July–14 August 1998', UN Doc. A/53/10 and Corr.1.

[40] See Tuiloma Neroni Slade and Roger S. Clark, 'Preamble and Final Clauses', in Lee, *The International Criminal Court*, pp. 421–50, at pp. 431–2.

[41] *Belilos* v. *Switzerland*, Series A, No. 132, 29 April 1988.   [42] Rome Statute, Art. 124.

[43] France was the twelfth State to ratify the Statute, in June 2000. Its ratification was the first to be accompanied by a declaration pursuant to Art. 124. See Slade and Clark, 'Preamble and Final Clauses', p. 443.

were probably exaggerated.[44] Serious war crimes likely to attract the attention of the Prosecutor and meet the Court's threshold for serious crimes will by and large also meet the definition of crimes against humanity. It would seem unlikely that the Court will be deprived of jurisdiction over very many specific offenders merely because of Article 124.[45]

It is not entirely clear what the effect of a declaration under Article 124 will be. If a State declares that it does not accept the Court's jurisdiction over war crimes, does this mean that its nationals cannot be prosecuted, even if the crime is committed on the territory of another State party? Elizabeth Wilmshurst of the United Kingdom foreign ministry argues that the 'common sense view' resulting from the negotiations of the Statute is that a declaration under Article 124 in effect insulates nationals of the State from prosecution by the Court. Similarly, she argues that after expiry of the declaration, the Court will be blocked from prosecuting war crimes committed during the period of the declaration.[46]

France made a declaration pursuant to Article 124 at the time of its ratification of the Statute.

Amendment

In domestic legal systems, criminal law requires a large degree of flexibility. Criminal behaviour evolves rapidly, and both procedural and substantive rules need to be adjusted regularly in order to cope with change. International justice is rather more cumbersome in this respect, and, to make matters worse, the drafters of the Statute attempted to reduce or eliminate judicial discretion in a variety of areas. Judges at the *ad hoc* tribunals were given a wide degree of latitude in their interpretation of the crimes themselves, the definition and application of defences, and the adjustment of rules of procedure and evidence. All of this was left to them by the relatively terse words of the statutes themselves. The Rome Statute sets out considerably more detailed rules with respect to defences and other general principles, and then further constrains any prospect of dis-

---

[44] See, for example, the comments of the International Committee of the Red Cross: UN Doc. A/C.6/53/SR.12.

[45] See also Kelly Dawn Askin, 'Crimes Within the jurisdiction of the International Criminal Court', (1999) 10 *Criminal Law Forum* 33, at p. 50, who notes that Art. 124 may in fact provide an incentive to States to ratify the Statute.

[46] Elizabeth Wilmshurst, 'Jurisdiction of the Court', in Lee, *The International Criminal Court*, pp. 127–41, at pp. 139–41.

cretion by adding the detailed Elements of Crimes and Rules of Procedure and Evidence to the mix. Experienced judges will no doubt find imaginative ways of pushing these limits to the utmost, but the fact remains that their manoeuvrability has been considerably hampered.

As a result, changes in the applicable law should require frequent adjustment by the States parties. Minor alterations can be effected by the Assembly of States Parties at any time through modification of the Elements and the Rules. Where amendment of the Statute is required, a complex and extremely cumbersome procedure is set out. Amendments during the first seven years from the entry into force of the Statute are excluded altogether. Assuming the Statute comes into force in 2002, then no amendment can be made until the end of the decade. Although any State party will be able to propose an amendment at any time,[47] the Statute institutionalizes the initial amendment process by providing for a Review Conference.[48] A Review Conference is not an unusual procedure in modern multilateral treaties. In the case of the Rome Statute, seven years after the entry into force of the Statute, the depositary of the treaty, who is the Secretary-General of the United Nations, is to convene the Review Conference in order to consider any amendments. Article 123 specifically refers to changes to the list of crimes contained in Article 5 of the Statute, but adds that this in no way limits the Review Conference's scope with respect to other amendments. A number of possible additional crimes were considered by the Rome Conference, and their advocates are likely to campaign for inclusion at the first Review Conference. These include drug trafficking, terrorism and a range of economic crimes, most of them already proscribed in existing international treaties. The Statute also provides that the Review Conference is to consider whether or not to retain Article 124, the provision allowing States parties to deny jurisdiction over war crimes for a seven-year period. The first Review Conference will also be the occasion to consider provisions concerning the crime of aggression.[49] At any future time, a majority of the States parties to the Statute may agree to convene additional review conferences.

In addition to the Review Conference context, amendments may also be proposed at any time subsequently. However, amendment of the Statute during the seven years that follow its entry into force would appear to be impossible. The text of an amendment is to be submitted by the proposing

---

[47] Rome Statute, Art. 121.   [48] *Ibid.*, Art. 123.   [49] *Ibid.*, Art. 5(2).

State party to the Secretary-General of the United Nations, who is to circulate it to all States parties. The next Assembly of States Parties will consider the amendment or, alternatively, decide to convene a Review Conference. Amendments are to be adopted by the Assembly of States Parties or by a Review Conference by consensus, failing which a majority of two-thirds of all States parties shall be required.

But amendments adopted by the Assembly of States Parties or by a Review Conference do not automatically enter into force. The States parties to the Statute must also deposit individual instruments of ratification or accession to such amendments. As a general rule, an amendment will not come into force until seven-eighths of the States parties have filed instruments of acceptance. When an amendment has been accepted by seven-eighths of the States parties, any State party unhappy with the change may give notice that it withdraws from the Statute. If new 'treaty crimes' are added to the jurisdiction of the Court, the Court cannot exercise jurisdiction for any new crimes added by amendment in the territory of a State or over the national of a State that has not made a specific declaration of acceptance.[50]

In the case of amendments to provisions of an institutional nature, these are in principle rather less controversial and the Statute does not require that they be ratified by States parties. Such amendments are to be adopted by consensus or by a two-thirds vote of the Assembly of States Parties or a Review Conference, and come into force six months later. The expression 'amendments of an institutional nature' is defined;[51] they include matters dealing with the number of judges, the composition of chambers, staff of the Court, and so on.

Signature, ratification, approval and accession

States were entitled to sign the Statute until 31 December 2000.[52] Although signature of a treaty may also, under certain circumstances, constitute a means of indicating its acceptance,[53] in the context of the Statute signature is only a preliminary act – 'a first step to participation'[54] – and must be followed by deposit of an instrument of ratification, approval or accession

---

[50] *Ibid.*, Art. 123(5).   [51] *Ibid.*, Art. 122(1).   [52] *Ibid.*, Art. 125(1).

[53] Vienna Convention on the Law of Treaties, *supra* note 37, Arts 11–12.

[54] *Reservations to the Convention on the Prevention and Punishment of the Crime of Genocide (Advisory Opinion)* [1951] ICJ Reports 16, p. 28.

for the State to become a party to the Statute. Customary law, as codified in the 1969 Vienna Convention on the Law of Treaties, requires that between the time of signature and ratification a State is obliged to refrain from acts which would defeat the object and purpose of a treaty, until it shall have made its intention clear not to become a party to the treaty.[55]

The terms 'ratification', 'acceptance', 'approval' and 'accession' describe the international act by which a State establishes on the international plane its consent to be bound by a treaty.[56] Although all four terms are acceptable,[57] the acts they describe are colloquially referred to as 'ratification'. States which have already signed the Statute deposit instruments of ratification, acceptance or approval. Those that have not deposit instruments of 'accession'. Deposit of these instruments is done with the depositary, who is designated as the Secretary-General of the United Nations.

The Statute will enter into force on the first day of the month after the sixtieth day following the date of the deposit of the sixtieth instrument of ratification, acceptance, approval or accession with the Secretary-General of the United Nations.[58] For States that ratify, accept, approve or accede after the entry into force of the Statute, it will enter into force for them on the first day of the month after the sixtieth day following the deposit of instruments of ratification, acceptance, approval or accession.[59] It is possible for States to withdraw from the Statute by sending a written notice to the Secretary-General of the United Nations. Withdrawal takes effect one year after the receipt of the notification, unless the State in question specifies a later date.[60] But a State that withdraws cannot escape obligations that arose while it was a party, including financial obligations.[61] A State that reacted to indictment of one of its senior officials by withdrawing from the Statute could not affect any pending investigation or trial. The Statute does not explain what would happen if there were enough withdrawals to bring the number of ratifications below the number of sixty.

Authentic texts

The plenary sessions and working groups of the Rome Conference took place with simultaneous translation in all six official languages of the

---

[55] Vienna Convention on the Law of Treaties, *supra* note 37, Art. 18.
[56] *Ibid.*, Art. 2(1)(b).
[57] Some States prefer one or the other term for constitutional or historical reasons: Slade and Clark, 'Preamble and Final Clauses', at p. 444.   [58] Rome Statute, Art. 126(1).
[59] *Ibid.*, Art. 126(2).   [60] *Ibid.*, Art. 127.   [61] *Ibid.*, Art. 127(2).

United Nations system, namely, English, French, Russian, Spanish, Arabic and Chinese. All documents were also available in these languages. The drafting committee, presided by M. Cherif Bassiouni, worked intensely on the various language versions in order to ensure the greatest degree of consistency and coherence. The six versions of the authentic text of the Statute, adopted the evening of 17 July 1998, are declared to be equally valid.[62] Because of the complexities of the Statute and the haste with which the Conference operated, there were inevitably some errors in the version that was actually voted upon on 17 July. Subsequently, corrections were circulated to the participants in the Conference for their concurrence and the official text is now slightly different from the one voted upon at the conclusion of the conference.[63]

[62] *Ibid.*, Art. 128.
[63] Roy Lee, 'The Rome Conference and Its Contributions to International Law', in Lee, *The International Criminal Court*, pp. 1–39, at pp. 11–12.

Appendices

Rome Statute of the International Criminal Court

Adopted by the United Nations Diplomatic Conference of Plenipotentiaries on the Establishment of an International Criminal Court on 17 July 1998.[1]

Preamble

The States Parties to this Statute,

Conscious that all peoples are united by common bonds, their cultures pieced together in a shared heritage, and concerned that this delicate mosaic may be shattered at any time,

Mindful that during this century millions of children, women and men have been victims of unimaginable atrocities that deeply shock the conscience of humanity,

Recognizing that such grave crimes threaten the peace, security and well-being of the world,

Affirming that the most serious crimes of concern to the international community as a whole must not go unpunished and that their effective prosecution must be ensured by taking measures at the national level and by enhancing international cooperation,

Determined to put an end to impunity for the perpetrators of these crimes and thus to contribute to the prevention of such crimes,

Recalling that it is the duty of every State to exercise its criminal jurisdiction over those responsible for international crimes,

Reaffirming the Purposes and Principles of the Charter of the United Nations, and in particular that all States shall refrain from the threat or use of force against the territorial integrity or political independence of any State, or in any other manner inconsistent with the Purposes of the United Nations,

Emphasizing in this connection that nothing in this Statute shall be taken as authorizing any State Party to intervene in an armed conflict in the internal affairs of any State,

---

[1] As corrected by the *procès-verbaux* of 10 November 1998 and 12 July 1999, 30 November 1999 and 8 May 2000.

Determined to these ends and for the sake of present and future generations, to establish an independent permanent International Criminal Court in relationship with the United Nations system, with jurisdiction over the most serious crimes of concern to the international community as a whole,

Emphasizing that the International Criminal Court established under this Statute shall be complementary to national criminal jurisdictions,

Resolved to guarantee lasting respect for and the enforcement of international justice,

Have agreed as follows:

Part 1 Establishment of the court

Article 1 The Court

An International Criminal Court ('the Court') is hereby established. It shall be a permanent institution and shall have the power to exercise its jurisdiction over persons for the most serious crimes of international concern, as referred to in this Statute, and shall be complementary to national criminal jurisdictions. The jurisdiction and functioning of the Court shall be governed by the provisions of this Statute.

Article 2 Relationship of the Court with the United Nations

The Court shall be brought into relationship with the United Nations through an agreement to be approved by the Assembly of States Parties to this Statute and thereafter concluded by the President of the Court on its behalf.

Article 3 Seat of the Court

1. The seat of the Court shall be established at The Hague in the Netherlands ('the host State').

2. The Court shall enter into a headquarters agreement with the host State, to be approved by the Assembly of States Parties and thereafter concluded by the President of the Court on its behalf.

3. The Court may sit elsewhere, whenever it considers it desirable, as provided in this Statute.

Article 4 Legal status and powers of the Court

1. The Court shall have international legal personality. It shall also have such legal capacity as may be necessary for the exercise of its functions and the fulfilment of its purposes.

2. The Court may exercise its functions and powers, as provided in this Statute, on the territory of any State Party and, by special agreement, on the territory of any other State.

Part 2 Jurisdiction, admissibility and applicable law

Article 5 Crimes within the jurisdiction of the Court

1. The jurisdiction of the Court shall be limited to the most serious crimes of concern to the international community as a whole. The Court has jurisdiction in accordance with this Statute with respect to the following crimes:

(a) The crime of genocide;
(b) Crimes against humanity;
(c) War crimes;
(d) The crime of aggression.

2. The Court shall exercise jurisdiction over the crime of aggression once a provision is adopted in accordance with articles 121 and 123 defining the crime and setting out the conditions under which the Court shall exercise jurisdiction with respect to this crime. Such a provision shall be consistent with the relevant provisions of the Charter of the United Nations.

Article 6 Genocide

For the purpose of this Statute, 'genocide' means any of the following acts committed with intent to destroy, in whole or in part, a national, ethnical, racial or religious group, as such:

(a) Killing members of the group;
(b) Causing serious bodily or mental harm to members of the group;
(c) Deliberately inflicting on the group conditions of life calculated to bring about its physical destruction in whole or in part;
(d) Imposing measures intended to prevent births within the group;
(e) Forcibly transferring children of the group to another group.

Article 7   Crimes against humanity

1. For the purpose of this Statute, 'crime against humanity' means any of the following acts when committed as part of a widespread or systematic attack directed against any civilian population, with knowledge of the attack:

(a) Murder;

(b) Extermination;

(c) Enslavement;

(d) Deportation or forcible transfer of population;

(e) Imprisonment or other severe deprivation of physical liberty in violation of fundamental rules of international law;

(f) Torture;

(g) Rape, sexual slavery, enforced prostitution, forced pregnancy, enforced sterilization, or any other form of sexual violence of comparable gravity;

(h) Persecution against any identifiable group or collectivity on political, racial, national, ethnic, cultural, religious, gender as defined in paragraph 3, or other grounds that are universally recognized as impermissible under international law, in connection with any act referred to in this paragraph or any crime within the jurisdiction of the Court;

(i) Enforced disappearance of persons;

(j) The crime of apartheid;

(k) Other inhumane acts of a similar character intentionally causing great suffering, or serious injury to body or to mental or physical health.

2. For the purpose of paragraph 1:

(a) 'Attack directed against any civilian population' means a course of conduct involving the multiple commission of acts referred to in paragraph 1 against any civilian population, pursuant to or in furtherance of a State or organizational policy to commit such attack;

(b) 'Extermination' includes the intentional infliction of conditions of life, *inter alia* the deprivation of access to food and medicine, calculated to bring about the destruction of part of a population;

(c) 'Enslavement' means the exercise of any or all of the powers attaching to the right of ownership over a person and includes the exercise of such power in the course of trafficking in persons, in particular women and children;

(d) 'Deportation or forcible transfer of population' means forced displacement of the persons concerned by expulsion or other coercive acts from the area in which they are lawfully present, without grounds permitted under international law;

(e) 'Torture' means the intentional infliction of severe pain or suffering, whether physical or mental, upon a person in the custody or under the control of the accused; except that torture shall not include pain or suffering arising only from, inherent in or incidental to, lawful sanctions;

(f) 'Forced pregnancy' means the unlawful confinement of a woman forcibly made pregnant, with the intent of affecting the ethnic composition of any population or carrying out other grave violations of international law. This definition shall not in any way be interpreted as affecting national laws relating to pregnancy;

(g) 'Persecution' means the intentional and severe deprivation of fundamental rights contrary to international law by reason of the identity of the group or collectivity;

(h) 'The crime of apartheid' means inhumane acts of a character similar to those referred to in paragraph 1, committed in the context of an institutionalized regime of systematic oppression and domination by one racial group over any other racial group or groups and committed with the intention of maintaining that regime;

(i) 'Enforced disappearance of persons' means the arrest, detention or abduction of persons by, or with the authorization, support or acquiescence of, a State or a political organization, followed by a refusal to acknowledge that deprivation of freedom or to give information on the fate or whereabouts of those persons, with the intention of removing them from the protection of the law for a prolonged period of time.

3. For the purpose of this Statute, it is understood that the term 'gender' refers to the two sexes, male and female, within the context of society. The term 'gender' does not indicate any meaning different from the above.

Article 8 War crimes

1. The Court shall have jurisdiction in respect of war crimes in particular when committed as part of a plan or policy or as part of a large-scale commission of such crimes.

2. For the purpose of this Statute, 'war crimes' means:

(a) Grave breaches of the Geneva Conventions of 12 August 1949, namely, any of the following acts against persons or property protected under the provisions of the relevant Geneva Convention:
(i)   Wilful killing;
(ii)   Torture or inhuman treatment, including biological experiments;
(iii) Wilfully causing great suffering, or serious injury to body or health;
(iv)   Extensive destruction and appropriation of property, not justified by military necessity and carried out unlawfully and wantonly;

(v)   Compelling a prisoner of war or other protected person to serve in the forces of a hostile Power;

(vi)   Wilfully depriving a prisoner of war or other protected person of the rights of fair and regular trial;

(vii)   Unlawful deportation or transfer or unlawful confinement;

(viii) Taking of hostages.

(b) Other serious violations of the laws and customs applicable in international armed conflict, within the established framework of international law, namely, any of the following acts:

(i)   Intentionally directing attacks against the civilian population as such or against individual civilians not taking direct part in hostilities;

(ii)   Intentionally directing attacks against civilian objects, that is, objects which are not military objectives;

(iii)   Intentionally directing attacks against personnel, installations, material, units or vehicles involved in a humanitarian assistance or peacekeeping mission in accordance with the Charter of the United Nations, as long as they are entitled to the protection given to civilians or civilian objects under the international law of armed conflict;

(iv)   Intentionally launching an attack in the knowledge that such attack will cause incidental loss of life or injury to civilians or damage to civilian objects or widespread, long-term and severe damage to the natural environment which would be clearly excessive in relation to the concrete and direct overall military advantage anticipated;

(v)   Attacking or bombarding, by whatever means, towns, villages, dwellings or buildings which are undefended and which are not military objectives;

(vi)   Killing or wounding a combatant who, having laid down his arms or having no longer means of defence, has surrendered at discretion;

(vii)   Making improper use of a flag of truce, of the flag or of the military insignia and uniform of the enemy or of the United Nations, as well as of the distinctive emblems of the Geneva Conventions, resulting in death or serious personal injury;

(viii) The transfer, directly or indirectly, by the Occupying Power of parts of its own civilian population into the territory it occupies, or the deportation or transfer of all or parts of the population of the occupied territory within or outside this territory;

(ix)   Intentionally directing attacks against buildings dedicated to religion, education, art, science or charitable purposes, historic monuments, hospitals and places where the sick and wounded are collected, provided they are not military objectives;

(x)   Subjecting persons who are in the power of an adverse party to physical mutilation or to medical or scientific experiments of any kind which are neither justified by the medical, dental or hospital treatment of the person concerned nor carried out in his or her interest, and which cause death to or seriously endanger the health of such person or persons;

(xi) Killing or wounding treacherously individuals belonging to the hostile nation or army;

(xii) Declaring that no quarter will be given;

(xiii) Destroying or seizing the enemy's property unless such destruction or seizure be imperatively demanded by the necessities of war;

(xiv) Declaring abolished, suspended or inadmissible in a court of law the rights and actions of the nationals of the hostile party;

(xv) Compelling the nationals of the hostile party to take part in the operations of war directed against their own country, even if they were in the belligerent's service before the commencement of the war;

(xvi) Pillaging a town or place, even when taken by assault;

(xvii) Employing poison or poisoned weapons;

(xviii) Employing asphyxiating, poisonous or other gases, and all analogous liquids, materials or devices;

(xix) Employing bullets which expand or flatten easily in the human body, such as bullets with a hard envelope which does not entirely cover the core or is pierced with incisions;

(xx) Employing weapons, projectiles and material and methods of warfare which are of a nature to cause superfluous injury or unnecessary suffering or which are inherently indiscriminate in violation of the international law of armed conflict, provided that such weapons, projectiles and material and methods of warfare are the subject of a comprehensive prohibition and are included in an annex to this Statute, by an amendment in accordance with the relevant provisions set forth in articles 121 and 123;

(xxi) Committing outrages upon personal dignity, in particular humiliating and degrading treatment;

(xxii) Committing rape, sexual slavery, enforced prostitution, forced pregnancy, as defined in article 7, paragraph 2 (f), enforced sterilization, or any other form of sexual violence also constituting a grave breach of the Geneva Conventions;

(xxiii) Utilizing the presence of a civilian or other protected person to render certain points, areas or military forces immune from military operations;

(xxiv) Intentionally directing attacks against buildings, material, medical units and transport, and personnel using the distinctive emblems of the Geneva Conventions in conformity with international law;

(xxv) Intentionally using starvation of civilians as a method of warfare by depriving them of objects indispensable to their survival, including wilfully impeding relief supplies as provided for under the Geneva Conventions;

(xxvi) Conscripting or enlisting children under the age of fifteen years into the national armed forces or using them to participate actively in hostilities.

(c) In the case of an armed conflict not of an international character, serious violations of article 3 common to the four Geneva Conventions of 12 August 1949, namely, any of the following acts committed against persons taking no active part in the hostilities, including members of armed forces who have laid down their arms and those placed *hors de combat* by sickness, wounds, detention or any other cause:

(i) Violence to life and person, in particular murder of all kinds, mutilation, cruel treatment and torture;

(ii) Committing outrages upon personal dignity, in particular humiliating and degrading treatment;

(iii) Taking of hostages;

(iv) The passing of sentences and the carrying out of executions without previous judgment pronounced by a regularly constituted court, affording all judicial guarantees which are generally recognized as indispensable.

(d) Paragraph 2 (c) applies to armed conflicts not of an international character and thus does not apply to situations of internal disturbances and tensions, such as riots, isolated and sporadic acts of violence or other acts of a similar nature.

(e) Other serious violations of the laws and customs applicable in armed conflicts not of an international character, within the established framework of international law, namely, any of the following acts:

(i) Intentionally directing attacks against the civilian population as such or against individual civilians not taking direct part in hostilities;

(ii) Intentionally directing attacks against buildings, material, medical units and transport, and personnel using the distinctive emblems of the Geneva Conventions in conformity with international law;

(iii) Intentionally directing attacks against personnel, installations, material, units or vehicles involved in a humanitarian assistance or peacekeeping mission in accordance with the Charter of the United Nations, as long as they are entitled to the protection given to civilians or civilian objects under the international law of armed conflict;

(iv) Intentionally directing attacks against buildings dedicated to religion, education, art, science or charitable purposes, historic monuments, hospitals and places where the sick and wounded are collected, provided they are not military objectives;

(v) Pillaging a town or place, even when taken by assault;

(vi) Committing rape, sexual slavery, enforced prostitution, forced pregnancy, as defined in article 7, paragraph 2 (f), enforced sterilization, and any other form of sexual violence also constituting a serious violation of article 3 common to the four Geneva Conventions;

(vii) Conscripting or enlisting children under the age of fifteen years into armed forces or groups or using them to participate actively in hostilities;

(viii) Ordering the displacement of the civilian population for reasons related to the conflict, unless the security of the civilians involved or imperative military reasons so demand;

(ix) Killing or wounding treacherously a combatant adversary;

(x) Declaring that no quarter will be given;

(xi) Subjecting persons who are in the power of another party to the conflict to physical mutilation or to medical or scientific experiments of any kind which are neither justified by the medical, dental or hospital treatment of the person concerned nor carried out in his or her interest, and which cause death to or seriously endanger the health of such person or persons;

(xii) Destroying or seizing the property of an adversary unless such destruction or seizure be imperatively demanded by the necessities of the conflict;

(f) Paragraph 2 (e) applies to armed conflicts not of an international character and thus does not apply to situations of internal disturbances and tensions, such as riots, isolated and sporadic acts of violence or other acts of a similar nature. It applies to armed conflicts that take place in the territory of a State when there is protracted armed conflict between governmental authorities and organized armed groups or between such groups.

3. Nothing in paragraph 2 (c) and (d) shall affect the responsibility of a Government to maintain or re-establish law and order in the State or to defend the unity and territorial integrity of the State, by all legitimate means.

Article 9 Elements of Crimes

1. Elements of Crimes shall assist the Court in the interpretation and application of articles 6, 7 and 8. They shall be adopted by a two-thirds majority of the members of the Assembly of States Parties.

2. Amendments to the Elements of Crimes may be proposed by:

(a) Any State Party;

(b) The judges acting by an absolute majority;

(c) The Prosecutor.

Such amendments shall be adopted by a two-thirds majority of the members of the Assembly of States Parties.

3. The Elements of Crimes and amendments thereto shall be consistent with this Statute.

Article 10

Nothing in this Part shall be interpreted as limiting or prejudicing in any way existing or developing rules of international law for purposes other than this Statute.

Article 11 Jurisdiction ratione temporis

1. The Court has jurisdiction only with respect to crimes committed after the entry into force of this Statute.

2. If a State becomes a Party to this Statute after its entry into force, the Court may exercise its jurisdiction only with respect to crimes committed after the entry into force of this Statute for that State, unless that State has made a declaration under article 12, paragraph 3.

Article 12 Preconditions to the exercise of jurisdiction

1. A State which becomes a Party to this Statute thereby accepts the jurisdiction of the Court with respect to the crimes referred to in article 5.

2. In the case of article 13, paragraph (a) or (c), the Court may exercise its jurisdiction if one or more of the following States are Parties to this Statute or have accepted the jurisdiction of the Court in accordance with paragraph 3:

(a) The State on the territory of which the conduct in question occurred or, if the crime was committed on board a vessel or aircraft, the State of registration of that vessel or aircraft;

(b) The State of which the person accused of the crime is a national.

3. If the acceptance of a State which is not a Party to this Statute is required under paragraph 2, that State may, by declaration lodged with the Registrar, accept the exercise of jurisdiction by the Court with respect to the crime in question. The accepting State shall cooperate with the Court without any delay or exception in accordance with Part 9.

Article 13 Exercise of jurisdiction

The Court may exercise its jurisdiction with respect to a crime referred to in article 5 in accordance with the provisions of this Statute if:

(a) A situation in which one or more of such crimes appears to have been committed is referred to the Prosecutor by a State Party in accordance with article 14;

(b) A situation in which one or more of such crimes appears to have been committed is referred to the Prosecutor by the Security Council acting under Chapter VII of the Charter of the United Nations; or

(c) The Prosecutor has initiated an investigation in respect of such a crime in accordance with article 15.

Article 14 Referral of a situation by a State Party

1. A State Party may refer to the Prosecutor a situation in which one or more crimes within the jurisdiction of the Court appear to have been committed requesting the Prosecutor to investigate the situation for the purpose of determining whether one or more specific persons should be charged with the commission of such crimes.

2. As far as possible, a referral shall specify the relevant circumstances and be accompanied by such supporting documentation as is available to the State referring the situation.

Article 15 Prosecutor

1. The Prosecutor may initiate investigations proprio motu on the basis of information on crimes within the jurisdiction of the Court.

2. The Prosecutor shall analyse the seriousness of the information received. For this purpose, he or she may seek additional information from States, organs of the United Nations, intergovernmental or non-governmental organizations, or other reliable sources that he or she deems appropriate, and may receive written or oral testimony at the seat of the Court.

3. If the Prosecutor concludes that there is a reasonable basis to proceed with an investigation, he or she shall submit to the Pre-Trial Chamber a request for authorization of an investigation, together with any supporting material collected. Victims may make representations to the Pre-Trial Chamber, in accordance with the Rules of Procedure and Evidence.

4. If the Pre-Trial Chamber, upon examination of the request and the supporting material, considers that there is a reasonable basis to proceed with an

investigation, and that the case appears to fall within the jurisdiction of the Court, it shall authorize the commencement of the investigation, without prejudice to subsequent determinations by the Court with regard to the jurisdiction and admissibility of a case.

5. The refusal of the Pre-Trial Chamber to authorize the investigation shall not preclude the presentation of a subsequent request by the Prosecutor based on new facts or evidence regarding the same situation.

6. If, after the preliminary examination referred to in paragraphs 1 and 2, the Prosecutor concludes that the information provided does not constitute a reasonable basis for an investigation, he or she shall inform those who provided the information. This shall not preclude the Prosecutor from considering further information submitted to him or her regarding the same situation in the light of new facts or evidence.

Article 16 Deferral of investigation or prosecution

No investigation or prosecution may be commenced or proceeded with under this Statute for a period of 12 months after the Security Council, in a resolution adopted under Chapter VII of the Charter of the United Nations, has requested the Court to that effect; that request may be renewed by the Council under the same conditions.

Article 17 Issues of admissibility

1. Having regard to paragraph 10 of the Preamble and article 1, the Court shall determine that a case is inadmissible where:

(a) The case is being investigated or prosecuted by a State which has jurisdiction over it, unless the State is unwilling or unable genuinely to carry out the investigation or prosecution;

(b) The case has been investigated by a State which has jurisdiction over it and the State has decided not to prosecute the person concerned, unless the decision resulted from the unwillingness or inability of the State genuinely to prosecute;

(c) The person concerned has already been tried for conduct which is the subject of the complaint, and a trial by the Court is not permitted under article 20, paragraph 3;

(d) The case is not of sufficient gravity to justify further action by the Court.

2. In order to determine unwillingness in a particular case, the Court shall consider, having regard to the principles of due process recognized by international law, whether one or more of the following exist, as applicable:

(a) The proceedings were or are being undertaken or the national decision was made for the purpose of shielding the person concerned from criminal responsibility for crimes within the jurisdiction of the Court referred to in article 5;

(b) There has been an unjustified delay in the proceedings which in the circumstances is inconsistent with an intent to bring the person concerned to justice;

(c) The proceedings were not or are not being conducted independently or impartially, and they were or are being conducted in a manner which, in the circumstances, is inconsistent with an intent to bring the person concerned to justice.

3. In order to determine inability in a particular case, the Court shall consider whether, due to a total or substantial collapse or unavailability of its national judicial system, the State is unable to obtain the accused or the necessary evidence and testimony or otherwise unable to carry out its proceedings.

Article 18 Preliminary rulings regarding admissibility

1. When a situation has been referred to the Court pursuant to article 13 (a) and the Prosecutor has determined that there would be a reasonable basis to commence an investigation, or the Prosecutor initiates an investigation pursuant to articles 13 (c) and 15, the Prosecutor shall notify all States Parties and those States which, taking into account the information available, would normally exercise jurisdiction over the crimes concerned. The Prosecutor may notify such States on a confidential basis and, where the Prosecutor believes it necessary to protect persons, prevent destruction of evidence or prevent the absconding of persons, may limit the scope of the information provided to States.

2. Within one month of receipt of that notice, a State may inform the Court that it is investigating or has investigated its nationals or others within its jurisdiction with respect to criminal acts which may constitute crimes referred to in article 5 and which relate to the information provided in the notification to States. At the request of that State, the Prosecutor shall defer to the State's investigation of those persons unless the Pre-Trial Chamber, on the application of the Prosecutor, decides to authorize the investigation.

3. The Prosecutor's deferral to a State's investigation shall be open to review by the Prosecutor six months after the date of deferral or at any time when there has been a significant change of circumstances based on the State's unwillingness or inability genuinely to carry out the investigation.

4. The State concerned or the Prosecutor may appeal to the Appeals Chamber against a ruling of the Pre-Trial Chamber, in accordance with article 82. The appeal may be heard on an expedited basis.

5. When the Prosecutor has deferred an investigation in accordance with paragraph 2, the Prosecutor may request that the State concerned periodically inform the Prosecutor of the progress of its investigations and any subsequent prosecutions. States Parties shall respond to such requests without undue delay.

6. Pending a ruling by the Pre-Trial Chamber, or at any time when the Prosecutor has deferred an investigation under this article, the Prosecutor may, on an exceptional basis, seek authority from the Pre-Trial Chamber to pursue necessary investigative steps for the purpose of preserving evidence where there is a unique opportunity to obtain important evidence or there is a significant risk that such evidence may not be subsequently available.

7. A State which has challenged a ruling of the Pre-Trial Chamber under this article may challenge the admissibility of a case under article 19 on the grounds of additional significant facts or significant change of circumstances.

Article 19 Challenges to the jurisdiction of the Court or the admissibility of a case

1. The Court shall satisfy itself that it has jurisdiction in any case brought before it. The Court may, on its own motion, determine the admissibility of a case in accordance with article 17.

2. Challenges to the admissibility of a case on the grounds referred to in article 17 or challenges to the jurisdiction of the Court may be made by:

(a) An accused or a person for whom a warrant of arrest or a summons to appear has been issued under article 58;

(b) A State which has jurisdiction over a case, on the ground that it is investigating or prosecuting the case or has investigated or prosecuted; or

(c) A State from which acceptance of jurisdiction is required under article 12.

3. The Prosecutor may seek a ruling from the Court regarding a question of jurisdiction or admissibility. In proceedings with respect to jurisdiction or admissibility, those who have referred the situation under article 13, as well as victims, may also submit observations to the Court.

4. The admissibility of a case or the jurisdiction of the Court may be challenged only once by any person or State referred to in paragraph 2. The challenge shall take place prior to or at the commencement of the trial. In

exceptional circumstances, the Court may grant leave for a challenge to be brought more than once or at a time later than the commencement of the trial. Challenges to the admissibility of a case, at the commencement of a trial, or subsequently with the leave of the Court, may be based only on article 17, paragraph 1 (c).

5. A State referred to in paragraph 2 (b) and (c) shall make a challenge at the earliest opportunity.

6. Prior to the confirmation of the charges, challenges to the admissibility of a case or challenges to the jurisdiction of the Court shall be referred to the Pre-Trial Chamber. After confirmation of the charges, they shall be referred to the Trial Chamber. Decisions with respect to jurisdiction or admissibility may be appealed to the Appeals Chamber in accordance with article 82.

7. If a challenge is made by a State referred to in paragraph 2 (b) or (c), the Prosecutor shall suspend the investigation until such time as the Court makes a determination in accordance with article 17.

8. Pending a ruling by the Court, the Prosecutor may seek authority from the Court:

(a) To pursue necessary investigative steps of the kind referred to in article 18, paragraph 6;

(b) To take a statement or testimony from a witness or complete the collection and examination of evidence which had begun prior to the making of the challenge; and

(c) In cooperation with the relevant States, to prevent the absconding of persons in respect of whom the Prosecutor has already requested a warrant of arrest under article 58.

9. The making of a challenge shall not affect the validity of any act performed by the Prosecutor or any order or warrant issued by the Court prior to the making of the challenge.

10. If the Court has decided that a case is inadmissible under article 17, the Prosecutor may submit a request for a review of the decision when he or she is fully satisfied that new facts have arisen which negate the basis on which the case had previously been found inadmissible under article 17.

11. If the Prosecutor, having regard to the matters referred to in article 17, defers an investigation, the Prosecutor may request that the relevant State make available to the Prosecutor information on the proceedings. That information shall, at the request of the State concerned, be confidential. If the Prosecutor thereafter decides to proceed with an investigation, he or she shall notify the State in respect of the proceedings of which deferral has taken place.

Article 20 Ne bis in idem

1. Except as provided in this Statute, no person shall be tried before the Court with respect to conduct which formed the basis of crimes for which the person has been convicted or acquitted by the Court.

2. No person shall be tried by another court for a crime referred to in article 5 for which that person has already been convicted or acquitted by the Court.

3. No person who has been tried by another court for conduct also proscribed under article 6, 7 or 8 shall be tried by the Court with respect to the same conduct unless the proceedings in the other court:

(a) Were for the purpose of shielding the person concerned from criminal responsibility for crimes within the jurisdiction of the Court; or

(b) Otherwise were not conducted independently or impartially in accordance with the norms of due process recognized by international law and were conducted in a manner which, in the circumstances, was inconsistent with an intent to bring the person concerned to justice.

Article 21 Applicable law

1. The Court shall apply:

(a) In the first place, this Statute, Elements of Crimes and its Rules of Procedure and Evidence;

(b) In the second place, where appropriate, applicable treaties and the principles and rules of international law, including the established principles of the international law of armed conflict;

(c) Failing that, general principles of law derived by the Court from national laws of legal systems of the world including, as appropriate, the national laws of States that would normally exercise jurisdiction over the crime, provided that those principles are not inconsistent with this Statute and with international law and internationally recognized norms and standards.

2. The Court may apply principles and rules of law as interpreted in its previous decisions.

3. The application and interpretation of law pursuant to this article must be consistent with internationally recognized human rights, and be without any adverse distinction founded on grounds such as gender as defined in article 7, paragraph 3, age, race, colour, language, religion or belief, political or other opinion, national, ethnic or social origin, wealth, birth or other status.

Part 3 General principles of criminal law

Article 22 Nullum crimen sine lege

1. A person shall not be criminally responsible under this Statute unless the conduct in question constitutes, at the time it takes place, a crime within the jurisdiction of the Court.

2. The definition of a crime shall be strictly construed and shall not be extended by analogy. In case of ambiguity, the definition shall be interpreted in favour of the person being investigated, prosecuted or convicted.

3. This article shall not affect the characterization of any conduct as criminal under international law independently of this Statute.

Article 23 Nulla poena sine lege

A person convicted by the Court may be punished only in accordance with this Statute.

Article 24 Non-retroactivity ratione personae

1. No person shall be criminally responsible under this Statute for conduct prior to the entry into force of the Statute.

2. In the event of a change in the law applicable to a given case prior to a final judgment, the law more favourable to the person being investigated, prosecuted or convicted shall apply.

Article 25 Individual criminal responsibility

1. The Court shall have jurisdiction over natural persons pursuant to this Statute.

2. A person who commits a crime within the jurisdiction of the Court shall be individually responsible and liable for punishment in accordance with this Statute.

3. In accordance with this Statute, a person shall be criminally responsible and liable for punishment for a crime within the jurisdiction of the Court if that person:

(a) Commits such a crime, whether as an individual, jointly with another or through another person, regardless of whether that other person is criminally responsible;

(b) Orders, solicits or induces the commission of such a crime which in fact occurs or is attempted;

(c) For the purpose of facilitating the commission of such a crime, aids, abets or otherwise assists in its commission or its attempted commission, including providing the means for its commission;

(d) In any other way contributes to the commission or attempted commission of such a crime by a group of persons acting with a common purpose. Such contribution shall be intentional and shall either:

    (i) Be made with the aim of furthering the criminal activity or criminal purpose of the group, where such activity or purpose involves the commission of a crime within the jurisdiction of the Court; or

    (ii) Be made in the knowledge of the intention of the group to commit the crime;

(e) In respect of the crime of genocide, directly and publicly incites others to commit genocide;

(f) Attempts to commit such a crime by taking action that commences its execution by means of a substantial step, but the crime does not occur because of circumstances independent of the person's intentions. However, a person who abandons the effort to commit the crime or otherwise prevents the completion of the crime shall not be liable for punishment under this Statute for the attempt to commit that crime if that person completely and voluntarily gave up the criminal purpose.

4. No provision in this Statute relating to individual criminal responsibility shall affect the responsibility of States under international law.

Article 26 Exclusion of jurisdiction over persons under eighteen

The Court shall have no jurisdiction over any person who was under the age of 18 at the time of the alleged commission of a crime.

Article 27 Irrelevance of official capacity

1. This Statute shall apply equally to all persons without any distinction based on official capacity. In particular, official capacity as a Head of State or Government, a member of a Government or parliament, an elected representative or a government official shall in no case exempt a person from criminal responsibility under this Statute, nor shall it, in and of itself, constitute a ground for reduction of sentence.

2. Immunities or special procedural rules which may attach to the official capacity of a person, whether under national or international law, shall not bar the Court from exercising its jurisdiction over such a person.

Article 28 Responsibility of commanders and other superiors

In addition to other grounds of criminal responsibility under this Statute for crimes within the jurisdiction of the Court:

(a) A military commander or person effectively acting as a military commander shall be criminally responsible for crimes within the jurisdiction of the Court committed by forces under his or her effective command and control, or effective authority and control as the case may be, as a result of his or her failure to exercise control properly over such forces, where:

   (i) That military commander or person either knew or, owing to the circumstances at the time, should have known that the forces were committing or about to commit such crimes; and

   (ii) That military commander or person failed to take all necessary and reasonable measures within his or her power to prevent or repress their commission or to submit the matter to the competent authorities for investigation and prosecution.

(b) With respect to superior and subordinate relationships not described in paragraph (a), a superior shall be criminally responsible for crimes within the jurisdiction of the Court committed by subordinates under his or her effective authority and control, as a result of his or her failure to exercise control properly over such subordinates, where:

   (i) The superior either knew, or consciously disregarded information which clearly indicated, that the subordinates were committing or about to commit such crimes;

   (ii) The crimes concerned activities that were within the effective responsibility and control of the superior; and

   (iii) The superior failed to take all necessary and reasonable measures within his or her power to prevent or repress their commission or to submit the matter to the competent authorities for investigation and prosecution.

Article 29 Non-applicability of statute of limitations

The crimes within the jurisdiction of the Court shall not be subject to any statute of limitations.

Article 30 Mental element

1. Unless otherwise provided, a person shall be criminally responsible and liable for punishment for a crime within the jurisdiction of the Court only if the material elements are committed with intent and knowledge.

2. For the purposes of this article, a person has intent where:

(a) In relation to conduct, that person means to engage in the conduct;

(b) In relation to a consequence, that person means to cause that consequence or is aware that it will occur in the ordinary course of events.

3. For the purposes of this article, 'knowledge' means awareness that a circumstance exists or a consequence will occur in the ordinary course of events. 'Know' and 'knowingly' shall be construed accordingly.

Article 31 Grounds for excluding criminal responsibility

1. In addition to other grounds for excluding criminal responsibility provided for in this Statute, a person shall not be criminally responsible if, at the time of that person's conduct:

(a) The person suffers from a mental disease or defect that destroys that person's capacity to appreciate the unlawfulness or nature of his or her conduct, or capacity to control his or her conduct to conform to the requirements of law;

(b) The person is in a state of intoxication that destroys that person's capacity to appreciate the unlawfulness or nature of his or her conduct, or capacity to control his or her conduct to conform to the requirements of law, unless the person has become voluntarily intoxicated under such circumstances that the person knew, or disregarded the risk, that, as a result of the intoxication, he or she was likely to engage in conduct constituting a crime within the jurisdiction of the Court;

(c) The person acts reasonably to defend himself or herself or another person or, in the case of war crimes, property which is essential for the survival of the person or another person or property which is essential for accomplishing a military mission, against an imminent and unlawful use of force in a manner proportionate to the degree of danger to the person or the other person or property protected. The fact that the person was involved in a defensive operation conducted by forces shall not in itself constitute a ground for excluding criminal responsibility under this subparagraph;

(d) The conduct which is alleged to constitute a crime within the jurisdiction of the Court has been caused by duress resulting from a threat of imminent death or of continuing or imminent serious bodily harm against that person or another person, and the person acts necessarily and reasonably to avoid this threat, provided that the person does not intend to cause a greater harm than the one sought to be avoided. Such a threat may either be:

(i)   Made by other persons; or

(ii)   Constituted by other circumstances beyond that person's control.

2. The Court shall determine the applicability of the grounds for excluding criminal responsibility provided for in this Statute to the case before it.

3. At trial, the Court may consider a ground for excluding criminal responsibility other than those referred to in paragraph 1 where such a ground is derived from applicable law as set forth in article 21. The procedures relating to the consideration of such a ground shall be provided for in the Rules of Procedure and Evidence.

Article 32 Mistake of fact or mistake of law

1. A mistake of fact shall be a ground for excluding criminal responsibility only if it negates the mental element required by the crime.

2. A mistake of law as to whether a particular type of conduct is a crime within the jurisdiction of the Court shall not be a ground for excluding criminal responsibility. A mistake of law may, however, be a ground for excluding criminal responsibility if it negates the mental element required by such a crime, or as provided for in article 33.

Article 33 Superior orders and prescription of law

1. The fact that a crime within the jurisdiction of the Court has been committed by a person pursuant to an order of a Government or of a superior, whether military or civilian, shall not relieve that person of criminal responsibility unless:

(a) The person was under a legal obligation to obey orders of the Government or the superior in question;
(b) The person did not know that the order was unlawful; and
(c) The order was not manifestly unlawful.

2. For the purposes of this article, orders to commit genocide or crimes against humanity are manifestly unlawful.

Part 4 Composition and administration of the court

Article 34 Organs of the Court

The Court shall be composed of the following organs:

(a) The Presidency;
(b) An Appeals Division, a Trial Division and a Pre-Trial Division;
(c) The Office of the Prosecutor;
(d) The Registry.

Article 35 Service of judges

1. All judges shall be elected as full-time members of the Court and shall be available to serve on that basis from the commencement of their terms of office.

2. The judges composing the Presidency shall serve on a full-time basis as soon as they are elected.

3. The Presidency may, on the basis of the workload of the Court and in consultation with its members, decide from time to time to what extent the remaining judges shall be required to serve on a full-time basis. Any such arrangement shall be without prejudice to the provisions of article 40.

4. The financial arrangements for judges not required to serve on a full-time basis shall be made in accordance with article 49.

Article 36 Qualifications, nomination and election of judges

1. Subject to the provisions of paragraph 2, there shall be 18 judges of the Court.

2.

(a) The Presidency, acting on behalf of the Court, may propose an increase in the number of judges specified in paragraph 1, indicating the reasons why this is considered necessary and appropriate. The Registrar shall promptly circulate any such proposal to all States Parties.

(b) Any such proposal shall then be considered at a meeting of the Assembly of States Parties to be convened in accordance with article 112. The proposal shall be considered adopted if approved at the meeting by a vote of two thirds of the members of the Assembly of States Parties and shall enter into force at such time as decided by the Assembly of States Parties.

(c)

    (i)   Once a proposal for an increase in the number of judges has been adopted under subparagraph (b), the election of the additional judges shall take place at the next session of the Assembly of States Parties in accordance with paragraphs 3 to 8, and article 37, paragraph 2;

    (ii)   Once a proposal for an increase in the number of judges has been adopted and brought into effect under subparagraphs (b) and (c) (i), it shall be open to the Presidency at any time thereafter, if the workload of the Court justifies it, to propose a reduction in the number of judges, provided that the number of judges shall not be reduced below that specified in paragraph 1. The proposal shall be dealt with in accordance with the procedure laid down in subparagraphs (a) and (b). In the event that the proposal is adopted, the number of judges shall be progressively decreased as the terms of office of serving judges expire, until the necessary number has been reached.

3.

(a) The judges shall be chosen from among persons of high moral character, impartiality and integrity who possess the qualifications required in their respective States for appointment to the highest judicial offices.

(b) Every candidate for election to the Court shall:

    (i)   Have established competence in criminal law and procedure, and the necessary relevant experience, whether as judge, prosecutor, advocate or in other similar capacity, in criminal proceedings; or

    (ii)   Have established competence in relevant areas of international law such as international humanitarian law and the law of human rights, and extensive experience in a professional legal capacity which is of relevance to the judicial work of the Court;

(c) Every candidate for election to the Court shall have an excellent knowledge of and be fluent in at least one of the working languages of the Court.

4.

(a) Nominations of candidates for election to the Court may be made by any State Party to this Statute, and shall be made either:

    (i)   By the procedure for the nomination of candidates for appointment to the highest judicial offices in the State in question; or

    (ii)   By the procedure provided for the nomination of candidates for the International Court of Justice in the Statute of that Court.

Nominations shall be accompanied by a statement in the necessary detail specifying how the candidate fulfils the requirements of paragraph 3.

(b) Each State Party may put forward one candidate for any given election who need not necessarily be a national of that State Party but shall in any case be a national of a State Party.

(c) The Assembly of States Parties may decide to establish, if appropriate, an Advisory Committee on nominations. In that event, the Committee's composition and mandate shall be established by the Assembly of States Parties.

5. For the purposes of the election, there shall be two lists of candidates:

List A containing the names of candidates with the qualifications specified in paragraph 3 (b) (i); and

List B containing the names of candidates with the qualifications specified in paragraph 3 (b) (ii).

A candidate with sufficient qualifications for both lists may choose on which list to appear. At the first election to the Court, at least nine judges shall be elected from list A and at least five judges from list B. Subsequent elections shall be so organized as to maintain the equivalent proportion on the Court of judges qualified on the two lists.

6.

(a) The judges shall be elected by secret ballot at a meeting of the Assembly of States Parties convened for that purpose under article 112. Subject to paragraph 7, the persons elected to the Court shall be the 18 candidates who obtain the highest number of votes and a two-thirds majority of the States Parties present and voting.

(b) In the event that a sufficient number of judges is not elected on the first ballot, successive ballots shall be held in accordance with the procedures laid down in subparagraph (a) until the remaining places have been filled.

7. No two judges may be nationals of the same State. A person who, for the purposes of membership of the Court, could be regarded as a national of more than one State shall be deemed to be a national of the State in which that person ordinarily exercises civil and political rights.

8.

(a) The States Parties shall, in the selection of judges, take into account the need, within the membership of the Court, for:
(i)   The representation of the principal legal systems of the world;
(ii) Equitable geographical representation; and
(iii) A fair representation of female and male judges.

(b) States Parties shall also take into account the need to include judges with legal expertise on specific issues, including, but not limited to, violence against women or children.

9.

(a) Subject to subparagraph (b), judges shall hold office for a term of nine years and, subject to subparagraph (c) and to article 37, paragraph 2, shall not be eligible for re-election.

(b) At the first election, one third of the judges elected shall be selected by lot to serve for a term of three years; one third of the judges elected shall be selected by lot to serve for a term of six years; and the remainder shall serve for a term of nine years.

(c) A judge who is selected to serve for a term of three years under subparagraph (b) shall be eligible for re-election for a full term.

10. Notwithstanding paragraph 9, a judge assigned to a Trial or Appeals Chamber in accordance with article 39 shall continue in office to complete any trial or appeal the hearing of which has already commenced before that Chamber.

Article 37 Judicial vacancies

1. In the event of a vacancy, an election shall be held in accordance with article 36 to fill the vacancy.

2. A judge elected to fill a vacancy shall serve for the remainder of the predecessor's term and, if that period is three years or less, shall be eligible for re-election for a full term under article 36.

Article 38 The Presidency

1. The President and the First and Second Vice-Presidents shall be elected by an absolute majority of the judges. They shall each serve for a term of three years or until the end of their respective terms of office as judges, whichever expires earlier. They shall be eligible for re-election once.

2. The First Vice-President shall act in place of the President in the event that the President is unavailable or disqualified. The Second Vice-President shall act in place of the President in the event that both the President and the First Vice-President are unavailable or disqualified.

3. The President, together with the First and Second Vice-Presidents, shall constitute the Presidency, which shall be responsible for:

(a) The proper administration of the Court, with the exception of the Office of the Prosecutor; and

(b) The other functions conferred upon it in accordance with this Statute.

4. In discharging its responsibility under paragraph 3 (a), the Presidency shall coordinate with and seek the concurrence of the Prosecutor on all matters of mutual concern.

Article 39 Chambers

1. As soon as possible after the election of the judges, the Court shall organize itself into the divisions specified in article 34, paragraph (b). The Appeals Division shall be composed of the President and four other judges, the Trial Division of not less than six judges and the Pre-Trial Division of not less than

six judges. The assignment of judges to divisions shall be based on the nature of the functions to be performed by each division and the qualifications and experience of the judges elected to the Court, in such a way that each division shall contain an appropriate combination of expertise in criminal law and procedure and in international law. The Trial and Pre-Trial Divisions shall be composed predominantly of judges with criminal trial experience.

2.

(a) The judicial functions of the Court shall be carried out in each division by Chambers.

(b)

(i) The Appeals Chamber shall be composed of all the judges of the Appeals Division;

(ii) The functions of the Trial Chamber shall be carried out by three judges of the Trial Division;

(iii) The functions of the Pre-Trial Chamber shall be carried out either by three judges of the Pre-Trial Division or by a single judge of that division in accordance with this Statute and the Rules of Procedure and Evidence;

(c) Nothing in this paragraph shall preclude the simultaneous constitution of more than one Trial Chamber or Pre-Trial Chamber when the efficient management of the Court's workload so requires.

3.

(a) Judges assigned to the Trial and Pre-Trial Divisions shall serve in those divisions for a period of three years, and thereafter until the completion of any case the hearing of which has already commenced in the division concerned.

(b) Judges assigned to the Appeals Division shall serve in that division for their entire term of office.

4. Judges assigned to the Appeals Division shall serve only in that division. Nothing in this article shall, however, preclude the temporary attachment of judges from the Trial Division to the Pre-Trial Division or vice versa, if the Presidency considers that the efficient management of the Court's workload so requires, provided that under no circumstances shall a judge who has participated in the pre-trial phase of a case be eligible to sit on the Trial Chamber hearing that case.

Article 40 Independence of the judges

1. The judges shall be independent in the performance of their functions.

2. Judges shall not engage in any activity which is likely to interfere with their judicial functions or to affect confidence in their independence.

3. Judges required to serve on a full-time basis at the seat of the Court shall not engage in any other occupation of a professional nature.

4. Any question regarding the application of paragraphs 2 and 3 shall be decided by an absolute majority of the judges. Where any such question concerns an individual judge, that judge shall not take part in the decision.

Article 41 Excusing and disqualification of judges

1. The Presidency may, at the request of a judge, excuse that judge from the exercise of a function under this Statute, in accordance with the Rules of Procedure and Evidence.

2.

(a) A judge shall not participate in any case in which his or her impartiality might reasonably be doubted on any ground. A judge shall be disqualified from a case in accordance with this paragraph if, *inter alia*, that judge has previously been involved in any capacity in that case before the Court or in a related criminal case at the national level involving the person being investigated or prosecuted. A judge shall also be disqualified on such other grounds as may be provided for in the Rules of Procedure and Evidence.

(b) The Prosecutor or the person being investigated or prosecuted may request the disqualification of a judge under this paragraph.

(c) Any question as to the disqualification of a judge shall be decided by an absolute majority of the judges. The challenged judge shall be entitled to present his or her comments on the matter, but shall not take part in the decision.

Article 42 The Office of the Prosecutor

1. The Office of the Prosecutor shall act independently as a separate organ of the Court. It shall be responsible for receiving referrals and any substantiated information on crimes within the jurisdiction of the Court, for examining them and for conducting investigations and prosecutions before the Court. A member of the Office shall not seek or act on instructions from any external source.

2. The Office shall be headed by the Prosecutor. The Prosecutor shall have full authority over the management and administration of the Office, including the staff, facilities and other resources thereof. The Prosecutor shall be assisted by one or more Deputy Prosecutors, who shall be entitled to carry out any of the acts required of the Prosecutor under this Statute. The Prosecutor and the Deputy Prosecutors shall be of different nationalities. They shall serve on a full-time basis.

3. The Prosecutor and the Deputy Prosecutors shall be persons of high moral character, be highly competent in and have extensive practical experience in the prosecution or trial of criminal cases. They shall have an excellent knowledge of and be fluent in at least one of the working languages of the Court.

4. The Prosecutor shall be elected by secret ballot by an absolute majority of the members of the Assembly of States Parties. The Deputy Prosecutors shall be elected in the same way from a list of candidates provided by the Prosecutor. The Prosecutor shall nominate three candidates for each position of Deputy Prosecutor to be filled. Unless a shorter term is decided upon at the time of their election, the Prosecutor and the Deputy Prosecutors shall hold office for a term of nine years and shall not be eligible for re-election.

5. Neither the Prosecutor nor a Deputy Prosecutor shall engage in any activity which is likely to interfere with his or her prosecutorial functions or to affect confidence in his or her independence. They shall not engage in any other occupation of a professional nature.

6. The Presidency may excuse the Prosecutor or a Deputy Prosecutor, at his or her request, from acting in a particular case.

7. Neither the Prosecutor nor a Deputy Prosecutor shall participate in any matter in which their impartiality might reasonably be doubted on any ground. They shall be disqualified from a case in accordance with this paragraph if, *inter alia*, they have previously been involved in any capacity in that case before the Court or in a related criminal case at the national level involving the person being investigated or prosecuted.

8. Any question as to the disqualification of the Prosecutor or a Deputy Prosecutor shall be decided by the Appeals Chamber.

(a) The person being investigated or prosecuted may at any time request the disqualification of the Prosecutor or a Deputy Prosecutor on the grounds set out in this article;

(b) The Prosecutor or the Deputy Prosecutor, as appropriate, shall be entitled to present his or her comments on the matter;

9. The Prosecutor shall appoint advisers with legal expertise on specific issues, including, but not limited to, sexual and gender violence and violence against children.

Article 43 *The Registry*

1. The Registry shall be responsible for the non-judicial aspects of the administration and servicing of the Court, without prejudice to the functions and powers of the Prosecutor in accordance with article 42.

2. The Registry shall be headed by the Registrar, who shall be the principal administrative officer of the Court. The Registrar shall exercise his or her functions under the authority of the President of the Court.

3. The Registrar and the Deputy Registrar shall be persons of high moral character, be highly competent and have an excellent knowledge of and be fluent in at least one of the working languages of the Court.

4. The judges shall elect the Registrar by an absolute majority by secret ballot, taking into account any recommendation by the Assembly of States Parties. If the need arises and upon the recommendation of the Registrar, the judges shall elect, in the same manner, a Deputy Registrar.

5. The Registrar shall hold office for a term of five years, shall be eligible for re-election once and shall serve on a full-time basis. The Deputy Registrar shall hold office for a term of five years or such shorter term as may be decided upon by an absolute majority of the judges, and may be elected on the basis that the Deputy Registrar shall be called upon to serve as required.

6. The Registrar shall set up a Victims and Witnesses Unit within the Registry. This Unit shall provide, in consultation with the Office of the Prosecutor, protective measures and security arrangements, counselling and other appropriate assistance for witnesses, victims who appear before the Court, and others who are at risk on account of testimony given by such witnesses. The Unit shall include staff with expertise in trauma, including trauma related to crimes of sexual violence.

Article 44 Staff

1. The Prosecutor and the Registrar shall appoint such qualified staff as may be required to their respective offices. In the case of the Prosecutor, this shall include the appointment of investigators.

2. In the employment of staff, the Prosecutor and the Registrar shall ensure the highest standards of efficiency, competency and integrity, and shall have regard, *mutatis mutandis*, to the criteria set forth in article 36, paragraph 8.

3. The Registrar, with the agreement of the Presidency and the Prosecutor, shall propose Staff Regulations which include the terms and conditions upon which the staff of the Court shall be appointed, remunerated and dismissed. The Staff Regulations shall be approved by the Assembly of States Parties.

4. The Court may, in exceptional circumstances, employ the expertise of gratis personnel offered by States Parties, intergovernmental organizations or non-governmental organizations to assist with the work of any of the organs of the Court. The Prosecutor may accept any such offer on behalf of the Office

of the Prosecutor. Such gratis personnel shall be employed in accordance with guidelines to be established by the Assembly of States Parties.

Article 45 Solemn undertaking

Before taking up their respective duties under this Statute, the judges, the Prosecutor, the Deputy Prosecutors, the Registrar and the Deputy Registrar shall each make a solemn undertaking in open court to exercise his or her respective functions impartially and conscientiously.

Article 46 Removal from office

1. A judge, the Prosecutor, a Deputy Prosecutor, the Registrar or the Deputy Registrar shall be removed from office if a decision to this effect is made in accordance with paragraph 2, in cases where that person:

(a) Is found to have committed serious misconduct or a serious breach of his or her duties under this Statute, as provided for in the Rules of Procedure and Evidence; or
(b) Is unable to exercise the functions required by this Statute.

2. A decision as to the removal from office of a judge, the Prosecutor or a Deputy Prosecutor under paragraph 1 shall be made by the Assembly of States Parties, by secret ballot:

(a) In the case of a judge, by a two-thirds majority of the States Parties upon a recommendation adopted by a two-thirds majority of the other judges;
(b) In the case of the Prosecutor, by an absolute majority of the States Parties;
(c) In the case of a Deputy Prosecutor, by an absolute majority of the States Parties upon the recommendation of the Prosecutor.

3. A decision as to the removal from office of the Registrar or Deputy Registrar shall be made by an absolute majority of the judges.

4. A judge, Prosecutor, Deputy Prosecutor, Registrar or Deputy Registrar whose conduct or ability to exercise the functions of the office as required by this Statute is challenged under this article shall have full opportunity to present and receive evidence and to make submissions in accordance with the Rules of Procedure and Evidence. The person in question shall not otherwise participate in the consideration of the matter.

Article 47 Disciplinary measures

A judge, Prosecutor, Deputy Prosecutor, Registrar or Deputy Registrar who has committed misconduct of a less serious nature than that set out in article 46, paragraph 1, shall be subject to disciplinary measures, in accordance with the Rules of Procedure and Evidence.

Article 48 Privileges and immunities

1. The Court shall enjoy in the territory of each State Party such privileges and immunities as are necessary for the fulfilment of its purposes.

2. The judges, the Prosecutor, the Deputy Prosecutors and the Registrar shall, when engaged on or with respect to the business of the Court, enjoy the same privileges and immunities as are accorded to heads of diplomatic missions and shall, after the expiry of their terms of office, continue to be accorded immunity from legal process of every kind in respect of words spoken or written and acts performed by them in their official capacity.

3. The Deputy Registrar, the staff of the Office of the Prosecutor and the staff of the Registry shall enjoy the privileges and immunities and facilities necessary for the performance of their functions, in accordance with the agreement on the privileges and immunities of the Court.

4. Counsel, experts, witnesses or any other person required to be present at the seat of the Court shall be accorded such treatment as is necessary for the proper functioning of the Court, in accordance with the agreement on the privileges and immunities of the Court.

5. The privileges and immunities of:

(a) A judge or the Prosecutor may be waived by an absolute majority of the judges;
(b) The Registrar may be waived by the Presidency;
(c) The Deputy Prosecutors and staff of the Office of the Prosecutor may be waived by the Prosecutor;
(d) The Deputy Registrar and staff of the Registry may be waived by the Registrar.

Article 49 Salaries, allowances and expenses

The judges, the Prosecutor, the Deputy Prosecutors, the Registrar and the Deputy Registrar shall receive such salaries, allowances and expenses as may be decided upon by the Assembly of States Parties. These salaries and allowances shall not be reduced during their terms of office.

Article 50 Official and working languages

1. The official languages of the Court shall be Arabic, Chinese, English, French, Russian and Spanish. The judgments of the Court, as well as other decisions resolving fundamental issues before the Court, shall be published in the official languages. The Presidency shall, in accordance with the criteria established by the Rules of Procedure and Evidence, determine which decisions may be considered as resolving fundamental issues for the purposes of this paragraph.

2. The working languages of the Court shall be English and French. The Rules of Procedure and Evidence shall determine the cases in which other official languages may be used as working languages.

3. At the request of any party to a proceeding or a State allowed to intervene in a proceeding, the Court shall authorize a language other than English or French to be used by such a party or State, provided that the Court considers such authorization to be adequately justified.

Article 51 Rules of Procedure and Evidence

1. The Rules of Procedure and Evidence shall enter into force upon adoption by a two-thirds majority of the members of the Assembly of States Parties.

2. Amendments to the Rules of Procedure and Evidence may be proposed by:

(a) Any State Party;
(b) The judges acting by an absolute majority; or
(c) The Prosecutor.

Such amendments shall enter into force upon adoption by a two-thirds majority of the members of the Assembly of States Parties.

3. After the adoption of the Rules of Procedure and Evidence, in urgent cases where the Rules do not provide for a specific situation before the Court, the judges may, by a two-thirds majority, draw up provisional Rules to be applied until adopted, amended or rejected at the next ordinary or special session of the Assembly of States Parties.

4. The Rules of Procedure and Evidence, amendments thereto and any provisional Rule shall be consistent with this Statute. Amendments to the Rules of Procedure and Evidence as well as provisional Rules shall not be applied retroactively to the detriment of the person who is being investigated or prosecuted or who has been convicted.

5. In the event of conflict between the Statute and the Rules of Procedure and Evidence, the Statute shall prevail.

Article 52 Regulations of the Court

1. The judges shall, in accordance with this Statute and the Rules of Procedure and Evidence, adopt, by an absolute majority, the Regulations of the Court necessary for its routine functioning.

2. The Prosecutor and the Registrar shall be consulted in the elaboration of the Regulations and any amendments thereto.

3. The Regulations and any amendments thereto shall take effect upon adoption unless otherwise decided by the judges. Immediately upon adoption, they shall be circulated to States Parties for comments. If within six months there are no objections from a majority of States Parties, they shall remain in force.

Part 5 Investigation and prosecution

Article 53 Initiation of an investigation

1. The Prosecutor shall, having evaluated the information made available to him or her, initiate an investigation unless he or she determines that there is no reasonable basis to proceed under this Statute. In deciding whether to initiate an investigation, the Prosecutor shall consider whether:

(a) The information available to the Prosecutor provides a reasonable basis to believe that a crime within the jurisdiction of the Court has been or is being committed;
(b) The case is or would be admissible under article 17; and
(c) Taking into account the gravity of the crime and the interests of victims, there are nonetheless substantial reasons to believe that an investigation would not serve the interests of justice.

If the Prosecutor determines that there is no reasonable basis to proceed and his or her determination is based solely on subparagraph (c) above, he or she shall inform the Pre-Trial Chamber.

2. If, upon investigation, the Prosecutor concludes that there is not a sufficient basis for a prosecution because:

(a) There is not a sufficient legal or factual basis to seek a warrant or summons under article 58;
(b) The case is inadmissible under article 17; or

(c) A prosecution is not in the interests of justice, taking into account all the circumstances, including the gravity of the crime, the interests of victims and the age or infirmity of the alleged perpetrator, and his or her role in the alleged crime

The Prosecutor shall inform the Pre-Trial Chamber and the State making a referral under article 14 or the Security Council in a case under article 13, paragraph (b), of his or her conclusion and the reasons for the conclusion.

3.

(a) At the request of the State making a referral under article 14 or the Security Council under article 13, paragraph (b), the Pre-Trial Chamber may review a decision of the Prosecutor under paragraph 1 or 2 not to proceed and may request the Prosecutor to reconsider that decision.

(b) In addition, the Pre-Trial Chamber may, on its own initiative, review a decision of the Prosecutor not to proceed if it is based solely on paragraph 1 (c) or 2 (c). In such a case, the decision of the Prosecutor shall be effective only if confirmed by the Pre-Trial Chamber.

4. The Prosecutor may, at any time, reconsider a decision whether to initiate an investigation or prosecution based on new facts or information.

Article 54 Duties and powers of the Prosecutor with respect to investigations

1. The Prosecutor shall:

(a) In order to establish the truth, extend the investigation to cover all facts and evidence relevant to an assessment of whether there is criminal responsibility under this Statute, and, in doing so, investigate incriminating and exonerating circumstances equally;

(b) Take appropriate measures to ensure the effective investigation and prosecution of crimes within the jurisdiction of the Court, and in doing so, respect the interests and personal circumstances of victims and witnesses, including age, gender as defined in article 7, paragraph 3, and health, and take into account the nature of the crime, in particular where it involves sexual violence, gender violence or violence against children; and

(c) Fully respect the rights of persons arising under this Statute.

2. The Prosecutor may conduct investigations on the territory of a State:

(a) In accordance with the provisions of Part 9; or

(b) As authorized by the Pre-Trial Chamber under article 57, paragraph 3 (d).

3. The Prosecutor may:

(a) Collect and examine evidence;
(b) Request the presence of and question persons being investigated, victims and witnesses;
(c) Seek the cooperation of any State or intergovernmental organization or arrangement in accordance with its respective competence and/or mandate;
(d) Enter into such arrangements or agreements, not inconsistent with this Statute, as may be necessary to facilitate the cooperation of a State, intergovernmental organization or person;
(e) Agree not to disclose, at any stage of the proceedings, documents or information that the Prosecutor obtains on the condition of confidentiality and solely for the purpose of generating new evidence, unless the provider of the information consents; and
(f) Take necessary measures, or request that necessary measures be taken, to ensure the confidentiality of information, the protection of any person or the preservation of evidence.

Article 55 Rights of persons during an investigation

1. In respect of an investigation under this Statute, a person:

(a) Shall not be compelled to incriminate himself or herself or to confess guilt;
(b) Shall not be subjected to any form of coercion, duress or threat, to torture or to any other form of cruel, inhuman or degrading treatment or punishment;
(c) Shall, if questioned in a language other than a language the person fully understands and speaks, have, free of any cost, the assistance of a competent interpreter and such translations as are necessary to meet the requirements of fairness and
(d) Shall not be subjected to arbitrary arrest or detention; and shall not be deprived of his or her liberty except on such grounds and in accordance with such procedures as are established in this Statute.

2. Where there are grounds to believe that a person has committed a crime within the jurisdiction of the Court and that person is about to be questioned either by the Prosecutor, or by national authorities pursuant to a request made under Part 9 of this Statute, that person shall also have the following rights of which he or she shall be informed prior to being questioned:

(a) To be informed, prior to being questioned, that there are grounds to believe that he or she has committed a crime within the jurisdiction of the Court;
(b) To remain silent, without such silence being a consideration in the determination of guilt or innocence;

(c) To have legal assistance of the person's choosing, or, if the person does not have legal assistance, to have legal assistance assigned to him or her, in any case where the interests of justice so require, and without payment by the person in any such case if the person does not have sufficient means to pay for it; and

(d) To be questioned in the presence of counsel unless the person has voluntarily waived his or her right to counsel.

Article 56 Role of the Pre-Trial Chamber in relation to a unique investigative opportunity

1.

(a) Where the Prosecutor considers an investigation to present a unique opportunity to take testimony or a statement from a witness or to examine, collect or test evidence, which may not be available subsequently for the purposes of a trial, the Prosecutor shall so inform the Pre-Trial Chamber.

(b) In that case, the Pre-Trial Chamber may, upon request of the Prosecutor, take such measures as may be necessary to ensure the efficiency and integrity of the proceedings and, in particular, to protect the rights of the defence.

(c) Unless the Pre-Trial Chamber orders otherwise, the Prosecutor shall provide the relevant information to the person who has been arrested or appeared in response to a summons in connection with the investigation referred to in subparagraph (a), in order that he or she may be heard on the matter.

2. The measures referred to in paragraph 1 (b) may include:

(a) Making recommendations or orders regarding procedures to be followed;

(b) Directing that a record be made of the proceedings;

(c) Appointing an expert to assist;

(d) Authorizing counsel for a person who has been arrested, or appeared before the Court in response to a summons, to participate, or where there has not yet been such an arrest or appearance or counsel has not been designated, appointing another counsel to attend and represent the interests of the defence;

(e) Naming one of its members or, if necessary, another available judge of the Pre-Trial or Trial Division to observe and make recommendations or orders regarding the collection and preservation of evidence and the questioning of persons;

(f) Taking such other action as may be necessary to collect or preserve evidence.

3.

(a) Where the Prosecutor has not sought measures pursuant to this article but the Pre-Trial Chamber considers that such measures are required to preserve evidence that it deems would be essential for the defence at trial, it shall consult with the Prosecutor as to whether there is good reason for the Prosecutor's failure to request the measures. If upon consultation, the Pre-Trial Chamber concludes that the Prosecutor's failure to request such measures is unjustified, the Pre-Trial Chamber may take such measures on its own initiative.

(b) A decision of the Pre-Trial Chamber to act on its own initiative under this paragraph may be appealed by the Prosecutor. The appeal shall be heard on an expedited basis.

4. The admissibility of evidence preserved or collected for trial pursuant to this article, or the record thereof, shall be governed at trial by article 69, and given such weight as determined by the Trial Chamber.

Article 57 Functions and powers of the Pre-Trial Chamber

1. Unless otherwise provided in this Statute, the Pre-Trial Chamber shall exercise its functions in accordance with the provisions of this article.

2.

(a) Orders or rulings of the Pre-Trial Chamber issued under articles 15, 18, 19, 54, paragraph 2, 61, paragraph 7, and 72 must be concurred in by a majority of its judges.

(b) In all other cases, a single judge of the Pre-Trial Chamber may exercise the functions provided for in this Statute, unless otherwise provided for in the Rules of Procedure and Evidence or by a majority of the Pre-Trial Chamber.

3. In addition to its other functions under this Statute, the Pre-Trial Chamber may:

(a) At the request of the Prosecutor, issue such orders and warrants as may be required for the purposes of an investigation;

(b) Upon the request of a person who has been arrested or has appeared pursuant to a summons under article 58, issue such orders, including measures such as those described in article 56, or seek such cooperation pursuant to Part 9 as may be necessary to assist the person in the preparation of his or her defence;

(c) Where necessary, provide for the protection and privacy of victims and witnesses, the preservation of evidence, the protection of persons who have been arrested or appeared in response to a summons, and the protection of national security information;

(d) Authorize the Prosecutor to take specific investigative steps within the territory of a State Party without having secured the cooperation of that State under Part 9 if, whenever possible having regard to the views of the State concerned, the Pre-Trial Chamber has determined in that case that the State is clearly unable to execute a request for cooperation due to the unavailability of any authority or any component of its judicial system competent to execute the request for cooperation under Part 9.

(e) Where a warrant of arrest or a summons has been issued under article 58, and having due regard to the strength of the evidence and the rights of the parties concerned, as provided for in this Statute and the Rules of Procedure and Evidence, seek the cooperation of States pursuant to article 93, paragraph 1 (k), to take protective measures for the purpose of forfeiture, in particular for the ultimate benefit of victims.

Article 58 Issuance by the Pre-Trial Chamber of a warrant of arrest or a summons to appear

1. At any time after the initiation of an investigation, the Pre-Trial Chamber shall, on the application of the Prosecutor, issue a warrant of arrest of a person if, having examined the application and the evidence or other information submitted by the Prosecutor, it is satisfied that:

(a) There are reasonable grounds to believe that the person has committed a crime within the jurisdiction of the Court; and

(b) The arrest of the person appears necessary:
   (i) To ensure the person's appearance at trial,
   (ii) To ensure that the person does not obstruct or endanger the investigation or the court proceedings, or
   (iii) Where applicable, to prevent the person from continuing with the commission of that crime or a related crime which is within the jurisdiction of the Court and which arises out of the same circumstances.

2. The application of the Prosecutor shall contain:

(a) The name of the person and any other relevant identifying information;

(b) A specific reference to the crimes within the jurisdiction of the Court which the person is alleged to have committed;

(c) A concise statement of the facts which are alleged to constitute those crimes;

(d) A summary of the evidence and any other information which establish reasonable grounds to believe that the person committed those crimes; and

(e) The reason why the Prosecutor believes that the arrest of the person is necessary.

3. The warrant of arrest shall contain:

(a) The name of the person and any other relevant identifying information;
(b) A specific reference to the crimes within the jurisdiction of the Court for which the person's arrest is sought; and
(c) A concise statement of the facts which are alleged to constitute those crimes.

4. The warrant of arrest shall remain in effect until otherwise ordered by the Court.

5. On the basis of the warrant of arrest, the Court may request the provisional arrest or the arrest and surrender of the person under Part 9.

6. The Prosecutor may request the Pre-Trial Chamber to amend the warrant of arrest by modifying or adding to the crimes specified therein. The Pre-Trial Chamber shall so amend the warrant if it is satisfied that there are reasonable grounds to believe that the person committed the modified or additional crimes.

7. As an alternative to seeking a warrant of arrest, the Prosecutor may submit an application requesting that the Pre-Trial Chamber issue a summons for the person to appear. If the Pre-Trial Chamber is satisfied that there are reasonable grounds to believe that the person committed the crime alleged and that a summons is sufficient to ensure the person's appearance, it shall issue the summons, with or without conditions restricting liberty (other than detention) if provided for by national law, for the person to appear. The summons shall contain:

(a) The name of the person and any other relevant identifying information;
(b) The specified date on which the person is to appear;
(c) A specific reference to the crimes within the jurisdiction of the Court which the person is alleged to have committed; and
(d) A concise statement of the facts which are alleged to constitute the crime.

The summons shall be served on the person.

Article 59 Arrest proceedings in the custodial State

1. A State Party which has received a request for provisional arrest or for arrest and surrender shall immediately take steps to arrest the person in question in accordance with its laws and the provisions of Part 9.

2. A person arrested shall be brought promptly before the competent judicial authority in the custodial State which shall determine, in accordance with the law of that State, that:

(a) The warrant applies to that person;
(b) The person has been arrested in accordance with the proper process; and
(c) The person's rights have been respected.

3. The person arrested shall have the right to apply to the competent authority in the custodial State for interim release pending surrender.

4. In reaching a decision on any such application, the competent authority in the custodial State shall consider whether, given the gravity of the alleged crimes, there are urgent and exceptional circumstances to justify interim release and whether necessary safeguards exist to ensure that the custodial State can fulfil its duty to surrender the person to the Court. It shall not be open to the competent authority of the custodial State to consider whether the warrant of arrest was properly issued in accordance with article 58, paragraph 1 (a) and (b).

5. The Pre-Trial Chamber shall be notified of any request for interim release and shall make recommendations to the competent authority in the custodial State. The competent authority in the custodial State shall give full consideration to such recommendations, including any recommendations on measures to prevent the escape of the person, before rendering its decision.

6. If the person is granted interim release, the Pre-Trial Chamber may request periodic reports on the status of the interim release.

7. Once ordered to be surrendered by the custodial State, the person shall be delivered to the Court as soon as possible.

Article 60   Initial proceedings before the Court

1. Upon the surrender of the person to the Court, or the person's appearance before the Court voluntarily or pursuant to a summons, the Pre-Trial Chamber shall satisfy itself that the person has been informed of the crimes which he or she is alleged to have committed, and of his or her rights under this Statute, including the right to apply for interim release pending trial.

2. A person subject to a warrant of arrest may apply for interim release pending trial. If the Pre-Trial Chamber is satisfied that the conditions set forth in article 58, paragraph 1, are met, the person shall continue to be detained. If it is not so satisfied, the Pre-Trial Chamber shall release the person, with or without conditions.

3. The Pre-Trial Chamber shall periodically review its ruling on the release or detention of the person, and may do so at any time on the request of the Prosecutor or the person. Upon such review, it may modify its ruling as to detention, release or conditions of release, if it is satisfied that changed circumstances so require.

4. The Pre-Trial Chamber shall ensure that a person is not detained for an unreasonable period prior to trial due to inexcusable delay by the Prosecutor. If such delay occurs, the Court shall consider releasing the person, with or without conditions.

5. If necessary, the Pre-Trial Chamber may issue a warrant of arrest to secure the presence of a person who has been released.

Article 61 Confirmation of the charges before trial

1. Subject to the provisions of paragraph 2, within a reasonable time after the person's surrender or voluntary appearance before the Court, the Pre-Trial Chamber shall hold a hearing to confirm the charges on which the Prosecutor intends to seek trial. The hearing shall be held in the presence of the Prosecutor and the person charged, as well as his or her counsel.

2. The Pre-Trial Chamber may, upon request of the Prosecutor or on its own motion, hold a hearing in the absence of the person charged to confirm the charges on which the Prosecutor intends to seek trial when the person has:

(a) Waived his or her right to be present; or
(b) Fled or cannot be found and all reasonable steps have been taken to secure his or her appearance before the Court and to inform the person of the charges and that a hearing to confirm those charges will be held.

In that case, the person shall be represented by counsel where the Pre-Trial Chamber determines that it is in the interests of justice.

3. Within a reasonable time before the hearing, the person shall:

(a) Be provided with a copy of the document containing the charges on which the Prosecutor intends to bring the person to trial; and
(b) Be informed of the evidence on which the Prosecutor intends to rely at the hearing.

The Pre-Trial Chamber may issue orders regarding the disclosure of information for the purposes of the hearing.

4. Before the hearing, the Prosecutor may continue the investigation and may amend or withdraw any charges. The person shall be given reasonable

notice before the hearing of any amendment to or withdrawal of charges. In case of a withdrawal of charges, the Prosecutor shall notify the Pre-Trial Chamber of the reasons for the withdrawal.

5. At the hearing, the Prosecutor shall support each charge with sufficient evidence to establish substantial grounds to believe that the person committed the crime charged. The Prosecutor may rely on documentary or summary evidence and need not call the witnesses expected to testify at the trial.

6. At the hearing, the person may:

(a) Object to the charges;
(b) Challenge the evidence presented by the Prosecutor; and
(c) Present evidence.

7. The Pre-Trial Chamber shall, on the basis of the hearing, determine whether there is sufficient evidence to establish substantial grounds to believe that the person committed each of the crimes charged. Based on its determination, the Pre-Trial Chamber shall:

(a) Confirm those charges in relation to which it has determined that there is sufficient evidence; and commit the person to a Trial Chamber for trial on the charges as confirmed;
(b) Decline to confirm those charges in relation to which it has determined that there is insufficient evidence;
(c) Adjourn the hearing and request the Prosecutor to consider:
  (i) Providing further evidence or conducting further investigation with respect to a particular charge; or
  (ii) Amending a charge because the evidence submitted appears to establish a different crime within the jurisdiction of the Court.

8. Where the Pre-Trial Chamber declines to confirm a charge, the Prosecutor shall not be precluded from subsequently requesting its confirmation if the request is supported by additional evidence.

9. After the charges are confirmed and before the trial has begun, the Prosecutor may, with the permission of the Pre-Trial Chamber and after notice to the accused, amend the charges. If the Prosecutor seeks to add additional charges or to substitute more serious charges, a hearing under this article to confirm those charges must be held. After commencement of the trial, the Prosecutor may, with the permission of the Trial Chamber, withdraw the charges.

10. Any warrant previously issued shall cease to have effect with respect to any charges which have not been confirmed by the Pre-Trial Chamber or which have been withdrawn by the Prosecutor.

11. Once the charges have been confirmed in accordance with this article, the Presidency shall constitute a Trial Chamber which, subject to paragraph 9 and to article 64, paragraph 4, shall be responsible for the conduct of subsequent proceedings and may exercise any function of the Pre-Trial Chamber that is relevant and capable of application in those proceedings.

Part 6 The trial

Article 62 Place of trial

Unless otherwise decided, the place of the trial shall be the seat of the Court.

[*Article 63 Trial in the presence of the accused*]

1. The accused shall be present during the trial.

2. If the accused, being present before the Court, continues to disrupt the trial, the Trial Chamber may remove the accused and shall make provision for him or her to observe the trial and instruct counsel from outside the courtroom, through the use of communications technology, if required. Such measures shall be taken only in exceptional circumstances after other reasonable alternatives have proved inadequate, and only for such duration as is strictly required.

Article 64 Functions and powers of the Trial Chamber

1. The functions and powers of the Trial Chamber set out in this article shall be exercised in accordance with this Statute and the Rules of Procedure and Evidence.

2. The Trial Chamber shall ensure that a trial is fair and expeditious and is conducted with full respect for the rights of the accused and due regard for the protection of victims and witnesses.

3. Upon assignment of a case for trial in accordance with this Statute, the Trial Chamber assigned to deal with the case shall:

(a) Confer with the parties and adopt such procedures as are necessary to facilitate the fair and expeditious conduct of the proceedings;
(b) Determine the language or languages to be used at trial; and
(c) Subject to any other relevant provisions of this Statute, provide for disclosure of documents or information not previously disclosed, sufficiently in advance of the commencement of the trial to enable adequate preparation for trial.

4. The Trial Chamber may, if necessary for its effective and fair functioning, refer preliminary issues to the Pre-Trial Chamber or, if necessary, to another available judge of the Pre-Trial Division.

5. Upon notice to the parties, the Trial Chamber may, as appropriate, direct that there be joinder or severance in respect of charges against more than one accused.

6. In performing its functions prior to trial or during the course of a trial, the Trial Chamber may, as necessary:

(a) Exercise any functions of the Pre-Trial Chamber referred to in article 61, paragraph 11;
(b) Require the attendance and testimony of witnesses and production of documents and other evidence by obtaining, if necessary, the assistance of States as provided in this Statute;
(c) Provide for the protection of confidential information;
(d) Order the production of evidence in addition to that already collected prior to the trial or presented during the trial by the parties;
(e) Provide for the protection of the accused, witnesses and victims; and
(f) Rule on any other relevant matters.

7. The trial shall be held in public. The Trial Chamber may, however, determine that special circumstances require that certain proceedings be in closed session for the purposes set forth in article 68, or to protect confidential or sensitive information to be given in evidence.

8.

(a) At the commencement of the trial, the Trial Chamber shall have read to the accused the charges previously confirmed by the Pre-Trial Chamber. The Trial Chamber shall satisfy itself that the accused understands the nature of the charges. It shall afford him or her the opportunity to make an admission of guilt in accordance with article 65 or to plead not guilty.
(b) At the trial, the presiding judge may give directions for the conduct of proceedings, including to ensure that they are conducted in a fair and impartial manner. Subject to any directions of the presiding judge, the parties may submit evidence in accordance with the provisions of this Statute.

9. The Trial Chamber shall have, *inter alia*, the power on application of a party or on its own motion to:

(a) Rule on the admissibility or relevance of evidence; and
(b) Take all necessary steps to maintain order in the course of a hearing.

10. The Trial Chamber shall ensure that a complete record of the trial, which accurately reflects the proceedings, is made and that it is maintained and preserved by the Registrar.

Article 65 Proceedings on an admission of guilt

1. Where the accused makes an admission of guilt pursuant to article 64, paragraph 8 (a), the Trial Chamber shall determine whether:

(a) The accused understands the nature and consequences of the admission of guilt;
(b) The admission is voluntarily made by the accused after sufficient consultation with defence counsel; and
(c) The admission of guilt is supported by the facts of the case that are contained in:
   (i)   The charges brought by the Prosecutor and admitted by the accused;
   (ii) Any materials presented by the Prosecutor which supplement the charges and which the accused accepts; and
   (iii) Any other evidence, such as the testimony of witnesses, presented by the Prosecutor or the accused.

2. Where the Trial Chamber is satisfied that the matters referred to in paragraph 1 are established, it shall consider the admission of guilt, together with any additional evidence presented, as establishing all the essential facts that are required to prove the crime to which the admission of guilt relates, and may convict the accused of that crime.

3. Where the Trial Chamber is not satisfied that the matters referred to in paragraph 1 are established, it shall consider the admission of guilt as not having been made, in which case it shall order that the trial be continued under the ordinary trial procedures provided by this Statute and may remit the case to another Trial Chamber.

4. Where the Trial Chamber is of the opinion that a more complete presentation of the facts of the case is required in the interests of justice, in particular the interests of the victims, the Trial Chamber may:

(a) Request the Prosecutor to present additional evidence, including the testimony of witnesses; or
(b) Order that the trial be continued under the ordinary trial procedures provided by this Statute, in which case it shall consider the admission of guilt as not having been made and may remit the case to another Trial Chamber.

5. Any discussions between the Prosecutor and the defence regarding modification of the charges, the admission of guilt or the penalty to be imposed shall not be binding on the Court.

Article 66 Presumption of innocence

1. Everyone shall be presumed innocent until proved guilty before the Court in accordance with the applicable law.

2. The onus is on the Prosecutor to prove the guilt of the accused.

3. In order to convict the accused, the Court must be convinced of the guilt of the accused beyond reasonable doubt.

Article 67 Rights of the accused

1. In the determination of any charge, the accused shall be entitled to a public hearing, having regard to the provisions of this Statute, to a fair hearing conducted impartially, and to the following minimum guarantees, in full equality:

(a) To be informed promptly and in detail of the nature, cause and content of the charge, in a language which the accused fully understands and speaks;

(b) To have adequate time and facilities for the preparation of the defence and to communicate freely with counsel of the accused's choosing in confidence;

(c) To be tried without undue delay;

(d) Subject to article 63, paragraph 2, to be present at the trial, to conduct the defence in person or through legal assistance of the accused's choosing, to be informed, if the accused does not have legal assistance, of this right and to have legal assistance assigned by the Court in any case where the interests of justice so require, and without payment if the accused lacks sufficient means to pay for it;

(e) To examine, or have examined, the witnesses against him or her and to obtain the attendance and examination of witnesses on his or her behalf under the same conditions as witnesses against him or her. The accused shall also be entitled to raise defences and to present other evidence admissible under this Statute;

(f) To have, free of any cost, the assistance of a competent interpreter and such translations as are necessary to meet the requirements of fairness, if any of the proceedings of or documents presented to the Court are not in a language which the accused fully understands and speaks;

(g) Not to be compelled to testify or to confess guilt and to remain silent, without such silence being a consideration in the determination of guilt or innocence;

(h) To make an unsworn oral or written statement in his or her defence; and
(i) Not to have imposed on him or her any reversal of the burden of proof or any onus of rebuttal.

2. In addition to any other disclosure provided for in this Statute, the Prosecutor shall, as soon as practicable, disclose to the defence evidence in the Prosecutor's possession or control which he or she believes shows or tends to show the innocence of the accused, or to mitigate the guilt of the accused, or which may affect the credibility of prosecution evidence. In case of doubt as to the application of this paragraph, the Court shall decide.

Article 68 Protection of the victims and witnesses and their participation in the proceedings

1. The Court shall take appropriate measures to protect the safety, physical and psychological well-being, dignity and privacy of victims and witnesses. In so doing, the Court shall have regard to all relevant factors, including age, gender as defined in article 7, paragraph 3, and health, and the nature of the crime, in particular, but not limited to, where the crime involves sexual or gender violence or violence against children. The Prosecutor shall take such measures particularly during the investigation and prosecution of such crimes. These measures shall not be prejudicial to or inconsistent with the rights of the accused and a fair and impartial trial.

2. As an exception to the principle of public hearings provided for in article 67, the Chambers of the Court may, to protect victims and witnesses or an accused, conduct any part of the proceedings *in camera* or allow the presentation of evidence by electronic or other special means. In particular, such measures shall be implemented in the case of a victim of sexual violence or a child who is a victim or a witness, unless otherwise ordered by the Court, having regard to all the circumstances, particularly the views of the victim or witness.

3. Where the personal interests of the victims are affected, the Court shall permit their views and concerns to be presented and considered at stages of the proceedings determined to be appropriate by the Court and in a manner which is not prejudicial to or inconsistent with the rights of the accused and a fair and impartial trial. Such views and concerns may be presented by the legal representatives of the victims where the Court considers it appropriate, in accordance with the Rules of Procedure and Evidence.

4. The Victims and Witnesses Unit may advise the Prosecutor and the Court on appropriate protective measures, security arrangements, counselling and assistance as referred to in article 43, paragraph 6.

5. Where the disclosure of evidence or information pursuant to this Statute may lead to the grave endangerment of the security of a witness or his or her family, the Prosecutor may, for the purposes of any proceedings conducted prior to the commencement of the trial, withhold such evidence or information and instead submit a summary thereof. Such measures shall be exercised in a manner which is not prejudicial to or inconsistent with the rights of the accused and a fair and impartial trial.

6. A State may make an application for necessary measures to be taken in respect of the protection of its servants or agents and the protection of confidential or sensitive information.

Article 69 Evidence

1. Before testifying, each witness shall, in accordance with the Rules of Procedure and Evidence, give an undertaking as to the truthfulness of the evidence to be given by that witness.

2. The testimony of a witness at trial shall be given in person, except to the extent provided by the measures set forth in article 68 or in the Rules of Procedure and Evidence. The Court may also permit the giving of viva voce (oral) or recorded testimony of a witness by means of video or audio technology, as well as the introduction of documents or written transcripts, subject to this Statute and in accordance with the Rules of Procedure and Evidence. These measures shall not be prejudicial to or inconsistent with the rights of the accused.

3. The parties may submit evidence relevant to the case, in accordance with article 64. The Court shall have the authority to request the submission of all evidence that it considers necessary for the determination of the truth.

4. The Court may rule on the relevance or admissibility of any evidence, taking into account, *inter alia*, the probative value of the evidence and any prejudice that such evidence may cause to a fair trial or to a fair evaluation of the testimony of a witness, in accordance with the Rules of Procedure and Evidence.

5. The Court shall respect and observe privileges on confidentiality as provided for in the Rules of Procedure and Evidence.

6. The Court shall not require proof of facts of common knowledge but may take judicial notice of them.

7. Evidence obtained by means of a violation of this Statute or internationally recognized human rights shall not be admissible if:

(a) The violation casts substantial doubt on the reliability of the evidence; or
(b) The admission of the evidence would be antithetical to and would seriously damage the integrity of the proceedings.

8. When deciding on the relevance or admissibility of evidence collected by a State, the Court shall not rule on the application of the State's national law.

Article 70 Offences against the administration of justice

1. The Court shall have jurisdiction over the following offences against its administration of justice when committed intentionally:

(a) Giving false testimony when under an obligation pursuant to article 69, paragraph 1, to tell the truth;
(b) Presenting evidence that the party knows is false or forged;
(c) Corruptly influencing a witness, obstructing or interfering with the attendance or testimony of a witness, retaliating against a witness for giving testimony or destroying, tampering with or interfering with the collection of evidence;
(d) Impeding, intimidating or corruptly influencing an official of the Court for the purpose of forcing or persuading the official not to perform, or to perform improperly, his or her duties;
(e) Retaliating against an official of the Court on account of duties performed by that or another official;
(f) Soliciting or accepting a bribe as an official of the Court in connection with his or her official duties.

2. The principles and procedures governing the Court's exercise of jurisdiction over offences under this article shall be those provided for in the Rules of Procedure and Evidence. The conditions for providing international cooperation to the Court with respect to its proceedings under this article shall be governed by the domestic laws of the requested State.

3. In the event of conviction, the Court may impose a term of imprisonment not exceeding five years, or a fine in accordance with the Rules of Procedure and Evidence, or both.

4.

(a) Each State Party shall extend its criminal laws penalizing offences against the integrity of its own investigative or judicial process to offences against the administration of justice referred to in this article, committed on its territory, or by one of its nationals;

(b) Upon request by the Court, whenever it deems it proper, the State Party shall submit the case to its competent authorities for the purpose of prosecution. Those authorities shall treat such cases with diligence and devote sufficient resources to enable them to be conducted effectively.

Article 71   Sanctions for misconduct before the Court

1. The Court may sanction persons present before it who commit misconduct, including disruption of its proceedings or deliberate refusal to comply with its directions, by administrative measures other than imprisonment, such as temporary or permanent removal from the courtroom, a fine or other similar measures provided for in the Rules of Procedure and Evidence.

2. The procedures governing the imposition of the measures set forth in paragraph 1 shall be those provided for in the Rules of Procedure and Evidence.

Article 72   Protection of national security information

1. This article applies in any case where the disclosure of the information or documents of a State would, in the opinion of that State, prejudice its national security interests. Such cases include those falling within the scope of article 56, paragraphs 2 and 3, article 61, paragraph 3, article 64, paragraph 3, article 67, paragraph 2, article 68, paragraph 6, article 87, paragraph 6 and article 93, as well as cases arising at any other stage of the proceedings where such disclosure may be at issue.

2. This article shall also apply when a person who has been requested to give information or evidence has refused to do so or has referred the matter to the State on the ground that disclosure would prejudice the national security interests of a State and the State concerned confirms that it is of the opinion that disclosure would prejudice its national security interests.

3. Nothing in this article shall prejudice the requirements of confidentiality applicable under article 54, paragraph 3 (e) and (f), or the application of article 73.

4. If a State learns that information or documents of the State are being, or are likely to be, disclosed at any stage of the proceedings, and it is of the opinion that disclosure would prejudice its national security interests, that State shall have the right to intervene in order to obtain resolution of the issue in accordance with this article.

5. If, in the opinion of a State, disclosure of information would prejudice its national security interests, all reasonable steps will be taken by the State,

acting in conjunction with the Prosecutor, the defence or the Pre-Trial Chamber or Trial Chamber, as the case may be, to seek to resolve the matter by cooperative means. Such steps may include:

(a) Modification or clarification of the request;

(b) A determination by the Court regarding the relevance of the information or evidence sought, or a determination as to whether the evidence, though relevant, could be or has been obtained from a source other than the requested State;

(c) Obtaining the information or evidence from a different source or in a different form; or

(d) Agreement on conditions under which the assistance could be provided including, among other things, providing summaries or redactions, limitations on disclosure, use of *in camera* or *ex parte* proceedings, or other protective measures permissible under the Statute and the Rules of Procedure and Evidence.

6. Once all reasonable steps have been taken to resolve the matter through cooperative means, and if the State considers that there are no means or conditions under which the information or documents could be provided or disclosed without prejudice to its national security interests, it shall so notify the Prosecutor or the Court of the specific reasons for its decision, unless a specific description of the reasons would itself necessarily result in such prejudice to the State's national security interests.

7. Thereafter, if the Court determines that the evidence is relevant and necessary for the establishment of the guilt or innocence of the accused, the Court may undertake the following actions:

(a) Where disclosure of the information or document is sought pursuant to a request for cooperation under Part 9 or the circumstances described in paragraph 2, and the State has invoked the ground for refusal referred to in article 93, paragraph 4:

    (i) The Court may, before making any conclusion referred to in subparagraph 7 (a) (ii), request further consultations for the purpose of considering the State's representations, which may include, as appropriate, hearings *in camera* and *ex parte*;

    (ii) If the Court concludes that, by invoking the ground for refusal under article 93, paragraph 4, in the circumstances of the case, the requested State is not acting in accordance with its obligations under this Statute, the Court may refer the matter in accordance with article 87, paragraph 7, specifying the reasons for its conclusion and

    (iii) The Court may make such inference in the trial of the accused as to the existence or non-existence of a fact, as may be appropriate in the circumstances; or

(b) In all other circumstances:
  (i)   Order disclosure; or
  (ii) To the extent it does not order disclosure, make such inference in the trial of the accused as to the existence or non-existence of a fact, as may be appropriate in the circumstances.

Article 73   Third-party information or documents

If a State Party is requested by the Court to provide a document or information in its custody, possession or control, which was disclosed to it in confidence by a State, intergovernmental organization or international organization, it shall seek the consent of the originator to disclose that document or information. If the originator is a State Party, it shall either consent to disclosure of the information or document or undertake to resolve the issue of disclosure with the Court, subject to the provisions of article 72. If the originator is not a State Party and refuses to consent to disclosure, the requested State shall inform the Court that it is unable to provide the document or information because of a pre-existing obligation of confidentiality to the originator.

Article 74   Requirements for the decision

1. All the judges of the Trial Chamber shall be present at each stage of the trial and throughout their deliberations. The Presidency may, on a case-by-case basis, designate, as available, one or more alternate judges to be present at each stage of the trial and to replace a member of the Trial Chamber if that member is unable to continue attending.

2. The Trial Chamber's decision shall be based on its evaluation of the evidence and the entire proceedings. The decision shall not exceed the facts and circumstances described in the charges and any amendments to the charges. The Court may base its decision only on evidence submitted and discussed before it at the trial.

3. The judges shall attempt to achieve unanimity in their decision, failing which the decision shall be taken by a majority of the judges.

4. The deliberations of the Trial Chamber shall remain secret.

5. The decision shall be in writing and shall contain a full and reasoned statement of the Trial Chamber's findings on the evidence and conclusions. The Trial Chamber shall issue one decision. When there is no unanimity, the

Trial Chamber's decision shall contain the views of the majority and the minority. The decision or a summary thereof shall be delivered in open court.

Article 75 Reparations to victims

1. The Court shall establish principles relating to reparations to, or in respect of, victims, including restitution, compensation and rehabilitation. On this basis, in its decision the Court may, either upon request or on its own motion in exceptional circumstances, determine the scope and extent of any damage, loss and injury to, or in respect of, victims and will state the principles on which it is acting.

2. The Court may make an order directly against a convicted person specifying appropriate reparations to, or in respect of, victims, including restitution, compensation and rehabilitation. Where appropriate, the Court may order that the award for reparations be made through the Trust Fund provided for in article 79.

3. Before making an order under this article, the Court may invite and shall take account of representations from or on behalf of the convicted person, victims, other interested persons or interested States.

4. In exercising its power under this article, the Court may, after a person is convicted of a crime within the jurisdiction of the Court, determine whether, in order to give effect to an order which it may make under this article, it is necessary to seek measures under article 93, paragraph 1.

5. A State Party shall give effect to a decision under this article as if the provisions of article 109 were applicable to this article.

6. Nothing in this article shall be interpreted as prejudicing the rights of victims under national or international law.

Article 76 Sentencing

1. In the event of a conviction, the Trial Chamber shall consider the appropriate sentence to be imposed and shall take into account the evidence presented and submissions made during the trial that are relevant to the sentence.

2. Except where article 65 applies and before the completion of the trial, the Trial Chamber may on its own motion and shall, at the request of the Prosecutor or the accused, hold a further hearing to hear any additional evidence or submissions relevant to the sentence, in accordance with the Rules of Procedure and Evidence.

3. Where paragraph 2 applies, any representations under article 75 shall be

heard during the further hearing referred to in paragraph 2 and, if necessary, during any additional hearing.

4. The sentence shall be pronounced in public and, wherever possible, in the presence of the accused.

Part 7 Penalties

Article 77 Applicable penalties

1. Subject to article 110, the Court may impose one of the following penalties on a person convicted of a crime referred to in article 5 of this Statute:

(a) Imprisonment for a specified number of years, which may not exceed a maximum of 30 years; or
(b) A term of life imprisonment when justified by the extreme gravity of the crime and the individual circumstances of the convicted person.

2. In addition to imprisonment, the Court may order:

(a) A fine under the criteria provided for in the Rules of Procedure and Evidence;
(b) A forfeiture of proceeds, property and assets derived directly or indirectly from that crime, without prejudice to the rights of bona fide third parties.

Article 78 Determination of the sentence

1. In determining the sentence, the Court shall, in accordance with the Rules of Procedure and Evidence, take into account such factors as the gravity of the crime and the individual circumstances of the convicted person.

2. In imposing a sentence of imprisonment, the Court shall deduct the time, if any, previously spent in detention in accordance with an order of the Court. The Court may deduct any time otherwise spent in detention in connection with conduct underlying the crime.

3. When a person has been convicted of more than one crime, the Court shall pronounce a sentence for each crime and a joint sentence specifying the total period of imprisonment. This period shall be no less than the highest individual sentence pronounced and shall not exceed 30 years' imprisonment or a sentence of life imprisonment in conformity with article 77, paragraph 1 (b).

Article 79 Trust Fund

1. A Trust Fund shall be established by decision of the Assembly of States Parties for the benefit of victims of crimes within the jurisdiction of the Court, and of the families of such victims.

2. The Court may order money and other property collected through fines or forfeiture to be transferred, by order of the Court, to the Trust Fund.

3. The Trust Fund shall be managed according to criteria to be determined by the Assembly of States Parties.

Article 80 Non-prejudice to national application of penalties and national laws

Nothing in this Part affects the application by States of penalties prescribed by their national law, nor the law of States which do not provide for penalties prescribed in this Part.

Part 8 Appeal and revision

Article 81 Appeal against decision of acquittal or conviction or against sentence

1. A decision under article 74 may be appealed in accordance with the Rules of Procedure and Evidence as follows:

(a) The Prosecutor may make an appeal on any of the following grounds:
    (i) Procedural error,
    (ii) Error of fact, or
    (iii) Error of law;
(b) The convicted person, or the Prosecutor on that person's behalf, may make an appeal on any of the following grounds:
    (i) Procedural error,
    (ii) Error of fact,
    (iii) Error of law, or
    (iv) Any other ground that affects the fairness or reliability of the proceedings or decision.

2.

(a) A sentence may be appealed, in accordance with the Rules of Procedure and Evidence, by the Prosecutor or the convicted person on the ground of disproportion between the crime and the sentence;
(b) If on an appeal against sentence the Court considers that there are grounds on

which the conviction might be set aside, wholly or in part, it may invite the Prosecutor and the convicted person to submit grounds under article 81, paragraph 1 (a) or (b), and may render a decision on conviction in accordance with article 83;

(c) The same procedure applies when the Court, on an appeal against conviction only, considers that there are grounds to reduce the sentence under paragraph 2 (a).

3.

(a) Unless the Trial Chamber orders otherwise, a convicted person shall remain in custody pending an appeal;

(b) When a convicted person's time in custody exceeds the sentence of imprisonment imposed, that person shall be released, except that if the Prosecutor is also appealing, the release may be subject to the conditions under subparagraph (c) below;

(c) In case of an acquittal, the accused shall be released immediately, subject to the following:

(i) Under exceptional circumstances, and having regard, *inter alia*, to the concrete risk of flight, the seriousness of the offence charged and the probability of success on appeal, the Trial Chamber, at the request of the Prosecutor, may maintain the detention of the person pending appeal;

(ii) A decision by the Trial Chamber under subparagraph (c) (i) may be appealed in accordance with the Rules of Procedure and Evidence.

4. Subject to the provisions of paragraph 3 (a) and (b), execution of the decision or sentence shall be suspended during the period allowed for appeal and for the duration of the appeal proceedings.

Article 82 Appeal against other decisions

1. Either party may appeal any of the following decisions in accordance with the Rules of Procedure and Evidence:

(a) A decision with respect to jurisdiction or admissibility;

(b) A decision granting or denying release of the person being investigated or prosecuted;

(c) A decision of the Pre-Trial Chamber to act on its own initiative under article 56, paragraph 3;

(d) A decision that involves an issue that would significantly affect the fair and expeditious conduct of the proceedings or the outcome of the trial, and for which, in the opinion of the Pre-Trial or Trial Chamber, an immediate resolution by the Appeals Chamber may materially advance the proceedings.

2. A decision of the Pre-Trial Chamber under article 57, paragraph 3 (d), may be appealed against by the State concerned or by the Prosecutor, with the leave of the Pre-Trial Chamber. The appeal shall be heard on an expedited basis.

3. An appeal shall not of itself have suspensive effect unless the Appeals Chamber so orders, upon request, in accordance with the Rules of Procedure and Evidence.

4. A legal representative of the victims, the convicted person or a bona fide owner of property adversely affected by an order under article 75 may appeal against the order for reparations, as provided in the Rules of Procedure and Evidence.

Article 83 Proceedings on appeal

1. For the purposes of proceedings under article 81 and this article, the Appeals Chamber shall have all the powers of the Trial Chamber.

2. If the Appeals Chamber finds that the proceedings appealed from were unfair in a way that affected the reliability of the decision or sentence, or that the decision or sentence appealed from was materially affected by error of fact or law or procedural error, it may:

(a) Reverse or amend the decision or sentence; or
(b) Order a new trial before a different Trial Chamber.

For these purposes, the Appeals Chamber may remand a factual issue to the original Trial Chamber for it to determine the issue and to report back accordingly, or may itself call evidence to determine the issue. When the decision or sentence has been appealed only by the person convicted, or the Prosecutor on that person's behalf, it cannot be amended to his or her detriment.

3. If in an appeal against sentence the Appeals Chamber finds that the sentence is disproportionate to the crime, it may vary the sentence in accordance with Part 7.

4. The judgment of the Appeals Chamber shall be taken by a majority of the judges and shall be delivered in open court. The judgment shall state the reasons on which it is based. When there is no unanimity, the judgment of the Appeals Chamber shall contain the views of the majority and the minority, but a judge may deliver a separate or dissenting opinion on a question of law.

5. The Appeals Chamber may deliver its judgment in the absence of the person acquitted or convicted.

Article 84 Revision of conviction or sentence

1. The convicted person or, after death, spouses, children, parents or one person alive at the time of the accused's death who has been given express written instructions from the accused to bring such a claim, or the Prosecutor on the person's behalf, may apply to the Appeals Chamber to revise the final judgment of conviction or sentence on the grounds that:

(a) New evidence has been discovered that:
  (i) Was not available at the time of trial, and such unavailability was not wholly or partially attributable to the party making application; and
  (ii) Is sufficiently important that had it been proved at trial it would have been likely to have resulted in a different verdict;
(b) It has been newly discovered that decisive evidence, taken into account at trial and upon which the conviction depends, was false, forged or falsified;
(c) One or more of the judges who participated in conviction or confirmation of the charges has committed, in that case, an act of serious misconduct or serious breach of duty of sufficient gravity to justify the removal of that judge or those judges from office under article 46.

2. The Appeals Chamber shall reject the application if it considers it to be unfounded. If it determines that the application is meritorious, it may, as appropriate:

(a) Reconvene the original Trial Chamber;
(b) Constitute a new Trial Chamber; or
(c) Retain jurisdiction over the matter,

with a view to, after hearing the parties in the manner set forth in the Rules of Procedure and Evidence, arriving at a determination on whether the judgment should be revised.

Article 85 Compensation to an arrested or convicted person

1. Anyone who has been the victim of unlawful arrest or detention shall have an enforceable right to compensation.

2. When a person has by a final decision been convicted of a criminal offence, and when subsequently his or her conviction has been reversed on the ground that a new or newly discovered fact shows conclusively that there has

been a miscarriage of justice, the person who has suffered punishment as a result of such conviction shall be compensated according to law, unless it is proved that the non-disclosure of the unknown fact in time is wholly or partly attributable to him or her.

3. In exceptional circumstances, where the Court finds conclusive facts showing that there has been a grave and manifest miscarriage of justice, it may in its discretion award compensation, according to the criteria provided in the Rules of Procedure and Evidence, to a person who has been released from detention following a final decision of acquittal or a termination of the proceedings for that reason.

Part 9 International cooperation and judicial assistance

Article 86 General obligation to cooperate

States Parties shall, in accordance with the provisions of this Statute, cooperate fully with the Court in its investigation and prosecution of crimes within the jurisdiction of the Court.

Article 87 Requests for cooperation: general provisions

1.

(a) The Court shall have the authority to make requests to States Parties for cooperation. The requests shall be transmitted through the diplomatic channel or any other appropriate channel as may be designated by each State Party upon ratification, acceptance, approval or accession. Subsequent changes to the designation shall be made by each State Party in accordance with the Rules of Procedure and Evidence.
(b) When appropriate, without prejudice to the provisions of subparagraph (a), requests may also be transmitted through the International Criminal Police Organization or any appropriate regional organization.

2. Requests for cooperation and any documents supporting the request shall either be in or be accompanied by a translation into an official language of the requested State or one of the working languages of the Court, in accordance with the choice made by that State upon ratification, acceptance, approval or accession. Subsequent changes to this choice shall be made in accordance with the Rules of Procedure and Evidence.

3. The requested State shall keep confidential a request for cooperation and any documents supporting the request, except to the extent that the disclosure is necessary for execution of the request.

4. In relation to any request for assistance presented under this Part, the Court may take such measures, including measures related to the protection of information, as may be necessary to ensure the safety or physical or psychological well-being of any victims, potential witnesses and their families. The Court may request that any information that is made available under this Part shall be provided and handled in a manner that protects the safety and physical or psychological well-being of any victims, potential witnesses and their families.

5. The Court may invite any State not party to this Statute to provide assistance under this Part on the basis of an ad hoc arrangement, an agreement with such State or any other appropriate basis. Where a State not party to this Statute, which has entered into an ad hoc arrangement or an agreement with the Court, fails to cooperate with requests pursuant to any such arrangement or agreement, the Court may so inform the Assembly of States Parties or, where the Security Council referred the matter to the Court, the Security Council.

6. The Court may ask any intergovernmental organization to provide information or documents. The Court may also ask for other forms of cooperation and assistance which may be agreed upon with such an organization and which are in accordance with its competence or mandate.

7. Where a State Party fails to comply with a request to cooperate by the Court contrary to the provisions of this Statute, thereby preventing the Court from exercising its functions and powers under this Statute, the Court may make a finding to that effect and refer the matter to the Assembly of States Parties or, where the Security Council referred the matter to the Court, to the Security Council.

Article 88 Availability of procedures under national law

States Parties shall ensure that there are procedures available under their national law for all of the forms of cooperation which are specified under this Part.

Article 89 Surrender of persons to the Court

1. The Court may transmit a request for the arrest and surrender of a person, together with the material supporting the request outlined in article 91, to any State on the territory of which that person may be found and shall request the cooperation of that State in the arrest and surrender of such a person. States Parties shall, in accordance with the provisions of this Part and

the procedure under their national law, comply with requests for arrest and surrender.

2. Where the person sought for surrender brings a challenge before a national court on the basis of the principle of ne bis in idem as provided in article 20, the requested State shall immediately consult with the Court to determine if there has been a relevant ruling on admissibility. If the case is admissible, the requested State shall proceed with the execution of the request. If an admissibility ruling is pending, the requested State may postpone the execution of the request for surrender of the person until the Court makes a determination on admissibility.

3.

(a) A State Party shall authorize, in accordance with its national procedural law, transportation through its territory of a person being surrendered to the Court by another State, except where transit through that State would impede or delay the surrender.

(b) A request by the Court for transit shall be transmitted in accordance with article 87. The request for transit shall contain:

(i) A description of the person being transported;

(ii) A brief statement of the facts of the case and their legal characterization; and

(iii) The warrant for arrest and surrender;

(c) A person being transported shall be detained in custody during the period of transit;

(d) No authorization is required if the person is transported by air and no landing is scheduled on the territory of the transit State;

(e) If an unscheduled landing occurs on the territory of the transit State, that State may require a request for transit from the Court as provided for in subparagraph (b). The transit State shall detain the person being transported until the request for transit is received and the transit is effected; provided that detention for purposes of this subparagraph may not be extended beyond 96 hours from the unscheduled landing unless the request is received within that time.

4. If the person sought is being proceeded against or is serving a sentence in the requested State for a crime different from that for which surrender to the Court is sought, the requested State, after making its decision to grant the request, shall consult with the Court.

Article 90   Competing requests

1. A State Party which receives a request from the Court for the surrender of a person under article 89 shall, if it also receives a request from any other State for the extradition of the same person for the same conduct which forms the basis of the crime for which the Court seeks the person's surrender, notify the Court and the requesting State of that fact.

2. Where the requesting State is a State Party, the requested State shall give priority to the request from the Court if:

(a) The Court has, pursuant to articles 18 or 19, made a determination that the case in respect of which surrender is sought is admissible and that determination takes into account the investigation or prosecution conducted by the requesting State in respect of its request for extradition; or

(b) The Court makes the determination described in subparagraph (a) pursuant to the requested State's notification under paragraph 1.

3. Where a determination under paragraph 2 (a) has not been made, the requested State may, at its discretion, pending the determination of the Court under paragraph 2 (b), proceed to deal with the request for extradition from the requesting State but shall not extradite the person until the Court has determined that the case is inadmissible. The Court's determination shall be made on an expedited basis.

4. If the requesting State is a State not Party to this Statute the requested State, if it is not under an international obligation to extradite the person to the requesting State, shall give priority to the request for surrender from the Court, if the Court has determined that the case is admissible.

5. Where a case under paragraph 4 has not been determined to be admissible by the Court, the requested State may, at its discretion, proceed to deal with the request for extradition from the requesting State.

6. In cases where paragraph 4 applies except that the requested State is under an existing international obligation to extradite the person to the requesting State not Party to this Statute, the requested State shall determine whether to surrender the person to the Court or extradite the person to the requesting State. In making its decision, the requested State shall consider all the relevant factors, including but not limited to:

(a) The respective dates of the requests;

(b) The interests of the requesting State including, where relevant, whether the crime was committed in its territory and the nationality of the victims and of the person sought; and

(c) The possibility of subsequent surrender between the Court and the requesting State.

7. Where a State Party which receives a request from the Court for the surrender of a person also receives a request from any State for the extradition of the same person for conduct other than that which constitutes the crime for which the Court seeks the person's surrender:

(a) The requested State shall, if it is not under an existing international obligation to extradite the person to the requesting State, give priority to the request from the Court;

(b) The requested State shall, if it is under an existing international obligation to extradite the person to the requesting State, determine whether to surrender the person to the Court or to extradite the person to the requesting State. In making its decision, the requested State shall consider all the relevant factors, including but not limited to those set out in paragraph 6, but shall give special consideration to the relative nature and gravity of the conduct in question.

8. Where pursuant to a notification under this article, the Court has determined a case to be inadmissible, and subsequently extradition to the requesting State is refused, the requested State shall notify the Court of this decision.

Article 91 Contents of request for arrest and surrender

1. A request for arrest and surrender shall be made in writing. In urgent cases, a request may be made by any medium capable of delivering a written record, provided that the request shall be confirmed through the channel provided for in article 87, paragraph 1 (a).

2. In the case of a request for the arrest and surrender of a person for whom a warrant of arrest has been issued by the Pre-Trial Chamber under article 58, the request shall contain or be supported by:

(a) Information describing the person sought, sufficient to identify the person, and information as to that person's probable location;

(b) A copy of the warrant of arrest; and

(c) Such documents, statements or information as may be necessary to meet the requirements for the surrender process in the requested State, except that those requirements should not be more burdensome than those applicable to requests for extradition pursuant to treaties or arrangements between the requested State and other States and should, if possible, be less burdensome, taking into account the distinct nature of the Court.

3. In the case of a request for the arrest and surrender of a person already convicted, the request shall contain or be supported by:

(a) A copy of any warrant of arrest for that person;
(b) A copy of the judgment of conviction;
(c) Information to demonstrate that the person sought is the one referred to in the judgment of conviction; and
(d) If the person sought has been sentenced, a copy of the sentence imposed and, in the case of a sentence for imprisonment, a statement of any time already served and the time remaining to be served.

4. Upon the request of the Court, a State Party shall consult with the Court, either generally or with respect to a specific matter, regarding any requirements under its national law that may apply under paragraph 2 (c). During the consultations, the State Party shall advise the Court of the specific requirements of its national law.

Article 92 Provisional arrest

1. In urgent cases, the Court may request the provisional arrest of the person sought, pending presentation of the request for surrender and the documents supporting the request as specified in article 91.

2. The request for provisional arrest shall be made by any medium capable of delivering a written record and shall contain:

(a) Information describing the person sought, sufficient to identify the person, and information as to that person's probable location;
(b) A concise statement of the crimes for which the person's arrest is sought and of the facts which are alleged to constitute those crimes, including, where possible, the date and location of the crime;
(c) A statement of the existence of a warrant of arrest or a judgment of conviction against the person sought; and
(d) A statement that a request for surrender of the person sought will follow.

3. A person who is provisionally arrested may be released from custody if the requested State has not received the request for surrender and the documents supporting the request as specified in article 91 within the time limits specified in the Rules of Procedure and Evidence. However, the person may consent to surrender before the expiration of this period if permitted by the law of the requested State. In such a case, the requested State shall proceed to surrender the person to the Court as soon as possible.

4. The fact that the person sought has been released from custody pursuant to paragraph 3 shall not prejudice the subsequent arrest and surrender of that person if the request for surrender and the documents supporting the request are delivered at a later date.

Article 93 Other forms of cooperation

1. States Parties shall, in accordance with the provisions of this Part and under procedures of national law, comply with requests by the Court to provide the following assistance in relation to investigations or prosecutions:

(a) The identification and whereabouts of persons or the location of items;

(b) The taking of evidence, including testimony under oath, and the production of evidence, including expert opinions and reports necessary to the Court;

(c) The questioning of any person being investigated or prosecuted;

(d) The service of documents, including judicial documents;

(e) Facilitating the voluntary appearance of persons as witnesses or experts before the Court;

(f) The temporary transfer of persons as provided in paragraph 7;

(g) The examination of places or sites, including the exhumation and examination of grave sites;

(h) The execution of searches and seizures;

(i) The provision of records and documents, including official records and documents;

(j) The protection of victims and witnesses and the preservation of evidence;

(k) The identification, tracing and freezing or seizure of proceeds, property and assets and instrumentalities of crimes for the purpose of eventual forfeiture, without prejudice to the rights of bona fide third parties; and

(l) Any other type of assistance which is not prohibited by the law of the requested State, with a view to facilitating the investigation and prosecution of crimes within the jurisdiction of the Court.

2. The Court shall have the authority to provide an assurance to a witness or an expert appearing before the Court that he or she will not be prosecuted, detained or subjected to any restriction of personal freedom by the Court in respect of any act or omission that preceded the departure of that person from the requested State.

3. Where execution of a particular measure of assistance detailed in a request presented under paragraph 1, is prohibited in the requested State on the basis of an existing fundamental legal principle of general application, the

requested State shall promptly consult with the Court to try to resolve the matter. In the consultations, consideration should be given to whether the assistance can be rendered in another manner or subject to conditions. If after consultations the matter cannot be resolved, the Court shall modify the request as necessary.

4. In accordance with article 72, a State Party may deny a request for assistance, in whole or in part, only if the request concerns the production of any documents or disclosure of evidence which relates to its national security.

5. Before denying a request for assistance under paragraph 1 (l), the requested State shall consider whether the assistance can be provided subject to specified conditions, or whether the assistance can be provided at a later date or in an alternative manner, provided that if the Court or the Prosecutor accepts the assistance subject to conditions, the Court or the Prosecutor shall abide by them.

6. If a request for assistance is denied, the requested State Party shall promptly inform the Court or the Prosecutor of the reasons for such denial.

7.

(a) The Court may request the temporary transfer of a person in custody for purposes of identification or for obtaining testimony or other assistance. The person may be transferred if the following conditions are fulfilled:
  (i)   The person freely gives his or her informed consent to the transfer; and
  (ii) The requested State agrees to the transfer, subject to such conditions as that State and the Court may agree.
(b) The person being transferred shall remain in custody. When the purposes of the transfer have been fulfilled, the Court shall return the person without delay to the requested State.

8.

(a) The Court shall ensure the confidentiality of documents and information, except as required for the investigation and proceedings described in the request.
(b) The requested State may, when necessary, transmit documents or information to the Prosecutor on a confidential basis. The Prosecutor may then use them solely for the purpose of generating new evidence;
(c) The requested State may, on its own motion or at the request of the Prosecutor, subsequently consent to the disclosure of such documents or information. They may then be used as evidence pursuant to the provisions of Parts 5 and 6 and in accordance with the Rules of Procedure and Evidence.

9.

(a)

   (i)   In the event that a State Party receives competing requests, other than for surrender or extradition, from the Court and from another State pursuant to an international obligation, the State Party shall endeavour, in consultation with the Court and the other State, to meet both requests, if necessary by postponing or attaching conditions to one or the other request.

   (ii)   Failing that, competing requests shall be resolved in accordance with the principles established in article 90.

(b) Where, however, the request from the Court concerns information, property or persons which are subject to the control of a third State or an international organization by virtue of an international agreement, the requested States shall so inform the Court and the Court shall direct its request to the third State or international organization.

10.

(a) The Court may, upon request, cooperate with and provide assistance to a State Party conducting an investigation into or trial in respect of conduct which constitutes a crime within the jurisdiction of the Court or which constitutes a serious crime under the national law of the requesting State.

(b)

   (i)   The assistance provided under subparagraph (a) shall include, *inter alia*:

      a.   The transmission of statements, documents or other types of evidence obtained in the course of an investigation or a trial conducted by the Court; and

      b.   The questioning of any person detained by order of the Court;

   (ii)   In the case of assistance under subparagraph (b) (i) (a):

      a.   If the documents or other types of evidence have been obtained with the assistance of a State, such transmission shall require the consent of that State;

      b.   If the statements, documents or other types of evidence have been provided by a witness or expert, such transmission shall be subject to the provisions of article 68.

(c) The Court may, under the conditions set out in this paragraph, grant a request for assistance under this paragraph from a State which is not a Party to this Statute.

Article 94 Postponement of execution of a request in respect of ongoing investigation or prosecution

1. If the immediate execution of a request would interfere with an ongoing investigation or prosecution of a case different from that to which the request relates, the requested State may postpone the execution of the request for a period of time agreed upon with the Court. However, the postponement shall be no longer than is necessary to complete the relevant investigation or prosecution in the requested State. Before making a decision to postpone, the requested State should consider whether the assistance may be immediately provided subject to certain conditions.

2. If a decision to postpone is taken pursuant to paragraph 1, the Prosecutor may, however, seek measures to preserve evidence, pursuant to article 93, paragraph 1 (j).

Article 95 Postponement of execution of a request in respect of an admissibility challenge

Where there is an admissibility challenge under consideration by the Court pursuant to article 18 or 19, the requested State may postpone the execution of a request under this Part pending a determination by the Court, unless the Court has specifically ordered that the Prosecutor may pursue the collection of such evidence pursuant to article 18 or 19.

Article 96 Contents of request for other forms of assistance under article 93

1. A request for other forms of assistance referred to in article 93 shall be made in writing. In urgent cases, a request may be made by any medium capable of delivering a written record, provided that the request shall be confirmed through the channel provided for in article 87, paragraph 1 (a).

2. The request shall, as applicable, contain or be supported by the following:

(a) A concise statement of the purpose of the request and the assistance sought, including the legal basis and the grounds for the request;
(b) As much detailed information as possible about the location or identification of any person or place that must be found or identified in order for the assistance sought to be provided;
(c) A concise statement of the essential facts underlying the request;
(d) The reasons for and details of any procedure or requirement to be followed;

(e) Such information as may be required under the law of the requested State in order to execute the request; and

(f) Any other information relevant in order for the assistance sought to be provided.

3. Upon the request of the Court, a State Party shall consult with the Court, either generally or with respect to a specific matter, regarding any requirements under its national law that may apply under paragraph 2 (e). During the consultations, the State Party shall advise the Court of the specific requirements of its national law.

4. The provisions of this article shall, where applicable, also apply in respect of a request for assistance made to the Court.

Article 97 Consultations

Where a State Party receives a request under this Part in relation to which it identifies problems which may impede or prevent the execution of the request, that State shall consult with the Court without delay in order to resolve the matter. Such problems may include, *inter alia*:

(a) Insufficient information to execute the request;

(b) In the case of a request for surrender, the fact that despite best efforts, the person sought cannot be located or that the investigation conducted has determined that the person in the requested State is clearly not the person named in the warrant; or

(c) The fact that execution of the request in its current form would require the requested State to breach a pre-existing treaty obligation undertaken with respect to another State.

Article 98 Cooperation with respect to waiver of immunity and consent to surrender

1. The Court may not proceed with a request for surrender or assistance which would require the requested State to act inconsistently with its obligations under international law with respect to the State or diplomatic immunity of a person or property of a third State, unless the Court can first obtain the cooperation of that third State for the waiver of the immunity.

2. The Court may not proceed with a request for surrender which would require the requested State to act inconsistently with its obligations under international agreements pursuant to which the consent of a sending State is required to surrender a person of that State to the Court, unless the Court can

first obtain the cooperation of the sending State for the giving of consent for the surrender.

Article 99 Execution of requests under articles 93 and 96

1. Requests for assistance shall be executed in accordance with the relevant procedure under the law of the requested State and, unless prohibited by such law, in the manner specified in the request, including following any procedure outlined therein or permitting persons specified in the request to be present at and assist in the execution process.

2. In the case of an urgent request, the documents or evidence produced in response shall, at the request of the Court, be sent urgently.

3. Replies from the requested State shall be transmitted in their original language and form.

4. Without prejudice to other articles in this Part, where it is necessary for the successful execution of a request which can be executed without any compulsory measures, including specifically the interview of or taking evidence from a person on a voluntary basis, including doing so without the presence of the authorities of the requested State Party if it is essential for the request to be executed, and the examination without modification of a public site or other public place, the Prosecutor may execute such request directly on the territory of a State as follows:

(a) When the State Party requested is a State on the territory of which the crime is alleged to have been committed, and there has been a determination of admissibility pursuant to article 18 or 19, the Prosecutor may directly execute such request following all possible consultations with the requested State Party;

(b) In other cases, the Prosecutor may execute such request following consultations with the requested State Party and subject to any reasonable conditions or concerns raised by that State Party. Where the requested State Party identifies problems with the execution of a request pursuant to this subparagraph it shall, without delay, consult with the Court to resolve the matter.

5. Provisions allowing a person heard or examined by the Court under article 72 to invoke restrictions designed to prevent disclosure of confidential information connected with national security shall also apply to the execution of requests for assistance under this article.

Article 100 Costs

1. The ordinary costs for execution of requests in the territory of the requested State shall be borne by that State, except for the following, which shall be borne by the Court:

(a) Costs associated with the travel and security of witnesses and experts or the transfer under article 93 of persons in custody;
(b) Costs of translation, interpretation and transcription;
(c) Travel and subsistence costs of the judges, the Prosecutor, the Deputy Prosecutors, the Registrar, the Deputy Registrar and staff of any organ of the Court;
(d) Costs of any expert opinion or report requested by the Court;
(e) Costs associated with the transport of a person being surrendered to the Court by a custodial State; and
(f) Following consultations, any extraordinary costs that may result from the execution of a request.

2. The provisions of paragraph 1 shall, as appropriate, apply to requests from States Parties to the Court. In that case, the Court shall bear the ordinary costs of execution.

Article 101 Rule of speciality

1. A person surrendered to the Court under this Statute shall not be proceeded against, punished or detained for any conduct committed prior to surrender, other than the conduct or course of conduct which forms the basis of the crimes for which that person has been surrendered.

2. The Court may request a waiver of the requirements of paragraph 1 from the State which surrendered the person to the Court and, if necessary, the Court shall provide additional information in accordance with article 91. States Parties shall have the authority to provide a waiver to the Court and should endeavour to do so.

Article 102 Use of terms

For the purposes of this Statute:

(a) 'surrender' means the delivering up of a person by a State to the Court, pursuant to this Statute.
(b) 'extradition' means the delivering up of a person by one State to another as provided by treaty, convention or national legislation.

Part 10 Enforcement

Article 103 Role of States in enforcement of sentences of imprisonment

1.

(a) A sentence of imprisonment shall be served in a State designated by the Court from a list of States which have indicated to the Court their willingness to accept sentenced persons.

(b) At the time of declaring its willingness to accept sentenced persons, a State may attach conditions to its acceptance as agreed by the Court and in accordance with this Part.

(c) A State designated in a particular case shall promptly inform the Court whether it accepts the Court's designation.

2.

(a) The State of enforcement shall notify the Court of any circumstances, including the exercise of any conditions agreed under paragraph 1, which could materially affect the terms or extent of the imprisonment. The Court shall be given at least 45 days' notice of any such known or foreseeable circumstances. During this period, the State of enforcement shall take no action that might prejudice its obligations under article 110.

(b) Where the Court cannot agree to the circumstances referred to in subparagraph (a), it shall notify the State of enforcement and proceed in accordance with article 104, paragraph 1.

3. In exercising its discretion to make a designation under paragraph 1, the Court shall take into account the following:

(a) The principle that States Parties should share the responsibility for enforcing sentences of imprisonment, in accordance with principles of equitable distribution, as provided in the Rules of Procedure and Evidence;

(b) The application of widely accepted international treaty standards governing the treatment of prisoners;

(c) The views of the sentenced person;

(d) The nationality of the sentenced person;

(e) Such other factors regarding the circumstances of the crime or the person sentenced, or the effective enforcement of the sentence, as may be appropriate in designating the State of enforcement.

4. If no State is designated under paragraph 1, the sentence of imprisonment shall be served in a prison facility made available by the host State, in accordance with the conditions set out in the headquarters agreement referred

to in article 3, paragraph 2. In such a case, the costs arising out of the enforcement of a sentence of imprisonment shall be borne by the Court.

Article 104 Change in designation of State of enforcement

1. The Court may, at any time, decide to transfer a sentenced person to a prison of another State.

2. A sentenced person may, at any time, apply to the Court to be transferred from the State of enforcement.

Article 105 Enforcement of the sentence

1. Subject to conditions which a State may have specified in accordance with article 103, paragraph 1 (b), the sentence of imprisonment shall be binding on the States Parties, which shall in no case modify it.

2. The Court alone shall have the right to decide any application for appeal and revision. The State of enforcement shall not impede the making of any such application by a sentenced person.

Article 106 Supervision of enforcement of sentences and conditions of imprisonment

1. The enforcement of a sentence of imprisonment shall be subject to the supervision of the Court and shall be consistent with widely accepted international treaty standards governing treatment of prisoners.

2. The conditions of imprisonment shall be governed by the law of the State of enforcement and shall be consistent with widely accepted international treaty standards governing treatment of prisoners; in no case shall such conditions be more or less favourable than those available to prisoners convicted of similar offences in the State of enforcement.

3. Communications between a sentenced person and the Court shall be unimpeded and confidential.

Article 107 Transfer of the person upon completion of sentence

1. Following completion of the sentence, a person who is not a national of the State of enforcement may, in accordance with the law of the State of enforcement, be transferred to a State which is obliged to receive him or her, or to another State which agrees to receive him or her, taking into account any wishes of the person to be transferred to that State, unless the State of enforcement authorizes the person to remain in its territory.

2. If no State bears the costs arising out of transferring the person to another State pursuant to paragraph 1, such costs shall be borne by the Court.

3. Subject to the provisions of article 108, the State of enforcement may also, in accordance with its national law, extradite or otherwise surrender the person to a State which has requested the extradition or surrender of the person for purposes of trial or enforcement of a sentence.

Article 108 Limitation on the prosecution or punishment of other offences

1. A sentenced person in the custody of the State of enforcement shall not be subject to prosecution or punishment or to extradition to a third State for any conduct engaged in prior to that person's delivery to the State of enforcement, unless such prosecution, punishment or extradition has been approved by the Court at the request of the State of enforcement.

2. The Court shall decide the matter after having heard the views of the sentenced person.

3. Paragraph 1 shall cease to apply if the sentenced person remains voluntarily for more than 30 days in the territory of the State of enforcement after having served the full sentence imposed by the Court, or returns to the territory of that State after having left it.

Article 109 Enforcement of fines and forfeiture measures

1. States Parties shall give effect to fines or forfeitures ordered by the Court under Part 7, without prejudice to the rights of bona fide third parties, and in accordance with the procedure of their national law.

2. If a State Party is unable to give effect to an order for forfeiture, it shall take measures to recover the value of the proceeds, property or assets ordered by the Court to be forfeited, without prejudice to the rights of bona fide third parties.

3. Property, or the proceeds of the sale of real property or, where appropriate, the sale of other property, which is obtained by a State Party as a result of its enforcement of a judgment of the Court shall be transferred to the Court.

Article 110 Review by the Court concerning reduction of sentence

1. The State of enforcement shall not release the person before expiry of the sentence pronounced by the Court.

2. The Court alone shall have the right to decide any reduction of sentence, and shall rule on the matter after having heard the person.

3. When the person has served two thirds of the sentence, or 25 years in the case of life imprisonment, the Court shall review the sentence to determine whether it should be reduced. Such a review shall not be conducted before that time.

4. In its review under paragraph 3, the Court may reduce the sentence if it finds that one or more of the following factors are present:

(a) The early and continuing willingness of the person to cooperate with the Court in its investigations and prosecutions;

(b) The voluntary assistance of the person in enabling the enforcement of the judgments and orders of the Court in other cases, and in particular providing assistance in locating assets subject to orders of fine, forfeiture or reparation which may be used for the benefit of victims; or

(c) Other factors establishing a clear and significant change of circumstances sufficient to justify the reduction of sentence, as provided in the Rules of Procedure and Evidence.

5. If the Court determines in its initial review under paragraph 3 that it is not appropriate to reduce the sentence, it shall thereafter review the question of reduction of sentence at such intervals and applying such criteria as provided for in the Rules of Procedure and Evidence.

Article 111 Escape

If a convicted person escapes from custody and flees the State of enforcement, that State may, after consultation with the Court, request the person's surrender from the State in which the person is located pursuant to existing bilateral or multilateral arrangements, or may request that the Court seek the person's surrender. It may direct that the person be delivered to the State in which he or she was serving the sentence or to another State designated by the Court.

Part 11 Assembly of States Parties

Article 112 Assembly of States Parties

1. An Assembly of States Parties to this Statute is hereby established. Each State Party shall have one representative in the Assembly who may be accompanied by alternates and advisers. Other States which have signed this Statute or the Final Act may be observers in the Assembly.

2. The Assembly shall:

(a) Consider and adopt, as appropriate, recommendations of the Preparatory Commission;
(b) Provide management oversight to the Presidency, the Prosecutor and the Registrar regarding the administration of the Court;
(c) Consider the reports and activities of the Bureau established under paragraph 3 and take appropriate action in regard thereto;
(d) Consider and decide the budget for the Court;
(e) Decide whether to alter, in accordance with article 36, the number of judges;
(f) Consider pursuant to article 87, paragraphs 5 and 7, any question relating to non-cooperation;
(g) Perform any other function consistent with this Statute or the Rules of Procedure and Evidence.

3.

(a) The Assembly shall have a Bureau consisting of a President, two Vice-Presidents and 18 members elected by the Assembly for three-year terms;
(b) The Bureau shall have a representative character, taking into account, in particular, equitable geographic distribution and the adequate representation of the principal legal systems of the world.
(c) The Bureau shall meet as often as necessary, but at least once a year. It shall assist the Assembly in the discharge of its responsibilities.

4. The Assembly may establish such subsidiary bodies as may be necessary, including an independent oversight mechanism for inspection, evaluation and investigation of the Court, in order to enhance its efficiency and economy.

5. The President of the Court, the Prosecutor and the Registrar or their representatives may participate, as appropriate, in meetings of the Assembly and of the Bureau.

6. The Assembly shall meet at the seat of the Court or at the Headquarters of the United Nations once a year and, when circumstances so require, hold special sessions. Except as otherwise specified in this Statute, special sessions shall be convened by the Bureau on its own initiative or at the request of one third of the States Parties.

7. Each State Party shall have one vote. Every effort shall be made to reach decisions by consensus in the Assembly and in the Bureau. If consensus cannot be reached, except as otherwise provided in the Statute:

(a) Decisions on matters of substance must be approved by a two-thirds majority of those present and voting provided that an absolute majority of States Parties constitutes the quorum for voting;

(b) Decisions on matters of procedure shall be taken by a simple majority of States Parties present and voting.

8. A State Party which is in arrears in the payment of its financial contributions towards the costs of the Court shall have no vote in the Assembly and in the Bureau if the amount of its arrears exceeds or equals the amount of the contributions due from it for the preceding two full years. The Assembly may, nevertheless, permit such a State Party to vote in the Assembly and in the Bureau if it is satisfied that the failure to pay is due to conditions beyond the control of the State Party.

9. The Assembly shall adopt its own rules of procedure.

10. The official and working languages of the Assembly shall be those of the General Assembly of the United Nations.

Article 113 Financial Regulations

Except as otherwise specifically provided, all financial matters related to the Court and the meetings of the Assembly of States Parties, including its Bureau and subsidiary bodies, shall be governed by this Statute and the Financial Regulations and Rules adopted by the Assembly of States Parties.

Article 114 Payment of expenses

Expenses of the Court and the Assembly of States Parties, including its Bureau and subsidiary bodies, shall be paid from the funds of the Court.

Article 115 Funds of the Court and of the Assembly of States Parties

The expenses of the Court and the Assembly of States Parties, including its Bureau and subsidiary bodies, as provided for in the budget decided by the Assembly of States Parties, shall be provided by the following sources:

(a) Assessed contributions made by States Parties;
(b) Funds provided by the United Nations, subject to the approval of the General Assembly, in particular in relation to the expenses incurred due to referrals by the Security Council.

Article 116 Voluntary contributions

Without prejudice to article 115, the Court may receive and utilize, as additional funds, voluntary contributions from Governments, international organizations, individuals, corporations and other entities, in accordance with relevant criteria adopted by the Assembly of States Parties.

Article 117 Assessment of contributions

The contributions of States Parties shall be assessed in accordance with an agreed scale of assessment, based on the scale adopted by the United Nations for its regular budget and adjusted in accordance with the principles on which that scale is based.

Article 118 Annual audit

The records, books and accounts of the Court, including its annual financial statements, shall be audited annually by an independent auditor.

Part 13 Final clauses

Article 119 Settlement of disputes

1. Any dispute concerning the judicial functions of the Court shall be settled by the decision of the Court.

2. Any other dispute between two or more States Parties relating to the interpretation or application of this Statute which is not settled through negotiations within three months of their commencement shall be referred to the Assembly of States Parties. The Assembly may itself seek to settle the dispute or may make recommendations on further means of settlement of the dispute, including referral to the International Court of Justice in conformity with the Statute of that Court.

Article 120 Reservations

No reservations may be made to this Statute.

Article 121 Amendments

1. After the expiry of seven years from the entry into force of this Statute, any State Party may propose amendments thereto. The text of any proposed amendment shall be submitted to the Secretary-General of the United Nations, who shall promptly circulate it to all States Parties.

2. No sooner than three months from the date of notification, the Assembly of States Parties, at its next meeting, shall, by a majority of those present and

voting, decide whether to take up the proposal. The Assembly may deal with the proposal directly or convene a Review Conference if the issue involved so warrants.

3. The adoption of an amendment at a meeting of the Assembly of States Parties or at a Review Conference on which consensus cannot be reached shall require a two-thirds majority of States Parties.

4. Except as provided in paragraph 5, an amendment shall enter into force for all States Parties one year after instruments of ratification or acceptance have been deposited with the Secretary-General of the United Nations by seven-eighths of them.

5. Any amendment to articles 5, 6, 7 and 8 of this Statute shall enter into force for those States Parties which have accepted the amendment one year after the deposit of their instruments of ratification or acceptance. In respect of a State Party which has not accepted the amendment, the Court shall not exercise its jurisdiction regarding a crime covered by the amendment when committed by that State Party's nationals or on its territory.

6. If an amendment has been accepted by seven-eighths of States Parties in accordance with paragraph 4, any State Party which has not accepted the amendment may withdraw from this Statute with immediate effect, notwithstanding article 127, paragraph 1, but subject to article 127, paragraph 2, by giving notice no later than one year after the entry into force of such amendment.

7. The Secretary-General of the United Nations shall circulate to all States Parties any amendment adopted at a meeting of the Assembly of States Parties or at a Review Conference.

Article 122 Amendments to provisions of an institutional nature

1. Amendments to provisions of this Statute which are of an exclusively institutional nature, namely, article 35, article 36, paragraphs 8 and 9, article 37, article 38, article 39, paragraphs 1 (first two sentences), 2 and 4, article 42, paragraphs 4 to 9, article 43, paragraphs 2 and 3, and articles 44, 46, 47 and 49, may be proposed at any time, notwithstanding article 121, paragraph 1, by any State Party. The text of any proposed amendment shall be submitted to the Secretary-General of the United Nations or such other person designated by the Assembly of States Parties who shall promptly circulate it to all States Parties and to others participating in the Assembly.

2. Amendments under this article on which consensus cannot be reached shall be adopted by the Assembly of States Parties or by a Review Conference, by a two-thirds majority of States Parties. Such amendments shall enter into

force for all States Parties six months after their adoption by the Assembly or, as the case may be, by the Conference.

Article 123 Review of the Statute

1. Seven years after the entry into force of this Statute the Secretary-General of the United Nations shall convene a Review Conference to consider any amendments to this Statute. Such review may include, but is not limited to, the list of crimes contained in article 5. The Conference shall be open to those participating in the Assembly of States Parties and on the same conditions.

2. At any time thereafter, at the request of a State Party and for the purposes set out in paragraph 1, the Secretary-General of the United Nations shall, upon approval by a majority of States Parties, convene a Review Conference.

3. The provisions of article 121, paragraphs 3 to 7, shall apply to the adoption and entry into force of any amendment to the Statute considered at a Review Conference.

Article 124 Transitional Provision

Notwithstanding article 12 paragraph 1, a State, on becoming a party to this Statute, may declare that, for a period of seven years after the entry into force of this Statute for the State concerned, it does not accept the jurisdiction of the Court with respect to the category of crimes referred to in article 8 when a crime is alleged to have been committed by its nationals or on its territory. A declaration under this article may be withdrawn at any time. The provisions of this article shall be reviewed at the Review Conference convened in accordance with article 123, paragraph 1.

Article 125 Signature, ratification, acceptance, approval or accession

1. This Statute shall be open for signature by all States in Rome, at the headquarters of the Food and Agriculture Organization of the United Nations, on 17 July 1998. Thereafter, it shall remain open for signature in Rome at the Ministry of Foreign Affairs of Italy until 17 October 1998. After that date, the Statute shall remain open for signature in New York, at United Nations Headquarters, until 31 December 2000.

2. This Statute is subject to ratification, acceptance or approval by signatory States. Instruments of ratification, acceptance or approval shall be deposited with the Secretary-General of the United Nations.

3. This Statute shall be open to accession by all States. Instruments of accession shall be deposited with the Secretary-General of the United Nations.

Article 126 Entry into force

1. This Statute shall enter into force on the first day of the month after the 60th day following the date of the deposit of the 60th instrument of ratification, acceptance, approval or accession with the Secretary-General of the United Nations.

2. For each State ratifying, accepting, approving or acceding to this Statute after the deposit of the 60th instrument of ratification, acceptance, approval or accession, the Statute shall enter into force on the first day of the month after the 60th day following the deposit by such State of its instrument of ratification, acceptance, approval or accession.

Article 127 Withdrawal

1. A State Party may, by written notification addressed to the Secretary-General of the United Nations, withdraw from this Statute. The withdrawal shall take effect one year after the date of receipt of the notification, unless the notification specifies a later date.

2. A State shall not be discharged, by reason of its withdrawal, from the obligations arising from this Statute while it was a Party to the Statute, including any financial obligations which may have accrued. Its withdrawal shall not affect any cooperation with the Court in connection with criminal investigations and proceedings in relation to which the withdrawing State had a duty to cooperate and which were commenced prior to the date on which the withdrawal became effective, nor shall it prejudice in any way the continued consideration of any matter which was already under consideration by the Court prior to the date on which the withdrawal became effective.

Article 128 Authentic texts

The original of this Statute, of which the Arabic, Chinese, English, French, Russian and Spanish texts are equally authentic, shall be deposited with the Secretary-General of the United Nations, who shall send certified copies thereof to all States.

IN WITNESS WHEREOF, the undersigned, being duly authorized thereto by their respective Governments, have signed this Statute.

DONE at Rome, this 17th day of July 1998.

Elements of Crimes

General introduction

1. Pursuant to article 9, the following Elements of Crimes shall assist the Court in the interpretation and application of articles 6, 7 and 8, consistent with the Statute. The provisions of the Statute, including article 21 and the general principles set out in Part 3, are applicable to the Elements of Crimes.

2. As stated in article 30, unless otherwise provided, a person shall be criminally responsible and liable for punishment for a crime within the jurisdiction of the Court only if the material elements are committed with intent and knowledge. Where no reference is made in the Elements of Crimes to a mental element for any particular conduct, consequence or circumstance listed, it is understood that the relevant mental element, i.e., intent, knowledge or both, set out in article 30 applies. Exceptions to the article 30 standard, based on the Statute, including applicable law under its relevant provisions, are indicated below.

3. Existence of intent and knowledge can be inferred from relevant facts and circumstances.

4. With respect to mental elements associated with elements involving value judgment, such as those using the terms 'inhumane' or 'severe', it is not necessary that the perpetrator personally completed a particular value judgment, unless otherwise indicated.

5. Grounds for excluding criminal responsibility or the absence thereof are generally not specified in the elements of crimes listed under each crime.[1]

6. The requirement of 'unlawfulness' found in the Statute or in other parts of international law, in particular international humanitarian law, is generally not specified in the elements of crimes.

7. The elements of crimes are generally structured in accordance with the following principles:
   - As the elements of crimes focus on the conduct, consequences and circumstances associated with each crime, they are generally listed in that order;

---

[1] This paragraph is without prejudice to the obligation of the Prosecutor under article 54, paragraph 1, of the Statute.

- When required, a particular mental element is listed after the affected conduct, consequence or circumstance;
- Contextual circumstances are listed last.

8. As used in the Elements of Crimes, the term 'perpetrator' is neutral as to guilt or innocence. The elements, including the appropriate mental elements, apply *mutatis mutandis* to all those whose criminal responsibility may fall under articles 25 and 28 of the Statute.

9. A particular conduct may constitute one or more crimes.

10. The use of short titles for the crimes has no legal effect.

Article 6   Genocide

Introduction

With respect to the last element listed for each crime:

- The term 'in the context of' would include the initial acts in an emerging pattern;
- The term 'manifest' is an objective qualification;
- Notwithstanding the normal requirement for a mental element provided for in article 30, and recognizing that knowledge of the circumstances will usually be addressed in proving genocidal intent, the appropriate requirement, if any, for a mental element regarding this circumstance will need to be decided by the Court on a case-by-case basis.

Article 6 (a)   Genocide by killing

Elements

1. The perpetrator killed[2] one or more persons.
2. Such person or persons belonged to a particular national, ethnical, racial or religious group.
3. The perpetrator intended to destroy, in whole or in part, that national, ethnical, racial or religious group, as such.
4. The conduct took place in the context of a manifest pattern of similar conduct directed against that group or was conduct that could itself effect such destruction.

---

[2] The term 'killed' is interchangeable with the term 'caused death'.

Article 6 (b) Genocide by causing serious bodily or mental harm

Elements

1. The perpetrator caused serious bodily or mental harm to one or more persons.[3]
2. Such person or persons belonged to a particular national, ethnical, racial or religious group.
3. The perpetrator intended to destroy, in whole or in part, that national, ethnical, racial or religious group, as such.
4. The conduct took place in the context of a manifest pattern of similar conduct directed against that group or was conduct that could itself effect such destruction.

Article 6 (c) Genocide by deliberately inflicting conditions of life calculated to bring about physical destruction

Elements

1. The perpetrator inflicted certain conditions of life upon one or more persons.
2. Such person or persons belonged to a particular national, ethnical, racial or religious group.
3. The perpetrator intended to destroy, in whole or in part, that national, ethnical, racial or religious group, as such.
4. The conditions of life were calculated to bring about the physical destruction of that group, in whole or in part.[4]
5. The conduct took place in the context of a manifest pattern of similar conduct directed against that group or was conduct that could itself effect such destruction.

Article 6 (d) Genocide by imposing measures intended to prevent births

Elements

1. The perpetrator imposed certain measures upon one or more persons.

---

[3] This conduct may include, but is not necessarily restricted to, acts of torture, rape, sexual violence or inhuman or degrading treatment.
[4] The term 'conditions of life' may include, but is not necessarily restricted to, deliberate deprivation of resources indispensable for survival, such as food or medical services, or systematic expulsion from homes.

2. Such person or persons belonged to a particular national, ethnical, racial or religious group.

3. The perpetrator intended to destroy, in whole or in part, that national, ethnical, racial or religious group, as such.

4. The measures imposed were intended to prevent births within that group.

5. The conduct took place in the context of a manifest pattern of similar conduct directed against that group or was conduct that could itself effect such destruction.

Article 6 (e) Genocide by forcibly transferring children

Elements

1. The perpetrator forcibly transferred one or more persons.[5]

2. Such person or persons belonged to a particular national, ethnical, racial or religious group.

3. The perpetrator intended to destroy, in whole or in part, that national, ethnical, racial or religious group, as such.

4. The transfer was from that group to another group.

5. The person or persons were under the age of 18 years.

6. The perpetrator knew, or should have known, that the person or persons were under the age of 18 years.

7. The conduct took place in the context of a manifest pattern of similar conduct directed against that group or was conduct that could itself effect such destruction.

Article 7 Crimes against humanity

Introduction

1. Since article 7 pertains to international criminal law, its provisions, consistent with article 22, must be strictly construed, taking into account that crimes against humanity as defined in article 7 are among the most serious crimes of concern to the international community as a whole, warrant and entail individual criminal responsibility, and require conduct which is impermissible under generally applicable international law, as recognized by the principal legal systems of the world.

---

[5] The term 'forcibly' is not restricted to physical force, but may include threat of force or coercion, such as that caused by fear of violence, duress, detention, psychological oppression or abuse of power, against such person or persons or another person, or by taking advantage of a coercive environment.

2. The last two elements for each crime against humanity describe the context in which the conduct must take place. These elements clarify the requisite participation in and knowledge of a widespread or systematic attack against a civilian population. However, the last element should not be interpreted as requiring proof that the perpetrator had knowledge of all characteristics of the attack or the precise details of the plan or policy of the State or organization. In the case of an emerging widespread or systematic attack against a civilian population, the intent clause of the last element indicates that this mental element is satisfied if the perpetrator intended to further such an attack.

3. 'Attack directed against a civilian population' in these context elements is understood to mean a course of conduct involving the multiple commission of acts referred to in article 7, paragraph 1, of the Statute against any civilian population, pursuant to or in furtherance of a State or organizational policy to commit such attack. The acts need not constitute a military attack. It is understood that 'policy to commit such attack' requires that the State or organization actively promote or encourage such an attack against a civilian population.[6]

Article 7 (1) (a) Crime against humanity of murder

Elements

1. The perpetrator killed[7] one or more persons.
2. The conduct was committed as part of a widespread or systematic attack directed against a civilian population.
3. The perpetrator knew that the conduct was part of or intended the conduct to be part of a widespread or systematic attack against a civilian population.

Article 7 (1) (b) Crime against humanity of extermination

Elements

1. The perpetrator killed[8] one or more persons, including by inflicting conditions of life calculated to bring about the destruction of part of a population.[9]

---

[6] A policy which has a civilian population as the object of the attack would be implemented by State or organizational action. Such a policy may, in exceptional circumstances, be implemented by a deliberate failure to take action, which is consciously aimed at encouraging such attack. The existence of such a policy cannot be inferred solely from the absence of governmental or organizational action.

[7] The term 'killed' is interchangeable with the term 'caused death'. This footnote applies to all elements which use either of these concepts.

[8] The conduct could be committed by different methods of killing, either directly or indirectly.

[9] The infliction of such conditions could include the deprivation of access to food and medicine.

2. The conduct constituted, or took place as part of,[10] a mass killing of members of a civilian population.
3. The conduct was committed as part of a widespread or systematic attack directed against a civilian population.
4. The perpetrator knew that the conduct was part of or intended the conduct to be part of a widespread or systematic attack directed against a civilian population.

Article 7 (1) (c) Crime against humanity of enslavement

Elements

1. The perpetrator exercised any or all of the powers attaching to the right of ownership over one or more persons, such as by purchasing, selling, lending or bartering such a person or persons, or by imposing on them a similar deprivation of liberty.[11]
2. The conduct was committed as part of a widespread or systematic attack directed against a civilian population.
3. The perpetrator knew that the conduct was part of or intended the conduct to be part of a widespread or systematic attack directed against a civilian population.

Article 7 (1) (d) Crime against humanity of deportation or forcible transfer of population

Elements

1. The perpetrator deported or forcibly[12] transferred,[13] without grounds permitted under international law, one or more persons to another State or location, by expulsion or other coercive acts.
2. Such person or persons were lawfully present in the area from which they were so deported or transferred.

---

[10] The term 'as part of' would include the initial conduct in a mass killing.

[11] It is understood that such deprivation of liberty may, in some circumstances, include exacting forced labour or otherwise reducing a person to a servile status as defined in the Supplementary Convention on the Abolition of Slavery, the Slave Trade, and Institutions and Practices Similar to Slavery of 1956. It is also understood that the conduct described in this element includes trafficking in persons, in particular women and children.

[12] The term 'forcibly' is not restricted to physical force, but may include threat of force or coercion, such as that caused by fear of violence, duress, detention, psychological oppression or abuse of power against such person or persons or another person, or by taking advantage of a coercive environment.

[13] 'Deported or forcibly transferred' is interchangeable with 'forcibly displaced'.

3. The perpetrator was aware of the factual circumstances that established the lawfulness of such presence.
4. The conduct was committed as part of a widespread or systematic attack directed against a civilian population.
5. The perpetrator knew that the conduct was part of or intended the conduct to be part of a widespread or systematic attack directed against a civilian population.

Article 7 (1) (e) Crime against humanity of imprisonment or other severe deprivation of physical liberty

Elements

1. The perpetrator imprisoned one or more persons or otherwise severely deprived one or more persons of physical liberty.
2. The gravity of the conduct was such that it was in violation of fundamental rules of international law.
3. The perpetrator was aware of the factual circumstances that established the gravity of the conduct.
4. The conduct was committed as part of a widespread or systematic attack directed against a civilian population.
5. The perpetrator knew that the conduct was part of or intended the conduct to be part of a widespread or systematic attack directed against a civilian population.

Article 7 (1) (f) Crime against humanity of torture[14]

Elements

1. The perpetrator inflicted severe physical or mental pain or suffering upon one or more persons.
2. Such person or persons were in the custody or under the control of the perpetrator.
3. Such pain or suffering did not arise only from, and was not inherent in or incidental to, lawful sanctions.
4. The conduct was committed as part of a widespread or systematic attack directed against a civilian population.
5. The perpetrator knew that the conduct was part of or intended the conduct to be part of a widespread or systematic attack directed against a civilian population.

[14] It is understood that no specific purpose need be proved for this crime.

Article 7 (1) (g)-1 Crime against humanity of rape

Elements

1. The perpetrator invaded[15] the body of a person by conduct resulting in penetration, however slight, of any part of the body of the victim or of the perpetrator with a sexual organ, or of the anal or genital opening of the victim with any object or any other part of the body.
2. The invasion was committed by force, or by threat of force or coercion, such as that caused by fear of violence, duress, detention, psychological oppression or abuse of power, against such person or another person, or by taking advantage of a coercive environment, or the invasion was committed against a person incapable of giving genuine consent.[16]
3. The conduct was committed as part of a widespread or systematic attack directed against a civilian population.
4. The perpetrator knew that the conduct was part of or intended the conduct to be part of a widespread or systematic attack directed against a civilian population.

Article 7 (1) (g)-2 Crime against humanity of sexual slavery[17]

Elements

1. The perpetrator exercised any or all of the powers attaching to the right of ownership over one or more persons, such as by purchasing, selling, lending or bartering such a person or persons, or by imposing on them a similar deprivation of liberty.[18]
2. The perpetrator caused such person or persons to engage in one or more acts of a sexual nature.
3. The conduct was committed as part of a widespread or systematic attack directed against a civilian population.

---

[15] The concept of 'invasion' is intended to be broad enough to be gender-neutral.
[16] It is understood that a person may be incapable of giving genuine consent if affected by natural, induced or age-related incapacity. This footnote also applies to the corresponding elements of article 7 (1) (g)-3, 5 and 6.
[17] Given the complex nature of this crime, it is recognized that its commission could involve more than one perpetrator as a part of a common criminal purpose.
[18] It is understood that such deprivation of liberty may, in some circumstances, include exacting forced labour or otherwise reducing a person to a servile status as defined in the Supplementary Convention on the Abolition of Slavery, the Slave Trade, and Institutions and Practices Similar to Slavery of 1956. It is also understood that the conduct described in this element includes trafficking in persons, in particular women and children.

4. The perpetrator knew that the conduct was part of or intended the conduct to be part of a widespread or systematic attack directed against a civilian population.

Article 7 (1) (g)-3 Crime against humanity of enforced prostitution

Elements

1. The perpetrator caused one or more persons to engage in one or more acts of a sexual nature by force, or by threat of force or coercion, such as that caused by fear of violence, duress, detention, psychological oppression or abuse of power, against such person or persons or another person, or by taking advantage of a coercive environment or such person's or persons' incapacity to give genuine consent.
2. The perpetrator or another person obtained or expected to obtain pecuniary or other advantage in exchange for or in connection with the acts of a sexual nature.
3. The conduct was committed as part of a widespread or systematic attack directed against a civilian population.
4. The perpetrator knew that the conduct was part of or intended the conduct to be part of a widespread or systematic attack directed against a civilian population.

Article 7 (1) (g)-4 Crime against humanity of forced pregnancy

Elements

1. The perpetrator confined one or more women forcibly made pregnant, with the intent of affecting the ethnic composition of any population or carrying out other grave violations of international law.
2. The conduct was committed as part of a widespread or systematic attack directed against a civilian population.
3. The perpetrator knew that the conduct was part of or intended the conduct to be part of a widespread or systematic attack directed against a civilian population.

Article 7 (1) (g)-5 Crime against humanity of enforced sterilization

Elements

1. The perpetrator deprived one or more persons of biological reproductive capacity.[19]
2. The conduct was neither justified by the medical or hospital treatment of the person or persons concerned nor carried out with their genuine consent.[20]
3. The conduct was committed as part of a widespread or systematic attack directed against a civilian population.
4. The perpetrator knew that the conduct was part of or intended the conduct to be part of a widespread or systematic attack directed against a civilian population.

Article 7 (1) (g)-6 Crime against humanity of sexual violence

Elements

1. The perpetrator committed an act of a sexual nature against one or more persons or caused such person or persons to engage in an act of a sexual nature by force, or by threat of force or coercion, such as that caused by fear of violence, duress, detention, psychological oppression or abuse of power, against such person or persons or another person, or by taking advantage of a coercive environment or such person's or persons' incapacity to give genuine consent.
2. Such conduct was of a gravity comparable to the other offences in article 7, paragraph 1 (g), of the Statute.
3. The perpetrator was aware of the factual circumstances that established the gravity of the conduct.
4. The conduct was committed as part of a widespread or systematic attack directed against a civilian population.
5. The perpetrator knew that the conduct was part of or intended the conduct to be part of a widespread or systematic attack directed against a civilian population.

---

[19] The deprivation is not intended to include birth-control measures which have a non-permanent effect in practice.
[20] It is understood that 'genuine consent' does not include consent obtained through deception.

Article 7 (1) (h) Crime against humanity of persecution

Elements

1. The perpetrator severely deprived, contrary to international law,[21] one or more persons of fundamental rights.
2. The perpetrator targeted such person or persons by reason of the identity of a group or collectivity or targeted the group or collectivity as such.
3. Such targeting was based on political, racial, national, ethnic, cultural, religious, gender as defined in article 7, paragraph 3, of the Statute, or other grounds that are universally recognized as impermissible under international law.
4. The conduct was committed in connection with any act referred to in article 7, paragraph 1, of the Statute or any crime within the jurisdiction of the Court.[22]
5. The conduct was committed as part of a widespread or systematic attack directed against a civilian population.
6. The perpetrator knew that the conduct was part of or intended the conduct to be part of a widespread or systematic attack directed against a civilian population.

Article 7 (1) (i) Crime against humanity of enforced disappearance of persons[23] [24]

Elements

1. The perpetrator:
   (a)   Arrested, detained[25] [26] or abducted one or more persons; or
   (b)   Refused to acknowledge the arrest, detention or abduction, or to give information on the fate or whereabouts of such person or persons.

---

[21] This requirement is without prejudice to paragraph 6 of the General Introduction to the Elements of Crimes.

[22] It is understood that no additional mental element is necessary for this element other than that inherent in element 6.

[23] Given the complex nature of this crime, it is recognized that its commission will normally involve more than one perpetrator as a part of a common criminal purpose.

[24] This crime falls under the jurisdiction of the Court only if the attack referred to in elements 7 and 8 occurs after the entry into force of the Statute.

[25] The word 'detained' would include a perpetrator who maintained an existing detention.

[26] It is understood that under certain circumstances an arrest or detention may have been lawful.

2.
(a)   Such arrest, detention or abduction was followed or accompanied by a refusal to acknowledge that deprivation of freedom or to give information on the fate or whereabouts of such person or persons; or

(b)   Such refusal was preceded or accompanied by that deprivation of freedom.

3.   The perpetrator was aware that:[27]
(a)   Such arrest, detention or abduction would be followed in the ordinary course of events by a refusal to acknowledge that deprivation of freedom or to give information on the fate or whereabouts of such person or persons;[28] or

(b)   Such refusal was preceded or accompanied by that deprivation of freedom.

4.   Such arrest, detention or abduction was carried out by, or with the authorization, support or acquiescence of, a State or a political organization.

5.   Such refusal to acknowledge that deprivation of freedom or to give information on the fate or whereabouts of such person or persons was carried out by, or with the authorization or support of, such State or political organization.

6.   The perpetrator intended to remove such person or persons from the protection of the law for a prolonged period of time.

7.   The conduct was committed as part of a widespread or systematic attack directed against a civilian population.

8.   The perpetrator knew that the conduct was part of or intended the conduct to be part of a widespread or systematic attack directed against a civilian population.

Article 7 (1) (j) Crime against humanity of apartheid

Elements

1.   The perpetrator committed an inhumane act against one or more persons.

2.   Such act was an act referred to in article 7, paragraph 1, of the Statute, or was an act of a character similar to any of those acts.[29]

3.   The perpetrator was aware of the factual circumstances that established the character of the act.

[27] This element, inserted because of the complexity of this crime, is without prejudice to the General Introduction to the Elements of Crimes.
[28] It is understood that, in the case of a perpetrator who maintained an existing detention, this element would be satisfied if the perpetrator was aware that such a refusal had already taken place.   [29] It is understood that 'character' refers to the nature and gravity of the act.

4. The conduct was committed in the context of an institutionalized regime of systematic oppression and domination by one racial group over any other racial group or groups.
5. The perpetrator intended to maintain such regime by that conduct.
6. The conduct was committed as part of a widespread or systematic attack directed against a civilian population.
7. The perpetrator knew that the conduct was part of or intended the conduct to be part of a widespread or systematic attack directed against a civilian population.

Article 7 (1) (k) Crime against humanity of other inhumane acts

Elements

1. The perpetrator inflicted great suffering, or serious injury to body or to mental or physical health, by means of an inhumane act.
2. Such act was of a character similar to any other act referred to in article 7, paragraph 1, of the Statute.[30]
3. The perpetrator was aware of the factual circumstances that established the character of the act.
4. The conduct was committed as part of a widespread or systematic attack directed against a civilian population.
5. The perpetrator knew that the conduct was part of or intended the conduct to be part of a widespread or systematic attack directed against a civilian population.

Article 8 War crimes

Introduction

The elements for war crimes under article 8, paragraph 2 (c) and (e), are subject to the limitations addressed in article 8, paragraph 2 (d) and (f), which are not elements of crimes.

The elements for war crimes under article 8, paragraph 2, of the Statute shall be interpreted within the established framework of the international law of armed conflict including, as appropriate, the international law of armed conflict applicable to armed conflict at sea.

With respect to the last two elements listed for each crime:

• There is no requirement for a legal evaluation by the perpetrator as to the existence of an armed conflict or its character as international or non-international;

---

[30] It is understood that 'character' refers to the nature and gravity of the act.

- In that context there is no requirement for awareness by the perpetrator of the facts that established the character of the conflict as international or non-international;
- There is only a requirement for the awareness of the factual circumstances that established the existence of an armed conflict that is implicit in the terms 'took place in the context of and was associated with'.

Article 8 (2) (a)

Article 8 (2) (a) (i) War crime of wilful killing

Elements

1. The perpetrator killed one or more persons.[31]
2. Such person or persons were protected under one or more of the Geneva Conventions of 1949.
3. The perpetrator was aware of the factual circumstances that established that protected status.[32] [33]
4. The conduct took place in the context of and was associated with an international armed conflict.[34]
5. The perpetrator was aware of factual circumstances that established the existence of an armed conflict.

Article 8 (2) (a) (ii)-1 War crime of torture

Elements[35]

1. The perpetrator inflicted severe physical or mental pain or suffering upon one or more persons.

---

[31] The term 'killed' is interchangeable with the term 'caused death'. This footnote applies to all elements which use either of these concepts.

[32] This mental element recognizes the interplay between articles 30 and 32. This footnote also applies to the corresponding element in each crime under article 8 (2) (a), and to the element in other crimes in article 8 (2) concerning the awareness of factual circumstances that establish the status of persons or property protected under the relevant international law of armed conflict.

[33] With respect to nationality, it is understood that the perpetrator needs only to know that the victim belonged to an adverse party to the conflict. This footnote also applies to the corresponding element in each crime under article 8 (2) (a).

[34] The term 'international armed conflict' includes military occupation. This footnote also applies to the corresponding element in each crime under article 8 (2) (a).

[35] As element 3 requires that all victims must be 'protected persons' under one or more of the Geneva Conventions of 1949, these elements do not include the custody or control requirement found in the elements of article 7 (1) (e).

2. The perpetrator inflicted the pain or suffering for such purposes as: obtaining information or a confession, punishment, intimidation or coercion or for any reason based on discrimination of any kind.
3. Such person or persons were protected under one or more of the Geneva Conventions of 1949.
4. The perpetrator was aware of the factual circumstances that established that protected status.
5. The conduct took place in the context of and was associated with an international armed conflict.
6. The perpetrator was aware of factual circumstances that established the existence of an armed conflict.

Article 8 (2) (a) (ii)-2 War crime of inhuman treatment

Elements

1. The perpetrator inflicted severe physical or mental pain or suffering upon one or more persons.
2. Such person or persons were protected under one or more of the Geneva Conventions of 1949.
3. The perpetrator was aware of the factual circumstances that established that protected status.
4. The conduct took place in the context of and was associated with an international armed conflict.
5. The perpetrator was aware of factual circumstances that established the existence of an armed conflict.

Article 8 (2) (a) (ii)-3 War crime of biological experiments

Elements

1. The perpetrator subjected one or more persons to a particular biological experiment.
2. The experiment seriously endangered the physical or mental health or integrity of such person or persons.
3. The intent of the experiment was non-therapeutic and it was neither justified by medical reasons nor carried out in such person's or persons' interest.
4. Such person or persons were protected under one or more of the Geneva Conventions of 1949.
5. The perpetrator was aware of the factual circumstances that established that protected status.
6. The conduct took place in the context of and was associated with an international armed conflict.

7. The perpetrator was aware of factual circumstances that established the existence of an armed conflict.

Article 8 (2) (a) (iii) War crime of wilfully causing great suffering

Elements

1. The perpetrator caused great physical or mental pain or suffering to, or serious injury to body or health of, one or more persons.
2. Such person or persons were protected under one or more of the Geneva Conventions of 1949.
3. The perpetrator was aware of the factual circumstances that established that protected status.
4. The conduct took place in the context of and was associated with an international armed conflict.
5. The perpetrator was aware of factual circumstances that established the existence of an armed conflict.

Article 8 (2) (a) (iv) War crime of destruction and appropriation of property

Elements

1. The perpetrator destroyed or appropriated certain property.
2. The destruction or appropriation was not justified by military necessity.
3. The destruction or appropriation was extensive and carried out wantonly.
4. Such property was protected under one or more of the Geneva Conventions of 1949.
5. The perpetrator was aware of the factual circumstances that established that protected status.
6. The conduct took place in the context of and was associated with an international armed conflict.
7. The perpetrator was aware of factual circumstances that established the existence of an armed conflict.

Article 8 (2) (a) (v) War crime of compelling service in hostile forces

Elements

1. The perpetrator coerced one or more persons, by act or threat, to take part in military operations against that person's own country or forces or otherwise serve in the forces of a hostile power.

2. Such person or persons were protected under one or more of the Geneva Conventions of 1949.
3. The perpetrator was aware of the factual circumstances that established that protected status.
4. The conduct took place in the context of and was associated with an international armed conflict.
5. The perpetrator was aware of factual circumstances that established the existence of an armed conflict.

Article 8 (2) (a) (vi) War crime of denying a fair trial

Elements

1. The perpetrator deprived one or more persons of a fair and regular trial by denying judicial guarantees as defined, in particular, in the third and the fourth Geneva Conventions of 1949.
2. Such person or persons were protected under one or more of the Geneva Conventions of 1949.
3. The perpetrator was aware of the factual circumstances that established that protected status.
4. The conduct took place in the context of and was associated with an international armed conflict.
5. The perpetrator was aware of factual circumstances that established the existence of an armed conflict.

Article 8 (2) (a) (vii)-1 War crime of unlawful deportation and transfer

Elements

1. The perpetrator deported or transferred one or more persons to another State or to another location.
2. Such person or persons were protected under one or more of the Geneva Conventions of 1949.
3. The perpetrator was aware of the factual circumstances that established that protected status.
4. The conduct took place in the context of and was associated with an international armed conflict.
5. The perpetrator was aware of factual circumstances that established the existence of an armed conflict.

Article 8 (2) (a) (vii)-2 War crime of unlawful confinement

Elements

1. The perpetrator confined or continued to confine one or more persons to a certain location.
2. Such person or persons were protected under one or more of the Geneva Conventions of 1949.
3. The perpetrator was aware of the factual circumstances that established that protected status.
4. The conduct took place in the context of and was associated with an international armed conflict.
5. The perpetrator was aware of factual circumstances that established the existence of an armed conflict.

Article 8 (2) (a) (viii) War crime of taking hostages

Elements

1. The perpetrator seized, detained or otherwise held hostage one or more persons.
2. The perpetrator threatened to kill, injure or continue to detain such person or persons.
3. The perpetrator intended to compel a State, an international organization, a natural or legal person or a group of persons to act or refrain from acting as an explicit or implicit condition for the safety or the release of such person or persons.
4. Such person or persons were protected under one or more of the Geneva Conventions of 1949.
5. The perpetrator was aware of the factual circumstances that established that protected status.
6. The conduct took place in the context of and was associated with an international armed conflict.
7. The perpetrator was aware of factual circumstances that established the existence of an armed conflict.

Article 8 (2) (b)

Article 8 (2) (b) (i) War crime of attacking civilians

Elements

1. The perpetrator directed an attack.
2. The object of the attack was a civilian population as such or individual civilians not taking direct part in hostilities.
3. The perpetrator intended the civilian population as such or individual civilians not taking direct part in hostilities to be the object of the attack.
4. The conduct took place in the context of and was associated with an international armed conflict.
5. The perpetrator was aware of factual circumstances that established the existence of an armed conflict.

Article 8 (2) (b) (ii) War crime of attacking civilian objects

Elements

1. The perpetrator directed an attack.
2. The object of the attack was civilian objects, that is, objects which are not military objectives.
3. The perpetrator intended such civilian objects to be the object of the attack.
4. The conduct took place in the context of and was associated with an international armed conflict.
5. The perpetrator was aware of factual circumstances that established the existence of an armed conflict.

Article 8 (2) (b) (iii) War crime of attacking personnel or objects involved in a humanitarian assistance or peacekeeping mission

Elements

1. The perpetrator directed an attack.
2. The object of the attack was personnel, installations, material, units or vehicles involved in a humanitarian assistance or peacekeeping mission in accordance with the Charter of the United Nations.
3. The perpetrator intended such personnel, installations, material, units or vehicles so involved to be the object of the attack.

4. Such personnel, installations, material, units or vehicles were entitled to that protection given to civilians or civilian objects under the international law of armed conflict.
5. The perpetrator was aware of the factual circumstances that established that protection.
6. The conduct took place in the context of and was associated with an international armed conflict.
7. The perpetrator was aware of factual circumstances that established the existence of an armed conflict.

Article 8 (2) (b) (iv) War crime of excessive incidental death, injury, or damage

Elements

1. The perpetrator launched an attack.
2. The attack was such that it would cause incidental death or injury to civilians or damage to civilian objects or widespread, long-term and severe damage to the natural environment and that such death, injury or damage would be of such an extent as to be clearly excessive in relation to the concrete and direct overall military advantage anticipated.[36]
3. The perpetrator knew that the attack would cause incidental death or injury to civilians or damage to civilian objects or widespread, long-term and severe damage to the natural environment and that such death, injury or damage would be of such an extent as to be clearly excessive in relation to the concrete and direct overall military advantage anticipated.[37]
4. The conduct took place in the context of and was associated with an international armed conflict.
5. The perpetrator was aware of factual circumstances that established the existence of an armed conflict.

---

[36] The expression 'concrete and direct overall military advantage' refers to a military advantage that is foreseeable by the perpetrator at the relevant time. Such advantage may or may not be temporally or geographically related to the object of the attack. The fact that this crime admits the possibility of lawful incidental injury and collateral damage does not in any way justify any violation of the law applicable in armed conflict. It does not address justifications for war or other rules related to jus ad bellum. It reflects the proportionality requirement inherent in determining the legality of any military activity undertaken in the context of an armed conflict.

[37] As opposed to the general rule set forth in paragraph 4 of the General Introduction, this knowledge element requires that the perpetrator make the value judgment as described therein. An evaluation of that value judgment must be based on the requisite information available to the perpetrator at the time.

Article 8 (2) (b) (v) War crime of attacking undefended places[38]

Elements

1. The perpetrator attacked one or more towns, villages, dwellings or buildings.
2. Such towns, villages, dwellings or buildings were open for unresisted occupation.
3. Such towns, villages, dwellings or buildings did not constitute military objectives.
4. The conduct took place in the context of and was associated with an international armed conflict.
5. The perpetrator was aware of factual circumstances that established the existence of an armed conflict.

Article 8 (2) (b) (vi) War crime of killing or wounding a person hors de combat

Elements

1. The perpetrator killed or injured one or more persons.
2. Such person or persons were *hors de combat.*
3. The perpetrator was aware of the factual circumstances that established this status.
4. The conduct took place in the context of and was associated with an international armed conflict.
5. The perpetrator was aware of factual circumstances that established the existence of an armed conflict.

Article 8 (2) (b) (vii)-1 War crime of improper use of a flag of truce

Elements

1. The perpetrator used a flag of truce.
2. The perpetrator made such use in order to feign an intention to negotiate when there was no such intention on the part of the perpetrator.
3. The perpetrator knew or should have known of the prohibited nature of such use.[39]

---

[38] The presence in the locality of persons specially protected under the Geneva Conventions of 1949 or of police forces retained for the sole purpose of maintaining law and order does not by itself render the locality a military objective.

[39] This mental element recognizes the interplay between article 30 and article 32. The term 'prohibited nature' denotes illegality.

4. The conduct resulted in death or serious personal injury.
5. The perpetrator knew that the conduct could result in death or serious personal injury.
6. The conduct took place in the context of and was associated with an international armed conflict.
7. The perpetrator was aware of factual circumstances that established the existence of an armed conflict.

Article 8 (2) (b) (vii)-2 War crime of improper use of a flag, insignia or uniform of the hostile party

Elements

1. The perpetrator used a flag, insignia or uniform of the hostile party.
2. The perpetrator made such use in a manner prohibited under the international law of armed conflict while engaged in an attack.
3. The perpetrator knew or should have known of the prohibited nature of such use.[40]
4. The conduct resulted in death or serious personal injury.
5. The perpetrator knew that the conduct could result in death or serious personal injury.
6. The conduct took place in the context of and was associated with an international armed conflict.
7. The perpetrator was aware of factual circumstances that established the existence of an armed conflict.

Article 8 (2) (b) (vii)-3 War crime of improper use of a flag, insignia or uniform of the United Nations

Elements

1. The perpetrator used a flag, insignia or uniform of the United Nations.
2. The perpetrator made such use in a manner prohibited under the international law of armed conflict.
3. The perpetrator knew of the prohibited nature of such use.[41]
4. The conduct resulted in death or serious personal injury.

[40] This mental element recognizes the interplay between article 30 and article 32. The term 'prohibited nature' denotes illegality.
[41] This mental element recognizes the interplay between article 30 and article 32. The 'should have known' test required in the other offences found in article 8 (2) (b) (vii) is not applicable here because of the variable and regulatory nature of the relevant prohibitions.

5. The perpetrator knew that the conduct could result in death or serious personal injury.
6. The conduct took place in the context of and was associated with an international armed conflict.
7. The perpetrator was aware of factual circumstances that established the existence of an armed conflict.

Article 8 (2) (b) (vii)-4 War crime of improper use of the distinctive emblems of the Geneva Conventions

Elements

1. The perpetrator used the distinctive emblems of the Geneva Conventions.
2. The perpetrator made such use for combatant purposes[42] in a manner prohibited under the international law of armed conflict.
3. The perpetrator knew or should have known of the prohibited nature of such use.[43]
4. The conduct resulted in death or serious personal injury.
5. The perpetrator knew that the conduct could result in death or serious personal injury.
6. The conduct took place in the context of and was associated with an international armed conflict.
7. The perpetrator was aware of factual circumstances that established the existence of an armed conflict.

Article 8 (2) (b) (viii) The transfer, directly or indirectly, by the Occupying Power of parts of its own civilian population into the territory it occupies, or the deportation or transfer of all or parts of the population of the occupied territory within or outside this territory

Elements

1. The perpetrator:
   (a)   Transferred,[44] directly or indirectly, parts of its own population into the territory it occupies; or

---

[42] 'Combatant purposes' in these circumstances means purposes directly related to hostilities and not including medical, religious or similar activities.

[43] This mental element recognizes the interplay between article 30 and article 32. The term 'prohibited nature' denotes illegality.

[44] The term 'transfer' needs to be interpreted in accordance with the relevant provisions of international humanitarian law.

(b) Deported or transferred all or parts of the population of the occupied territory within or outside this territory.

2. The conduct took place in the context of and was associated with an international armed conflict.

3. The perpetrator was aware of factual circumstances that established the existence of an armed conflict.

Article 8 (2) (b) (ix) War crime of attacking protected objects[45]

Elements

1. The perpetrator directed an attack.

2. The object of the attack was one or more buildings dedicated to religion, education, art, science or charitable purposes, historic monuments, hospitals or places where the sick and wounded are collected, which were not military objectives.

3. The perpetrator intended such building or buildings dedicated to religion, education, art, science or charitable purposes, historic monuments, hospitals or places where the sick and wounded are collected, which were not military objectives, to be the object of the attack.

4. The conduct took place in the context of and was associated with an international armed conflict.

5. The perpetrator was aware of factual circumstances that established the existence of an armed conflict.

Article 8 (2) (b) (x)-1 War crime of mutilation

Elements

1. The perpetrator subjected one or more persons to mutilation, in particular by permanently disfiguring the person or persons, or by permanently disabling or removing an organ or appendage.

2. The conduct caused death or seriously endangered the physical or mental health of such person or persons.

3. The conduct was neither justified by the medical, dental or hospital treatment of the person or persons concerned nor carried out in such person's or persons' interest.[46]

---

[45] The presence in the locality of persons specially protected under the Geneva Conventions of 1949 or of police forces retained for the sole purpose of maintaining law and order does not by itself render the locality a military objective.

[46] Consent is not a defence to this crime. The crime prohibits any medical procedure which is not

4. Such person or persons were in the power of an adverse party.
5. The conduct took place in the context of and was associated with an international armed conflict.
6. The perpetrator was aware of factual circumstances that established the existence of an armed conflict.

Article 8 (2) (b) (x)-2 War crime of medical or scientific experiments

Elements

1. The perpetrator subjected one or more persons to a medical or scientific experiment.
2. The experiment caused death or seriously endangered the physical or mental health or integrity of such person or persons.
3. The conduct was neither justified by the medical, dental or hospital treatment of such person or persons concerned nor carried out in such person's or persons' interest.
4. Such person or persons were in the power of an adverse party.
5. The conduct took place in the context of and was associated with an international armed conflict.
6. The perpetrator was aware of factual circumstances that established the existence of an armed conflict.

Article 8 (2) (b) (xi) War crime of treacherously killing or wounding

Elements

1. The perpetrator invited the confidence or belief of one or more persons that they were entitled to, or were obliged to accord, protection under rules of international law applicable in armed conflict.
2. The perpetrator intended to betray that confidence or belief.
3. The perpetrator killed or injured such person or persons.
4. The perpetrator made use of that confidence or belief in killing or injuring such person or persons.
5. Such person or persons belonged to an adverse party.

footnote 46 (*cont.*)
indicated by the state of health of the person concerned and which is not consistent with generally accepted medical standards which would be applied under similar medical circumstances to persons who are nationals of the party conducting the procedure and who are in no way deprived of liberty. This footnote also applies to the same element for article 8 (2) (b) (x)-2.

6. The conduct took place in the context of and was associated with an international armed conflict.
7. The perpetrator was aware of factual circumstances that established the existence of an armed conflict.

Article 8 (2) (b) (xii) War crime of denying quarter

Elements

1. The perpetrator declared or ordered that there shall be no survivors.
2. Such declaration or order was given in order to threaten an adversary or to conduct hostilities on the basis that there shall be no survivors.
3. The perpetrator was in a position of effective command or control over the subordinate forces to which the declaration or order was directed.
4. The conduct took place in the context of and was associated with an international armed conflict.
5. The perpetrator was aware of factual circumstances that established the existence of an armed conflict.

Article 8 (2) (b) (xiii) War crime of destroying or seizing the enemy's property

Elements

1. The perpetrator destroyed or seized certain property.
2. Such property was property of a hostile party.
3. Such property was protected from that destruction or seizure under the international law of armed conflict.
4. The perpetrator was aware of the factual circumstances that established the status of the property.
5. The destruction or seizure was not justified by military necessity.
6. The conduct took place in the context of and was associated with an international armed conflict.
7. The perpetrator was aware of factual circumstances that established the existence of an armed conflict.

Article 8 (2) (b) (xiv) War crime of depriving the nationals of the hostile power of rights or actions

Elements

1. The perpetrator effected the abolition, suspension or termination of admissibility in a court of law of certain rights or actions.

2. The abolition, suspension or termination was directed at the nationals of a hostile party.
3. The perpetrator intended the abolition, suspension or termination to be directed at the nationals of a hostile party.
4. The conduct took place in the context of and was associated with an international armed conflict.
5. The perpetrator was aware of factual circumstances that established the existence of an armed conflict.

Article 8 (2) (b) (xv) War crime of compelling participation in military operations

Elements

1. The perpetrator coerced one or more persons by act or threat to take part in military operations against that person's own country or forces.
2. Such person or persons were nationals of a hostile party.
3. The conduct took place in the context of and was associated with an international armed conflict.
4. The perpetrator was aware of factual circumstances that established the existence of an armed conflict.

Article 8 (2) (b) (xvi) War crime of pillaging

Elements

1. The perpetrator appropriated certain property.
2. The perpetrator intended to deprive the owner of the property and to appropriate it for private or personal use.[47]
3. The appropriation was without the consent of the owner.
4. The conduct took place in the context of and was associated with an international armed conflict.
5. The perpetrator was aware of factual circumstances that established the existence of an armed conflict.

---

[47] As indicated by the use of the term 'private or personal use', appropriations justified by military necessity cannot constitute the crime of pillaging.

Article 8 (2) (b) (xvii) War crime of employing poison or poisoned weapons

Elements

1. The perpetrator employed a substance or a weapon that releases a substance as a result of its employment.
2. The substance was such that it causes death or serious damage to health in the ordinary course of events, through its toxic properties.
3. The conduct took place in the context of and was associated with an international armed conflict.
4. The perpetrator was aware of factual circumstances that established the existence of an armed conflict.

Article 8 (2) (b) (xviii) War crime of employing prohibited gases, liquids, materials or devices

Elements

1. The perpetrator employed a gas or other analogous substance or device.
2. The gas, substance or device was such that it causes death or serious damage to health in the ordinary course of events, through its asphyxiating or toxic properties.[48]
3. The conduct took place in the context of and was associated with an international armed conflict.
4. The perpetrator was aware of factual circumstances that established the existence of an armed conflict.

Article 8 (2) (b) (xix) War crime of employing prohibited bullets

Elements

1. The perpetrator employed certain bullets.
2. The bullets were such that their use violates the international law of armed conflict because they expand or flatten easily in the human body.
3. The perpetrator was aware that the nature of the bullets was such that their employment would uselessly aggravate suffering or the wounding effect.

---

[48] Nothing in this element shall be interpreted as limiting or prejudicing in any way existing or developing rules of international law with respect to development, production, stockpiling and use of chemical weapons.

4. The conduct took place in the context of and was associated with an international armed conflict.
5. The perpetrator was aware of factual circumstances that established the existence of an armed conflict.

Article 8 (2) (b) (xx) War crime of employing weapons, projectiles or materials or methods of warfare listed in the Annex to the Statute

Elements

[Elements will have to be drafted once weapons, projectiles or material or methods of warfare have been included in an annex to the Statute.]

Article 8 (2) (b) (xxi) War crime of outrages upon personal dignity

Elements

1. The perpetrator humiliated, degraded or otherwise violated the dignity of one or more persons.[49]
2. The severity of the humiliation, degradation or other violation was of such degree as to be generally recognized as an outrage upon personal dignity.
3. The conduct took place in the context of and was associated with an international armed conflict.
4. The perpetrator was aware of factual circumstances that established the existence of an armed conflict.

Article 8 (2) (b) (xxii)-1 War crime of rape

Elements

1. The perpetrator invaded[50] the body of a person by conduct resulting in penetration, however slight, of any part of the body of the victim or of the perpetrator with a sexual organ, or of the anal or genital opening of the victim with any object or any other part of the body.
2. The invasion was committed by force, or by threat of force or coercion, such as that caused by fear of violence, duress, detention, psychological oppression or abuse of power, against such person or another person, or by taking advantage

[49] For this crime, 'persons' can include dead persons. It is understood that the victim need not personally be aware of the existence of the humiliation or degradation or other violation. This element takes into account relevant aspects of the cultural background of the victim.
[50] The concept of 'invasion' is intended to be broad enough to be gender-neutral.

of a coercive environment, or the invasion was committed against a person incapable of giving genuine consent.[51]

3. The conduct took place in the context of and was associated with an international armed conflict.

4. The perpetrator was aware of factual circumstances that established the existence of an armed conflict.

Article 8 (2) (b) (xxii)-2 War crime of sexual slavery[52]

Elements

1. The perpetrator exercised any or all of the powers attaching to the right of ownership over one or more persons, such as by purchasing, selling, lending or bartering such a person or persons, or by imposing on them a similar deprivation of liberty.[53]

2. The perpetrator caused such person or persons to engage in one or more acts of a sexual nature.

3. The conduct took place in the context of and was associated with an international armed conflict.

4. The perpetrator was aware of factual circumstances that established the existence of an armed conflict.

Article 8 (2) (b) (xxii)-3 War crime of enforced prostitution

Elements

1. The perpetrator caused one or more persons to engage in one or more acts of a sexual nature by force, or by threat of force or coercion, such as that caused by fear of violence, duress, detention, psychological oppression or abuse of power, against such person or persons or another person, or by taking advantage of a coercive environment or such person's or persons' incapacity to give genuine consent.

---

[51] It is understood that a person may be incapable of giving genuine consent if affected by natural, induced or age-related incapacity. This footnote also applies to the corresponding elements of article 8 (2) (b) (xxii)-3, 5 and 6.

[52] Given the complex nature of this crime, it is recognized that its commission could involve more than one perpetrator as a part of a common criminal purpose.

[53] It is understood that such deprivation of liberty may, in some circumstances, include exacting forced labour or otherwise reducing a person to servile status as defined in the Supplementary Convention on the Abolition of Slavery, the Slave Trade, and Institutions and Practices Similar to Slavery of 1956. It is also understood that the conduct described in this element includes trafficking in persons, in particular women and children.

2. The perpetrator or another person obtained or expected to obtain pecuniary or other advantage in exchange for or in connection with the acts of a sexual nature.
3. The conduct took place in the context of and was associated with an international armed conflict.
4. The perpetrator was aware of factual circumstances that established the existence of an armed conflict.

Article 8 (2) (b) (xxii)-4 War crime of forced pregnancy

Elements

1. The perpetrator confined one or more women forcibly made pregnant, with the intent of affecting the ethnic composition of any population or carrying out other grave violations of international law.
2. The conduct took place in the context of and was associated with an international armed conflict.
3. The perpetrator was aware of factual circumstances that established the existence of an armed conflict.

Article 8 (2) (b) (xxii)-5 War crime of enforced sterilization

Elements

1. The perpetrator deprived one or more persons of biological reproductive capacity.[54]
2. The conduct was neither justified by the medical or hospital treatment of the person or persons concerned nor carried out with their genuine consent.[55]
3. The conduct took place in the context of and was associated with an international armed conflict.
4. The perpetrator was aware of factual circumstances that established the existence of an armed conflict.

Article 8 (2) (b) (xxii)-6 War crime of sexual violence

Elements

1. The perpetrator committed an act of a sexual nature against one or more persons or caused such person or persons to engage in an act of a sexual

---

[54] The deprivation is not intended to include birth-control measures which have a non-permanent effect in practice.

[55] It is understood that 'genuine consent' does not include consent obtained through deception.

nature by force, or by threat of force or coercion, such as that caused by fear of violence, duress, detention, psychological oppression or abuse of power, against such person or persons or another person, or by taking advantage of a coercive environment or such person's or persons' incapacity to give genuine consent.

2. The conduct was of a gravity comparable to that of a grave breach of the Geneva Conventions.

3. The perpetrator was aware of the factual circumstances that established the gravity of the conduct.

4. The conduct took place in the context of and was associated with an international armed conflict.

5. The perpetrator was aware of factual circumstances that established the existence of an armed conflict.

Article 8 (2) (b) (xxiii) War crime of using protected persons as shields

Elements

1. The perpetrator moved or otherwise took advantage of the location of one or more civilians or other persons protected under the international law of armed conflict.

2. The perpetrator intended to shield a military objective from attack or shield, favour or impede military operations.

3. The conduct took place in the context of and was associated with an international armed conflict.

4. The perpetrator was aware of factual circumstances that established the existence of an armed conflict.

Article 8 (2) (b) (xxiv) War crime of attacking objects or persons using the distinctive emblems of the Geneva Conventions

Elements

1. The perpetrator attacked one or more persons, buildings, medical units or transports or other objects using, in conformity with international law, a distinctive emblem or other method of identification indicating protection under the Geneva Conventions.

2. The perpetrator intended such persons, buildings, units or transports or other objects so using such identification to be the object of the attack.

3. The conduct took place in the context of and was associated with an international armed conflict.

4. The perpetrator was aware of factual circumstances that established the existence of an armed conflict.

Article 8 (2) (b) (xxv) War crime of starvation as a method of warfare

Elements

1. The perpetrator deprived civilians of objects indispensable to their survival.
2. The perpetrator intended to starve civilians as a method of warfare.
3. The conduct took place in the context of and was associated with an international armed conflict.
4. The perpetrator was aware of factual circumstances that established the existence of an armed conflict.

Article 8 (2) (b) (xxvi) War crime of using, conscripting or enlisting children

Elements

1. The perpetrator conscripted or enlisted one or more persons into the national armed forces or used one or more persons to participate actively in hostilities.
2. Such person or persons were under the age of 15 years.
3. The perpetrator knew or should have known that such person or persons were under the age of 15 years.
4. The conduct took place in the context of and was associated with an international armed conflict.
5. The perpetrator was aware of factual circumstances that established the existence of an armed conflict.

Article 8 (2) (c)

Article 8 (2) (c) (i)-1 War crime of murder

Elements

1. The perpetrator killed one or more persons.
2. Such person or persons were either *hors de combat*, or were civilians, medical personnel, or religious personnel[56] taking no active part in the hostilities.
3. The perpetrator was aware of the factual circumstances that established this status.

---

[56] The term 'religious personnel' includes those non-confessional non-combatant military personnel carrying out a similar function.

4. The conduct took place in the context of and was associated with an armed conflict not of an international character.
5. The perpetrator was aware of factual circumstances that established the existence of an armed conflict.

Article 8 (2) (c) (i)-2 War crime of mutilation

Elements

1. The perpetrator subjected one or more persons to mutilation, in particular by permanently disfiguring the person or persons, or by permanently disabling or removing an organ or appendage.
2. The conduct was neither justified by the medical, dental or hospital treatment of the person or persons concerned nor carried out in such person's or persons' interests.
3. Such person or persons were either *hors de combat*, or were civilians, medical personnel or religious personnel taking no active part in the hostilities.
4. The perpetrator was aware of the factual circumstances that established this status.
5. The conduct took place in the context of and was associated with an armed conflict not of an international character.
6. The perpetrator was aware of factual circumstances that established the existence of an armed conflict.

Article 8 (2) (c) (i)-3 War crime of cruel treatment

Elements

1. The perpetrator inflicted severe physical or mental pain or suffering upon one or more persons.
2. Such person or persons were either *hors de combat*, or were civilians, medical personnel, or religious personnel taking no active part in the hostilities.
3. The perpetrator was aware of the factual circumstances that established this status.
4. The conduct took place in the context of and was associated with an armed conflict not of an international character.
5. The perpetrator was aware of factual circumstances that established the existence of an armed conflict.

Article 8 (2) (c) (i)-4 War crime of torture

Elements

1. The perpetrator inflicted severe physical or mental pain or suffering upon one or more persons.
2. The perpetrator inflicted the pain or suffering for such purposes as: obtaining information or a confession, punishment, intimidation or coercion or for any reason based on discrimination of any kind.
3. Such person or persons were either *hors de combat*, or were civilians, medical personnel or religious personnel taking no active part in the hostilities.
4. The perpetrator was aware of the factual circumstances that established this status.
5. The conduct took place in the context of and was associated with an armed conflict not of an international character.
6. The perpetrator was aware of factual circumstances that established the existence of an armed conflict.

Article 8 (2) (c) (ii) War crime of outrages upon personal dignity

Elements

1. The perpetrator humiliated, degraded or otherwise violated the dignity of one or more persons.[57]
2. The severity of the humiliation, degradation or other violation was of such degree as to be generally recognized as an outrage upon personal dignity.
3. Such person or persons were either *hors de combat*, or were civilians, medical personnel or religious personnel taking no active part in the hostilities.
4. The perpetrator was aware of the factual circumstances that established this status.
5. The conduct took place in the context of and was associated with an armed conflict not of an international character.
6. The perpetrator was aware of factual circumstances that established the existence of an armed conflict.

---

[57] For this crime, 'persons' can include dead persons. It is understood that the victim need not personally be aware of the existence of the humiliation or degradation or other violation. This element takes into account relevant aspects of the cultural background of the victim.

Article 8 (2) (c) (iii) War crime of taking hostages

Elements

1. The perpetrator seized, detained or otherwise held hostage one or more persons.
2. The perpetrator threatened to kill, injure or continue to detain such person or persons.
3. The perpetrator intended to compel a State, an international organization, a natural or legal person or a group of persons to act or refrain from acting as an explicit or implicit condition for the safety or the release of such person or persons.
4. Such person or persons were either *hors de combat,* or were civilians, medical personnel or religious personnel taking no active part in the hostilities.
5. The perpetrator was aware of the factual circumstances that established this status.
6. The conduct took place in the context of and was associated with an armed conflict not of an international character.
7. The perpetrator was aware of factual circumstances that established the existence of an armed conflict.

Article 8 (2) (c) (iv) War crime of sentencing or execution without due process

Elements

1. The perpetrator passed sentence or executed one or more persons.[58]
2. Such person or persons were either *hors de combat,* or were civilians, medical personnel or religious personnel taking no active part in the hostilities.
3. The perpetrator was aware of the factual circumstances that established this status.
4. There was no previous judgment pronounced by a court, or the court that rendered judgment was not 'regularly constituted', that is, it did not afford the essential guarantees of independence and impartiality, or the court that rendered judgment did not afford all other judicial guarantees generally recognized as indispensable under international law.[59]

---

[58] The elements laid down in these documents do not address the different forms of individual criminal responsibility, as enunciated in articles 25 and 28 of the Statute.
[59] With respect to elements 4 and 5, the Court should consider whether, in the light of all relevant circumstances, the cumulative effect of factors with respect to guarantees deprived the person or persons of a fair trial.

5. The perpetrator was aware of the absence of a previous judgment or of the denial of relevant guarantees and the fact that they are essential or indispensable to a fair trial.
6. The conduct took place in the context of and was associated with an armed conflict not of an international character.
7. The perpetrator was aware of factual circumstances that established the existence of an armed conflict.

Article 8 (2) (e)

Article 8 (2) (e) (i) War crime of attacking civilians

Elements

1. The perpetrator directed an attack.
2. The object of the attack was a civilian population as such or individual civilians not taking direct part in hostilities.
3. The perpetrator intended the civilian population as such or individual civilians not taking direct part in hostilities to be the object of the attack.
4. The conduct took place in the context of and was associated with an armed conflict not of an international character.
5. The perpetrator was aware of factual circumstances that established the existence of an armed conflict.

Article 8 (2) (e) (ii) War crime of attacking objects or persons using the distinctive emblems of the Geneva Conventions

Elements

1. The perpetrator attacked one or more persons, buildings, medical units or transports or other objects using, in conformity with international law, a distinctive emblem or other method of identification indicating protection under the Geneva Conventions.
2. The perpetrator intended such persons, buildings, units or transports or other objects so using such identification to be the object of the attack.
3. The conduct took place in the context of and was associated with an armed conflict not of an international character.
4. The perpetrator was aware of factual circumstances that established the existence of an armed conflict.

Article 8 (2) (e) (iii) War crime of attacking personnel or objects involved in a humanitarian assistance or peacekeeping mission

Elements

1. The perpetrator directed an attack.
2. The object of the attack was personnel, installations, material, units or vehicles involved in a humanitarian assistance or peacekeeping mission in accordance with the Charter of the United Nations.
3. The perpetrator intended such personnel, installations, material, units or vehicles so involved to be the object of the attack.
4. Such personnel, installations, material, units or vehicles were entitled to that protection given to civilians or civilian objects under the international law of armed conflict.
5. The perpetrator was aware of the factual circumstances that established that protection.
6. The conduct took place in the context of and was associated with an armed conflict not of an international character.
7. The perpetrator was aware of factual circumstances that established the existence of an armed conflict.

Article 8 (2) (e) (iv) War crime of attacking protected objects[60]

Elements

1. The perpetrator directed an attack.
2. The object of the attack was one or more buildings dedicated to religion, education, art, science or charitable purposes, historic monuments, hospitals or places where the sick and wounded are collected, which were not military objectives.
3. The perpetrator intended such building or buildings dedicated to religion, education, art, science or charitable purposes, historic monuments, hospitals or places where the sick and wounded are collected, which were not military objectives, to be the object of the attack.
4. The conduct took place in the context of and was associated with an armed conflict not of an international character.

---

[60] The presence in the locality of persons specially protected under the Geneva Conventions of 1949 or of police forces retained for the sole purpose of maintaining law and order does not by itself render the locality a military objective.

5. The perpetrator was aware of factual circumstances that established the existence of an armed conflict.

Article 8 (2) (e) (v) War crime of pillaging

Elements

1. The perpetrator appropriated certain property.
2. The perpetrator intended to deprive the owner of the property and to appropriate it for private or personal use.[61]
3. The appropriation was without the consent of the owner.
4. The conduct took place in the context of and was associated with an armed conflict not of an international character.
5. The perpetrator was aware of factual circumstances that established the existence of an armed conflict.

Article 8 (2) (e) (vi)-1 War crime of rape

Elements

1. The perpetrator invaded[62] the body of a person by conduct resulting in penetration, however slight, of any part of the body of the victim or of the perpetrator with a sexual organ, or of the anal or genital opening of the victim with any object or any other part of the body.
2. The invasion was committed by force, or by threat of force or coercion, such as that caused by fear of violence, duress, detention, psychological oppression or abuse of power, against such person or another person, or by taking advantage of a coercive environment, or the invasion was committed against a person incapable of giving genuine consent.[63]
3. The conduct took place in the context of and was associated with an armed conflict not of an international character.
4. The perpetrator was aware of factual circumstances that established the existence of an armed conflict.

---

[61] As indicated by the use of the term 'private or personal use', appropriations justified by military necessity cannot constitute the crime of pillaging.

[62] The concept of 'invasion' is intended to be broad enough to be gender-neutral.

[63] It is understood that a person may be incapable of giving genuine consent if affected by natural, induced or age-related incapacity. This footnote also applies to the corresponding elements in article 8 (2) (e) (vi)-3, 5 and 6.

Article 8 (2) (e) (vi)-2 War crime of sexual slavery[64]

Elements

1. The perpetrator exercised any or all of the powers attaching to the right of ownership over one or more persons, such as by purchasing, selling, lending or bartering such a person or persons, or by imposing on them a similar deprivation of liberty.[65]
2. The perpetrator caused such person or persons to engage in one or more acts of a sexual nature.
3. The conduct took place in the context of and was associated with an armed conflict not of an international character.
4. The perpetrator was aware of factual circumstances that established the existence of an armed conflict.

Article 8 (2) (e) (vi)-3 War crime of enforced prostitution

Elements

1. The perpetrator caused one or more persons to engage in one or more acts of a sexual nature by force, or by threat of force or coercion, such as that caused by fear of violence, duress, detention, psychological oppression or abuse of power, against such person or persons or another person, or by taking advantage of a coercive environment or such person's or persons' incapacity to give genuine consent.
2. The perpetrator or another person obtained or expected to obtain pecuniary or other advantage in exchange for or in connection with the acts of a sexual nature.
3. The conduct took place in the context of and was associated with an armed conflict not of an international character.
4. The perpetrator was aware of factual circumstances that established the existence of an armed conflict.

---

[64] Given the complex nature of this crime, it is recognized that its commission could involve more than one perpetrator as a part of a common criminal purpose.

[65] It is understood that such deprivation of liberty may, in some circumstances, include exacting forced labour or otherwise reducing a person to servile status as defined in the Supplementary Convention on the Abolition of Slavery, the Slave Trade, and Institutions and Practices Similar to Slavery of 1956. It is also understood that the conduct described in this element includes trafficking in persons, in particular women and children.

Article 8 (2) (e) (vi)-4 War crime of forced pregnancy

Elements

1. The perpetrator confined one or more women forcibly made pregnant, with the intent of affecting the ethnic composition of any population or carrying out other grave violations of international law.
2. The conduct took place in the context of and was associated with an armed conflict not of an international character.
3. The perpetrator was aware of factual circumstances that established the existence of an armed conflict.

Article 8 (2) (e) (vi)-5 War crime of enforced sterilization

Elements

1. The perpetrator deprived one or more persons of biological reproductive capacity.[66]
2. The conduct was neither justified by the medical or hospital treatment of the person or persons concerned nor carried out with their genuine consent.[67]
3. The conduct took place in the context of and was associated with an armed conflict not of an international character.
4. The perpetrator was aware of factual circumstances that established the existence of an armed conflict.

Article 8 (2) (e) (vi)-6 War crime of sexual violence

Elements

1. The perpetrator committed an act of a sexual nature against one or more persons or caused such person or persons to engage in an act of a sexual nature by force, or by threat of force or coercion, such as that caused by fear of violence, duress, detention, psychological oppression or abuse of power, against such person or persons or another person, or by taking advantage of a coercive environment or such person's or persons' incapacity to give genuine consent.

---

[66] The deprivation is not intended to include birth-control measures which have a non-permanent effect in practice.
[67] It is understood that 'genuine consent' does not include consent obtained through deception.

2. The conduct was of a gravity comparable to that of a serious violation of article 3 common to the four Geneva Conventions.
3. The perpetrator was aware of the factual circumstances that established the gravity of the conduct.
4. The conduct took place in the context of and was associated with an armed conflict not of an international character.
5. The perpetrator was aware of factual circumstances that established the existence of an armed conflict.

Article 8 (2) (e) (vii) War crime of using, conscripting and enlisting children

Elements

1. The perpetrator conscripted or enlisted one or more persons into an armed force or group or used one or more persons to participate actively in hostilities.
2. Such person or persons were under the age of 15 years.
3. The perpetrator knew or should have known that such person or persons were under the age of 15 years.
4. The conduct took place in the context of and was associated with an armed conflict not of an international character.
5. The perpetrator was aware of factual circumstances that established the existence of an armed conflict.

Article 8 (2) (e) (viii) War crime of displacing civilians

Elements

1. The perpetrator ordered a displacement of a civilian population.
2. Such order was not justified by the security of the civilians involved or by military necessity.
3. The perpetrator was in a position to effect such displacement by giving such order.
4. The conduct took place in the context of and was associated with an armed conflict not of an international character.
5. The perpetrator was aware of factual circumstances that established the existence of an armed conflict.

Article 8 (2) (e) (ix) War crime of treacherously killing or wounding

Elements

1. The perpetrator invited the confidence or belief of one or more combatant adversaries that they were entitled to, or were obliged to accord, protection under rules of international law applicable in armed conflict.
2. The perpetrator intended to betray that confidence or belief.
3. The perpetrator killed or injured such person or persons.
4. The perpetrator made use of that confidence or belief in killing or injuring such person or persons.
5. Such person or persons belonged to an adverse party.
6. The conduct took place in the context of and was associated with an armed conflict not of an international character.
7. The perpetrator was aware of factual circumstances that established the existence of an armed conflict.

Article 8 (2) (e) (x) War crime of denying quarter

Elements

1. The perpetrator declared or ordered that there shall be no survivors.
2. Such declaration or order was given in order to threaten an adversary or to conduct hostilities on the basis that there shall be no survivors.
3. The perpetrator was in a position of effective command or control over the subordinate forces to which the declaration or order was directed.
4. The conduct took place in the context of and was associated with an armed conflict not of an international character.
5. The perpetrator was aware of factual circumstances that established the existence of an armed conflict.

Article 8 (2) (e) (xi)-1 War crime of mutilation

Elements

1. The perpetrator subjected one or more persons to mutilation, in particular by permanently disfiguring the person or persons, or by permanently disabling or removing an organ or appendage.
2. The conduct caused death or seriously endangered the physical or mental health of such person or persons.

3. The conduct was neither justified by the medical, dental or hospital treatment of the person or persons concerned nor carried out in such person's or persons' interest.[68]
4. Such person or persons were in the power of another party to the conflict.
5. The conduct took place in the context of and was associated with an armed conflict not of an international character.
6. The perpetrator was aware of factual circumstances that established the existence of an armed conflict.

Article 8 (2) (e) (xi)-2 War crime of medical or scientific experiments

Elements

1. The perpetrator subjected one or more persons to a medical or scientific experiment.
2. The experiment caused the death or seriously endangered the physical or mental health or integrity of such person or persons.
3. The conduct was neither justified by the medical, dental or hospital treatment of such person or persons concerned nor carried out in such person's or persons' interest.
4. Such person or persons were in the power of another party to the conflict.
5. The conduct took place in the context of and was associated with an armed conflict not of an international character.
6. The perpetrator was aware of factual circumstances that established the existence of an armed conflict.

Article 8 (2) (e) (xii) War crime of destroying or seizing the enemy's property

Elements

1. The perpetrator destroyed or seized certain property.
2. Such property was property of an adversary.
3. Such property was protected from that destruction or seizure under the international law of armed conflict.

---

[68] Consent is not a defence to this crime. The crime prohibits any medical procedure which is not indicated by the state of health of the person concerned and which is not consistent with generally accepted medical standards which would be applied under similar medical circumstances to persons who are nationals of the party conducting the procedure and who are in no way deprived of liberty. This footnote also applies to the similar element in article 8(2)(e) (xi)-2.

292 INTRODUCTION TO THE INTERNATIONAL CRIMINAL COURT

4. The perpetrator was aware of the factual circumstances that established the status of the property.
5. The destruction or seizure was not required by military necessity.
6. The conduct took place in the context of and was associated with an armed conflict not of an international character.
7. The perpetrator was aware of factual circumstances that established the existence of an armed conflict.

Rules of Procedure and Evidence

Explanatory note

The Rules of Procedure and Evidence are an instrument for the application of the Rome Statute of the International Criminal Court, to which they are subordinate in all cases. In elaborating the Rules of Procedure and Evidence, care has been taken to avoid rephrasing and, to the extent possible, repeating the provisions of the Statute. Direct references to the Statute have been included in the Rules, where appropriate, in order to emphasize the relationship between the Rules and the Rome Statute, as provided for in article 51, in particular, paragraphs 4 and 5.

In all cases, the Rules of Procedure and Evidence should be read in conjunction with and subject to the provisions of the Statute.

The Rules of Procedure and Evidence of the International Criminal Court do not affect the procedural rules for any national court or legal system for the purpose of national proceedings.

In connection with rule 41, the Preparatory Commission considered whether the application of the rule would be facilitated by including a provision in the Regulations of the Court that at least one of the judges of the Chamber in which the case is heard knows the official language used as a working language in a given case. The Assembly of States Parties is invited to give further consideration to this issue.

Chapter 1 General provisions

Rule 1 Use of terms

In the present document:

- 'article' refers to articles of the Rome Statute;
- 'Chamber' refers to a Chamber of the Court;
- 'Part' refers to the Parts of the Rome Statute;
- 'Presiding Judge' refers to the Presiding Judge of a Chamber;

- 'the President' refers to the President of the Court;
- 'the Regulations' refers to the Regulations of the Court;
- 'the Rules' refers to the Rules of Procedure and Evidence.

Rule 2 Authentic texts

The Rules have been adopted in the official languages of the Court established by article 50, paragraph 1. All texts are equally authentic.

Rule 3 Amendments

1. Amendments to the rules that are proposed in accordance with article 51, paragraph 2, shall be forwarded to the President of the Bureau of the Assembly of States Parties.

2. The President of the Bureau of the Assembly of States Parties shall ensure that all proposed amendments are translated into the official languages of the Court and are transmitted to the States Parties.

3. The procedure described in sub-rules 1 and 2 shall also apply to the provisional rules referred to in article 51, paragraph 3.

Chapter 2 Composition and administration of the Court

Section I General provisions relating to the composition and administration of the Court

Rule 4 Plenary sessions

1. The judges shall meet in plenary session not later than two months after their election. At that first session, after having made their solemn undertaking, in conformity with rule 5, the judges shall:

(a) Elect the President and Vice-Presidents;
(b) Assign judges to divisions.

2. The judges shall meet subsequently in plenary session at least once a year to exercise their functions under the Statute, the Rules and the Regulations and, if necessary, in special plenary sessions convened by the President on his or her own motion or at the request of one half of the judges.

3. The quorum for each plenary session shall be two-thirds of the judges.

4. Unless otherwise provided in the Statute or the Rules, the decisions of the plenary sessions shall be taken by the majority of the judges present. In the

event of an equality of votes, the President, or the judge acting in the place of the President, shall have a casting vote.

5. The Regulations shall be adopted as soon as possible in plenary sessions.

6.

Rule 5 Solemn undertaking under article 45

1. As provided in article 45, before exercising their functions under the Statute, the following solemn undertakings shall be made:

(a) In the case of a judge:
    'I solemnly undertake that I will perform my duties and exercise my powers as a judge of the International Criminal Court honourably, faithfully, impartially and conscientiously, and that I will respect the confidentiality of investigations and prosecutions and the secrecy of deliberations.';
(b) In the case of the Prosecutor, a Deputy Prosecutor, the Registrar and the Deputy Registrar of the Court:
    'I solemnly undertake that I will perform my duties and exercise my powers as (title) of the International Criminal Court honourably, faithfully, impartially and conscientiously, and that I will respect the confidentiality of investigations and prosecutions.'

2. The undertaking, signed by the person making it and witnessed by the President or a Vice-President of the Bureau of the Assembly of States Parties, shall be filed with the Registry and kept in the records of the Court.

Rule 6 Solemn undertaking by the staff of the Office of the Prosecutor, the Registry, interpreters and translators

1. Upon commencing employment, every staff member of the Office of the Prosecutor and the Registry shall make the following undertaking:

'I solemnly undertake that I will perform my duties and exercise my powers as (title) of the International Criminal Court honourably, faithfully, impartially and conscientiously, and that I will respect the confidentiality of investigations and prosecutions.';

The undertaking, signed by the person making it and witnessed, as appropriate, by the Prosecutor, the Deputy Prosecutor, the Registrar or the Deputy Registrar, shall be filed with the Registry and kept in the records of the Court.

2. Before performing any duties, an interpreter or a translator shall make the following undertaking:

'I solemnly declare that I will perform my duties faithfully, impartially and with full respect for the duty of confidentiality.';

The undertaking, signed by the person making it and witnessed by the President of the Court or his or her representative, shall be filed with the Registry and kept in the records of the Court.

Rule 7 *Single judge under article 39, paragraph 2 (b) (iii)*

1. Whenever the Pre-Trial Chamber designates a judge as a single judge in accordance with article 39, paragraph 2 (b) (iii), it shall do so on the basis of objective pre-established criteria.

2. The designated judge shall make the appropriate decisions on those questions on which decision by the full Chamber is not expressly provided for in the Statute or the Rules.

3. The Pre-Trial Chamber, on its own motion or, if appropriate, at the request of a party, may decide that the functions of the single judge be exercised by the full Chamber.

Rule 8 *Code of Professional Conduct*

1. The Presidency, on the basis of a proposal made by the Registrar, shall draw up a draft Code of Professional Conduct for counsel, after having consulted the Prosecutor. In the preparation of the proposal, the Registrar shall conduct the consultations in accordance with rule 20, sub-rule 3.

2. The draft Code shall then be transmitted to the Assembly of States Parties, for the purpose of adoption, according to article 112, paragraph 7.

3. The Code shall contain procedures for its amendment.

Section II The Office of the Prosecutor

Rule 9 *Operation of the Office of the Prosecutor*

In discharging his or her responsibility for the management and administration of the Office of the Prosecutor, the Prosecutor shall put in place regulations to govern the operation of the Office. In preparing or amending these regulations, the Prosecutor shall consult with the Registrar on any matters that may affect the operation of the Registry.

Rule 10 Retention of information and evidence

The Prosecutor shall be responsible for the retention, storage and security of information and physical evidence obtained in the course of the investigations by his or her Office.

Rule 11 Delegation of the Prosecutor's functions

Except for the inherent powers of the Prosecutor set forth in the Statute, *inter alia*, those described in articles 15 and 53, the Prosecutor or a Deputy Prosecutor may authorize staff members of the Office of the Prosecutor, other than those referred to in article 44, paragraph 4, to represent him or her in the exercise of his or her functions.

Section III The Registry

Subsection 1 General provisions relating to the Registry

Rule 12 Qualifications and election of the Registrar and the Deputy Registrar

1. As soon as it is elected, the Presidency shall establish a list of candidates who satisfy the criteria laid down in article 43, paragraph 3, and shall transmit the list to the Assembly of States Parties with a request for any recommendations.

2. Upon receipt of any recommendations from the Assembly of States Parties, the President shall, without delay, transmit the list together with the recommendations to the plenary session.

3. As provided for in article 43, paragraph 4, the Court, meeting in plenary session, shall, as soon as possible, elect the Registrar by an absolute majority, taking into account any recommendations by the Assembly of States Parties. In the event that no candidate obtains an absolute majority on the first ballot, successive ballots shall be held until one candidate obtains an absolute majority.

4. If the need for a Deputy Registrar arises, the Registrar may make a recommendation to the President to that effect. The President shall convene a plenary session to decide on the matter. If the Court, meeting in plenary session, decides by an absolute majority that a Deputy Registrar is to be elected, the Registrar shall submit a list of candidates to the Court.

5. The Deputy Registrar shall be elected by the Court, meeting in plenary session, in the same manner as the Registrar.

Rule 13 Functions of the Registrar

1. Without prejudice to the authority of the Office of the Prosecutor under the Statute to receive, obtain and provide information and to establish channels of communication for this purpose, the Registrar shall serve as the channel of communication of the Court.

2. The Registrar shall also be responsible for the internal security of the Court in consultation with the Presidency and the Prosecutor, as well as the host State.

Rule 14 Operation of the Registry

1. In discharging his or her responsibility for the organization and management of the Registry, the Registrar shall put in place regulations to govern the operation of the Registry. In preparing or amending these regulations, the Registrar shall consult with the Prosecutor on any matters which may affect the operation of the Office of the Prosecutor. The regulations shall be approved by the Presidency.

2. The regulations shall provide for defence counsel to have access to appropriate and reasonable administrative assistance from the Registry.

Rule 15 Records

1. The Registrar shall keep a database containing all the particulars of each case brought before the Court, subject to any order of a judge or Chamber providing for the non-disclosure of any document or information, and to the protection of sensitive personal data. Information on the database shall be available to the public in the working languages of the Court.

2. The Registrar shall also maintain the other records of the Court.

Subsection 2 Victims and Witnesses Unit

Rule 16 Responsibilities of the Registrar relating to victims and witnesses

1. In relation to victims, the Registrar shall be responsible for the performance of the following functions in accordance with the Statute and these Rules:

(a) Providing notice or notification to victims or their legal representatives;
(b) Assisting them in obtaining legal advice and organizing their legal representa-

tion, and providing their legal representatives with adequate support, assistance and information, including such facilities as may be necessary for the direct performance of their duty, for the purpose of protecting their rights during all stages of the proceedings in accordance with rules 89 to 91;

(c) Assisting them in participating in the different phases of the proceedings in accordance with rules 89 to 91;

(d) Taking gender-sensitive measures to facilitate the participation of victims of sexual violence at all stages of the proceedings.

2. In relation to victims, witnesses and others who are at risk on account of testimony given by such witnesses, the Registrar shall be responsible for the performance of the following functions in accordance with the Statute and these Rules:

(a) Informing them of their rights under the Statute and the Rules, and of the existence, functions and availability of the Victims and Witnesses Unit;

(b) Ensuring that they are aware, in a timely manner, of the relevant decisions of the Court that may have an impact on their interests, subject to provisions on confidentiality.

3. For the fulfilment of his or her functions, the Registrar may keep a special register for victims who have expressed their intention to participate in relation to a specific case.

4. Agreements on relocation and provision of support services on the territory of a State of traumatized or threatened victims, witnesses and others who are at risk on account of testimony given by such witnesses may be negotiated with the States by the Registrar on behalf of the Court. Such agreements may remain confidential.

Rule 17 Functions of the Unit

1. The Victims and Witnesses Unit shall exercise its functions in accordance with article 43, paragraph 6.

2. The Victims and Witnesses Unit shall, *inter alia*, perform the following functions, in accordance with the Statute and the Rules, and in consultation with the Chamber, the Prosecutor and the defence, as appropriate:

(a) With respect to all witnesses, victims who appear before the Court, and others who are at risk on account of testimony given by such witnesses, in accordance with their particular needs and circumstances:

(i) Providing them with adequate protective and security measures and formulating long- and short-term plans for their protection;

     (ii)   Recommending to the organs of the Court the adoption of protection measures and also advising relevant States of such measures;

    (iii)   Assisting them in obtaining medical, psychological and other appropriate assistance;

    (iv)   Making available to the Court and the parties training in issues of trauma, sexual violence, security and confidentiality;

    (v)   Recommending, in consultation with the Office of the Prosecutor, the elaboration of a code of conduct, emphasizing the vital nature of security and confidentiality for investigators of the Court and of the defence and all intergovernmental and non-governmental organizations acting at the request of the Court, as appropriate;

    (vi)   Cooperating with States, where necessary, in providing any of the measures stipulated in this rule;

(b) With respect to witnesses:

    (i)   Advising them where to obtain legal advice for the purpose of protecting their rights, in particular in relation to their testimony;

    (ii)   Assisting them when they are called to testify before the Court;

    (iii)   Taking gender-sensitive measures to facilitate the testimony of victims of sexual violence at all stages of the proceedings.

3. In performing its functions, the Unit shall give due regard to the particular needs of children, elderly persons and persons with disabilities. In order to facilitate the participation and protection of children as witnesses, the Unit may assign, as appropriate, and with the agreement of the parents or the legal guardian, a child-support person to assist a child through all stages of the proceedings.

Rule 18 Responsibilities of the Unit

For the efficient and effective performance of its work, the Victims and Witnesses Unit shall:

(a) Ensure that the staff in the Unit maintain confidentiality at all times;

(b) While recognizing the specific interests of the Office of the Prosecutor, the defence and the witnesses, respect the interests of the witness, including, where necessary, by maintaining an appropriate separation of the services provided to the Prosecution and defence witnesses, and act impartially when cooperating with all parties and in accordance with the rulings and decisions of the Chambers;

(c) Have administrative and technical assistance available for witnesses, victims who appear before the Court, and others who are at risk on account of testimony given by such witnesses, during all stages of the proceedings and thereafter, as reasonably appropriate;

(d) Ensure training of its staff with respect to victims' and witnesses' security, integrity and dignity, including matters related to gender and cultural sensitivity;

(e) Where appropriate, cooperate with intergovernmental and non-governmental organizations.

Rule 19 Expertise in the Unit

In addition to the staff mentioned in article 43, paragraph 6, and subject to article 44, the Victims and Witnesses Unit may include, as appropriate, persons with expertise, *inter alia*, in the following areas:

(a) Witness protection and security;

(b) Legal and administrative matters, including areas of humanitarian and criminal law;

(c) Logistics administration;

(d) Psychology in criminal proceedings;

(e) Gender and cultural diversity;

(f) Children, in particular traumatized children;

(g) Elderly persons, in particular in connection with armed conflict and exile trauma;

(h) Persons with disabilities;

(i) Social work and counselling;

(j) Health care;

(k) Interpretation and translation.

Subsection 3 Counsel for the defence

Rule 20 Responsibilities of the Registrar relating to the rights of the defence

1. In accordance with article 43, paragraph 1, the Registrar shall organize the staff of the Registry in a manner that promotes the rights of the defence, consistent with the principle of fair trial as defined in the Statute. For that purpose, the Registrar shall, *inter alia*:

(a) Facilitate the protection of confidentiality, as defined in article 67, paragraph 1 (b);

(b) Provide support, assistance, and information to all defence counsel appearing before the Court and, as appropriate, support for professional investigators necessary for the efficient and effective conduct of the defence;

(c) Assist arrested persons, persons to whom article 55, paragraph 2, applies and the accused in obtaining legal advice and the assistance of legal counsel;

(d) Advise the Prosecutor and the Chambers, as necessary, on relevant defence-related issues;

(e) Provide the defence with such facilities as may be necessary for the direct performance of the duty of the defence;

(f) Facilitate the dissemination of information and case law of the Court to defence counsel and, as appropriate, cooperate with national defence and bar associations or any independent representative body of counsel and legal associations referred to in sub-rule 3 to promote the specialization and training of lawyers in the law of the Statute and the Rules.

2. The Registrar shall carry out the functions stipulated in sub-rule 1, including the financial administration of the Registry, in such a manner as to ensure the professional independence of defence counsel.

3. For purposes such as the management of legal assistance in accordance with rule 21 and the development of a Code of Professional Conduct in accordance with rule 8, the Registrar shall consult, as appropriate, with any independent representative body of counsel or legal associations, including any such body the establishment of which may be facilitated by the Assembly of States Parties.

Rule 21 Assignment of legal assistance

1. Subject to article 55, paragraph 2 (c), and article 67, paragraph 1 (d), criteria and procedures for assignment of legal assistance shall be established in the Regulations, based on a proposal by the Registrar, following consultations with any independent representative body of counsel or legal associations, as referred to in rule 20, sub-rule 3.

2. The Registrar shall create and maintain a list of counsel who meet the criteria set forth in rule 22 and the Regulations. The person shall freely choose his or her counsel from this list or other counsel who meets the required criteria and is willing to be included in the list.

3. A person may seek from the Presidency a review of a decision to refuse a request for assignment of counsel. The decision of the Presidency shall be final. If a request is refused, a further request may be made by a person to the Registrar, upon showing a change in circumstances.

4. A person choosing to represent himself or herself shall so notify the Registrar in writing at the first opportunity.

5. Where a person claims to have insufficient means to pay for legal assistance and this is subsequently found not to be so, the Chamber dealing with the case at that time may make an order of contribution to recover the cost of providing counsel.

Rule 22 Appointment and qualifications of Counsel for the defence

1. A counsel for the defence shall have established competence in international or criminal law and procedure, as well as the necessary relevant experience, whether as judge, prosecutor, advocate or in other similar capacity, in criminal proceedings. A counsel for the defence shall have an excellent knowledge of and be fluent in at least one of the working languages of the Court. Counsel for the defence may be assisted by other persons, including professors of law, with relevant expertise.

2. Counsel for the defence engaged by a person exercising his or her right under the Statute to retain legal counsel of his or her choosing shall file a power of attorney with the Registrar at the earliest opportunity.

3. In the performance of their duties, Counsel for the defence shall be subject to the Statute, the Rules, the Regulations, the Code of Professional Conduct for counsel adopted in accordance with rule 8 and any other document adopted by the Court that may be relevant to the performance of their duties.

Section IV Situations that may affect the functioning of the Court

Subsection 1 Removal from office and disciplinary measures

Rule 23 General principle

A judge, the Prosecutor, a Deputy Prosecutor, the Registrar and a Deputy Registrar shall be removed from office or shall be subject to disciplinary measures in such cases and with such guarantees as are established in the Statute and the Rules.

Rule 24 Definition of serious misconduct and serious breach of duty

1. For the purposes of article 46, paragraph 1 (a), 'serious misconduct' shall be constituted by conduct that:

(a) If it occurs in the course of official duties, is incompatible with official functions, and causes or is likely to cause serious harm to the proper administration of justice before the Court or the proper internal functioning of the Court, such as:

   (i) Disclosing facts or information that he or she has acquired in the course of his or her duties or on a matter which is *sub judice*, where such disclosure is seriously prejudicial to the judicial proceedings or to any person;

(ii)   Concealing information or circumstances of a nature sufficiently serious to have precluded him or her from holding office;

(iii)   Abuse of judicial office in order to obtain unwarranted favourable treatment from any authorities, officials or professionals; or

(b) If it occurs outside the course of official duties, is of a grave nature that causes or is likely to cause serious harm to the standing of the Court.

2. For the purposes of article 46, paragraph 1 (a), a 'serious breach of duty' occurs where a person has been grossly negligent in the performance of his or her duties or has knowingly acted in contravention of those duties. This may include, *inter alia*, situations where the person:

(a) Fails to comply with the duty to request to be excused, knowing that there are grounds for doing so;

(b) Repeatedly causes unwarranted delay in the initiation, prosecution or trial of cases, or in the exercise of judicial powers.

Rule 25 Definition of misconduct of a less serious nature

1. For the purposes of article 47, 'misconduct of a less serious nature' shall be constituted by conduct that:

(a) If it occurs in the course of official duties, causes or is likely to cause harm to the proper administration of justice before the Court or the proper internal functioning of the Court, such as:

(i)   Interfering in the exercise of the functions of a person referred to in article 47;

(ii)   Repeatedly failing to comply with or ignoring requests made by the Presiding Judge or by the Presidency in the exercise of their lawful authority;

(iii)   Failing to enforce the disciplinary measures to which the Registrar or a Deputy Registrar and other officers of the Court are subject when a judge knows or should know of a serious breach of duty on their part; or

(b) If it occurs outside the course of official duties, causes or is likely to cause harm to the standing of the Court.

2. Nothing in this rule precludes the possibility of the conduct set out in sub-rule 1 (a) constituting 'serious misconduct' or 'serious breach of duty' for the purposes of article 46, paragraph 1 (a).

Rule 26 Receipt of complaints

1. For the purposes of article 46, paragraph 1, and article 47, any complaint concerning any conduct defined under rules 24 and 25 shall include the grounds on which it is based, the identity of the complainant and, if available, any relevant evidence. The complaint shall remain confidential.

2. All complaints shall be transmitted to the Presidency, which may also initiate proceedings on its own motion, and which shall, pursuant to the Regulations, set aside anonymous or manifestly unfounded complaints and transmit the other complaints to the competent organ. The Presidency shall be assisted in this task by one or more judges, appointed on the basis of automatic rotation, in accordance with the Regulations.

Rule 27 Common provisions on the rights of the defence

1. In any case in which removal from office under article 46 or disciplinary measures under article 47 is under consideration, the person concerned shall be so informed in a written statement.

2. The person concerned shall be afforded full opportunity to present and receive evidence, to make written submissions and to supply answers to any questions put to him or her.

3. The person may be represented by counsel during the process established under this rule.

Rule 28 Suspension from duty

Where an allegation against a person who is the subject of a complaint is of a sufficiently serious nature, the person may be suspended from duty pending the final decision of the competent organ.

Rule 29 Procedure in the event of a request for removal from office

1. In the case of a judge, the Registrar or a Deputy Registrar, the question of removal from office shall be put to a vote at a plenary session.

2. The Presidency shall advise the President of the Bureau of the Assembly of States Parties in writing of any recommendation adopted in the case of a judge, and any decision adopted in the case of the Registrar or a Deputy Registrar.

3. The Prosecutor shall advise the President of the Bureau of the Assembly of States Parties in writing of any recommendation he or she makes in the case of a Deputy Prosecutor.

4. Where the conduct is found not to amount to serious misconduct or a serious breach of duty, it may be decided in accordance with article 47 that the person concerned has engaged in misconduct of a less serious nature and a disciplinary measure imposed.

Rule 30 Procedure in the event of a request for disciplinary measures

1. In the case of a judge, the Registrar or a Deputy Registrar, any decision to impose a disciplinary measure shall be taken by the Presidency.

2. In the case of the Prosecutor, any decision to impose a disciplinary measure shall be taken by an absolute majority of the Bureau of the Assembly of States Parties.

3. In the case of a Deputy Prosecutor:

(a) Any decision to give a reprimand shall be taken by the Prosecutor;
(b) Any decision to impose a pecuniary sanction shall be taken by an absolute majority of the Bureau of the Assembly of States Parties upon the recommendation of the Prosecutor.

4. Reprimands shall be recorded in writing and shall be transmitted to the President of the Bureau of the Assembly of States Parties.

Rule 31 Removal from office

Once removal from office has been pronounced, it shall take effect immediately. The person concerned shall cease to form part of the Court, including for unfinished cases in which he or she was taking part.

Rule 32 Disciplinary measures

The disciplinary measures that may be imposed are:

(a) A reprimand; or
(b) A pecuniary sanction that may not exceed six months of the salary paid by the Court to the person concerned.

Subsection 2   Excusing, disqualification, death and resignation

Rule 33   Excusing of a judge, the Prosecutor or a Deputy Prosecutor

1. A judge, the Prosecutor or a Deputy Prosecutor seeking to be excused from his or her functions shall make a request in writing to the Presidency, setting out the grounds upon which he or she should be excused.

2. The Presidency shall treat the request as confidential and shall not make public the reasons for its decision without the consent of the person concerned.

Rule 34   Disqualification of a judge, the Prosecutor or a Deputy Prosecutor

1. In addition to the grounds set out in article 41, paragraph 2, and article 42, paragraph 7, the grounds for disqualification of a judge, the Prosecutor or a Deputy Prosecutor shall include, *inter alia*, the following:

(a) Personal interest in the case, including a spousal, parental or other close family, personal or professional relationship, or a subordinate relationship, with any of the parties;

(b) Involvement, in his or her private capacity, in any legal proceedings initiated prior to his or her involvement in the case, or initiated by him or her subsequently, in which the person being investigated or prosecuted was or is an opposing party;

(c) Performance of functions, prior to taking office, during which he or she could be expected to have formed an opinion on the case in question, on the parties or on their legal representatives that, objectively, could adversely affect the required impartiality of the person concerned;

(d) Expression of opinions, through the communications media, in writing or in public actions, that, objectively, could adversely affect the required impartiality of the person concerned.

2. Subject to the provisions set out in article 41, paragraph 2, and article 42, paragraph 8, a request for disqualification shall be made in writing as soon as there is knowledge of the grounds on which it is based. The request shall state the grounds and attach any relevant evidence, and shall be transmitted to the person concerned, who shall be entitled to present written submissions.

3. Any question relating to the disqualification of the Prosecutor or a Deputy Prosecutor shall be decided by a majority of the judges of the Appeals Chamber.

Rule 35 Duty of a judge, the Prosecutor or a Deputy Prosecutor to request to be excused

Where a judge, the Prosecutor or a Deputy Prosecutor has reason to believe that a ground for disqualification exists in relation to him or her, he or she shall make a request to be excused and shall not wait for a request for disqualification to be made in accordance with article 41, paragraph 2, or article 42, paragraph 7, and rule 34. The request shall be made and the Presidency shall deal with it in accordance with rule 33.

Rule 36 Death of a judge, the Prosecutor, a Deputy Prosecutor, the Registrar or a Deputy Registrar

The Presidency shall inform, in writing, the President of the Bureau of the Assembly of States Parties of the death of a judge, the Prosecutor, a Deputy Prosecutor, the Registrar or a Deputy Registrar.

Rule 37 Resignation of a judge, the Prosecutor, a Deputy Prosecutor, the Registrar or a Deputy Registrar

1. A judge, the Prosecutor, a Deputy Prosecutor, the Registrar or a Deputy Registrar shall communicate to the Presidency, in writing, his or her decision to resign. The Presidency shall inform, in writing, the President of the Bureau of the Assembly of States Parties.

2. A judge, the Prosecutor, a Deputy Prosecutor, the Registrar or a Deputy Registrar shall endeavour to give notice of the date on which his or her resignation will take effect at least six months in advance. Before the resignation of a judge takes effect, he or she shall make every effort to discharge his or her outstanding responsibilities.

Subsection 3 Replacements and alternate judges

Rule 38 Replacements

1. A judge may be replaced for objective and justified reasons, *inter alia*:

(a) Resignation;
(b) Accepted excuse;
(c) Disqualification;
(d) Removal from office;
(e) Death.

2. Replacement shall take place in accordance with the pre-established procedure in the Statute, the Rules and the Regulations.

Rule 39 Alternate judges

Where an alternate judge has been assigned by the Presidency to a Trial Chamber pursuant to article 74, paragraph 1, he or she shall sit through all proceedings and deliberations of the case, but may not take any part therein and shall not exercise any of the functions of the members of the Trial Chamber hearing the case, unless and until he or she is required to replace a member of the Trial Chamber if that member is unable to continue attending. Alternate judges shall be designated in accordance with a procedure pre-established by the Court.

Section V Publication, languages and translation

Rule 40 Publication of decisions in official languages of the Court

1. For the purposes of article 50, paragraph 1, the following decisions shall be considered as resolving fundamental issues:

(a) All decisions of the Appeals Division;
(b) All decisions of the Court on its jurisdiction or on the admissibility of a case pursuant to articles 17, 18, 19 and 20;
(c) All decisions of a Trial Chamber on guilt or innocence, sentencing and reparations to victims pursuant to articles 74, 75 and 76;
(d) All decisions of a Pre-Trial Chamber pursuant to article 57, paragraph 3 (d).

2. Decisions on confirmation of charges under article 61, paragraph 7, and on offences against the administration of justice under article 70, paragraph 3, shall be published in all the official languages of the Court when the Presidency determines that they resolve fundamental issues.

3. The Presidency may decide to publish other decisions in all the official languages when such decisions concern major issues relating to the interpretation or the implementation of the Statute or concern a major issue of general interest.

Rule 41 Working languages of the Court

1. For the purposes of article 50, paragraph 2, the Presidency shall authorize the use of an official language of the Court as a working language when:

(a) That language is understood and spoken by the majority of those involved in a case before the Court and any of the participants in the proceedings so requests; or

(b) The Prosecutor and the defence so request.

2. The Presidency may authorize the use of an official language of the Court as a working language if it considers that it would facilitate the efficiency of the proceedings.

Rule 42 Translation and interpretation services

The Court shall arrange for the translation and interpretation services necessary to ensure the implementation of its obligations under the Statute and the Rules.

Rule 43 Procedure applicable to the publication of documents of the Court

The Court shall ensure that all documents subject to publication in accordance with the Statute and the Rules respect the duty to protect the confidentiality of the proceedings and the security of victims and witnesses.

Chapter 3 Jurisdiction and admissibility

Section I Declarations and referrals relating to articles 11, 12, 13 and 14

Rule 44 Declaration provided for in article 12, paragraph 3

1. The Registrar, at the request of the Prosecutor, may inquire of a State that is not a Party to the Statute or that has become a Party to the Statute after its entry into force, on a confidential basis, whether it intends to make the declaration provided for in article 12, paragraph 3.

2. When a State lodges, or declares to the Registrar its intent to lodge, a declaration with the Registrar pursuant to article 12, paragraph 3, or when the Registrar acts pursuant to sub-rule 1, the Registrar shall inform the State concerned that the declaration under article 12, paragraph 3, has as a consequence the acceptance of jurisdiction with respect to the crimes referred to in article 5 of relevance to the situation and the provisions of Part 9, and any rules thereunder concerning States Parties, shall apply.

Rule 45   Referral of a situation to the Prosecutor

A referral of a situation to the Prosecutor shall be in writing.

Section II   Initiation of investigations under article 15

Rule 46   Information provided to the Prosecutor under article 15, paragraphs 1 and 2

Where information is submitted under article 15, paragraph 1, or where oral or written testimony is received pursuant to article 15, paragraph 2, at the seat of the Court, the Prosecutor shall protect the confidentiality of such information and testimony or take any other necessary measures, pursuant to his or her duties under the Statute.

Rule 47   Testimony under article 15, paragraph 2

1. The provisions of rules 111 and 112 shall apply, *mutatis mutandis*, to testimony received by the Prosecutor pursuant to article 15, paragraph 2.

2. When the Prosecutor considers that there is a serious risk that it might not be possible for the testimony to be taken subsequently, he or she may request the Pre-Trial Chamber to take such measures as may be necessary to ensure the efficiency and integrity of the proceedings and, in particular, to appoint a counsel or a judge from the Pre-Trial Chamber to be present during the taking of the testimony in order to protect the rights of the defence. If the testimony is subsequently presented in the proceedings, its admissibility shall be governed by article 69, paragraph 4, and given such weight as determined by the relevant Chamber.

Rule 48   Determination of reasonable basis to proceed with an investigation under article 15, paragraph 3

In determining whether there is a reasonable basis to proceed with an investigation under article 15, paragraph 3, the Prosecutor shall consider the factors set out in article 53, paragraph 1 (a) to (c).

Rule 49   Decision and notice under article 15, paragraph 6

1. Where a decision under article 15, paragraph 6, is taken, the Prosecutor shall promptly ensure that notice is provided, including reasons for his or her

decision, in a manner that prevents any danger to the safety, well-being and privacy of those who provided information to him or her under article 15, paragraphs 1 and 2, or the integrity of investigations or proceedings.

2. The notice shall also advise of the possibility of submitting further information regarding the same situation in the light of new facts and evidence.

Rule 50 Procedure for authorization by the Pre-Trial Chamber of the commencement of the investigation

1. When the Prosecutor intends to seek authorization from the Pre-Trial Chamber to initiate an investigation pursuant to article 15, paragraph 3, the Prosecutor shall inform victims, known to him or her or to the Victims and Witnesses Unit, or their legal representatives, unless the Prosecutor decides that doing so would pose a danger to the integrity of the investigation or the life or well-being of victims and witnesses. The Prosecutor may also give notice by general means in order to reach groups of victims if he or she determines in the particular circumstances of the case that such notice could not pose a danger to the integrity and effective conduct of the investigation or to the security and well-being of victims and witnesses. In performing these functions, the Prosecutor may seek the assistance of the Victims and Witnesses Unit as appropriate.

2. A request for authorization by the Prosecutor shall be in writing.

3. Following information given in accordance with sub-rule 1, victims may make representations in writing to the Pre-Trial Chamber within such time limit as set forth in the Regulations.

4. The Pre-Trial Chamber, in deciding on the procedure to be followed, may request additional information from the Prosecutor and from any of the victims who have made representations, and, if it considers it appropriate, may hold a hearing.

5. The Pre-Trial Chamber shall issue its decision, including its reasons, as to whether to authorize the commencement of the investigation in accordance with article 15, paragraph 4, with respect to all or any part of the request by the Prosecutor. The Chamber shall give notice of the decision to victims who have made representations.

6. The above procedure shall also apply to a new request to the Pre-Trial Chamber pursuant to article 15, paragraph 5.

Section III Challenges and preliminary rulings under articles 17, 18 and 19

Rule 51 Information provided under article 17

In considering the matters referred to in article 17, paragraph 2, and in the context of the circumstances of the case, the Court may consider, *inter alia*, information that the State referred to in article 17, paragraph 1, may choose to bring to the attention of the Court showing that its courts meet internationally recognized norms and standards for the independent and impartial prosecution of similar conduct, or that the State has confirmed in writing to the Prosecutor that the case is being investigated or prosecuted.

Rule 52 Notification provided for in article 18, paragraph 1

1. Subject to the limitations provided for in article 18, paragraph 1, the notification shall contain information about the acts that may constitute crimes referred to in article 5, relevant for the purposes of article 18, paragraph 2.

2. A State may request additional information from the Prosecutor to assist it in the application of article 18, paragraph 2. Such a request shall not affect the one-month time limit provided for in article 18, paragraph 2, and shall be responded to by the Prosecutor on an expedited basis.

Rule 53 Deferral provided for in article 18, paragraph 2

When a State requests a deferral pursuant to article 18, paragraph 2, that State shall make this request in writing and provide information concerning its investigation, taking into account article 18, paragraph 2. The Prosecutor may request additional information from that State.

Rule 54 Application by the Prosecutor under article 18, paragraph 2

1. An application submitted by the Prosecutor to the Pre-Trial Chamber in accordance with article 18, paragraph 2, shall be in writing and shall contain the basis for the application. The information provided by the State under rule 53 shall be communicated by the Prosecutor to the Pre-Trial Chamber.

2. The Prosecutor shall inform that State in writing when he or she makes an application to the Pre-Trial Chamber under article 18, paragraph 2, and shall include in the notice a summary of the basis of the application.

Rule 55 Proceedings concerning article 18, paragraph 2

1. The Pre-Trial Chamber shall decide on the procedure to be followed and may take appropriate measures for the proper conduct of the proceedings. It may hold a hearing.

2. The Pre-Trial Chamber shall examine the Prosecutor's application and any observations submitted by a State that requested a deferral in accordance with article 18, paragraph 2, and shall consider the factors in article 17 in deciding whether to authorize an investigation.

3. The decision and the basis for the decision of the Pre-Trial Chamber shall be communicated as soon as possible to the Prosecutor and to the State that requested a deferral of an investigation.

Rule 56 Application by the Prosecutor following review under article 18, paragraph 3

1. Following a review by the Prosecutor as set forth in article 18, paragraph 3, the Prosecutor may apply to the Pre-Trial Chamber for authorization in accordance with article 18, paragraph 2. The application to the Pre-Trial Chamber shall be in writing and shall contain the basis for the application.

2. Any further information provided by the State under article 18, paragraph 5, shall be communicated by the Prosecutor to the Pre-Trial Chamber.

3. The proceedings shall be conducted in accordance with rules 54, sub-rule 2, and 55.

Rule 57 Provisional measures under article 18, paragraph 6

An application to the Pre-Trial Chamber by the Prosecutor in the circumstances provided for in article 18, paragraph 6, shall be considered *ex parte* and *in camera*. The Pre-Trial Chamber shall rule on the application on an expedited basis.

Rule 58 Proceedings under article 19

1. A request or application made under article 19 shall be in writing and contain the basis for it.

2. When a Chamber receives a request or application raising a challenge or question concerning its jurisdiction or the admissibility of a case in accordance with article 19, paragraph 2 or 3, or is acting on its own motion as pro-

vided for in article 19, paragraph 1, it shall decide on the procedure to be followed and may take appropriate measures for the proper conduct of the proceedings. It may hold a hearing. It may join the challenge or question to a confirmation or a trial proceeding as long as this does not cause undue delay, and in this circumstance shall hear and decide on the challenge or question first.

3. The Court shall transmit a request or application received under sub-rule 2 to the Prosecutor and to the person referred to in article 19, paragraph 2, who has been surrendered to the Court or who has appeared voluntarily or pursuant to a summons, and shall allow them to submit written observations to the request or application within a period of time determined by the Chamber.

4. The Court shall rule on any challenge or question of jurisdiction first and then on any challenge or question of admissibility.

Rule 59 Participation in proceedings under article 19, paragraph 3

1. For the purpose of article 19, paragraph 3, the Registrar shall inform the following of any question or challenge of jurisdiction or admissibility which has arisen pursuant to article 19, paragraphs 1, 2 and 3:

(a) Those who have referred a situation pursuant to article 13;
(b) The victims who have already communicated with the Court in relation to that case or their legal representatives.

2. The Registrar shall provide those referred to in sub-rule 1, in a manner consistent with the duty of the Court regarding the confidentiality of information, the protection of any person and the preservation of evidence, with a summary of the grounds on which the jurisdiction of the Court or the admissibility of the case has been challenged.

3. Those receiving the information, as provided for in sub-rule 1, may make representation in writing to the competent Chamber within such time limit as it considers appropriate.

Rule 60 Competent organ to receive challenges

If a challenge to the jurisdiction of the Court or to the admissibility of a case is made after a confirmation of the charges but before the constitution or designation of the Trial Chamber, it shall be addressed to the Presidency, which shall refer it to the Trial Chamber as soon as the latter is constituted or designated in accordance with rule 130.

Rule 61 Provisional measures under article 19, paragraph 8

When the Prosecutor makes application to the competent Chamber in the circumstances provided for in article 19, paragraph 8, rule 57 shall apply.

Rule 62 Proceedings under article 19, paragraph 10

1. If the Prosecutor makes a request under article 19, paragraph 10, he or she shall make the request to the Chamber that made the latest ruling on admissibility. The provisions of rules 58, 59 and 61 shall be applicable.

2. The State or States whose challenge to admissibility under article 19, paragraph 2, provoked the decision of inadmissibility provided for in article 19, paragraph 10, shall be notified of the request of the Prosecutor and shall be given a time limit within which to make representations.

Chapter 4 Provisions relating to various stages of the proceedings

Section I Evidence

Rule 63 General provisions relating to evidence

1. The rules of evidence set forth in this chapter, together with article 69, shall apply in proceedings before all Chambers.

2. A Chamber shall have the authority, in accordance with the discretion described in article 64, paragraph 9, to assess freely all evidence submitted in order to determine its relevance or admissibility in accordance with article 69.

3. A Chamber shall rule on an application of a party or on its own motion, made under article 64, subparagraph 9 (a), concerning admissibility when it is based on the grounds set out in article 69, paragraph 7.

4. Without prejudice to article 66, paragraph 3, a Chamber shall not impose a legal requirement that corroboration is required in order to prove any crime within the jurisdiction of the Court, in particular, crimes of sexual violence.

5. The Chambers shall not apply national laws governing evidence, other than in accordance with article 21.

Rule 64 Procedure relating to the relevance or admissibility of evidence

1. An issue relating to relevance or admissibility must be raised at the time when the evidence is submitted to a Chamber. Exceptionally, when those issues were not known at the time when the evidence was submitted, it may be

raised immediately after the issue has become known. The Chamber may request that the issue be raised in writing. The written motion shall be communicated by the Court to all those who participate in the proceedings, unless otherwise decided by the Court.

2. A Chamber shall give reasons for any rulings it makes on evidentiary matters. These reasons shall be placed in the record of the proceedings if they have not already been incorporated into the record during the course of the proceedings in accordance with article 64, paragraph 10, and rule 137, sub-rule 1.

3. Evidence ruled irrelevant or inadmissible shall not be considered by the Chamber.

Rule 65 Compellability of witnesses

1. A witness who appears before the Court is compellable by the Court to provide testimony, unless otherwise provided for in the Statute and the Rules, in particular rules 73, 74 and 75.

2. Rule 171 applies to a witness appearing before the Court who is compellable to provide testimony under sub-rule 1.

Rule 66 Solemn undertaking

1. Except as described in sub-rule 2, every witness shall, in accordance with article 69, paragraph 1, make the following solemn undertaking before testifying:

'I solemnly declare that I will speak the truth, the whole truth and nothing but the truth.'

2. A person under the age of 18 or a person whose judgment has been impaired and who, in the opinion of the Chamber, does not understand the nature of a solemn undertaking may be allowed to testify without this solemn undertaking if the Chamber considers that the person is able to describe matters of which he or she has knowledge and that the person understands the meaning of the duty to speak the truth.

3. Before testifying, the witness shall be informed of the offence defined in article 70, paragraph 1 (a).

Rule 67 Live testimony by means of audio or video-link technology

1. In accordance with article 69, paragraph 2, a Chamber may allow a witness to give *viva voce* (oral) testimony before the Chamber by means of

audio or video technology, provided that such technology permits the witness to be examined by the Prosecutor, the defence, and by the Chamber itself, at the time that the witness so testifies.

2. The examination of a witness under this rule shall be conducted in accordance with the relevant rules of this chapter.

3. The Chamber, with the assistance of the Registry, shall ensure that the venue chosen for the conduct of the audio or video-link testimony is conducive to the giving of truthful and open testimony and to the safety, physical and psychological well-being, dignity and privacy of the witness.

Rule 68 Prior recorded testimony

When the Pre-Trial Chamber has not taken measures under article 56, the Trial Chamber may, in accordance with article 69, paragraph 2, allow the introduction of previously recorded audio or video testimony of a witness, or the transcript or other documented evidence of such testimony, provided that:

(a) If the witness who gave the previously recorded testimony is not present before the Trial Chamber, both the Prosecutor and the defence had the opportunity to examine the witness during the recording; or

(b) If the witness who gave the previously recorded testimony is present before the Trial Chamber, he or she does not object to the submission of the previously recorded testimony and the Prosecutor, the defence and the Chamber have the opportunity to examine the witness during the proceedings.

Rule 69 Agreements as to evidence

The Prosecutor and the defence may agree that an alleged fact, which is contained in the charges, the contents of a document, the expected testimony of a witness or other evidence is not contested and, accordingly, a Chamber may consider such alleged fact as being proven, unless the Chamber is of the opinion that a more complete presentation of the alleged facts is required in the interests of justice, in particular the interests of the victims.

Rule 70 Principles of evidence in cases of sexual violence

In cases of sexual violence, the Court shall be guided by and, where appropriate, apply the following principles:

(a) Consent cannot be inferred by reason of any words or conduct of a victim where force, threat of force, coercion or taking an advantage of a coercive environment undermined the victim's ability to give voluntary and genuine consent;

(b) Consent cannot be inferred by reason of any words or conduct of a victim where the victim is incapable of giving genuine consent;

(c) Consent cannot be inferred by reason of the silence of, or lack of resistance by, a victim to the alleged sexual violence;

(d) Credibility, character or predisposition to sexual availability of a victim or witness cannot be inferred by reason of the sexual nature of the prior or subsequent conduct of a victim or witness.

Rule 71 Evidence of other sexual conduct

In the light of the definition and nature of the crimes within the jurisdiction of the Court, and subject to article 69, paragraph 4, a Chamber shall not admit evidence of the prior or subsequent sexual conduct of a victim or witness.

Rule 72 In camera *procedure to consider relevance or admissibility of evidence*

1. Where there is an intention to introduce or elicit, including by means of the questioning of a victim or witness, evidence that the victim consented to an alleged crime of sexual violence, or evidence of the words, conduct, silence or lack of resistance of a victim or witness as referred to in principles (a) through (d) of rule 70, notification shall be provided to the Court which shall describe the substance of the evidence intended to be introduced or elicited and the relevance of the evidence to the issues in the case.

2. In deciding whether the evidence referred to in sub-rule 1 is relevant or admissible, a Chamber shall hear *in camera* the views of the Prosecutor, the defence, the witness and the victim or his or her legal representative, if any, and shall take into account whether that evidence has a sufficient degree of probative value to an issue in the case and the prejudice that such evidence may cause, in accordance with article 69, paragraph 4. For this purpose, the Chamber shall have regard to article 21, paragraph 3, and articles 67 and 68, and shall be guided by principles (a) to (d) of rule 70, especially with respect to the proposed questioning of a victim.

3. Where the Chamber determines that the evidence referred to in sub-rule 2 is admissible in the proceedings, the Chamber shall state on the record the specific purpose for which the evidence is admissible. In evaluating the evidence during the proceedings, the Chamber shall apply principles (a) to (d) of rule 70.

Rule 73   Privileged communications and information

1. Without prejudice to article 67, paragraph 1 (b), communications made in the context of the professional relationship between a person and his or her legal counsel shall be regarded as privileged, and consequently not subject to disclosure, unless:

(a) The person consents in writing to such disclosure; or
(b) The person voluntarily disclosed the content of the communication to a third party, and that third party then gives evidence of that disclosure.

2. Having regard to rule 63, sub-rule 5, communications made in the context of a class of professional or other confidential relationships shall be regarded as privileged, and consequently not subject to disclosure, under the same terms as in sub-rules 1 (a) and 1 (b) if a Chamber decides in respect of that class that:

(a) Communications occurring within that class of relationship are made in the course of a confidential relationship producing a reasonable expectation of privacy and non-disclosure;
(b) Confidentiality is essential to the nature and type of relationship between the person and the confidant; and
(c) Recognition of the privilege would further the objectives of the Statute and the Rules.

3. In making a decision under sub-rule 2, the Court shall give particular regard to recognizing as privileged those communications made in the context of the professional relationship between a person and his or her medical doctor, psychiatrist, psychologist or counsellor, in particular those related to or involving victims, or between a person and a member of a religious clergy; and in the latter case, the Court shall recognize as privileged those communications made in the context of a sacred confession where it is an integral part of the practice of that religion.

4. The Court shall regard as privileged, and consequently not subject to disclosure, including by way of testimony of any present or past official or employee of the International Committee of the Red Cross (ICRC), any information, documents or other evidence which it came into the possession of in the course, or as a consequence of, the performance by ICRC of its functions under the Statutes of the International Red Cross and Red Crescent Movement, unless:

(a) After consultations undertaken pursuant to sub-rule 6, ICRC does not object in writing to such disclosure, or otherwise has waived this privilege; or

(b) Such information, documents or other evidence is contained in public statements and documents of ICRC.

5. Nothing in sub-rule 4 shall affect the admissibility of the same evidence obtained from a source other than ICRC and its officials or employees when such evidence has also been acquired by this source independently of ICRC and its officials or employees.

6. If the Court determines that ICRC information, documents or other evidence are of great importance for a particular case, consultations shall be held between the Court and ICRC in order to seek to resolve the matter by cooperative means, bearing in mind the circumstances of the case, the relevance of the evidence sought, whether the evidence could be obtained from a source other than ICRC, the interests of justice and of victims, and the performance of the Court's and ICRC's functions.

Rule 74 Self-incrimination by a witness

1. Unless a witness has been notified pursuant to rule 190, the Chamber shall notify a witness of the provisions of this rule before his or her testimony.

2. Where the Court determines that an assurance with respect to self-incrimination should be provided to a particular witness, it shall provide the assurances under sub-rule 3, paragraph (c), before the witness attends, directly or pursuant to a request under article 93, paragraph (1) (e).

3.

(a) A witness may object to making any statement that might tend to incriminate him or her.

(b) Where the witness has attended after receiving an assurance under sub-rule 2, the Court may require the witness to answer the question or questions.

(c) In the case of other witnesses, the Chamber may require the witness to answer the question or questions, after assuring the witness that the evidence provided in response to the questions:

(i)   Will be kept confidential and will not be disclosed to the public or any State; and

(ii)   Will not be used either directly or indirectly against that person in any subsequent prosecution by the Court, except under articles 70 and 71.

4. Before giving such an assurance, the Chamber shall seek the views of the Prosecutor, *ex parte*, to determine if the assurance should be given to this particular witness.

5. In determining whether to require the witness to answer, the Chamber shall consider:

(a) The importance of the anticipated evidence;
(b) Whether the witness would be providing unique evidence;
(c) The nature of the possible incrimination, if known; and
(d) The sufficiency of the protections for the witness, in the particular circumstances.

6. If the Chamber determines that it would not be appropriate to provide an assurance to this witness, it shall not require the witness to answer the question. If the Chamber determines not to require the witness to answer, it may still continue the questioning of the witness on other matters.

7. In order to give effect to the assurance, the Chamber shall:

(a) Order that the evidence of the witness be given *in camera*;
(b) Order that the identity of the witness and the content of the evidence given shall not be disclosed, in any manner, and provide that the breach of any such order will be subject to sanction under article 71;
(c) Specifically advise the Prosecutor, the accused, the defence counsel, the legal representative of the victim and any Court staff present of the consequences of a breach of the order under subparagraph (b);
(d) Order the sealing of any record of the proceedings; and
(e) Use protective measures with respect to any decision of the Court to ensure that the identity of the witness and the content of the evidence given are not disclosed.

8. Where the Prosecutor is aware that the testimony of any witness may raise issues with respect to self-incrimination, he or she shall request an *in camera* hearing and advise the Chamber of this, in advance of the testimony of the witness. The Chamber may impose the measures outlined in sub-rule 7 for all or a part of the testimony of that witness.

9. The accused, the defence counsel or the witness may advise the Prosecutor or the Chamber that the testimony of a witness will raise issues of self-incrimination before the witness testifies and the Chamber may take the measures outlined in sub-rule 7.

10. If an issue of self-incrimination arises in the course of the proceedings, the Chamber shall suspend the taking of the testimony and provide the witness with an opportunity to obtain legal advice if he or she so requests for the purpose of the application of the rule.

Rule 75 Incrimination by family members

1. A witness appearing before the Court, who is a spouse, child or parent of an accused person, shall not be required by a Chamber to make any statement

that might tend to incriminate that accused person. However, the witness may choose to make such statement.

2. In evaluating the testimony of a witness, a Chamber may take into account that the witness, referred to in sub-rule 1, objected to reply to a question which was intended to contradict a previous statement made by the witness, or the witness was selective in choosing which questions to answer.

Section II Disclosure

Rule 76 Pre-trial disclosure relating to prosecution witnesses

1. The Prosecutor shall provide the defence with the names of witnesses whom the Prosecutor intends to call to testify and copies of any prior statements made by those witnesses. This shall be done sufficiently in advance to enable the adequate preparation of the defence.

2. The Prosecutor shall subsequently advise the defence of the names of any additional prosecution witnesses and provide copies of their statements when the decision is made to call those witnesses.

3. The statements of prosecution witnesses shall be made available in original and in a language which the accused fully understands and speaks.

4. This rule is subject to the protection and privacy of victims and witnesses and the protection of confidential information as provided for in the Statute and rules 81 and 82.

Rule 77 Inspection of material in possession or control of the Prosecutor

The Prosecutor shall, subject to the restrictions on disclosure as provided for in the Statute and in rules 81 and 82, permit the defence to inspect any books, documents, photographs and other tangible objects in the possession or control of the Prosecutor, which are material to the preparation of the defence or are intended for use by the Prosecutor as evidence for the purposes of the confirmation hearing or at trial, as the case may be, or were obtained from or belonged to the person.

Rule 78 Inspection of material in possession or control of the defence

The defence shall permit the Prosecutor to inspect any books, documents, photographs and other tangible objects in the possession or control of the defence, which are intended for use by the defence as evidence for the purposes of the confirmation hearing or at trial.

Rule 79 Disclosure by the defence

1. The defence shall notify the Prosecutor of its intent to:

(a) Raise the existence of an alibi, in which case the notification shall specify the place or places at which the accused claims to have been present at the time of the alleged crime and the names of witnesses and any other evidence upon which the accused intends to rely to establish the alibi; or
(b) Raise a ground for excluding criminal responsibility provided for in article 31, paragraph 1, in which case the notification shall specify the names of witnesses and any other evidence upon which the accused intends to rely to establish the ground.

2. With due regard to time limits set forth in other rules, notification under sub-rule 1 shall be given sufficiently in advance to enable the Prosecutor to prepare adequately and to respond. The Chamber dealing with the matter may grant the Prosecutor an adjournment to address the issue raised by the defence.

3. Failure of the defence to provide notice under this rule shall not limit its right to raise matters dealt with in sub-rule 1 and to present evidence.

4. This rule does not prevent a Chamber from ordering disclosure of any other evidence.

Rule 80 Procedures for raising a ground for excluding criminal responsibility under article 31, paragraph 3

1. The defence shall give notice to both the Trial Chamber and the Prosecutor if it intends to raise a ground for excluding criminal responsibility under article 31, paragraph 3. This shall be done sufficiently in advance of the commencement of the trial to enable the Prosecutor to prepare adequately for trial.

2. Following notice given under sub-rule 1, the Trial Chamber shall hear both the Prosecutor and the defence before deciding whether the defence can raise a ground for excluding criminal responsibility.

3. If the defence is permitted to raise the ground, the Trial Chamber may grant the Prosecutor an adjournment to address that ground.

Rule 81 Restrictions on disclosure

1. Reports, memoranda or other internal documents prepared by a party, its assistants or representatives in connection with the investigation or preparation of the case are not subject to disclosure.

2. Where material or information is in the possession or control of the Prosecutor which must be disclosed in accordance with the Statute, but disclosure may prejudice further or ongoing investigations, the Prosecutor may apply to the Chamber dealing with the matter for a ruling as to whether the material or information must be disclosed to the defence. The matter shall be heard on an *ex parte* basis by the Chamber. However, the Prosecutor may not introduce such material or information into evidence during the confirmation hearing or the trial without adequate prior disclosure to the accused.

3. Where steps have been taken to ensure the confidentiality of information, in accordance with articles 54, 57, 64, 72 and 93, and, in accordance with article 68, to protect the safety of witnesses and victims and members of their families, such information shall not be disclosed, except in accordance with those articles. When the disclosure of such information may create a risk to the safety of the witness, the Court shall take measures to inform the witness in advance.

4. The Chamber dealing with the matter shall, on its own motion or at the request of the Prosecutor, the accused or any State, take the necessary steps to ensure the confidentiality of information, in accordance with articles 54, 72 and 93, and, in accordance with article 68, to protect the safety of witnesses and victims and members of their families, including by authorizing the non-disclosure of their identity prior to the commencement of the trial.

5. Where material or information is in the possession or control of the Prosecutor which is withheld under article 68, paragraph 5, such material and information may not be subsequently introduced into evidence during the confirmation hearing or the trial without adequate prior disclosure to the accused.

6. Where material or information is in the possession or control of the defence which is subject to disclosure, it may be withheld in circumstances similar to those which would allow the Prosecutor to rely on article 68, paragraph 5, and a summary thereof submitted instead. Such material and information may not be subsequently introduced into evidence during the confirmation hearing or the trial without adequate prior disclosure to the Prosecutor.

Rule 82 Restrictions on disclosure of material and information protected under article 54, paragraph 3 (e)

1. Where material or information is in the possession or control of the Prosecutor which is protected under article 54, paragraph 3 (e), the Prosecutor may not subsequently introduce such material or information into

evidence without the prior consent of the provider of the material or information and adequate prior disclosure to the accused.

2. If the Prosecutor introduces material or information protected under article 54, paragraph 3 (e), into evidence, a Chamber may not order the production of additional evidence received from the provider of the initial material or information, nor may a Chamber for the purpose of obtaining such additional evidence itself summon the provider or a representative of the provider as a witness or order their attendance.

3. If the Prosecutor calls a witness to introduce in evidence any material or information which has been protected under article 54, paragraph 3 (e), a Chamber may not compel that witness to answer any question relating to the material or information or its origin, if the witness declines to answer on grounds of confidentiality.

4. The right of the accused to challenge evidence which has been protected under article 54, paragraph 3 (e), shall remain unaffected subject only to the limitations contained in sub-rules 2 and 3.

5. A Chamber dealing with the matter may order, upon application by the defence, that, in the interests of justice, material or information in the possession of the accused, which has been provided to the accused under the same conditions as set forth in article 54, paragraph 3 (e), and which is to be introduced into evidence, shall be subject *mutatis mutandis* to sub-rules 1, 2 and 3.

Rule 83 Ruling on exculpatory evidence under article 67, paragraph 2

The Prosecutor may request as soon as practicable a hearing on an *ex parte* basis before the Chamber dealing with the matter for the purpose of obtaining a ruling under article 67, paragraph 2.

Rule 84 Disclosure and additional evidence for trial

In order to enable the parties to prepare for trial and to facilitate the fair and expeditious conduct of the proceedings, the Trial Chamber shall, in accordance with article 64, paragraphs 3 (c) and 6 (d), and article 67, paragraph (2), and subject to article 68, paragraph 5, make any necessary orders for the disclosure of documents or information not previously disclosed and for the production of additional evidence. To avoid delay and to ensure that the trial commences on the set date, any such orders shall include strict time limits which shall be kept under review by the Trial Chamber.

Section III Victims and witnesses

Subsection 1 Definition and general principle relating to victims

Rule 85 Definition of victims

For the purposes of the Statute and the Rules of Procedure and Evidence:

(a) 'Victims' means natural persons who have suffered harm as a result of the commission of any crime within the jurisdiction of the Court;

(b) Victims may include organizations or institutions that have sustained direct harm to any of their property, which is dedicated to religion, education, art or science or charitable purposes, and to their historic monuments, hospitals and other places and objects for humanitarian purposes.

Rule 86 General principle

A Chamber in making any direction or order, and other organs of the Court in performing their functions under the Statute or the Rules, shall take into account the needs of all victims and witnesses in accordance with article 68, in particular, children, elderly persons, persons with disabilities and victims of sexual or gender violence.

Subsection 2 Protection of victims and witnesses

Rule 87 Protective measures

1. Upon the motion of the Prosecutor or the defence or upon the request of a witness or a victim or his or her legal representative, if any, or on its own motion, and after having consulted with the Victims and Witnesses Unit, as appropriate, a Chamber may order measures to protect a victim, a witness or another person at risk on account of testimony given by a witness pursuant to article 68, paragraphs 1 and 2. The Chamber shall seek to obtain, whenever possible, the consent of the person in respect of whom the protective measure is sought prior to ordering the protective measure.

2. A motion or request under sub-rule 1 shall be governed by rule 134, provided that:

(a) Such a motion or request shall not be submitted *ex parte*;

(b) A request by a witness or by a victim or his or her legal representative, if any, shall be served on both the Prosecutor and the defence, each of whom shall have the opportunity to respond;

(c) A motion or request affecting a particular witness or a particular victim shall be served on that witness or victim or his or her legal representative, if any, in addition to the other party, each of whom shall have the opportunity to respond;

(d) When the Chamber proceeds on its own motion, notice and opportunity to respond shall be given to the Prosecutor and the defence, and to any witness or any victim or his or her legal representative, if any, who would be affected by such protective measure; and

(e) A motion or request may be filed under seal, and, if so filed, shall remain sealed until otherwise ordered by a Chamber. Responses to motions or requests filed under seal shall also be filed under seal.

3. A Chamber may, on a motion or request under sub-rule 1, hold a hearing which shall be conducted *in camera*, to determine whether to order measures to prevent the release to the public or press and information agencies, of the identity or the location of a victim, a witness or other person at risk on account of testimony given by a witness by ordering, *inter alia*:

(a) That the name of the victim, witness or other person at risk on account of testimony given by a witness or any information which could lead to his or her identification, be expunged from the public records of the Chamber;

(b) That the Prosecutor, the defence or any other participant in the proceedings be prohibited from disclosing such information to a third party;

(c) That testimony be presented by electronic or other special means, including the use of technical means enabling the alteration of pictures or voice, the use of audio-visual technology, in particular videoconferencing and closed-circuit television, and the exclusive use of the sound media;

(d) That a pseudonym be used for a victim, a witness or other person at risk on account of testimony given by a witness; or

(e) That a Chamber conduct part of its proceedings *in camera*.

Rule 88 Special measures

1. Upon the motion of the Prosecutor or the defence, or upon the request of a witness or a victim or his or her legal representative, if any, or on its own motion, and after having consulted with the Victims and Witnesses Unit, as appropriate, a Chamber may, taking into account the views of the victim or witness, order special measures such as but not limited to measures to facilitate the testimony of a traumatized victim or witness, a child, an elderly person or a victim of sexual violence, pursuant to article 68, paragraphs 1 and 2. The Chamber shall seek to obtain, whenever possible, the consent of the

person in respect of whom the special measure is sought prior to ordering that measure.

2. A Chamber may hold a hearing on a motion or a request under sub-rule 1, if necessary *in camera* or *ex parte*, to determine whether to order any such special measure, including but not limited to an order that a counsel, a legal representative, a psychologist or a family member be permitted to attend during the testimony of the victim or the witness.

3. For *inter partes* motions or requests filed under this rule, the provisions of rule 87, sub-rules 2 (b) to (d), shall apply *mutatis mutandis.*

4. A motion or request filed under this rule may be filed under seal, and if so filed shall remain sealed until otherwise ordered by a Chamber. Any responses to *inter partes* motions or requests filed under seal shall also be filed under seal.

5. Taking into consideration that violations of the privacy of a witness or victim may create risk to his or her security, a Chamber shall be vigilant in controlling the manner of questioning a witness or victim so as to avoid any harassment or intimidation, paying particular attention to attacks on victims of crimes of sexual violence.

Subsection 3 Participation of victims in the proceedings

Rule 89 Application for participation of victims in the proceedings

1. In order to present their views and concerns, victims shall make written application to the Registrar, who shall transmit the application to the relevant Chamber. Subject to the provisions of the Statute, in particular article 68, paragraph 1, the Registrar shall provide a copy of the application to the Prosecutor and the defence, who shall be entitled to reply within a time limit to be set by the Chamber. Subject to the provisions of sub-rule 2, the Chamber shall then specify the proceedings and manner in which participation is considered appropriate, which may include making opening and closing statements.

2. The Chamber, on its own initiative or on the application of the Prosecutor or the defence, may reject the application if it considers that the person is not a victim or that the criteria set forth in article 68, paragraph 3, are not otherwise fulfilled. A victim whose application has been rejected may file a new application later in the proceedings.

3. An application referred to in this rule may also be made by a person acting with the consent of the victim, or a person acting on behalf of a victim, in the case of a victim who is a child or, when necessary, a victim who is disabled.

4. Where there are a number of applications, the Chamber may consider the applications in such a manner so as to ensure the effectiveness of the proceedings and may issue one decision.

Rule 90 Legal representatives of victims

1. A victim shall be free to choose a legal representative.

2. Where there are a number of victims, the Chamber may, for the purposes of ensuring the effectiveness of the proceedings, request the victims or particular groups of victims, if necessary with the assistance of the Registry, to choose a common legal representative or representatives. In facilitating the coordination of victim representation, the Registry may provide assistance, *inter alia*, by referring the victims to a list of counsel, maintained by the Registry, or suggesting one or more common legal representatives.

3. If the victims are unable to choose a common legal representative or representatives within a time limit that the Chamber may decide, the Chamber may request the Registrar to choose one or more common legal representatives.

4. The Chamber and the Registry shall take all reasonable steps to ensure that in the selection of common legal representatives, the distinct interests of the victims, particularly as provided in article 68, paragraph 1, are represented and that any conflict of interest is avoided.

5. A victim or group of victims who lack the necessary means to pay for a common legal representative chosen by the Court may receive assistance from the Registry, including, as appropriate, financial assistance.

6. A legal representative of a victim or victims shall have the qualifications set forth in rule 22, sub-rule 1.

Rule 91 Participation of legal representatives in the proceedings

1. A Chamber may modify a previous ruling under rule 89.

2. A legal representative of a victim shall be entitled to attend and participate in the proceedings in accordance with the terms of the ruling of the Chamber and any modification thereof given under rules 89 and 90. This shall include participation in hearings unless, in the circumstances of the case, the Chamber concerned is of the view that the representative's intervention should be confined to written observations or submissions. The Prosecutor and the defence shall be allowed to reply to any oral or written observation by the legal representative for victims.

3.

(a) When a legal representative attends and participates in accordance with this rule, and wishes to question a witness, including questioning under rules 67 and 68, an expert or the accused, the legal representative must make application to the Chamber. The Chamber may require the legal representative to provide a written note of the questions and in that case the questions shall be communicated to the Prosecutor and, if appropriate, the defence, who shall be allowed to make observations within a time limit set by the Chamber.

(b) The Chamber shall then issue a ruling on the request, taking into account the stage of the proceedings, the rights of the accused, the interests of witnesses, the need for a fair, impartial and expeditious trial and in order to give effect to article 68, paragraph 3. The ruling may include directions on the manner and order of the questions and the production of documents in accordance with the powers of the Chamber under article 64. The Chamber may, if it considers it appropriate, put the question to the witness, expert or accused on behalf of the victim's legal representative.

4. For a hearing limited to reparations under article 75, the restrictions on questioning by the legal representative set forth in sub-rule 2 shall not apply. In that case, the legal representative may, with the permission of the Chamber concerned, question witnesses, experts and the person concerned.

Rule 92 Notification to victims and their legal representatives

1. This rule on notification to victims and their legal representatives shall apply to all proceedings before the Court, except in proceedings provided for in Part 2.

2. In order to allow victims to apply for participation in the proceedings in accordance with rule 89, the Court shall notify victims concerning the decision of the Prosecutor not to initiate an investigation or not to prosecute pursuant to article 53. Such a notification shall be given to victims or their legal representatives who have already participated in the proceedings or, as far as possible, to those who have communicated with the Court in respect of the situation or case in question. The Chamber may order the measures outlined in sub-rule 8 if it considers it appropriate in the particular circumstances.

3. In order to allow victims to apply for participation in the proceedings in accordance with rule 89, the Court shall notify victims regarding its decision to hold a hearing to confirm charges pursuant to article 61. Such a notification shall be given to victims or their legal representatives who have already

participated in the proceedings or, as far as possible, to those who have communicated with the Court in respect of the case in question.

4. When a notification for participation as provided for in sub-rules 2 and 3 has been given, any subsequent notification as referred to in sub-rules 5 and 6 shall only be provided to victims or their legal representatives who may participate in the proceedings in accordance with a ruling of the Chamber pursuant to rule 89 and any modification thereof.

5. In a manner consistent with the ruling made under rules 89 to 91 *ter*, victims or their legal representatives participating in proceedings shall, in respect of those proceedings, be notified by the Registrar in a timely manner of:

(a) Proceedings before the Court, including the date of hearings and any postponements thereof, and the date of delivery of the decision;
(b) Requests, submissions, motions and other documents relating to such requests, submissions or motions.

6. Where victims or their legal representatives have participated in a certain stage of the proceedings, the Registrar shall notify them as soon as possible of the decisions of the Court in those proceedings.

7. Notifications as referred to in sub-rules 5 and 6 shall be in writing or, where written notification is not possible, in any other form as appropriate. The Registry shall keep a record of all notifications. Where necessary, the Registrar may seek the cooperation of States Parties in accordance with article 93, paragraph 1 (d) and (l).

8. For notification as referred to in sub-rule 3 and otherwise at the request of a Chamber, the Registrar shall take necessary measures to give adequate publicity to the proceedings. In doing so, the Registrar may seek in accordance with Part 9 the cooperation of relevant States Parties, and seek the assistance of intergovernmental organizations.

Rule 93 Views of victims or their legal representatives

A Chamber may seek the views of victims or their legal representatives participating pursuant to rules 89 to 91 on any issue, *inter alia*, in relation to issues referred to in rules 107, 109, 125, 128, 136, 139 and 191. In addition, a Chamber may seek the views of other victims, as appropriate.

Subsection 4 Reparations to victims

Rule 94 Procedure upon request

1. A victim's request for reparations under article 75 shall be made in writing and filed with the Registrar. It shall contain the following particulars:

(a) The identity and address of the claimant;

(b) A description of the injury, loss or harm;

(c) The location and date of the incident and, to the extent possible, the identity of the person or persons the victim believes to be responsible for the injury, loss or harm;

(d) Where restitution of assets, property or other tangible items is sought, a description of them;

(e) Claims for compensation;

(f) Claims for rehabilitation and other forms of remedy;

(g) To the extent possible, any relevant supporting documentation, including names and addresses of witnesses.

2. At commencement of the trial and subject to any protective measures, the Court shall ask the Registrar to provide notification of the request to the person or persons named in the request or identified in the charges and, to the extent possible, to any interested persons or any interested States. Those notified shall file with the Registry any representation made under article 75, paragraph 3.

Rule 95 Procedure on the motion of the Court

1. In cases where the Court intends to proceed on its own motion pursuant to article 75, paragraph 1, it shall ask the Registrar to provide notification of its intention to the person or persons against whom the Court is considering making a determination, and, to the extent possible, to victims, interested persons and interested States. Those notified shall file with the Registry any representation made under article 75, paragraph 3.

2. If, as a result of notification under sub-rule 1:

(a) A victim makes a request for reparations, that request will be determined as if it had been brought under rule 94;

(b) A victim requests that the Court does not make an order for reparations, the Court shall not proceed to make an individual order in respect of that victim.

Rule 96   Publication of reparation proceedings

1. Without prejudice to any other rules on notification of proceedings, the Registrar shall, insofar as practicable, notify the victims or their legal representatives and the person or persons concerned. The Registrar shall also, having regard to any information provided by the Prosecutor, take all the necessary measures to give adequate publicity of the reparations proceedings before the Court, to the extent possible, to other victims, interested persons and interested States.

2. In taking the measures described in sub-rule 1, the Court may seek in accordance with Part 9 the cooperation of relevant States Parties, and seek the assistance of intergovernmental organizations in order to give publicity, as widely as possible and by all possible means, to the reparation proceedings before the Court.

Rule 97   Assessment of reparations

1. Taking into account the scope and extent of any damage, loss or injury, the Court may award reparations on an individualized basis or, where it deems it appropriate, on a collective basis or both.

2. At the request of victims or their legal representatives, or at the request of the convicted person, or on its own motion, the Court may appoint appropriate experts to assist it in determining the scope, extent of any damage, loss and injury to, or in respect of victims and to suggest various options concerning the appropriate types and modalities of reparations. The Court shall invite, as appropriate, victims or their legal representatives, the convicted person as well as interested persons and interested States to make observations on the reports of the experts.

3. In all cases, the Court shall respect the rights of victims and the convicted person.

Rule 98   Trust Fund

1. Individual awards for reparations shall be made directly against a convicted person.

2. The Court may order that an award for reparations against a convicted person be deposited with the Trust Fund where at the time of making the order it is impossible or impracticable to make individual awards directly to

each victim. The award for reparations thus deposited in the Trust Fund shall be separated from other resources of the Trust Fund and shall be forwarded to each victim as soon as possible.

3. The Court may order that an award for reparations against a convicted person be made through the Trust Fund where the number of the victims and the scope, forms and modalities of reparations makes a collective award more appropriate.

4. Following consultations with interested States and the Trust Fund, the Court may order that an award for reparations be made through the Trust Fund to an intergovernmental, international or national organization approved by the Trust Fund.

5. Other resources of the Trust Fund may be used for the benefit of victims subject to the provisions of article 79.

Rule 99 Cooperation and protective measures for the purpose of forfeiture under articles 57, paragraph 3 (e), and 75, paragraph 4

1. The Pre-Trial Chamber, pursuant to article 57, paragraph 3 (e), or the Trial Chamber, pursuant to article 75, paragraph 4, may, on its own motion or on the application of the Prosecutor or at the request of the victims or their legal representatives who have made a request for reparations or who have given a written undertaking to do so, determine whether measures should be requested.

2. Notice is not required unless the Court determines, in the particular circumstances of the case, that notification could not jeopardize the effectiveness of the measures requested. In the latter case, the Registrar shall provide notification of the proceedings to the person against whom a request is made and so far as is possible to any interested persons or interested States.

3. If an order is made without prior notification, the relevant Chamber shall request the Registrar, as soon as is consistent with the effectiveness of the measures requested, to notify those against whom a request is made and, to the extent possible, to any interested persons or any interested States and invite them to make observations as to whether the order should be revoked or otherwise modified.

4. The Court may make orders as to the timing and conduct of any proceedings necessary to determine these issues.

Section IV Miscellaneous provisions

Rule 100 Place of the proceedings

1. In a particular case, where the Court considers that it would be in the interests of justice, it may decide to sit in a State other than the host State.

2. An application or recommendation changing the place where the Court sits may be filed at any time after the initiation of an investigation, either by the Prosecutor, the defence or by a majority of the judges of the Court. Such an application or recommendation shall be addressed to the Presidency. It shall be made in writing and specify in which State the Court would sit. The Presidency shall satisfy itself of the views of the relevant Chamber.

3. The Presidency shall consult the State where the Court intends to sit. If that State agrees that the Court can sit in that State, then the decision to sit in a State other than the host State shall be taken by the judges, in plenary session, by a two-thirds majority.

Rule 101 Time limits

1. In making any order setting time limits regarding the conduct of any proceedings, the Court shall have regard to the need to facilitate fair and expeditious proceedings, bearing in mind in particular the rights of the defence and the victims.

2. Taking into account the rights of the accused, in particular under article 67, paragraph (1) (c), all those participating in the proceedings to whom any order is directed shall endeavour to act as expeditiously as possible, within the time limit ordered by the Court.

Rule 102 Communications other than in writing

Where a person is unable, due to a disability or illiteracy, to make a written request, application, observation or other communication to the Court, the person may make such request, application, observation or communication in audio, video or other electronic form.

Rule 103 Amicus curiae and other forms of submission

1. At any stage of the proceedings, a Chamber may, if it considers it desirable for the proper determination of the case, invite or grant leave to a State,

organization or person to submit, in writing or orally, any observation on any issue that the Chamber deems appropriate.

2. The Prosecutor and the defence shall have the opportunity to respond to the observations submitted under sub-rule 1.

3. A written observation submitted under sub-rule 1 shall be filed with the Registrar, who shall provide copies to the Prosecutor and the defence. The Chamber shall determine what time limits shall apply to the filing of such observations.

Chapter 5 Investigation and prosecution

Section I Decision of the Prosecutor regarding the initiation of an investigation under article 53, paragraphs 1 and 2

Rule 104 Evaluation of information by the Prosecutor

1. In acting pursuant to article 53, paragraph 1, the Prosecutor shall, in evaluating the information made available to him or her, analyse the seriousness of the information received.

2. For the purposes of sub-rule 1, the Prosecutor may seek additional information from States, organs of the United Nations, intergovernmental and non-governmental organizations, or other reliable sources that he or she deems appropriate, and may receive written or oral testimony at the seat of the Court. The procedure set out in rule 47 shall apply to the receiving of such testimony.

Rule 105 Notification of a decision by the Prosecutor not to initiate an investigation

1. When the Prosecutor decides not to initiate an investigation under article 53, paragraph 1, he or she shall promptly inform in writing the State or States that referred a situation under article 14, or the Security Council in respect of a situation covered by article 13, paragraph (b).

2. When the Prosecutor decides not to submit to the Pre-Trial Chamber a request for authorization of an investigation, rule 49 shall apply.

3. The notification referred to in sub-rule 1 shall contain the conclusion of the Prosecutor and, having regard to article 68, paragraph 1, the reasons for the conclusion.

4. In case the Prosecutor decides not to investigate solely on the basis of

article 53, paragraph 1 (c), he or she shall inform in writing the Pre-Trial Chamber promptly after making that decision.

5. The notification shall contain the conclusion of the Prosecutor and the reasons for the conclusion.

Rule 106 Notification of a decision by the Prosecutor not to prosecute

1. When the Prosecutor decides that there is not a sufficient basis for prosecution under article 53, paragraph 2, he or she shall promptly inform in writing the Pre-Trial Chamber, together with the State or States that referred a situation under article 14, or the Security Council in respect of a situation covered by article 13, paragraph (b).

2. The notifications referred to in sub-rule 1 shall contain the conclusion of the Prosecutor and, having regard to article 68, paragraph 1, the reasons for the conclusion.

Section II Procedure under article 53, paragraph 3

Rule 107 Request for review under article 53, paragraph 3 (a)

1. A request under article 53, paragraph 3, for a review of a decision by the Prosecutor not to initiate an investigation or not to prosecute, shall be made in writing, and be supported with reasons, within 90 days following the notification given under rule 105 or 106.

2. The Pre-Trial Chamber may request the Prosecutor to transmit the information or documents in his or her possession, or summaries thereof, that the Chamber considers necessary for the conduct of the review.

3. The Pre-Trial Chamber shall take such measures as are necessary under articles 54, 72 and 93 to protect the information and documents referred to in sub-rule 2 and, under article 68, paragraph 5, to protect the safety of witnesses and victims and members of their families.

4. When a State or the Security Council makes a request referred to in sub-rule 1, the Pre-Trial Chamber may seek further observations from them.

5. Where an issue of jurisdiction or admissibility of the case is raised, rule 2.15 shall apply.

Rule 108 Decision of the Pre-Trial Chamber under article 53, paragraph 3 (a)

1. A decision of the Pre-Trial Chamber under article 53, paragraph 3 (a), must be concurred in by a majority of its judges and shall contain reasons. It shall be communicated to all those who participated in the review.

2. Where the Pre-Trial Chamber requests the Prosecutor to review, in whole or in part, his or her decision not to initiate an investigation or not to prosecute, the Prosecutor shall reconsider that decision as soon as possible.

3. Once the Prosecutor has taken a final decision, he or she shall notify the Pre-Trial Chamber in writing. This notification shall contain the conclusion of the Prosecutor and the reasons for the conclusion. It shall be communicated to all those who participated in the review.

Rule 109 Review by the Pre-Trial Chamber under article 53, paragraph 3 (b)

1. Within 180 days following a notification given under rule 105 or 106, the Pre-Trial Chamber may on its own initiative decide to review a decision of the Prosecutor taken solely under article 53, paragraph 1 (c) or 2 (c). The Pre-Trial Chamber shall inform the Prosecutor of its intention to review his or her decision and shall establish a time limit within which the Prosecutor may submit observations and other material.

2. In cases where a request has been submitted to the Pre-Trial Chamber by a State or by the Security Council, they shall also be informed and may submit observations in accordance with rule 107.

Rule 110 Decision by the Pre-Trial Chamber under article 53, paragraph 3 (b)

1. A decision by the Pre-Trial Chamber to confirm or not to confirm a decision taken by the Prosecutor solely under article 53, paragraph 1 (c) or 2 (c), must be concurred in by a majority of its judges and shall contain reasons. It shall be communicated to all those who participated in the review.

2. When the Pre-Trial Chamber does not confirm the decision by the Prosecutor referred to in sub-rule 1, he or she shall proceed with the investigation or prosecution.

Section III Collection of evidence

Rule 111 Record of questioning in general

1. A record shall be made of formal statements made by any person who is questioned in connection with an investigation or with proceedings. The record shall be signed by the person who records and conducts the questioning and by the person who is questioned and his or her counsel, if present, and, where applicable, the Prosecutor or the judge who is present. The record shall note the date, time and place of, and all persons present during the

questioning. It shall also be noted when someone has not signed the record as well as the reasons therefor.

2. When the Prosecutor or national authorities question a person, due regard shall be given to article 55. When a person is informed of his or her rights under article 55, paragraph 2, the fact that this information has been provided shall be noted in the record.

Rule 112 Recording of questioning in particular cases

1. Whenever the Prosecutor questions a person to whom article 55, paragraph 2, applies, or for whom a warrant of arrest or a summons to appear has been issued under article 58, paragraph 7, the questioning shall be audio- or video-recorded, in accordance with the following procedure:

(a) The person questioned shall be informed, in a language he or she fully understands and speaks, that the questioning is to be audio- or video-recorded, and that the person concerned may object if he or she so wishes. The fact that this information has been provided and the response given by the person concerned shall be noted in the record. The person may, before replying, speak in private with his or her counsel, if present. If the person questioned refuses to be audio- or video-recorded, the procedure in rule 111 shall be followed;

(b) A waiver of the right to be questioned in the presence of counsel shall be recorded in writing and, if possible, be audio- or video-recorded;

(c) In the event of an interruption in the course of questioning, the fact and the time of the interruption shall be recorded before the audio- or video-recording ends as well as the time of resumption of the questioning;

(d) At the conclusion of the questioning, the person questioned shall be offered the opportunity to clarify anything he or she has said and to add anything he or she may wish. The time of conclusion of the questioning shall be noted;

(e) The tape shall be transcribed as soon as practicable after the conclusion of the questioning and a copy of the transcript supplied to the person questioned together with a copy of the recorded tape or, if multiple recording apparatus was used, one of the original recorded tapes;

(f) The original tape or one of the original tapes shall be sealed in the presence of the person questioned and his or her counsel, if present, under the signature of the Prosecutor and the person questioned and the counsel, if present.

2. The Prosecutor shall make every reasonable effort to record the questioning in accordance with sub-rule 1. As an exception, a person may be questioned without the questioning being audio- or video-recorded where the circumstances prevent such recording taking place. In this case, the reasons

for not recording the questioning shall be stated in writing and the procedure in rule 111 shall be followed.

3. When, pursuant to sub-rule 1 (a) or 2, the questioning is not audio- or video-recorded, the person questioned shall be provided with a copy of his or her statement.

4. The Prosecutor may choose to follow the procedure in this rule when questioning other persons than those mentioned in sub-rule 1, in particular where the use of such procedures could assist in reducing any subsequent traumatization of a victim of sexual or gender violence, a child or a person with disabilities in providing their evidence. The Prosecutor may make an application to the relevant Chamber.

5. The Pre-Trial Chamber may, in pursuance of article 56, paragraph 2, order that the procedure in this rule be applied to the questioning of any person.

Rule 113 Collection of information regarding the state of health of the person concerned

1. The Pre-Trial Chamber may, on its own initiative or at the request of the Prosecutor, the person concerned or his or her counsel, order that a person having the rights in article 55, paragraph 2, be given a medical, psychological or psychiatric examination. In making its determination, the Pre-Trial Chamber shall consider the nature and purpose of the examination and whether the person consents to the examination.

2. The Pre-Trial Chamber shall appoint one or more experts from the list of experts approved by the Registrar, or an expert approved by the Pre-Trial Chamber at the request of a party.

Rule 114 Unique investigative opportunity under article 56

1. Upon being advised by the Prosecutor in accordance with article 56, paragraph 1 (a), the Pre-Trial Chamber shall hold consultations without delay with the Prosecutor and, subject to the provisions of article 56, paragraph 1 (c), with the person who has been arrested or who has appeared before the Court pursuant to summons and his or her counsel, in order to determine the measures to be taken and the modalities of their implementation, which may include measures to ensure that the right to communicate under article 67, paragraph 1 (b), is protected.

2. A decision of the Pre-Trial Chamber to take measures pursuant to article

56, paragraph 3, must be concurred in by a majority of its judges after consultations with the Prosecutor. During the consultations, the Prosecutor may advise the Pre-Trial Chamber that intended measures could jeopardize the proper conduct of the investigation.

Rule 115 Collection of evidence in the territory of a State Party under article 57, paragraph 3 (d)

1. Where the Prosecutor considers that article 57, paragraph 3 (d), applies, the Prosecutor may submit a written request to the Pre-Trial Chamber for authorization to take certain measures in the territory of the State Party in question. After a submission of such a request, the Pre-Trial Chamber shall, whenever possible, inform and invite views from the State Party concerned.

2. In arriving at its determination as to whether the request is well founded, the Pre-Trial Chamber shall take into account any views expressed by the State Party concerned. The Pre-Trial Chamber may, on its own initiative or at the request of the Prosecutor or the State Party concerned, decide to hold a hearing.

3. An authorization under article 57, paragraph 3 (d), shall be issued in the form of an order and shall state the reasons, based on the criteria set forth in that paragraph. The order may specify procedures to be followed in carrying out such collection of evidence.

Rule 116 Collection of evidence at the request of the defence under article 57, paragraph 3 (b)

1. The Pre-Trial Chamber shall issue an order or seek cooperation under article 57, paragraph 3 (b), where it is satisfied:

(a) That such an order would facilitate the collection of evidence that may be material to the proper determination of the issues being adjudicated, or to the proper preparation of the person's defence; and
(b) In a case of cooperation under Part 9, that sufficient information to comply with article 96, paragraph 2, has been provided.

2. Before taking a decision whether to issue an order or seek cooperation under article 57, paragraph 3 (b), the Pre-Trial Chamber may seek the views of the Prosecutor.

Section IV Procedures in respect of restriction and deprivation of liberty

Rule 117 Detention in the custodial State

1. The Court shall take measures to ensure that it is informed of the arrest of a person in response to a request made by the Court under article 89 or 92. Once so informed, the Court shall ensure that the person receives a copy of the arrest warrant issued by the Pre-Trial Chamber under article 58 and any relevant provisions of the Statute. The documents shall be made available in a language that the person fully understands and speaks.

2. At any time after arrest, the person may make a request to the Pre-Trial Chamber for the appointment of counsel to assist with proceedings before the Court and the Pre-Trial Chamber shall take a decision on such request.

3. A challenge as to whether the warrant of arrest was properly issued in accordance with article 58, paragraph 1 (a) and (b), shall be made in writing to the Pre-Trial Chamber. The application shall set out the basis for the challenge. After having obtained the views of the Prosecutor, the Pre-Trial Chamber shall decide on the application without delay.

4. When the competent authority of the custodial State notifies the Pre-Trial Chamber that a request for release has been made by the person arrested, in accordance with article 59, paragraph 5, the Pre-Trial Chamber shall provide its recommendations within any time limit set by the custodial State.

5. When the Pre-Trial Chamber is informed that the person has been granted interim release by the competent authority of the custodial State, the Pre-Trial Chamber shall inform the custodial State how and when it would like to receive periodic reports on the status of the interim release.

Rule 118 Pre-trial detention at the seat of the Court

1. If the person surrendered to the Court makes an initial request for interim release pending trial, either upon first appearance in accordance with rule 121 or subsequently, the Pre-Trial Chamber shall decide upon the request without delay, after seeking the views of the Prosecutor.

2. The Pre-Trial Chamber shall review its ruling on the release or detention of a person in accordance with article 60, paragraph 3, at least every 120 days and may do so at any time on the request of the person or the Prosecutor.

3. After the first appearance, a request for interim release must be made in writing. The Prosecutor shall be given notice of such a request. The Pre-Trial Chamber shall decide after having received observations in writing of the

Prosecutor and the detained person. The Pre-Trial Chamber may decide to hold a hearing, at the request of the Prosecutor or the detained person or on its own initiative. A hearing must be held at least once every year.

Rule 119 Conditional release

1. The Pre-Trial Chamber may set one or more conditions restricting liberty, including the following:

(a) The person must not travel beyond territorial limits set by the Pre-Trial Chamber without the explicit agreement of the Chamber;

(b) The person must not go to certain places or associate with certain persons as specified by the Pre-Trial Chamber;

(c) The person must not contact directly or indirectly victims or witnesses;

(d) The person must not engage in certain professional activities;

(e) The person must reside at a particular address as specified by the Pre-Trial Chamber;

(f) The person must respond when summoned by an authority or qualified person designated by the Pre-Trial Chamber;

(g) The person must post bond or provide real or personal security or surety, for which the amount and the schedule and mode of payment shall be determined by the Pre-Trial Chamber;

(h) The person must supply the Registrar with all identity documents, particularly his or her passport.

2. At the request of the person concerned or the Prosecutor or on its own initiative, the Pre-Trial Chamber may at any time decide to amend the conditions set pursuant to sub-rule 1.

3. Before imposing or amending any conditions restricting liberty, the Pre-Trial Chamber shall seek the views of the Prosecutor, the person concerned, any relevant State and victims that have communicated with the Court in that case and whom the Chamber considers could be at risk as a result of a release or conditions imposed.

4. If the Pre-Trial Chamber is convinced that the person concerned has failed to comply with one or more of the obligations imposed, it may, on such basis, at the request of the Prosecutor or on its own initiative, issue a warrant of arrest in respect of the person.

5. When the Pre-Trial Chamber issues a summons to appear pursuant to article 58, paragraph 7, and intends to set conditions restricting liberty, it shall ascertain the relevant provisions of the national law of the State receiving the summons. In a manner that is in keeping with the national law of the State

receiving the summons, the Pre-Trial Chamber shall proceed in accordance with sub-rules 1, 2 and 3. If the Pre-Trial Chamber receives information that the person concerned has failed to comply with conditions imposed, it shall proceed in accordance with sub-rule 4.

Rule 120 Instruments of restraint

Personal instruments of restraint shall not be used except as a precaution against escape, for the protection of the person in the custody of the Court and others or for other security reasons, and shall be removed when the person appears before a Chamber.

Section V Proceedings with regard to the confirmation of charges under article 61

Rule 121 Proceedings before the confirmation hearing

1. A person subject to a warrant of arrest or a summons to appear under article 58 shall appear before the Pre-Trial Chamber, in the presence of the Prosecutor, promptly upon arriving at the Court. Subject to the provisions of articles 60 and 61, the person shall enjoy the rights set forth in article 67. At this first appearance, the Pre-Trial Chamber shall set the date on which it intends to hold a hearing to confirm the charges. It shall ensure that this date, and any postponements under sub-rule 7, are made public.

2. In accordance with article 61, paragraph 3, the Pre-Trial Chamber shall take the necessary decisions regarding disclosure between the Prosecutor and the person in respect of whom a warrant of arrest or a summons to appear has been issued. During disclosure:

(a) The person concerned may be assisted or represented by the counsel of his or her choice or by a counsel assigned to him or her;

(b) The Pre-Trial Chamber shall hold status conferences to ensure that disclosure takes place under satisfactory conditions. For each case, a judge of the Pre-Trial Chamber shall be appointed to organize such status conferences, on his or her own motion, or at the request of the Prosecutor or the person;

(c) All evidence disclosed between the Prosecutor and the person for the purposes of the confirmation hearing shall be communicated to the Pre-Trial Chamber.

3. The Prosecutor shall provide to the Pre-Trial Chamber and the person, no later than 30 days before the date of the confirmation hearing, a detailed

description of the charges together with a list of the evidence which he or she intends to present at the hearing.

4. Where the Prosecutor intends to amend the charges pursuant to article 61, paragraph 4, he or she shall notify the Pre-Trial Chamber and the person no later than 15 days before the date of the hearing of the amended charges together with a list of evidence that the Prosecutor intends to bring in support of those charges at the hearing.

5. Where the Prosecutor intends to present new evidence at the hearing, he or she shall provide the Pre-Trial Chamber and the person with a list of that evidence no later than 15 days before the date of the hearing.

6. If the person intends to present evidence under article 61, paragraph 6, he or she shall provide a list of that evidence to the Pre-Trial Chamber no later than 15 days before the date of the hearing. The Pre-Trial Chamber shall transmit the list to the Prosecutor without delay. The person shall provide a list of evidence that he or she intends to present in response to any amended charges or a new list of evidence provided by the Prosecutor.

7. The Prosecutor or the person may ask the Pre-Trial Chamber to postpone the date of the confirmation hearing. The Pre-Trial Chamber may also, on its own motion, decide to postpone the hearing.

8. The Pre-Trial Chamber shall not take into consideration charges and evidence presented after the time limit, or any extension thereof, has expired.

9. The Prosecutor and the person may lodge written submissions with the Pre-Trial Chamber, on points of fact and on law, including grounds for excluding criminal responsibility set forth in article 31, paragraph 1, no later than three days before the date of the hearing. A copy of these submissions shall be transmitted immediately to the Prosecutor or the person, as the case may be.

10. The Registry shall create and maintain a full and accurate record of all proceedings before the Pre-Trial Chamber, including all documents transmitted to the Chamber pursuant to this rule. Subject to any restrictions concerning confidentiality and the protection of national security information, the record may be consulted by the Prosecutor, the person and victims or their legal representatives participating in the proceedings pursuant to rules 89 to 91.

Rule 122 Proceedings at the confirmation hearing in the presence of the person charged

1. The Presiding Judge of the Pre-Trial Chamber shall ask the officer of the Registry assisting the Chamber to read out the charges as presented by the

Prosecutor. The Presiding Judge shall determine how the hearing is to be conducted and, in particular, may establish the order and the conditions under which he or she intends the evidence contained in the record of the proceedings to be presented.

2. If a question or challenge concerning jurisdiction or admissibility arises, rule 58 applies.

3. Before hearing the matter on the merits, the Presiding Judge of the Pre-Trial Chamber shall ask the Prosecutor and the person whether they intend to raise objections or make observations concerning an issue related to the proper conduct of the proceedings prior to the confirmation hearing.

4. At no subsequent point may the objections and observations made under sub-rule 3 be raised or made again in the confirmation or trial proceedings.

5. If objections or observations referred to in sub-rule 3 are presented, the Presiding Judge of the Pre-Trial Chamber shall invite those referred to in sub-rule 3 to present their arguments, in the order which he or she shall establish. The person shall have the right to reply.

6. If the objections raised or observations made are those referred to in sub-rule 3, the Pre-Trial Chamber shall decide whether to join the issue raised with the examination of the charges and the evidence, or to separate them, in which case it shall adjourn the confirmation hearing and render a decision on the issues raised.

7. During the hearing on the merits, the Prosecutor and the person shall present their arguments in accordance with article 61, paragraphs 5 and 6.

8. The Pre-Trial Chamber shall permit the Prosecutor and the person, in that order, to make final observations.

9. Subject to the provisions of article 61, article 69 shall apply *mutatis mutandis* at the confirmation hearing.

Rule 123 Measures to ensure the presence of the person concerned at the confirmation hearing

1. When a warrant of arrest or summons to appear in accordance with article 58, paragraph 7, has been issued for a person by the Pre-Trial Chamber and the person is arrested or served with the summons, the Pre-Trial Chamber shall ensure that the person is notified of the provisions of article 61, paragraph 2.

2. The Pre-Trial Chamber may hold consultations with the Prosecutor, at the request of the latter or on its own initiative, in order to determine whether

there is cause to hold a hearing on confirmation of charges under the conditions set forth in article 61, paragraph 2 (b). When the person concerned has a counsel known to the Court, the consultations shall be held in the presence of the counsel unless the Pre-Trial Chamber decides otherwise.

3. The Pre-Trial Chamber shall ensure that a warrant of arrest for the person concerned has been issued and, if the warrant of arrest has not been executed within a reasonable period of time after the issuance of the warrant, that all reasonable measures have been taken to locate and arrest the person.

Rule 124 Waiver of the right to be present at the confirmation hearing

1. If the person concerned is available to the Court but wishes to waive the right to be present at the hearing on confirmation of charges, he or she shall submit a written request to the Pre-Trial Chamber, which may then hold consultations with the Prosecutor and the person concerned, assisted or represented by his or her counsel.

2. A confirmation hearing pursuant to article 61, paragraph 2 (a), shall only be held when the Pre-Trial Chamber is satisfied that the person concerned understands the right to be present at the hearing and the consequences of waiving this right.

3. The Pre-Trial Chamber may authorize and make provision for the person to observe the hearing from outside the courtroom through the use of communications technology, if required.

4. The waiving of the right to be present at the hearing does not prevent the Pre-Trial Chamber from receiving written observations on issues before the Chamber from the person concerned.

*Rule 125 Decision to hold the confirmation hearing in the absence of the
person concerned*

1. After holding consultations under rules 123 and 124, the Pre-Trial Chamber shall decide whether there is cause to hold a hearing on confirmation of charges in the absence of the person concerned, and in that case, whether the person may be represented by counsel. The Pre-Trial Chamber shall, when appropriate, set a date for the hearing and make the date public.

2. The decision of the Pre-Trial Chamber shall be notified to the Prosecutor and, if possible, to the person concerned or his or her counsel.

3. If the Pre-Trial Chamber decides not to hold a hearing on confirmation of charges in the absence of the person concerned, and the person is not avail-

able to the Court, the confirmation of charges may not take place until the person is available to the Court. The Pre-Trial Chamber may review its decision at any time, at the request of the Prosecutor or on its own initiative.

4. If the Pre-Trial Chamber decides not to hold a hearing on confirmation of charges in the absence of the person concerned, and the person is available to the Court, it shall order the person to appear.

Rule 126 Confirmation hearing in the absence of the person concerned

1. The provisions of rules 121 and 122 shall apply *mutatis mutandis* to the preparation for and holding of a hearing on confirmation of charges in the absence of the person concerned.

2. If the Pre-Trial Chamber has determined that the person concerned shall be represented by counsel, the counsel shall have the opportunity to exercise the rights of that person.

3. When the person who has fled is subsequently arrested and the Court has confirmed the charges upon which the Prosecutor intends to pursue the trial, the person charged shall be committed to the Trial Chamber established under article 61, paragraph 11. The person charged may request in writing that the Trial Chamber refer issues to the Pre-Trial Chamber that are necessary for the Chamber's effective and fair functioning in accordance with article 64, paragraph 4.

Section VI Closure of the pre-trial phase

Rule 127 Procedure in the event of different decisions on multiple charges

If the Pre-Trial Chamber is ready to confirm some of the charges but adjourns the hearing on other charges under article 61, paragraph 7 (c), it may decide that the committal of the person concerned to the Trial Chamber on the charges that it is ready to confirm shall be deferred pending the continuation of the hearing. The Pre-Trial Chamber may then establish a time limit within which the Prosecutor may proceed in accordance with article 61, paragraph 7 (c) (i) or (ii).

Rule 128 Amendment of the charges

1. If the Prosecutor seeks to amend charges already confirmed before the trial has begun, in accordance with article 61, the Prosecutor shall make a written request to the Pre-Trial Chamber, and that Chamber shall so notify the accused.

2. Before deciding whether to authorize the amendment, the Pre-Trial Chamber may request the accused and the Prosecutor to submit written observations on certain issues of fact or law.

3. If the Pre-Trial Chamber determines that the amendments proposed by the Prosecutor constitute additional or more serious charges, it shall proceed, as appropriate, in accordance with rules 121 and 122 or rules 123 to 126.

Rule 129 Notification of the decision on the confirmation of charges

The decision of the Pre-Trial Chamber on the confirmation of charges and the committal of the accused to the Trial Chamber shall be notified, if possible, to the Prosecutor, the person concerned and his or her counsel. Such decision and the record of the proceedings of the Pre-Trial Chamber shall be transmitted to the Presidency.

Rule 130 Constitution of the Trial Chamber

When the Presidency constitutes a Trial Chamber and refers the case to it, the Presidency shall transmit the decision of the Pre-Trial Chamber and the record of the proceedings to the Trial Chamber. The Presidency may also refer the case to a previously constituted Trial Chamber.

Chapter 6 Trial procedure

Rule 131 Record of the proceedings transmitted by the Pre-Trial Chamber

1. The Registrar shall maintain the record of the proceedings transmitted by the Pre-Trial Chamber, pursuant to rule 121, sub-rule 10.

2. Subject to any restrictions concerning confidentiality and the protection of national security information, the record may be consulted by the Prosecutor, the defence, the representatives of States when they participate in the proceedings, and the victims or their legal representatives participating in the proceedings pursuant to rules 89 to 91.

Rule 132 Status conferences

1. Promptly after it is constituted, the Trial Chamber shall hold a status conference in order to set the date of the trial. The Trial Chamber, on its own motion, or at the request of the Prosecutor or the defence, may postpone the date of the trial. The Trial Chamber shall notify the trial date to all those par-

ticipating in the proceedings. The Trial Chamber shall ensure that this date and any postponements are made public.

2. In order to facilitate the fair and expeditious conduct of the proceedings, the Trial Chamber may confer with the parties by holding status conferences as necessary.

Rule 133 Motions challenging admissibility or jurisdiction

Challenges to the jurisdiction of the Court or the admissibility of the case at the commencement of the trial, or subsequently with the leave of the Court, shall be dealt with by the Presiding Judge and the Trial Chamber in accordance with rule 58.

Rule 134 Motions relating to the trial proceedings

1. Prior to the commencement of the trial, the Trial Chamber on its own motion, or at the request of the Prosecutor or the defence, may rule on any issue concerning the conduct of the proceedings. Any request from the Prosecutor or the defence shall be in writing and, unless the request is for an *ex parte* procedure, served on the other party. For all requests other than those submitted for an *ex parte* procedure, the other party shall have the opportunity to file a response.

2. At the commencement of the trial, the Trial Chamber shall ask the Prosecutor and the defence whether they have any objections or observations concerning the conduct of the proceedings which have arisen since the confirmation hearings. Such objections or observations may not be raised or made again on a subsequent occasion in the trial proceedings, without leave of the Trial Chamber in this proceeding.

3. After the commencement of the trial, the Trial Chamber, on its own motion, or at the request of the Prosecutor or the defence, may rule on issues that arise during the course of the trial.

Rule 135 Medical examination of the accused

1. The Trial Chamber may, for the purpose of discharging its obligations under article 64, paragraph 8 (a), or for any other reasons, or at the request of a party, order a medical, psychiatric or psychological examination of the accused, under the conditions set forth in rule 113.

2. The Trial Chamber shall place its reasons for any such order on the record.

3. The Trial Chamber shall appoint one or more experts from the list of experts approved by the Registrar, or an expert approved by the Trial Chamber at the request of a party.

4. Where the Trial Chamber is satisfied that the accused is unfit to stand trial, it shall order that the trial be adjourned. The Trial Chamber may, on its own motion or at the request of the Prosecution or the defence, review the case of the accused. In any event, the case shall be reviewed every 120 days unless there are reasons to do otherwise. If necessary, the Trial Chamber may order further examinations of the accused. When the Trial Chamber is satisfied that the accused has become fit to stand trial it shall proceed in accordance with rule 132.

Rule 136 Joint and separate trials

1. Persons accused jointly shall be tried together unless the Trial Chamber, on its own motion or at the request of the Prosecutor or the defence, orders that separate trials are necessary, in order to avoid serious prejudice to the accused, to protect the interests of justice or because a person jointly accused has made an admission of guilt and can be proceeded against in accordance with article 65, paragraph 2.

2. In joint trials, each accused shall be accorded the same rights as if such accused were being tried separately.

Rule 137 Record of the trial proceedings

1. In accordance with article 64, paragraph 10, the Registrar shall take measures to make, and preserve, a full and accurate record of all proceedings, including transcripts, audio- and video-recordings and other means of capturing sound or image.

2. A Trial Chamber may order the disclosure of all or part of the record of closed proceedings when the reasons for ordering its non-disclosure no longer exist.

3. The Trial Chamber may authorize persons, other than the Registrar, to take photographs, audio- and video-recordings and other means of capturing the sound or image of the trial.

Rule 138 Custody of evidence

The Registrar shall retain and preserve, as necessary, all the evidence and other materials offered during the hearing, subject to any order of the Trial Chamber.

Rule 139 Decision on admission of guilt

1. After having proceeded in accordance with article 65, paragraph 1, the Trial Chamber, in order to decide whether to proceed in accordance with article 65, paragraph 4, may invite the views of the Prosecutor and the defence.

2. The Trial Chamber shall then make its decision on the admission of guilt and shall give reasons for this decision, which shall be placed on the record.

Rule 140 Directions for the conduct of the proceedings and testimony

1. If the Presiding Judge does not give directions under article 64, paragraph 8, the Prosecutor and the defence shall agree on the order and manner in which the evidence shall be submitted to the Trial Chamber. If no agreement can be reached, the Presiding Judge shall issue directions.

2. In all cases, subject to article 64, paragraphs 8 (b) and 9, article 69, paragraph 4, and rule 88, sub-rule 5, a witness may be questioned as follows:

(a) A party that submits evidence in accordance with article 69, paragraph 3, by way of a witness, has the right to question that witness;
(b) The Prosecution and the defence have the right to question that witness about relevant matters related to the witness's testimony and its reliability, the credibility of the witness and other relevant matters;
(c) The Trial Chamber has the right to question a witness before or after a witness is questioned by a participant referred to in sub-rules 2 (a) or (b);
(d) The defence shall have the right to be the last to examine a witness.

3. Unless otherwise ordered by the Trial Chamber, a witness other than an expert, or an investigator if he or she has not yet testified, shall not be present when the testimony of another witness is given. However, a witness who has heard the testimony of another witness shall not for that reason alone be disqualified from testifying. When a witness testifies after hearing the testimony of others, this fact shall be noted in the record and considered by the Trial Chamber when evaluating the evidence.

Rule 141 Closure of evidence and closing statements

1. The Presiding Judge shall declare when the submission of evidence is closed.

2. The Presiding Judge shall invite the Prosecutor and the defence to make their closing statements. The defence shall always have the opportunity to speak last.

Rule 142   *Deliberations*

1. After the closing statements, the Trial Chamber shall retire to deliberate, *in camera*. The Trial Chamber shall inform all those who participated in the proceedings of the date on which the Trial Chamber will pronounce its decision. The pronouncement shall be made within a reasonable period of time after the Trial Chamber has retired to deliberate.

2. When there is more than one charge, the Trial Chamber shall decide separately on each charge. When there is more than one accused, the Trial Chamber shall decide separately on the charges against each accused.

Rule 143   *Additional hearings on matters related to sentence or reparations*

Pursuant to article 76, paragraphs 2 and 3, for the purpose of holding a further hearing on matters related to sentence and, if applicable, reparations, the Presiding Judge shall set the date of the further hearing. This hearing can be postponed, in exceptional circumstances, by the Trial Chamber, on its own motion or at the request of the Prosecutor, the defence or the legal representatives of the victims participating in the proceedings pursuant to rules 89 to 91 and, in respect of reparations hearings, those victims who have made a request under rule 94.

Rule 144   *Delivery of the decisions of the Trial Chamber*

1. Decisions of the Trial Chamber concerning admissibility of a case, the jurisdiction of the Court, criminal responsibility of the accused, sentence and reparations shall be pronounced in public and, wherever possible, in the presence of the accused, the Prosecutor, the victims or the legal representatives of the victims participating in the proceedings pursuant to rules 89 to 91, and the representatives of the States which have participated in the proceedings.

2. Copies of all the above-mentioned decisions shall be provided as soon as possible to:

(a) All those who participated in the proceedings, in a working language of the Court;

(b) The accused, in a language he or she fully understands or speaks, if necessary to meet the requirements of fairness under article 67, paragraph 1 (f).

Chapter 7 Penalties

Rule 145 Determination of sentence

1. In its determination of the sentence pursuant to article 78, paragraph 1, the Court shall:

(a) Bear in mind that the totality of any sentence of imprisonment and fine, as the case may be, imposed under article 77 must reflect the culpability of the convicted person;

(b) Balance all the relevant factors, including any mitigating and aggravating factors and consider the circumstances both of the convicted person and of the crime;

(c) In addition to the factors mentioned in article 78, paragraph 1, give consideration, *inter alia*, to the extent of the damage caused, in particular the harm caused to the victims and their families, the nature of the unlawful behaviour and the means employed to execute the crime; the degree of participation of the convicted person; the degree of intent; the circumstances of manner, time and location; and the age, education, social and economic condition of the convicted person.

2. In addition to the factors mentioned above, the Court shall take into account, as appropriate:

(a) Mitigating circumstances such as:

    (i)   The circumstances falling short of constituting grounds for exclusion of criminal responsibility, such as substantially diminished mental capacity or duress;

    (ii)   The convicted person's conduct after the act, including any efforts by the person to compensate the victims and any cooperation with the Court;

(b) As aggravating circumstances:

    (i)   Any relevant prior criminal convictions for crimes under the jurisdiction of the Court or of a similar nature;

    (ii)   Abuse of power or official capacity;

    (iii)   Commission of the crime where the victim is particularly defenceless;

    (iv)   Commission of the crime with particular cruelty or where there were multiple victims;

    (v)   Commission of the crime for any motive involving discrimination on any of the grounds referred to in article 21, paragraph 3;

    (vi)   Other circumstances which, although not enumerated above, by virtue of their nature are similar to those mentioned.

3. Life imprisonment may be imposed when justified by the extreme gravity of the crime and the individual circumstances of the convicted person, as evidenced by the existence of one or more aggravating circumstances.

Rule 146 Imposition of fines under article 77

1. In determining whether to order a fine under article 77, paragraph 2 (a), and in fixing the amount of the fine, the Court shall determine whether imprisonment is a sufficient penalty. The Court shall give due consideration to the financial capacity of the convicted person, including any orders for forfeiture in accordance with article 77, paragraph 2 (b), and, as appropriate, any orders for reparation in accordance with article 75. The Court shall take into account, in addition to the factors referred to in rule 145, whether and to what degree the crime was motivated by personal financial gain.

2. A fine imposed under article 77, paragraph 2 (a), shall be set at an appropriate level. To this end, the Court shall, in addition to the factors referred to above, in particular take into consideration the damage and injuries caused as well as the proportionate gains derived from the crime by the perpetrator. Under no circumstances may the total amount exceed 75 per cent of the value of the convicted person's identifiable assets, liquid or realizable, and property, after deduction of an appropriate amount that would satisfy the financial needs of the convicted person and his or her dependants.

3. In imposing a fine, the Court shall allow the convicted person a reasonable period in which to pay the fine. The Court may provide for payment of a lump sum or by way of instalments during that period.

4. In imposing a fine, the Court may, as an option, calculate it according to a system of daily fines. In such cases, the minimum duration shall be 30 days and the maximum duration five years. The Court shall decide the total amount in accordance with sub-rules 1 and 2. It shall determine the amount of daily payment in the light of the individual circumstances of the convicted person, including the financial needs of his or her dependants.

5. If the convicted person does not pay the fine imposed in accordance with the conditions set above, appropriate measures may be taken by the Court pursuant to rules 217 to 222 and in accordance with article 109. Where, in cases of continued wilful non-payment, the Presidency, on its own motion or at the request of the Prosecutor, is satisfied that all available enforcement measures have been exhausted, it may as a last resort extend the term of imprisonment for a period not to exceed a quarter of such term or five years, whichever is less. In the determination of such period of extension, the Presidency shall take into account the amount of the fine, imposed and paid.

Any such extension shall not apply in the case of life imprisonment. The extension may not lead to a total period of imprisonment in excess of 30 years.

6. In order to determine whether to order an extension and the period involved, the Presidency shall sit *in camera* for the purpose of obtaining the views of the sentenced person and the Prosecutor. The sentenced person shall have the right to be assisted by counsel.

7. In imposing a fine, the Court shall warn the convicted person that failure to pay the fine in accordance with the conditions set out above, may result in an extension of the period of imprisonment as described in this rule.

Rule 147 Orders of forfeiture

1. In accordance with article 76, paragraphs 2 and 3 and rules 63, sub-rule 1, and 143, at any hearing to consider an order of forfeiture, a Chamber shall hear evidence as to the identification and location of specific proceeds, property or assets which have been derived directly or indirectly from the crime.

2. If before or during the hearing, a Chamber becomes aware of any bona fide third party who appears to have an interest in relevant proceeds, property or assets, it shall give notice to that third party.

3. The Prosecutor, the convicted person and any bona fide third party with an interest in the relevant proceeds, property or assets may submit evidence relevant to the issue.

4. After considering any evidence submitted, a Chamber may issue an order of forfeiture in relation to specific proceeds, property or assets if it is satisfied that these have been derived directly or indirectly from the crime.

Rule 148 Orders to transfer fines or forfeitures to the Trust Fund

Before making an order pursuant to article 79, paragraph 2, a Chamber may request the representatives of the Fund to submit written or oral observations to it.

Chapter 8 Appeal and revision

Section I General provisions

Rule 149 Rules governing proceedings in the Appeals Chamber

Parts 5 and 6 and rules governing proceedings and the submission of evidence in the Pre-Trial and Trial Chambers shall apply *mutatis mutandis* to proceedings in the Appeals Chamber.

Section II Appeals against convictions, acquittals, sentences and reparation orders

Rule 150 Appeal

1. Subject to sub-rule 2, an appeal against a decision of conviction or acquittal under article 74, a sentence under article 76 or a reparation order under article 75 may be filed not later than 30 days from the date on which the party filing the appeal is notified of the decision, the sentence or the reparation order.

2. The Appeals Chamber may extend the time limit set out in sub-rule 1, for good cause, upon the application of the party seeking to file the appeal.

3. The appeal shall be filed with the Registrar.

4. If an appeal is not filed as set out in sub-rules 1 to 3, the decision, the sentence or the reparation order of the Trial Chamber shall become final.

Rule 151 Procedure for the appeal

1. Upon the filing of an appeal under rule 150, the Registrar shall transmit the trial record to the Appeals Chamber.

2. The Registrar shall notify all parties who participated in the proceedings before the Trial Chamber that an appeal has been filed.

Rule 152 Discontinuance of the appeal

1. Any party who has filed an appeal may discontinue the appeal at any time before judgment has been delivered. In such case, the party shall file with the Registrar a written notice of discontinuance of appeal. The Registrar shall inform the other parties that such a notice has been filed.

2. If the Prosecutor has filed an appeal on behalf of a convicted person in accordance with article 81, paragraph 1 (b), before filing any notice of discontinuance, the Prosecutor shall inform the convicted person that he or she intends to discontinue the appeal in order to give him or her the opportunity to continue the appeal proceedings.

Rule 153 Judgment on appeals against reparation orders

1. The Appeals Chamber may confirm, reverse or amend a reparation order made under article 75.

2. The judgment of the Appeals Chamber shall be delivered in accordance with article 83, paragraphs 4 and 5.

Section III Appeals against other decisions

Rule 154 Appeals that do not require the leave of the Court

1. An appeal may be filed under article 81, paragraph 3 (c) (ii), or article 82, paragraph 1 (a) or (b), not later than five days from the date upon which the party filing the appeal is notified of the decision.

2. An appeal may be filed under article 82, paragraph 1 (c), not later than two days from the date upon which the party filing the appeal is notified of the decision.

3. Rule 150, sub-rules 3 and 4, shall apply to appeals filed under sub-rules 1 and 2 of this rule.

Rule 155 Appeals that require leave of the Court

1. When a party wishes to appeal a decision under article 82, paragraph 1 (d), or article 82, paragraph 2, that party shall, within five days of being notified of that decision, make a written application to the Chamber that gave the decision, setting out the reasons for the request for leave to appeal.

2. The Chamber shall render a decision and shall notify all parties who participated in the proceedings that gave rise to the decision referred to in sub-rule 1.

Rule 156 Procedure for the appeal

1. As soon as an appeal has been filed under rule 154 or as soon as leave to appeal has been granted under rule 155, the Registrar shall transmit to the Appeals Chamber the record of the proceedings of the Chamber that made the decision that is the subject of the appeal.

2. The Registrar shall give notice of the appeal to all parties who participated in the proceedings before the Chamber that gave the decision that is the subject of the appeal, unless they have already been notified by the Chamber under rule 155, sub-rule 2.

3. The appeal proceedings shall be in writing unless the Appeals Chamber decides to convene a hearing.

4. The appeal shall be heard as expeditiously as possible.

5. When filing the appeal, the party appealing may request that the appeal have suspensive effect in accordance with article 82, paragraph 3.

Rule 157   Discontinuance of the appeal

Any party who has filed an appeal under rule 154 or who has obtained the leave of a Chamber to appeal a decision under rule 155 may discontinue the appeal at any time before judgment has been delivered. In such case, the party shall file with the Registrar a written notice of discontinuance of appeal. The Registrar shall inform the other parties that such a notice has been filed.

Rule 158   Judgment on the appeal

1. An Appeals Chamber which considers an appeal referred to in this section may confirm, reverse or amend the decision appealed.

2. The judgment of the Appeals Chamber shall be delivered in accordance with article 83, paragraph 4.

Section IV   Revision of conviction or sentence

Rule 159   Application for revision

1. An application for revision provided for in article 84, paragraph 1, shall be in writing and shall set out the grounds on which the revision is sought. It shall as far as possible be accompanied by supporting material.

2. The determination on whether the application is meritorious shall be taken by a majority of the judges of the Appeals Chamber and shall be supported by reasons in writing.

3. Notification of the decision shall be sent to the applicant and, as far as possible, to all the parties who participated in the proceedings related to the initial decision.

Rule 160   Transfer for the purpose of revision

1. For the conduct of the hearing provided for in rule 161, the relevant Chamber shall issue its order sufficiently in advance to enable the transfer of the sentenced person to the seat of the Court, as appropriate.

2. The determination of the Court shall be communicated without delay to the State of enforcement.

3. The provisions of rule 206, sub-rule 3, shall be applicable.

Rule 161 Determination on revision

1. On a date which it shall determine and shall communicate to the applicant and to all those having received notification under rule 159, sub-rule 3, the relevant Chamber shall hold a hearing to determine whether the conviction or sentence should be revised.

2. For the conduct of the hearing, the relevant Chamber shall exercise, *mutatis mutandis*, all the powers of the Trial Chamber pursuant to Part 6 and the rules governing proceedings and the submission of evidence in the Pre-Trial and Trial Chambers.

3. The determination on revision shall be governed by the applicable provisions of article 83, paragraph 4.

Chapter 9 Offences and misconduct against the Court

Section I Offences against the administration of justice under article 70

Rule 162 Exercise of jurisdiction

1. Before deciding whether to exercise jurisdiction, the Court may consult with States Parties that may have jurisdiction over the offence.

2. In making a decision whether or not to exercise jurisdiction, the Court may consider, in particular:

(a) The availability and effectiveness of prosecution in a State Party;
(b) The seriousness of an offence;
(c) The possible joinder of charges under article 70 with charges under articles 5 to 8;
(d) The need to expedite proceedings;
(e) Links with an ongoing investigation or a trial before the Court; and
(f) Evidentiary considerations.

3. The Court shall give favourable consideration to a request from the host State for a waiver of the power of the Court to exercise jurisdiction in cases where the host State considers such a waiver to be of particular importance.

4. If the Court decides not to exercise its jurisdiction, it may request a State Party to exercise jurisdiction pursuant to article 70, paragraph 4.

Rule 163 Application of the Statute and the Rules

1. Unless otherwise provided in sub-rules 2 and 3, rule 162 and rules 164 to 169, the Statute and the Rules shall apply *mutatis mutandis* to the Court's

investigation, prosecution and punishment of offences defined in article 70.

2. The provisions of Part 2, and any rules thereunder, shall not apply, with the exception of article 21.

3. The provisions of Part 10, and any rules thereunder, shall not apply, with the exception of articles 103, 107, 109 and 111.

Rule 164 Periods of limitation

1. If the Court exercises jurisdiction in accordance with rule 162, it shall apply the periods of limitation set forth in this rule.

2. Offences defined in article 70 shall be subject to a period of limitation of five years from the date on which the offence was committed, provided that during this period no investigation or prosecution has been initiated. The period of limitation shall be interrupted, if an investigation or prosecution has been initiated during this period, either before the Court or by a State Party with jurisdiction over the case pursuant to article 70, paragraph 4 (a).

3. Enforcement of sanctions imposed with respect to offences defined in article 70 shall be subject to a period of limitation of 10 years from the date on which the sanction has become final. The period of limitation shall be interrupted with the detention of the convicted person or while the person concerned is outside the territory of the States Parties.

Rule 165 Investigation, prosecution and trial

1. The Prosecutor may initiate and conduct investigations with respect to the offences defined in article 70 on his or her own initiative, on the basis of information communicated by a Chamber or any reliable source.

2. Articles 53 and 59, and any rules thereunder, shall not apply.

3. For purposes of article 61, the Pre-Trial Chamber may make any of the determinations set forth in that article on the basis of written submissions, without a hearing, unless the interests of justice otherwise require.

4. A Trial Chamber may, as appropriate and taking into account the rights of the defence, direct that there be joinder of charges under article 70 with charges under articles 5 to 8.

Rule 166 Sanctions under article 70

1. If the Court imposes sanctions with respect to article 70, this rule shall apply.

2. Article 77, and any rules thereunder, shall not apply, with the exception of an order of forfeiture under article 77, paragraph 2 (b), which may be ordered in addition to imprisonment or a fine or both.

3. Each offence may be separately fined and those fines may be cumulative. Under no circumstances may the total amount exceed 50 per cent of the value of the convicted person's identifiable assets, liquid or realizable, and property, after deduction of an appropriate amount that would satisfy the financial needs of the convicted person and his or her dependants.

4. In imposing a fine the Court shall allow the convicted person a reasonable period in which to pay the fine. The Court may provide for payment of a lump sum or by way of instalments during that period.

5. If the convicted person does not pay a fine imposed in accordance with the conditions set forth in sub-rule 4, appropriate measures may be taken by the Court pursuant to rules 217 to 222 and in accordance with article 109. Where, in cases of continued wilful non-payment, the Court, on its own motion or at the request of the Prosecutor, is satisfied that all available enforcement measures have been exhausted, it may as a last resort impose a term of imprisonment in accordance with article 70, paragraph 3. In the determination of such term of imprisonment, the Court shall take into account the amount of fine paid.

Rule 167 International cooperation and judicial assistance

1. With regard to offences under article 70, the Court may request a State to provide any form of international cooperation or judicial assistance corresponding to those forms set forth in Part 9. In any such request, the Court shall indicate that the basis for the request is an investigation or prosecution of offences under article 70.

2. The conditions for providing international cooperation or judicial assistance to the Court with respect to offences under article 70 shall be those set forth in article 70, paragraph 2.

Rule 168 Ne bis in idem

In respect of offences under article 70, no person shall be tried before the Court with respect to conduct which formed the basis of an offence for which the person has already been convicted or acquitted by the Court or another court.

Rule 169 Immediate arrest

In the case of an alleged offence under article 70 committed in the presence of a Chamber, the Prosecutor may orally request that Chamber to order the immediate arrest of the person concerned.

Section II Misconduct before the Court under article 71

Rule 170 Disruption of proceedings

Having regard to article 63, paragraph 2, the Presiding Judge of the Chamber dealing with the matter may, after giving a warning:

(a) Order a person disrupting the proceedings of the Court to leave or be removed from the courtroom; or,
(b) In case of repeated misconduct, order the interdiction of that person from attending the proceedings.

Rule 171 Refusal to comply with a direction by the Court

1. When the misconduct consists of deliberate refusal to comply with an oral or written direction by the Court, not covered by rule 170, and that direction is accompanied by a warning of sanctions in case of breach, the Presiding Judge of the Chamber dealing with the matter may order the interdiction of that person from the proceedings for a period not exceeding 30 days or, if the misconduct is of a more serious nature, impose a fine.

2. If the person committing misconduct as described in sub-rule 1 is an official of the Court, or a defence counsel, or a legal representative of victims, the Presiding Judge of the Chamber dealing with the matter may also order the interdiction of that person from exercising his or her functions before the Court for a period not exceeding 30 days.

3. If the Presiding Judge in cases under sub-rules 1 and 2 considers that a longer period of interdiction is appropriate, the Presiding Judge shall refer the matter to the Presidency, which may hold a hearing to determine whether to order a longer or permanent period of interdiction.

4. A fine imposed under sub-rule 1 shall not exceed 2,000 euros, or the equivalent amount in any currency, provided that in cases of continuing misconduct, a new fine may be imposed on each day that the misconduct continues, and such fines shall be cumulative.

5. The person concerned shall be given an opportunity to be heard before a sanction for misconduct, as described in this rule, is imposed.

Rule 172 Conduct covered by both articles 70 and 71

If conduct covered by article 71 also constitutes one of the offences defined in article 70, the Court shall proceed in accordance with article 70 and rules 162 to 169.

Chapter 10 Compensation to an arrested or convicted person

Rule 173 Request for compensation

1. Anyone seeking compensation on any of the grounds indicated in article 85 shall submit a request, in writing, to the Presidency, which shall designate a Chamber composed of three judges to consider the request. These judges shall not have participated in any earlier judgment of the Court regarding the person making the request.

2. The request for compensation shall be submitted not later than six months from the date the person making the request was notified of the decision of the Court concerning:

(a) The unlawfulness of the arrest or detention under article 85, paragraph 1;
(b) The reversal of the conviction under article 85, paragraph 2;
(c) The existence of a grave and manifest miscarriage of justice under article 85, paragraph 3.

3. The request shall contain the grounds and the amount of compensation requested.

4. The person requesting compensation shall be entitled to legal assistance.

Rule 174 Procedure for seeking compensation

1. A request for compensation and any other written observation by the person filing the request shall be transmitted to the Prosecutor, who shall have an opportunity to respond in writing. Any observations by the Prosecutor shall be notified to the person filing the request.

2. The Chamber designated under rule 173, sub-rule 1, may either hold a hearing or determine the matter on the basis of the request and any written observations by the Prosecutor and the person filing the request. A hearing shall be held if the Prosecutor or the person seeking compensation so requests.

3. The decision shall be taken by the majority of the judges. The decision shall be notified to the Prosecutor and to the person filing the request.

Rule 175 Amount of compensation

In establishing the amount of any compensation in conformity with article 85, paragraph 3, the Chamber designated under rule 173, sub-rule 1, shall take into consideration the consequences of the grave and manifest miscarriage of justice on the personal, family, social and professional situation of the person filing the request.

Chapter 11 International cooperation and judicial assistance

Section I Requests for cooperation under article 87

Rule 176 Organs of the Court responsible for the transmission and receipt of any communications relating to international cooperation and judicial assistance

1. Upon and subsequent to the establishment of the Court, the Registrar shall obtain from the Secretary-General of the United Nations any communication made by States pursuant to article 87, paragraphs 1 (a) and 2.

2. The Registrar shall transmit the requests for cooperation made by the Chambers and shall receive the responses, information and documents from requested States. The Office of the Prosecutor shall transmit the requests for cooperation made by the Prosecutor and shall receive the responses, information and documents from requested States.

3. The Registrar shall be the recipient of any communication from States concerning subsequent changes in the designation of the national channels charged with receiving requests for cooperation, as well as of any change in the language in which requests for cooperation should be made, and shall, upon request, make such information available to States Parties as may be appropriate.

4. The provisions of sub-rule 2 are applicable *mutatis mutandis* where the Court requests information, documents or other forms of cooperation and assistance from an intergovernmental organization.

5. The Registrar shall transmit any communications referred to in sub-rules 1 and 3 and rule 177, sub-rule 2, as appropriate, to the Presidency or the Office of the Prosecutor, or both.

Rule 177 Channels of communication

1. Communications concerning the national authority charged with receiving requests for cooperation made upon ratification, acceptance,

approval or accession shall provide all relevant information about such authorities.

2. When an intergovernmental organization is asked to assist the Court under article 87, paragraph 6, the Registrar shall, when necessary, ascertain its designated channel of communication and obtain all relevant information relating thereto.

Rule 178 Language chosen by States Parties under article 87, paragraph 2

1. When a requested State Party has more than one official language, it may indicate upon ratification, acceptance, approval or accession that requests for cooperation and any supporting documents can be drafted in any one of its official languages.

2. When the requested State Party has not chosen a language for communication with the Court upon ratification, acceptance, accession or approval, the request for cooperation shall either be in or be accompanied by a translation into one of the working languages of the Court pursuant to article 87, paragraph 2.

Rule 179 Language of requests directed to States not party to the Statute

When a State not party to the Statute has agreed to provide assistance to the Court under article 87, paragraph 5, and has not made a choice of language for such requests, the requests for cooperation shall either be in or be accompanied by a translation into one of the working languages of the Court.

Rule 180 Changes in the channels of communication or the languages of requests for cooperation

1. Changes concerning the channel of communication or the language a State has chosen under article 87, paragraph 2, shall be communicated in writing to the Registrar at the earliest opportunity.

2. Such changes shall take effect in respect of requests for cooperation made by the Court at a time agreed between the Court and the State or, in the absence of such an agreement, 45 days after the Court has received the communication and, in all cases, without prejudice to current requests or requests in progress.

Section II Surrender, transit and competing requests under articles 89 and 90

Rule 181 Challenge to admissibility of a case before a national court

When a situation described in article 89, paragraph 2, arises, and without prejudice to the provisions of article 19 and of rules 58 to 62 on procedures applicable to challenges to the jurisdiction of the Court or the admissibility of a case, the Chamber dealing with the case, if the admissibility ruling is still pending, shall take steps to obtain from the requested State all the relevant information about the *ne bis in idem* challenge brought by the person.

Rule 182 Request for transit under article 89, paragraph 3 (e)

1. In situations described in article 89, paragraph 3 (e), the Court may transmit the request for transit by any medium capable of delivering a written record.

2. When the time limit provided for in article 89, paragraph 3 (e), has expired and the person concerned has been released, such a release is without prejudice to a subsequent arrest of the person in accordance with the provisions of article 89 or article 92.

Rule 183 Possible temporary surrender

Following the consultations referred to in article 89, paragraph 4, the requested State may temporarily surrender the person sought in accordance with conditions determined between the requested State and the Court. In such case the person shall be kept in custody during his or her presence before the Court and shall be transferred to the requested State once his or her presence before the Court is no longer required, at the latest when the proceedings have been completed.

Rule 184 Arrangements for surrender

1. The requested State shall immediately inform the Registrar when the person sought by the Court is available for surrender.

2. The person shall be surrendered to the Court by the date and in the manner agreed upon between the authorities of the requested State and the Registrar.

3. If circumstances prevent the surrender of the person by the date agreed,

the authorities of the requested State and the Registrar shall agree upon a new date and manner by which the person shall be surrendered.

4. The Registrar shall maintain contact with the authorities of the host State in relation to the arrangements for the surrender of the person to the Court.

Rule 185 Release of a person from the custody of the Court other than upon completion of sentence

1. Subject to sub-rule 2, where a person surrendered to the Court is released from the custody of the Court because the Court does not have jurisdiction, the case is inadmissible under article 17, paragraph 1 (b), (c) or (d), the charges have not been confirmed under article 61, the person has been acquitted at trial or on appeal, or for any other reason, the Court shall, as soon as possible, make such arrangements as it considers appropriate for the transfer of the person, taking into account the views of the person, to a State which is obliged to receive him or her, to another State which agrees to receive him or her, or to a State which has requested his or her extradition with the consent of the original surrendering State. In this case, the host State shall facilitate the transfer in accordance with the agreement referred to in article 3, paragraph 2, and the related arrangements.

2. Where the Court has determined that the case is inadmissible under article 17, paragraph 1 (a), the Court shall make arrangements, as appropriate, for the transfer of the person to a State whose investigation or prosecution has formed the basis of the successful challenge to admissibility, unless the State that originally surrendered the person requests his or her return.

Rule 186 Competing requests in the context of a challenge to the admissibility of the case

In situations described in article 90, paragraph 8, the requested State shall provide the notification of its decision to the Prosecutor in order to enable him or her to act in accordance with article 19, paragraph 10.

Section III Documents for arrest and surrender under articles 91 and 92

Rule 187 Translation of documents accompanying request for surrender

For the purposes of article 67, paragraph 1 (a), and in accordance with rule 117, sub-rule 1, the request under article 91 shall be accompanied, as appropriate, by a translation of the warrant of arrest or of the judgment of conviction and by a translation of the text of any relevant provisions of the Statute, in a language that the person fully understands and speaks.

Rule 188 Time limit for submission of documents after provisional arrest

For the purposes of article 92, paragraph 3, the time limit for receipt by the requested State of the request for surrender and the documents supporting the request shall be 60 days from the date of the provisional arrest.

Rule 189 Transmission of documents supporting the request

When a person has consented to surrender in accordance with the provisions of article 92, paragraph 3, and the requested State proceeds to surrender the person to the Court, the Court shall not be required to provide the documents described in article 91 unless the requested State indicates otherwise.

Section IV Cooperation under article 93

Rule 190 Instruction on self-incrimination accompanying request for witness

When making a request under article 93, paragraph 1 (e), with respect to a witness, the Court shall annex an instruction, concerning rule 74 relating to self-incrimination, to be provided to the witness in question, in a language that the person fully understands and speaks.

Rule 191 Assurance provided by the Court under article 93, paragraph 2

The Chamber dealing with the case, on its own motion or at the request of the Prosecutor, defence or witness or expert concerned, may decide, after taking into account the views of the Prosecutor and the witness or expert concerned, to provide the assurance described in article 93, paragraph 2.

Rule 192 Transfer of a person in custody

1. Transfer of a person in custody to the Court in accordance with article 93, paragraph 7, shall be arranged by the national authorities concerned in liaison with the Registrar and the authorities of the host State.

2. The Registrar shall ensure the proper conduct of the transfer, including the supervision of the person while in the custody of the Court.

3. The person in custody before the Court shall have the right to raise

matters concerning the conditions of his or her detention with the relevant Chamber.

4. In accordance with article 93, paragraph 7 (b), when the purposes of the transfer have been fulfilled, the Registrar shall arrange for the return of the person in custody to the requested State.

Rule 193 *Temporary transfer of the person from the State of enforcement*

1. The Chamber that is considering the case may order the temporary transfer from the State of enforcement to the seat of the Court of any person sentenced by the Court whose testimony or other assistance is necessary to the Court. The provisions of article 93, paragraph 7, shall not apply.

2. The Registrar shall ensure the proper conduct of the transfer, in liaison with the authorities of the State of enforcement and the authorities of the host State. When the purposes of the transfer have been fulfilled, the Court shall return the sentenced person to the State of enforcement.

3. The person shall be kept in custody during his or her presence before the Court. The entire period of detention spent at the seat of the Court shall be deducted from the sentence remaining to be served.

Rule 194 *Cooperation requested from the Court*

1. In accordance with article 93, paragraph 10, and consistent with article 96, *mutatis mutandis*, a State may transmit to the Court a request for cooperation or assistance to the Court, either in or accompanied by a translation into one of the working languages of the Court.

2. Requests described in sub-rule 1 are to be sent to the Registrar, which shall transmit them, as appropriate, either to the Prosecutor or to the Chamber concerned.

3. If protective measures within the meaning of article 68 have been adopted, the Prosecutor or Chamber, as appropriate, shall consider the views of the Chamber which ordered the measures as well as those of the relevant victim or witness, before deciding on the request.

4. If the request relates to documents or evidence as described in article 93, paragraph 10 (b) (ii), the Prosecutor or Chamber, as appropriate, shall obtain the written consent of the relevant State before proceeding with the request.

5. When the Court decides to grant the request for cooperation or assistance from a State, the request shall be executed, insofar as possible, following

any procedure outlined therein by the requesting State and permitting persons specified in the request to be present.

Section V Cooperation under article 98

Rule 195 Provision of information

1. When a requested State notifies the Court that a request for surrender or assistance raises a problem of execution in respect of article 98, the requested State shall provide any information relevant to assist the Court in the application of article 98. Any concerned third State or sending State may provide additional information to assist the Court.

2. The Court may not proceed with a request for the surrender of a person without the consent of a sending State if, under article 98, paragraph 2, such a request would be inconsistent with obligations under an international agreement pursuant to which the consent of a sending State is required prior to the surrender of a person of that State to the Court.

Section VI Rule of speciality under article 101

Rule 196 Provision of views on article 101, paragraph 1

A person surrendered to the Court may provide views on a perceived violation of the provisions of article 101, paragraph 1.

Rule 197 Extension of the surrender

When the Court has requested a waiver of the requirements of article 101, paragraph 1, the requested State may ask the Court to obtain and provide the views of the person surrendered to the Court.

Chapter 12 Enforcement

Section I Role of States in enforcement of sentences of imprisonment and change in designation of State of enforcement under articles 103 and 104

Rule 198 Communications between the Court and States

Unless the context otherwise requires, article 87 and rules 176 to 180 shall apply, as appropriate, to communications between the Court and a State on matters relating to enforcement of sentences.

Rule 199 Organ responsible under Part 10

Unless provided otherwise in the Rules, the functions of the Court under Part 10 shall be exercised by the Presidency.

Rule 200 List of States of enforcement

1. A list of States that have indicated their willingness to accept sentenced persons shall be established and maintained by the Registrar.

2. The Presidency shall not include a State on the list provided for in article 103, paragraph (1), if it does not agree with the conditions that such a State attaches to its acceptance. The Presidency may request any additional information from that State prior to taking a decision.

3. A State that has attached conditions of acceptance may at any time withdraw such conditions. Any amendments or additions to such conditions shall be subject to confirmation by the Presidency.

4. A State may at any time inform the Registrar of its withdrawal from the list. Such withdrawal shall not affect the enforcement of the sentences in respect of persons that the State has already accepted.

5. The Court may enter bilateral arrangements with States with a view to establishing a framework for the acceptance of prisoners sentenced by the Court. Such arrangements shall be consistent with the Statute.

Rule 201 Principles of equitable distribution

Principles of equitable distribution for purposes of article 103, paragraph 3, shall include:

(a) The principle of equitable geographical distribution;
(b) The need to afford each State on the list an opportunity to receive sentenced persons;
(c) The number of sentenced persons already received by that State and other States of enforcement;
(d) Any other relevant factors.

Rule 202 Timing of delivery of the sentenced person to the State of enforcement

The delivery of a sentenced person from the Court to the designated State of enforcement shall not take place unless the decision on the conviction and the decision on the sentence have become final.

Rule 203 Views of the sentenced person

1. The Presidency shall give notice in writing to the sentenced person that it is addressing the designation of a State of enforcement. The sentenced person shall, within such time limit as the Presidency shall prescribe, submit in writing his or her views on the question to the Presidency.

2. The Presidency may allow the sentenced person to make oral representations.

3. The Presidency shall allow the sentenced person:

(a) To be assisted, as appropriate, by a competent interpreter and to benefit from any translation necessary for the presentation of his or her views;
(b) To be granted adequate time and facilities necessary to prepare for the presentation of his or her views.

Rule 204 Information relating to designation

When the Presidency notifies the designated State of its decision, it shall also transmit the following information and documents:

(a) The name, nationality, date and place of birth of the sentenced person;
(b) A copy of the final judgment of conviction and of the sentence imposed;
(c) The length and commencement date of the sentence and the time remaining to be served;
(d) After having heard the views of the sentenced person, any necessary information concerning the state of his or her health, including any medical treatment that he or she is receiving.

Rule 205 Rejection of designation in a particular case

Where a State in a particular case rejects the designation by the Presidency, the Presidency may designate another State.

Rule 206 Delivery of the sentenced person to the State of enforcement

1. The Registrar shall inform the Prosecutor and the sentenced person of the State designated to enforce the sentence.

2. The sentenced person shall be delivered to the State of enforcement as soon as possible after the designated State of enforcement accepts.

3. The Registrar shall ensure the proper conduct of the delivery of the

person in consultation with the authorities of the State of enforcement and the host State.

Rule 207 Transit

1. No authorization is required if the sentenced person is transported by air and no landing is scheduled on the territory of the transit State. If an unscheduled landing occurs on the territory of the transit State, that State shall, to the extent possible under the procedure of national law, detain the sentenced person in custody until a request for transit as provided in sub-rule 2 or a request under article 89, paragraph 1, or article 92 is received.

2. To the extent possible under the procedure of national law, a State Party shall authorize the transit of a sentenced person through its territory and the provisions of article 89, paragraph 3 (b) and (c), and articles 105 and 108 and any rules relating thereto shall, as appropriate, apply. A copy of the final judgment of conviction and of the sentence imposed shall be attached to such request for transit.

Rule 208 Costs

1. The ordinary costs for the enforcement of the sentence in the territory of the State of enforcement shall be borne by that State.

2. Other costs, including those for the transport of the sentenced person and those referred to in article 100, paragraph 1 (c), (d) and (e), shall be borne by the Court.

Rule 209 Change in designation of State of enforcement

1. The Presidency, acting on its own motion or at the request of the sentenced person or the Prosecutor, may at any time act in accordance with article 104, paragraph 1.

2. The request of the sentenced person or of the Prosecutor shall be made in writing and shall set out the grounds upon which the transfer is sought.

Rule 210 Procedure for change in the designation of a State of enforcement

1. Before deciding to change the designation of a State of enforcement, the Presidency may:

(a) Request views from the State of enforcement;

(b) Consider written or oral presentations of the sentenced person and the Prosecutor;

(c) Consider written or oral expert opinion concerning, *inter alia*, the sentenced person;

(d) Obtain any other relevant information from any reliable sources.

2. The provisions of rule 203, sub-rule 3, shall apply, as appropriate.

3. If the Presidency refuses to change the designation of the State of enforcement, it shall, as soon as possible, inform the sentenced person, the Prosecutor and the Registrar of its decision and of the reasons therefor. It shall also inform the State of enforcement.

Section II   Enforcement, supervision and transfer under articles 105, 106 and 107

Rule 211   Supervision of enforcement of sentences and conditions of imprisonment

1. In order to supervise the enforcement of sentences of imprisonment, the Presidency:

(a) Shall, in consultation with the State of enforcement, ensure that in establishing appropriate arrangements for the exercise by any sentenced person of his or her right to communicate with the Court about the conditions of imprisonment, the provisions of article 106, paragraph 3, shall be respected;

(b) May, when necessary, request any information, report or expert opinion from the State of enforcement or from any reliable sources;

(c) May, where appropriate, delegate a judge of the Court or a member of the staff of the Court who will be responsible, after notifying the State of enforcement, for meeting the sentenced person and hearing his or her views, without the presence of national authorities;

(d) May, where appropriate, give the State of enforcement an opportunity to comment on the views expressed by the sentenced person under sub-rule 1 (c).

2. When a sentenced person is eligible for a prison programme or benefit available under the domestic law of the State of enforcement which may entail some activity outside the prison facility, the State of enforcement shall communicate that fact to the Presidency, together with any relevant information or observation, to enable the Court to exercise its supervisory function.

Rule 212   Information on location of the person for enforcement of fines,
forfeitures or reparation measures

For the purpose of enforcement of fines and forfeiture measures and of reparation measures ordered by the Court, the Presidency may, at any time or at
least 30 days before the scheduled completion of the sentence served by the
sentenced person, request the State of enforcement to transmit to it the relevant information concerning the intention of that State to authorize the
person to remain in its territory or the location where it intends to transfer the
person.

Rule 213   Procedure for article 107, paragraph 3

With respect to article 107, paragraph 3, the procedure set out in rules 214 and
215 shall apply, as appropriate.

**Section III   Limitation on the prosecution or punishment of other offences
under article 108**

Rule 214   Request to prosecute or enforce a sentence for prior conduct

1. For the application of article 108, when the State of enforcement wishes
to prosecute or enforce a sentence against the sentenced person for any
conduct engaged in prior to that person's transfer, it shall notify its intention
to the Presidency and transmit to it the following documents:

(a) A statement of the facts of the case and their legal characterization;
(b) A copy of any applicable legal provisions, including those concerning the
statute of limitation and the applicable penalties;
(c) A copy of any sentence, warrant of arrest or other document having the same
force, or of any other legal writ which the State intends to enforce;
(d) A protocol containing views of the sentenced person obtained after the person
has been informed sufficiently about the proceedings.

2. In the event of a request for extradition made by another State, the State
of enforcement shall transmit the entire request to the Presidency with a
protocol containing the views of the sentenced person obtained after informing the person sufficiently about the extradition request.

3. The Presidency may in all cases request any document or additional
information from the State of enforcement or the State requesting extradition.

4. If the person was surrendered to the Court by a State other than the State of enforcement or the State seeking extradition, the Presidency shall consult with the State that surrendered the person and take into account any views expressed by that State.

5. Any information or documents transmitted to the Presidency under sub-rules 1 to 4 shall be transmitted to the Prosecutor, who may comment.

6. The Presidency may decide to conduct a hearing.

Rule 215   Decision on request to prosecute or enforce a sentence

1. The Presidency shall make a determination as soon as possible. This determination shall be notified to all those who have participated in the proceedings.

2. If the request submitted under sub-rules 1 or 2 concerns the enforcement of a sentence, the sentenced person may serve that sentence in the State designated by the Court to enforce the sentence pronounced by it or be extradited to a third State only after having served the full sentence pronounced by the Court, subject to the provisions of article 110.

3. The Presidency may authorize the temporary extradition of the sentenced person to a third State for prosecution only if it has obtained assurances which it deems to be sufficient that the sentenced person will be kept in custody in the third State and transferred back to the State responsible for enforcement of the sentence pronounced by the Court, after the prosecution.

Rule 216   Information on enforcement

The Presidency shall request the State of enforcement to inform it of any important event concerning the sentenced person, and of any prosecution of that person for events subsequent to his or her transfer.

Section IV   Enforcement of fines, forfeiture measures and reparation orders under article 109

Rule 217   Cooperation and measures for enforcement of fines, forfeiture or reparation orders

For the enforcement of fines, forfeiture or reparation orders, the Presidency shall, as appropriate, seek cooperation and measures for enforcement in accordance with Part 9, as well as transmit copies of relevant orders to any State with which the sentenced person appears to have direct connection by reason of either nationality, domicile or habitual residence or by virtue of the location of the sentenced person's assets and property or with which the victim has such connection. The Presidency shall, as appropriate, inform the State of any third-party claims or of the fact that no claim was presented by a person who received notification of any proceedings conducted pursuant to article 75.

Rule 218 Orders for forfeiture and reparations

1. In order to enable States to give effect to an order for forfeiture, the order shall specify:

(a) The identity of the person against whom the order has been issued;
(b) The proceeds, property and assets that have been ordered by the Court to be forfeited; and
(c) That if the State Party is unable to give effect to the order for forfeiture in relation to the specified proceeds, property or assets, it shall take measures to recover the value of the same.

2. In the request for cooperation and measures for enforcement, the Court shall also provide available information as to the location of the proceeds, property and assets that are covered by the order for forfeiture.

3. In order to enable States to give effect to an order for reparations, the order shall specify:

(a) The identity of the person against whom the order has been issued;
(b) In respect of reparations of a financial nature, the identity of the victims to whom individual reparations have been granted, and, where the award for reparations shall be deposited with the Trust Fund, the particulars of the Trust Fund for the deposit of the award; and
(c) The scope and nature of the reparations ordered by the Court, including, where applicable, the property and assets for which restitution has been ordered.

4. Where the Court awards reparations on an individual basis, a copy of the reparation order shall be transmitted to the victim concerned.

Rule 219 Non-modification of orders for reparation

The Presidency shall, when transmitting copies of orders for reparations to States Parties under rule 217, inform them that, in giving effect to an order for reparations, the national authorities shall not modify the reparations specified by the Court, the scope or the extent of any damage, loss or injury determined by the Court or the principles stated in the order, and shall facilitate the enforcement of such order.

Rule 220 Non-modification of judgments in which fines were imposed

When transmitting copies of judgments in which fines were imposed to States Parties for the purpose of enforcement in accordance with article 109 and rule 217, the Presidency shall inform them that in enforcing the fines imposed, national authorities shall not modify them.

Rule 221 Decision on disposition or allocation of property or assets

1. The Presidency shall, after having consulted, as appropriate, with the Prosecutor, the sentenced person, the victims or their legal representatives, the national authorities of the State of enforcement or any relevant third party, or representatives of the Trust Fund provided for in article 79, decide on all matters related to the disposition or allocation of property or assets realized through enforcement of an order of the Court.

2. In all cases, when the Presidency decides on the disposition or allocation of property or assets belonging to the sentenced person, it shall give priority to the enforcement of measures concerning reparations to victims.

Rule 222 Assistance for service or any other measure

The Presidency shall assist the State in the enforcement of fines, forfeiture or reparation orders, as requested, with the service of any relevant notification on the sentenced person or any other relevant persons, or the carrying out of any other measures necessary for the enforcement of the order under the procedure of the national law of the enforcement State.

Section V Review concerning reduction of sentence under article 110

Rule 223 Criteria for review concerning reduction of sentence

In reviewing the question of reduction of sentence pursuant to article 110, paragraphs 3 and 5, the three judges of the Appeals Chamber shall take into account the criteria listed in article 110, paragraph 4 (a) and (b), and the following criteria:

(a) The conduct of the sentenced person while in detention, which shows a genuine dissociation from his or her crime;

(b) The prospect of the resocialization and successful resettlement of the sentenced person;

(c) Whether the early release of the sentenced person would give rise to significant social instability;

(d) Any significant action taken by the sentenced person for the benefit of the victims as well as any impact on the victims and their families as a result of the early release;

(e) Individual circumstances of the sentenced person, including a worsening state of physical or mental health or advanced age.

Rule 224 Procedure for review concerning reduction of sentence

1. For the application of article 110, paragraph 3, three judges of the Appeals Chamber appointed by that Chamber shall conduct a hearing, unless they decide otherwise in a particular case, for exceptional reasons. The hearing shall be conducted with the sentenced person, who may be assisted by his or her counsel, with interpretation, as may be required. Those three judges shall invite the Prosecutor, the State of enforcement of any penalty under article 77 or any reparation order pursuant to article 75 and, to the extent possible, the victims or their legal representatives who participated in the proceedings, to participate in the hearing or to submit written observations. Under exceptional circumstances, this hearing may be conducted by way of a video-conference or in the State of enforcement by a judge delegated by the Appeals Chamber.

2. The same three judges shall communicate the decision and the reasons for it to all those who participated in the review proceedings as soon as possible.

3. For the application of article 110, paragraph 5, three judges of the Appeals Chamber appointed by that Chamber shall review the question of reduction of sentence every three years, unless it establishes a shorter interval in its decision taken pursuant to article 110, paragraph 3. In case of a significant change in circumstances, those three judges may permit the sentenced person to apply for a review within the three-year period or such shorter period as may have been set by the three judges.

4. For any review under article 110, paragraph 5, three judges of the Appeals Chamber appointed by that Chamber shall invite written representations from the sentenced person or his or her counsel, the Prosecutor, the State of enforcement of any penalty under article 77 and any reparation order pursuant to article 75 and, to the extent possible, the victims or their legal representatives who participated in the proceedings. The three judges may also decide to hold a hearing.

5. The decision and the reasons for it shall be communicated to all those who participated in the review proceedings as soon as possible.

Section VI Escape

Rule 225 Measures under article 111 in the event of escape

1. If the sentenced person has escaped, the State of enforcement shall, as soon as possible, advise the Registrar by any medium capable of delivering a written record. The Presidency shall then proceed in accordance with Part 9.

2. However, if the State in which the sentenced person is located agrees to surrender him or her to the State of enforcement, pursuant to either international agreements or its national legislation, the State of enforcement shall so advise the Registrar in writing. The person shall be surrendered to the State of enforcement as soon as possible, if necessary in consultation with the Registrar, who shall provide all necessary assistance, including, if necessary, the presentation of requests for transit to the States concerned, in accordance with rule 207. The costs associated with the surrender of the sentenced person shall be borne by the Court if no State assumes responsibility for them.

3. If the sentenced person is surrendered to the Court pursuant to Part 9, the Court shall transfer him or her to the State of enforcement. Nevertheless, the Presidency may, acting on its own motion or at the request of the Prosecutor or of the initial State of enforcement and in accordance with article 103 and rules 203 to 206, designate another State, including the State to the territory of which the sentenced person has fled.

4. In all cases, the entire period of detention in the territory of the State in which the sentenced person was in custody after his or her escape and, where sub-rule 3 is applicable, the period of detention at the seat of the Court following the surrender of the sentenced person from the State in which he or she was located shall be deducted from the sentence remaining to be served.

BIBLIOGRAPHY

Ambos, Kai, 'Establishing an International Criminal Court and International Criminal Code: Observations from an International Criminal Law Viewpoint', (1996) 7 *European Journal of International Law* 519
  'The Role of the Prosecutor of an International Criminal Court from a Comparative Perspective', 1997 *ICJ Review* 45
Annan, K., 'Advocating for an International Criminal Court', (1997) 21 *Fordham International Law Journal* 363
Arbour, Louise, Eser, Albin, Ambos, Kai and Sanders, Andrew, eds, *The Prosecutor of a Permanent International Criminal Court*, Freiburg im Breisgau: Edition Iuscrim, 2000
Armstead, J. H. Jr, 'The International Criminal Court: History, Development and Status', (1998) 38 *Santa Clara Law Review* 745
Arsanjani, Mahnoush H., 'The Rome Statute of the International Criminal Court', (1999) 93 *American Journal of International Law* 22
Askin, Kelly Dawn, 'Crimes Within the Jurisdiction of the International Criminal Court', (1999) 10 *Criminal Law Forum* 33
Bachrach, M., 'The Permanent International Criminal Court: An Examination of the Statutory Debate', (1998) 5 *ILSA Journal of International and Comparative Law* 139
Baez, Jose A., 'An International Crimes Court: Further Tales of the King of Corinth', (1993) 23 *Georgia Journal of International and Comparative Law* 289
Bassiouni, M. Cherif, 'Enforcing Human Rights Through International Criminal Law and Through an International Criminal Tribunal', in Henkin, Louis, and Hargrove, John L., eds, *Human Rights: An Agenda for the Next Century*, Washington: American Society of International Law, 1994
  'From Versailles to Rwanda in Seventy-Five Years: The Need to Establish a Permanent International Criminal Court', (1997) 10 *Harvard Human Rights Journal* 11
  'Historical Survey: 1919–1998', (1999) 13*quater Nouvelles études pénales* 1.
  'Observations Concerning the 1997–98 Preparatory Committee's Work', (1997) 29 *Denver Journal of International Law and Policy* 397

383

'Observations Concerning the 1997–98 Preparatory Committee's Work',
(1997) 13 *Nouvelles études pénales* 5

'Observations on the Structure of the (Zutphen) Consolidated Text', (1998)
13*bis Nouvelles études pénales* 5

'The Time Has Come for an International Criminal Court', (1991) 1 *Indiana
International and Comparative Law Review* 1

ed., *The Statute of the International Criminal Court: A Documentary History*,
Ardsley, NY: Transnational Publishers, 1998

Bassiouni, M. Cherif and Christopher L. Blakesley, 'The Need for an International
Criminal Court in the New International World Order', (1992) 25
Vanderbilt Journal of Transnational Law 151

Behrens, Hans-Jörg, 'Investigation, Trial and Appeal in the International Criminal
Court Statute (Parts V, VI, VIII)', (1998) 6 *European Journal of Crime,
Criminal Law and Criminal Justice* 113

Berg, Bradley E., 'The 1994 ILC Draft Statute for an International Criminal Court:
A Principled Appraisal of Jurisdictional Structure', (1996) 28 *Case Western
Reserve Journal of International Law* 221

Bergsmo, Morten, 'The Establishment of the International Tribunal on War
Crimes', (1993) 14 *Human Rights Law Journal* 371

'The Jurisdictional Regime of the International Criminal Court (Part II,
Articles 11–19)', (1998) 6 *European Journal of Crime, Criminal Law and
Criminal Justice* 29

Blakesley, Christopher L., 'Commentary on Parts 5 & 6 of the Zutphen
Intersessional Draft: General Principles of Criminal Law', (1998) 13*bis
Nouvelles études pénales* 69

'Introduction au projet de convention portant création d'un tribunal pénal
international', (1992) 62 *Revue internationale de droit pénal* 345

'Jurisdiction, Definition of Crimes, and Triggering Mechanisms', (1997) 29
Denver Journal of International Law and Policy 233, (1997) 13 *Nouvelles
études pénales* 177

'Model Draft Statute for the International Criminal Court Based on the
Preparatory Committee's Text to the Diplomatic Conference, Rome, June
15–July 17, 1997, Parts 5 & 6', (1998) 13*ter Nouvelles études pénales* 83

'Obstacles to the Creation of a Permanent War Crimes Tribunal', (1994) 18
Fletcher Forum of World Affairs 77

Bleich, Jeffrey L., 'Complementarity', (1997) 13 *Nouvelles études pénales* 231;
(1997) 29 *Denver Journal of International Law and Policy* 281

'Cooperation with National Systems,' (1997) 13 *Nouvelles études pénales* 245;
(1997) 29 *Denver Journal of International Law and Policy* 293

Boister, Neil, 'The Exclusion of Treaty Crimes from the Jurisdiction of the

Proposed International Criminal Court: Law, Pragmatism, Politics', (1998)
    3 *Journal of Armed Conflict Law* 27
Borchers, Patrick J., 'International Criminal Tribunals: A Jurisprudential
    Thought', (1997) 60 *Albany Law Review* 653
Bos, Adrian, '1948–1998: The Universal Declaration of Human Rights and the
    Statute of the International Criminal Court', (1998) 22 *Fordham
    International Law Journal* 229
Bourdon, William, 'Rôle de la société civile et des ONG', in *La Cour pénale
    internationale*, Paris: La Documentation française, 1999, pp. 89–96
Bourdon, William and Duverger, Emmanuelle, *La cour pénale internationale*,
    Paris: Seuil, 2000
Broms, B., 'The Establishment of an International Criminal Court', in Dinstein,
    Yoram and Tabory, Mala, eds, *War Crimes In International Law*, The Hague,
    Boston and London: Martinus Nijhoff Publishers, 1996, pp. 183–96
Broomhall, Bruce, 'Looking Forward to the Establishment of an International
    Criminal Court: Between State Consent and the Rule of Law', (1997) 8
    Criminal Law Forum 317
'The International Criminal Court: A Checklist for National Implementation',
    (1999) 13*quater Nouvelles études pénales* 113
'The International Criminal Court: Overview and Cooperation with States',
    (1999) 13*quater Nouvelles études pénales* 45
Brown, Bartram S., 'Nationality and Internationality in International
    Humanitarian Law', (1998) 34 *Stanford Journal of International Law* 347
'Primacy or Complementarity: Reconciling the Jurisdiction of National Courts
    and International Criminal Tribunals', (1998) 23 *Yale Journal of
    International Law* 383
Brown, Daniel J., 'The International Criminal Court and Trial in Absentia', (1999)
    24 *Brooklyn Journal of International Law* 763
Buchet, Antoine, 'Organisation de la Cour et procédure', in *La Cour pénale
    internationale*, Paris: La Documentation française, 1999, pp. 27–40
Burns, Peter, 'An International Criminal Tribunal: The Difficult Union of
    Principle and Politics', (1994) 5 *Criminal Law Forum* 341
Butler, A. Hays, 'A Selective and Annotated Bibliography of the International
    Criminal Court', (1999) 10 *Criminal Law Forum* 121
Caflisch, Lucius, 'Réflexions sur la création d'une Cour criminelle internationale',
    in Makaczyk, Jerzy, *Essays in Honour of Krzystof Skubiszewski*, The Hague:
    Kluwer, 1996, pp. 859–90
Carnahan, Burrus M., 'Lincoln, Lieber and the Laws of War: The Origins and
    Limits of the Principle of Military Necessity', (1998) 92 *American Journal of
    International Law* 213

Cassese, A., 'Reflections on International Criminal Justice', (1998) 61 *Modern Law Review* 1

Champy, Guillaume, 'Inquisitoire – accusatoire devant les juridictions pénales internationales', (1997) 68 *Revue internationale de droit pénal* 149

Chesterman, S., 'Never Again . . . And Again: Law, Order and the Gender of War Crimes in Bosnia and Beyond', (1997) 22 *Yale Journal of International Law* 299

Chin, Lionel Yee Woon, 'Not Just a War Crime Court: The Penal Regime Established by the Rome Statute of the International Criminal Court', (1998) 10 *Singapore Academy Law Journal* 321

Chinkin, C., 'Due Process and Witness Anonymity', (1997) 91 *American Journal of International Law* 75

'Rape and Sexual Abuse of Women in International Law', (1994) 5 *European Journal of International Law* 326

Clark, Roger S., 'Commentary on Parts 1 and 4 of the Zutphen Intersessional Draft', (1998) 13*bis Nouvelles études pénales* 55

'Methods of Warfare that Cause Unnecessary Suffering are Inherently Indiscriminate', (1998) 28 *California Western International Law Journal* 379

'The Proposed International Criminal Court: Its Establishment and Its Relationship with the United Nations', (1997) 8 *Criminal Law Forum* 411

Clark, Roger S. and Sann, Madeleine, eds, *The Prosecution of International War Crimes*, New Brunswick: Transaction Publishers, 1996

Condorelli, Luigi, La Rosa, Anne-Marie and Scherrer, Sylvie, *Les Nations Unies et le droit international humanitaire*, Paris: Éditions Pedone, 1997

Crawford, James, 'The ILC Adopts a Statute for an International Criminal Court', (1995) 89 *American Journal of International Law* 404

'The ILC's Draft Statute of an International Tribunal', (1994) 88 *American Journal of International Law* 140

Cryer, Robert, 'Commentary on the Rome Statute for an International Criminal Court: A Cadenza for the Song of Those Who Died in Vain?', (1998) 3 *Journal of Armed Conflict Law* 271

David, Eric, 'Le projet de Cour criminelle internationale permanente', in Destexhe, A. and Foret, M., ed., *De Nuremberg à La Haye et Arusha*, Brussels: Bruylant, 1997, pp. 129–136

David, M., 'Grotius Repudiated: The American Objections to the International Criminal Court and the Commitment to International Law', (1999) 20 *Michigan Journal of International Law* 337

Decaux, Emmanuel, 'Actions au regard de la souveraineté des États et moyens d'investigation', in *La Cour pénale internationale*, Paris: La Documentation française, 1999, pp. 77–88

Deming, Stuart H., 'War Crimes and International Criminal Law', (1995) 28
Akron Law Review 421

Derby, Daniel H., 'An International Criminal Court for the Future', (1995) 5
Transnational Law and Contemporary Problems 307

'Model Draft Statute for the International Criminal Court Based on the
Preparatory Committee's Text to the Diplomatic Conference, Rome, June
15–July 17, 1997, Part 4', (1998) 13*ter Nouvelles études pénales* 64

Deschênes, Jules, 'Toward International Criminal Justice', (1994) 5 *Criminal Law
Forum* 249

Dinstein, Yoram and Tabory, Mala, *War Crimes In International Law*, The Hague,
Boston and London: Martinus Nijhoff Publishers, 1996

Dobelle, Jean-François, 'Positions des Etats dans la negociation', in *La Cour pénale
internationale*, Paris: La Documentation française, 1999, pp. 11–26

Donat-Cattin, David, 'Crimes Against Humanity', in Lattanzi, Flavia, ed., *The
International Criminal Court, Comments on the Draft Statute*, Naples:
Editoriale Scientifica, 1998, pp. 49–78

'The Role of Victims in the ICC Proceedings', in Lattanzi, Flavia, ed., *The
International Criminal Court, Comments on the Draft Statute*, Naples:
Editoriale Scientifica, 1998, pp. 251–72

Dormann, Knut, 'The First and Second Sessions of the Preparatory Commission
for the International Criminal Court', (1999) 2 *Yearbook of International
Humanitarian Law* 283

Dugard, John, 'Obstacles in the Way of an International Criminal Court', (1997)
56 *Cambridge Law Journal* 337

Erb, Nicole Eva, 'Gender-Based Crimes under the Draft Statute for the Permanent
International Criminal Court', (1998) 29 *Columbia Human Rights Law
Review* 401

Eser, Albin, 'The Need for a General Part, Commentaries on the International Law
Commission's 1991 Draft Code of Crimes Against the Peace and Security of
Mankind', (1993) 11 *Nouvelles études pénales* 43

Fenrick, William J., 'Should Crimes Against Humanity Replace War Crimes?',
(1999) 37 *Columbia Journal of Transnational Law* 767

Ferencz, Benjamin B., 'An International Criminal Code and Court: Where They
Stand and Where They're Going', (1992) 30 *Columbia Journal of
Transnational Law* 375

*An International Criminal Court: A Step Toward World Peace: A Documentary
History and Analysis*, Dobbs Ferry, NY: Oceana Publications, 1990

'International Criminal Courts: The Legacy of Nuremberg', (1997) 10 *Pace
International Law Journal* 201

Forsythe, David P., 'International Criminal Courts: A Political View', (1997) 15
Netherlands Quarterly of Human Rights 5

Gaeta, Paola, 'The Defence of Superior Orders: The Statute of the International
    Criminal Court Versus Customary International Law', (1999) 10 *European
    Journal of International Law* 172
Gallant, Kenneth S., 'Securing the Presence of Defendants before the International
    Tribunal for the Former Yugoslavia: Breaking with Extradition', (1994) 5
    Criminal Law Forum 557
Gerber, Steven J., 'Commentary on Parts 10 and 11 of the Zutphen Intersessional
    Draft: General Principles of Criminal Law', (1998) 13*bis Nouvelles études
    pénales* 105
    'Model Draft Statute for the International Criminal Court Based on the
    Preparatory Committee's Text to the Diplomatic Conference, Rome, June
    15–July 17, 1997, Parts 11, 12 & 13', (1998) 13*ter Nouvelles études pénales*
    141
Gianaris, William N., 'The New World Order and the Need for an International
    Criminal Court', (1992) 16 *Fordham International Law Journal* 88
Gilmore, William C., 'The Proposed International Criminal Court: Recent
    Developments', (1995) 5 *Transnational Law and Contemporary Problems* 264
Gowlland-Debbas, Vera, 'The Relationship Between the Security Council and the
    Projected International Criminal Court', (1998) 3 *Journal of Armed Conflict
    Law* 97
Graefrath, Bernhard, 'Universal Criminal Jurisdiction and an International
    Criminal Court', (1990) 1 *European Journal of International Law* 67
Greenberg, Michael D., 'Creating an International Criminal Court', (1992) 10
    Boston University International Law Journal 119
Guffey-Landers, Nancy E., 'Establishing an International Criminal Court: Will It
    Do Justice?', (1996) 20 *Maryland Journal of International Law and Trade* 199
Gustafson, C., 'International Criminal Courts: Some Dissident Views on the
    Continuation of War by Penal Means', (1998) 21 *Houston Journal of
    International Law* 51
Hall, Christopher Keith, 'The First Proposal for a Permanent International
    Criminal Court', (1998) 322 *International Review of the Red Cross* 57
    'The Fifth Session of the UN Preparatory Committee on the Establishment of
    an International Criminal Court', (1998) 92 *American Journal of
    International Law* 331
    'The First Two Sessions of the UN Preparatory Committee on the
    Establishment of an International Criminal Court', (1997) 91 *American
    Journal of International Law* 177
    'The Sixth Session of the UN Preparatory Committee on the Establishment of
    an International Criminal Court', (1998) 92 *American Journal of
    International Law* 548
    'The Third and Fourth Sessions of the UN Preparatory Committee on the

Establishment of an International Criminal Court', (1998) 92 *American Journal of International Law* 124

Harris, David, 'Progress and Problems in Establishing an International Criminal Court', (1998) 3 *Journal of Armed Conflict Law* 1

Harris, Kenneth, 'Development of Rules of International Criminal Procedure Applicable to the International Adjudication Process: Arriving at a Body of Criminal Procedure Law for the ICC', (1998) 17 *Nouvelles études pénales* 389

Harris, Whitney R., 'A Call for an International War Crimes Court: Learning from Nuremberg', (1992) 23 *University of Toledo Law Review* 229

Hogan-Doran, J. and Van Ginkel, B.T., 'Aggression as a Crime under International Law and the Prosecution of Individuals by the Proposed International Criminal Court', (1996) 43 *Netherlands International Law Review* 321

Howard, Robert J., 'An Economic Paradigm for the Debate Concerning the Jurisdictional Extent of the International Criminal Court', (1998) 8 *Touro International Law Review* 117

Hwang, Phyllis, 'Defining Crimes Against Humanity in the Rome Statute of the International Criminal Court', (1998) 22 *Fordham International Law Journal* 457

Jamison, Sandra L., 'A Permanent International Court: A Proposal that Overcomes Past Objections', (1995) 23 *Denver Journal of International Law and Policy* 419

Jarasch, Frank, 'Establishment, Organization and Financing of the International Criminal Court (Parts I, IV, XI–XIII)', (1998) 6 *European Journal of Crime, Criminal Law and Criminal Justice* 9

Johnson, D. H. N., 'Draft Code of Offenses Against the Peace and Security of Mankind', (1955) 4 *International and Comparative Law Quarterly* 445

Jones, John R. W. D., 'The Implications of the Peace Agreement for the International Criminal Tribunal for the Former Yugoslavia', (1996) 7 *European Journal of International Law* 226

Josipovic, Ivo, *The Hague: Implementing Criminal Law*, Zagreb: Hrvatski Pravni Centar, 2000

Joyner, Christopher and Posteraro, Christopher C., 'The United States and the International Criminal Court: Rethinking the Struggle Between National Interests and International Justice', (1999) 10 *Criminal Law Forum* 359

Kaul, Hans-Peter, 'Special Note: The Struggle for the International Criminal Courts Jurisdiction', (1998) 6 *European Journal of Crime, Criminal Law and Criminal Justice* 48

'Towards a Permanent International Criminal Tribunal, Some Observations of a Negotiator', (1997) 18 *Human Rights Law Journal* 169

Kaul, Hans-Peter and Kress, Claus, 'Jurisdiction and Cooperation in the Statute of the International Criminal Court: Principles and Compromises', (1999) 2 *Yearbook of International Humanitarian Law* 143

King, Henry T. and Theofrastous, Theodore C., 'From Nuremberg to Rome: A Step Backward for US Foreign Policy', (1999) 31 *Case Western Reserve Journal of International Law* 47

Kirsch, Philippe and Holmes, John T., 'The Rome Conference on an International Criminal Court: The Negotiating Process', (1999) 93 *American Journal of International Law* 2

Koenig, Dorean Marguerite, 'Commentary on Parts 7 & 8 of the Zutphen Intersessional Draft: General Principles of Criminal Law', (1998) 13*bis Nouvelles études pénales* 95

Koenig, Dorean M. and Joyner, Christopher C., 'Model Draft Statute for the International Criminal Court Based on the Preparatory Committee's Text to the Diplomatic Conference, Rome, June 15–July 17, 1997, Parts 7 & 8', (1998) 13*ter Nouvelles études pénales* 111

Kress, Claus, 'Investigation, Trial and Appeal in the International Criminal Court Statute (Parts V, VI, VIII)', (1998) 6 *European Journal of Crime, Criminal Law and Criminal Justice* 126

Krohne, S. W., 'The United States and the World Need an International Criminal Court as an Ally in the War Against Terrorism', (1997) 8 *Indiana International and Comparative Law Review* 159

La Rosa, Anne-Marie, 'A Tremendous Challenge for the International Criminal Tribunals: Reconciling the Requirements of International Humanitarian Law with those of Fair Trial', (1997) 321 *International Review of the Red Cross* 635

Lattanzi, Flavia, ed., *The International Criminal Court, Comments on the Draft Statute*, Naples: Editoriale Scientifica, 1998

Lattanzi, Flavia and Sciso, Elena, eds, *Dai Tribunali penali internazionali ad hoc a una corte permanente*, Naples: Editoriale Scientifica, 1996

Lee, Roy, ed., *The International Criminal Court, The Making of the Rome Statute, Issues, Negotiations, Results*, The Hague: Kluwer Law International, 1999

Legomsky, Stephen H., 'Commentary on Part 9 of the Zutphen Intersessional Draft: General Principles of Criminal Law', (1998) 13*bis Nouvelles études pénales* 101

Liang, Yuen-Li, 'The Question of the Establishment of an International Criminal Jurisdiction', (1949) 43 *American Journal of International Law* 478

MacPherson, B. F., 'Building an International Criminal Court for the 21st Century', (1998) 13 *Connecticut Journal of International Law* 1

MacSweeney, Daniel, 'International Standards of Fairness, Criminal Procedure and the International Criminal Court', (1997) 68 *Revue internationale de droit pénal* 233

Marquart, Paul D., 'Law Without Borders: The Constitutionality of an International Criminal Court', (1995) 33 *Columbia Journal of Transnational Law* 73

Massot, Jean, 'Introduction dans l'ordre juridique français', in *La Cour pénale internationale*, Paris: La Documentation française, 1999, pp. 55–60

Matthew, Peter, 'The Proposed International Criminal Court: A Commentary on the Legal and Political Debates Regarding Jurisdiction that Threaten the Establishment of an Effective Court', (1997) 24 *Syracuse Journal of International Law and Commerce* 177

McCormack, Timothy L. H. and Simpson, Gerry, eds, *The Law of War Crimes: National and International Approaches*, The Hague: Kluwer Law International, 1997

McCoubrey, Hilaire, 'War Crimes Jurisdiction and a Permanent International Criminal Court: Advantages and Difficulties', (1998) 3 *Journal of Armed Conflict Law* 9

McKeon, Patricia A., 'An International Criminal Court: Balancing the Principle of Sovereignty Against the Demands for International Justice', (1997) 12 *St John's Journal of Legal Commentary* 535

Meron, Theodor, 'International Criminalization of Internal Atrocities,' (1995) 89 *American Journal of International Law* 554

'Is International Law Moving Towards Criminalization?', (1998) 9 *European Journal of International Law* 18

'Rape as a Crime under International Humanitarian Law', (1993) 87 *American Journal of International Law* 424

'The Continuing Role of Custom in the Formation of International Humanitarian Law', (1996) 90 *American Journal of International Law* 238

'War Crimes Law Comes of Age', (1998) 92 *American Journal of International Law* 462

Momtaz, Djamchid, 'War Crimes in Non-International Armed Conflicts under the Statute of the International Criminal Court', (1999) 2 *Yearbook of International Humanitarian Law* 177

Moshan, Brook Sari, 'Women, War, and Words: The Gender Component in the Permanent International Criminal Court's Definition of Crimes Against Humanity', (1998) 22 *Fordham International Law Journal* 154

Nanda, Ved, 'The Establishment of an International Criminal Court: Challenges Ahead', (1998) 20 *Human Rights Quarterly* 413

Nsereko, Daniel D. Ntanda, 'The International Criminal Court: Jurisdictional and Related Issues', (1999) 10 *Criminal Law Forum* 87

Paust, Jordan J., 'Nullum Crimen and Related Claims', (1997) 13 *Nouvelles études pénales* 275, (1997) 29 *Denver Journal of International Law Policy* 321

'The Preparatory Committee's "Definition of Crimes" – War Crimes', (1997) 8 *Criminal Law Forum* 431

Paust, Jordan J., Wexler, Leila Sadat and Wise, Edward M., 'Commentary on Part 2 of the Zutphen Intersessional Draft: General Principles of Criminal Law', (1998) 13*bis Nouvelles études pénales* 27

Pejic, Jelena, 'Creating a Permanent International Criminal Court: The Obstacles to Independence and Effectiveness', (1998) 29 *Columbia Human Rights Law Review* 291

'The Tribunal and the ICC: Do Precedents Matter?', (1997) 60 *Albany Law Review* 841

Pellet, Alain, 'Compétence matérielle et modalités de saisine', in *La Cour pénale internationale*, Paris: La Documentation française, 1999, pp. 41–54

Pesce, Marina, 'Le statut de la victime devant le Tribunal pénal', (1996) 1 *L'observateur des Nations Unies* 101

Peter, M. D., 'The Proposed International Criminal Court: A Commentary on the Legal and Political Debates Regarding Jurisdiction that Threaten the Establishment of an Effective Court', (1997) 24 *Syracuse Journal of International Law and Commerce* 177

Petera, A. Rohan, 'Towards the Establishment of an International Criminal Court', (1994) 20 *Commonwealth Law Bulletin* 298

Pfanner, Toni, 'The Establishment of a Permanent International Criminal Court: ICRC Expectations of the Rome Diplomatic Conference', (1998) 322 *International Review of the Red Cross* 21

Philips, Ruth B., 'The International Criminal Court Statute: Jurisdiction and Admissibility', (1999) 10 *Criminal Law Forum* 61

Pickard, Daniel B., 'Proposed Sentencing Guidelines for the International Criminal Court', (1997) 20 *Loyola of Los Angeles International and Comparative Law Journal* 123

Piotrowicz, Ryszard, 'Crime and Punishment, or the Establishment of a True International Court of Justice', (1998) 72 *Australian Law Journal* 844

Politi, Mauro, 'The Establishment of an International Criminal Court at a Crossroads: Issues and Prospects After the First Session of the Preparatory Committee', (1997) 13 *Nouvelles études pénales* 115

Ratner, Steven R. and Abrams, Jason S., *Accountability for Human Rights Atrocities in International Law: Beyond the Nuremberg Legacy*, Oxford: Clarendon Press, 1997

Rayfuse, Rosemary, 'The Draft Code of Crimes Against the Peace and Security of Mankind: Eating Disorders at the International Law Commission', (1997) 8 *Criminal Law Forum* 52

Roberge, Marie-Claude, 'The New International Criminal Court: A Preliminary Assessment', (1998) 325 *International Review of the Red Cross* 671

Robinson, Darryl, 'Defining "Crimes Against Humanity" at the Rome Conference', (1999) 93 *American Journal of International Law* 43

Robinson, Darryl and von Hebel, Herman, 'War Crimes in Internal Conflicts: Article 8 of the ICC Statute', (1999) 2 *Yearbook of International Humanitarian Law* 193

Rosenne, Shabtai, 'The Jurisdiction of the International Criminal Court', (1999) 2 *Yearbook of International Humanitarian Law* 119

Rowe, Peter, 'Duress as a Defence to War Crimes after Erdemovic? A Laboratory for a Permanent Court', (1998) 1 *Yearbook of International Humanitarian Law* 210

Sadat, Leila Nadya and Carden, S. Richard, 'The New International Criminal Court: An Uneasy Revolution', (2000) 88 *Georgetown Law Journal* 381

Sarooshi, Danesh, 'The Statute of the International Criminal Court', (1999) 48 *International and Comparative Law Quarterly* 387

Schabas, William A., 'General Principles of Criminal Law in the International Criminal Court Statute (Part III)', (1998) 6 *European Journal of Crime, Criminal Law and Criminal Justice* 84

'La cour criminelle internationale: Un pas de plus contre l'impunité', in *The Impact of International Law on the Practice of Law*, The Hague: Kluwer Law International, 1999, pp. 3–16

'Life, Death and the Crime of Crimes: Supreme Penalties and the ICC Statute', (2000) 2 *Punishment and Society* 263

'Sentencing and the International Tribunals: For a Human Rights Approach', (1997) 7 *Duke Journal of Comparative and International Law* 461

'The Follow Up to Rome: Preparing for Entry into Force of the International Criminal Court Statute', (1999) 20 *Human Rights Law Journal* 157

Scharf, Michael P., 'Getting Serious About an International Criminal Court', (1994) 6 *Pace International Law Review* 103

'Model Draft Statute for the International Criminal Court Based on the Preparatory Committee's Text to the Diplomatic Conference, Rome, June 15–July 17, 1997, Parts 9 & 10', (1998) 13*ter Nouvelles études pénales* 120

'The Amnesty Exception to the Jurisdiction of the International Criminal Court', (1999) 32 *Cornell International Law Journal* 507

'The Jury is Still Out on the Need for an International Criminal Court', (1991) 1 *Duke Journal of International and Comparative Law Review* 135

'The Politics of Establishing an International Criminal Court', (1995) 6 *Duke Journal of International and Comparative Law Review* 167

Scheffer, David J., 'The United States and the International Criminal Court', (1999) 93 *American Journal of International Law* 12

Sellers, Patricia Viseur and Okuizumi, Kaoru, 'International Prosecution of Sexual Assaults', (1997) 7 *Transnational Law and Contemporary Problems* 45

Shaw, Malcolm N., 'The International Criminal Court – Some Procedural and Evidential Issues', (1998) 3 *Journal of Armed Conflict Law* 65

Shelton, Dinah, ed., *International Crimes, Peace, and Human Rights: The Role of the International Criminal Court*, Ardsley, NY: Transnational Publishers, 2000

Sluiter, G., 'An International Criminal Court is Hereby Established', (1998) 3 *Netherlands Quarterly of Human Rights* 413

Stevens, Lyn L., 'Towards a Permanent International Criminal Court', (1998) 6 *European Journal of Crime, Criminal Law and Criminal Justice* 236

Stoelting, David, 'Status Report on the International Criminal Court', (1999) 3 *Hofstra Law and Policy Symposium* 233

Sunga, Lyal S., 'The Crimes Within the Jurisdiction of the International Criminal Court (Part II, Articles 5–10)', (1998) 6 *European Journal of Crime, Criminal Law and Criminal Justice* 61

Swaak-Goldman, Olivia Q., 'The Crime of Persecution in International Law', (1998) 11 *Leiden Journal of International Law* 145

Tavernier, Paul, 'Vers une juridiction pénale internationale?', in Thuan, Cao Huy and Fenet, Alain, *Mutations internationales et évolutions des normes*, Paris: Presses universitaires de France, 1994, pp. 137–54

Tomuschat, Christian, 'A System of International Criminal Prosecution is Taking Shape', (1993) 50 *ICJ Review* 56

'International Criminal Prosecution: The Precedent of Nuremberg Confirmed', (1994) 5 *Criminal Law Forum* 237

Triffterer, Otto, ed., *Commentary on the Rome Statute of the International Criminal Court, Observers' Notes, Article by Article*, Baden-Baden: Nomos, 1999

van Boven, Theo C., 'The European Union and the International Criminal Court', (1998) 5 *Maastricht Journal of European Comparative Law* 325

van Schaack, Beth, 'The Definition of Crimes Against Humanity: Resolving the Incoherence', (1999) 37 *Columbia Journal of Transnational Law* 787

van Zyl Smit, Dirk, 'Life Imprisonment as an Ultimate Penalty in International Law: A Human Rights Perspective', (1998) 10 *Criminal Law Forum* 1

von Hebel, Herman, Lammers, Johan G. and Schukking, Jolien, eds, *Reflections on the International Criminal Court: Essays in Honour of Adriaan Bos*, The Hague: T. M. C. Asser, 1999

Wallach, Evan J., 'The Procedural and Evidentiary Rules of the Post-World War II War Crimes Trials: Did They Provide an Outline for International Legal Procedure?', (1999) 37 *Columbia Journal of Transnational Law* 851

Warbrick, Colin, 'International Criminal Courts and Fair Trial', (1998) 3 *Journal of Armed Conflict Law* 45

'The United Nations System: A Place for Criminal Courts?', (1995) 5 *Transnational Law and Contemporary Problems* 237

Warrick, Thomas S., 'Organization of the International Criminal Court:

Administrative and Financial Issues', (1997) 25 *Denver Journal of International Law and Policy* 333

'Organization of the International Criminal Court: Administrative and Financial Issues', (1997) 13 *Nouvelles études pénales* 37

Wedgwood, Ruth, 'The International Criminal Court: An American View', (1999) 10 *European Journal of International Law* 93

Wexler, Leila Sadat, 'First Committee Report on Jurisdiction, Definition of Crimes and Complementarity', (1997) 29 *Denver Journal of International Law and Policy* 221

'First Committee Report on Jurisdiction, Definition of Crimes and Complementarity', (1997) 13 *Nouvelles études pénales* 163

'The Proposed Permanent International Criminal Court: An Appraisal', (1996) 29 *Cornell International Law Journal* 665

Wexler, Leila Sadat and Clark, Roger S., 'Commentary on Part 1 of the Zutphen Intersessional Draft: General Principles of Criminal Law', (1998) 13*bis Nouvelles études pénales* 17

Wexler, Leila Sadat and Paust, Jordan J., 'Model Draft Statute for the International Criminal Court Based on the Preparatory Committee's Text to the Diplomatic Conference, Rome, June 15–July 17, 1997, Preamble, Parts 1 & 2', (1998) 13*ter Nouvelles études pénales* 1

Wise, Edward M., 'Commentary on Parts 2 and 3 of the Zutphen Intersessional Draft: General Principles of Criminal Law', (1998) 13*bis Nouvelles études pénales* 43

'General Rules of Criminal Law' (1997) 13 *Nouvelles études pénales* 267 (1997) 29 *Denver Journal of International Law and Policy* 313

'Model Draft Statute for the International Criminal Court Based on the Preparatory Committee's Text to the Diplomatic Conference, Rome, June 15–July 17, 1997, Part 3', (1998) 13*ter Nouvelles études pénales* 39

Yee, Sien Ho, 'A Proposal to Reorganize Article 23 of the ILC Draft Statute for an International Criminal Court', (1996) 19 *Hastings International and Comparative Law Review* 529

Zwanenburg, Marten, 'The Statute for an International Criminal Court and the United States: Peacekeepers under Fire?', (1999) 10 *European Journal of International Law* 124

INDEX